Corporate Taxation, Group Debt Funding and Base Erosion

EUCOTAX Series on European Taxation

VOLUME 67

Series Editors

Introduction

EUCOTAX (European Universities Cooperating on Taxes) is a network of tax institutes currently consisting of eleven universities: WU (Vienna University of Economics and Business) in Austria, Katholieke Universiteit Leuven in Belgium, Corvinus University of Budapest, Hungary, Université Paris-I Panthéon-Sorbonne in France, Universität Osnabrück in Germany, Libera, Università Internazionale di Studi Sociali in Rome (and Università degli Studi di Bologna for the research part), in Italy, Fiscaal Instituut Tilburg at Tilburg University in the Netherlands, Universidad de Barcelona in Spain, Uppsala University in Sweden, Queen Mary and Westfield College at the University of London in the United Kingdom, and Georgetown University in Washington DC, United States of America. The network aims at initiating and coordinating both comparative education in taxation, through the organization of activities such as winter courses and guest lectures, and comparative research in the field, by means of joint research projects, international conferences and exchange of researchers between various countries.

Contents/Subjects

The EUCOTAX series covers a wide range of topics in European tax law. For example tax treaties, EC case law, tax planning, exchange of information and VAT. The series is well-known for its high-quality research and practical solutions.

Objective

The series aims to provide insights on new developments in European taxation.

Readership

Practitioners and academics dealing with European tax law.

Frequency of Publication

2-3 new volumes published each year.

The titles published in this series are listed at the end of this volume.

Corporate Taxation, Group Debt Funding and Base Erosion

New Perspectives on the EU Anti-Tax Avoidance Directive

Edited by

Gianluigi Bizioli
Mario Grandinetti
Leopoldo Parada
Giuseppe Vanz
Alessandro Vicini Ronchetti

Wolters Kluwer

Published by:
Kluwer Law International B.V.
PO Box 316
2400 AH Alphen aan den Rijn
The Netherlands
E-mail: international-sales@wolterskluwer.com
Website: lrus.wolterskluwer.com

Sold and distributed in North, Central and South America by:
Wolters Kluwer Legal & Regulatory U.S.
7201 McKinney Circle
Frederick, MD 21704
United States of America
Email: customer.service@wolterskluwer.com

Sold and distributed in all other countries by:
Air Business Subscriptions
Rockwood House
Haywards Heath
West Sussex
RH16 3DH
United Kingdom
Email: international-customerservice@wolterskluwer.com

ISBN 978-94-035-1170-2

e-Book: ISBN 978-94-035-1231-0
web-PDF: ISBN 978-94-035-1232-7

Editors

Gianluigi Bizioli is Professor of Tax Law and International and EU Tax Law in the Department of Law at the University of Bergamo. He also teaches Tax Law at the *Accademia della Guardia di Finanza* in Bergamo. He is Member of the Board of Professors of the Ph.D. Program in Business and Law of the University of Bergamo and Co-Director of the *Rivista di Diritto Finanziario e Scienza delle Finanze*. He is Author of more than ninety books and articles, especially in the field of constitutional tax law and European and International tax law. Since 2018 he is the Italian member of the Academic Committee of the European Association of Tax Law Professors and *Of Counsel* at the Italian practice of PwC Tax and Legal Services.

Mario Grandinetti is a researcher and assistant professor of Tax Law at the University of Turin, where he regularly lectures both undergraduate (Tax Law) and graduate (International, European and Comparative Tax Lax) courses. In 2018, he was habilitated to Associate Professorship by the National Scientific Committee. He holds a Ph.D. in Public and Tax Law in the European dimension from the University of Bergamo (Italy) and has been a visiting researcher at several institutions, for example the Max Planck Institute in Intellectual Property and Tax Law of Munich (Germany) and the University of Valencia (Spain). In 2010, he was awarded a scholarship for young researchers by the Giovanni Goria Foundation. Mario authored a monograph and several contributions published on journals and in books, both in Italy and abroad. He also edited the book *Corporate Tax Base in the Light of the Ias/Ifrs and Eu Directive 2013/34. A Comparative Approach.*

Dr. Leopoldo Parada, L.L.M., is a lecturer in Tax Law at the University of Leeds School of Law in the United Kingdom. He is also Visiting Professor of International and EU Tax Law at the University of Turin in Italy. Formerly, he worked as a research associate at the Max Planck Institute for Tax Law and Public Finance in Munich and held a postdoctoral research position at the IBFD in Amsterdam. In the past, he also practiced full-time as a lawyer and tax advisor in Chile, Brazil and the United States. He is a member of the Tax Committee of Experts of the Joint Italian Arab Chamber of

Commerce (JIACC), the Chilean Bar Association and a former member of the American Bar Association (ABA) Section of Taxation.

Giuseppe Vanz is an associate professor of Tax Law in the Department of Management at the University of Turin in Italy. He graduated in Law at the University of Turin and is Author of two monographs: *I poteri conoscitivi e di controllo dell'amministrazione finanziaria*, Cedam ed., 2012, concerning the investigation powers of the tax authorities, and, together with I. Manzoni, *Il diritto tributario. Profili teorici e sistematici*, Giappichelli ed., 2008, concerning the general profiles of tax law. He is also the author of articles in different areas of tax law. He is admitted to the bar and practices before the Supreme Court in Italy.

Alessandro Vicini Ronchetti is a researcher and assistant professor of Tax Law at the University of Turin, where he regularly lectures both undergraduate (Tax Law) and graduate (International, European and Comparative Tax Lax) courses. In 2017, he was habilitated to Associate Professorship by the National Scientific Committee. He holds a Ph.D. in International and European Tax Law from the University of Genoa (Italy) and has been a visiting researcher at the University of Valencia (Spain). His areas of expertise are domestic company taxation, European and International Taxation, VAT and the Taxation of Groups. Alessandro authored a monograph and several contributions published on journals and in books.

Contributors

Aitor Navarro Ibarrola, is Assistant professor at Universidad Carlos III de Madrid. He specializes in transfer pricing, corporate taxation and international taxation matters and has published several contributions referred to such topics. His book *Transactional Adjustments in Transfer Pricing* was awarded with the 2019 IBFD Frans Vanistendael Award for International Tax Law. He lectures on Spanish Tax Law as well as European Union and International Tax Law in several undergraduate and L.L.M. programs, as well as seminars and conferences referred to the field of tax law. He is also the deputy director of the L.L.M. in Taxation program at Universidad Carlos III.

Andrés Báez Moreno is Associate Professor of Tax Law at the Universidad Carlos III de Madrid and a lawyer at the Madrid Bar. He has been a visiting predoctoral and postdoctoral researcher at the University of Münster, the University of Cologne, the University of Padua and IBFD and currently holds a Scholarship of the Max Planck Institute for Tax Law and Public Finance in Munich. His areas of expertise are domestic company taxation (in particular, commercial and tax accounting) and international taxation, fields in which he has published two books and more than thirty articles and contributions.

Daniel Reich studied Law in Heidelberg, Germany, from 2012 to 2018 and has been working as a research assistant to Prof. Dr. Ekkehart Reimer at the University of Heidelberg since July 2018.

F. Alfredo Garcia Prats is Professor of Financial and Tax Law at the University of Valencia (Spain). He holds a Jean Monnet Chair on EU Tax Law and Policy and has been Coordinator of the Centre of Excellence Jean Monnet on European Fiscal and Economic Integration of the University of Valencia. He has written more than twenty books and book chapters and more than 100 articles in domestic and international tax law reviews. He also serves as of counsel of Montero-Aramburu S.L.P. He can be contacted at alfredo.garcia@uv.es.

Dr. Federica Pitrone is the Head of International tax at Intesa Sanpaolo. Before joining Intesa Sanpaolo, she was a postdoctoral research fellow at IBFD Academic and Assistant Professor at Maastricht University (the Netherlands). She has been a visiting researcher at the Max Planck Institute for Tax Law and Public Finance, Munich (Germany) and at the Institute for Austrian and International Tax Law, WU, Vienna (Austria). Here, she has also been teaching assistant on European Tax Law. Furthermore, she has been a guest researcher of the International Tax Program at New York University (United States). She holds a Ph.D. in Tax Law (2014) from the Luiss Guido Carli University, Rome (Italy), where she has also been a research and teaching associate. She is a member of IFA and the Max Planck Alumni Association.

Prof. Giuseppe Melis, is a full professor of Tax Law at LUISS Guido Carli, Rome. He holds a Ph.D. in Tax Law at the Second University of Naples and an M.Sc. in International Tax Planning at La Sapienza University in Rome. He is Director of the Master in 'Tax Law, Accounting and Tax Planning' at LUISS Business School. He is also a member of the Council of the Italian branch of International Fiscal Association, tax lawyer and tax accountant; member of the Scientific Committee of the journal *Diritto e pratica tributaria internazionale*; member of the Executive Committee of the journal *Diritto e pratica tributaria*; founder and member of the Scientific Committee of the journal *Diritto e processo tributario. Dialogo con le Corti.* Author of two monographs, one handbook and over 120 articles, among which 50 have been published in A-Class Reviews.

Dr. Harm van den Broek works as associate professor of Tax Law and deputy head of the Tax Law Department of Radboud University Nijmegen (The Netherlands). His research and teaching activities are focused on Corporate Income Tax and European Tax Law. In 2011 he defended his Ph.D. thesis, entitled 'Cross-Border Mergers Within the EU. Proposals to Remove the Remaining Tax Obstacles', which was published in the EUCOTAX Series of Kluwer Law International and was nominated for the first Ph.D. Thesis Award of the Dutch Association of Tax Scholars in 2012. Many years he had combined his academic activities with his activities as Tax Adviser, in particular in the field of European Tax Law. During the academic year 2016-2017, he was Visiting Professor at the Università degli Studi di Torino. Harm van den Broek also acts as Deputy Judge at the Tax Chamber of the Court of Appeal of 's-Hertogenbosch.

Jakob Bundgaard Ph.D., is the managing director of CORIT Advisory. He advises leading companies broadly on tax law issues and strategic matters. He possesses a special expertise within the field of corporate taxation, international tax law, EU law, financial instruments, transactions and structuring, corporate finance and taxation of digital enterprises.

Concurrently with his counseling activities, Jakob has, for several years, been active in the academic world. Jakob is a professor of international tax law at the University of Aalborg and honorary professor of international tax law at the University of Aarhus. In addition, Jakob is the author of a significant number of publications on tax law issues and is often invited as a key-note speaker for other advisors, tax authorities, universities and at conferences.

Marco Barassi is Associate Professor of Tax Law in the Department of Law at the University of Bergamo, Italy. He is Member of the European Association of Tax Law Professors and Member of the Board of Professors of the Ph.D. in Business & Law. His main areas of interest are comparative tax law, European and international taxation and company taxation.

Michael Tell, Ph.D. is a partner of CORIT Advisory. He advises broadly on all matters within corporate tax and international tax and is a leading expert on corporate financing and tax, with a specific emphasis on international interest limitation legislation. Michael is active in the academia and has authored numerous articles within international tax law.

Peter Essers is Professor of Tax Law at Tilburg University, the Netherlands, specializing in national and international personal and corporate income tax. He is Director of the European Tax College and coordinator of EUCOTAX (European and US Universities Cooperating On TAXes). He has been Visiting Professor of many universities in the world and Chairman of the Academic Committee of the European Association of Tax Law Professors (EATLP). Besides, he is a member of the Dutch Senate and chairman of the Dutch Association of Tax Science. He has published numerous publications in the field of national and international tax law.

Werner Haslehner is Professor of Law with the Faculty of Law, Economics and Finance at the University of Luxembourg, where he holds the ATOZ Chair for European and International Taxation, and the Director of its L.L.M. Program in EU and International Tax Law. He joined the Faculty as Associate Professor in 2013 after holding full-time academic positions at JKU Linz the LSE and was appointed Full Professor in 2015. He has been a visiting professor at the University of Paris I Sorbonne in 2018 and at the University of Turin in 2019. His research interests cover all aspects of international taxation, including the impact of EU law, and tax policy.

Summary of Contents

Table of Contents

PART I The Interest Limitation Rule in the ATAD: Targeting Base Erosion

CHAPTER 1

Group Debt Funding and Base Erosion: An Introduction

Peter Essers

§1.01 GENERAL

Basically, companies have two options for financing their activities: through equity or through debt. Both alternatives have their own characteristics, mainly based on civil law. However, in practice, especially in group structures, the way companies want to finance their activities is predominantly determined by tax aspects instead of civil law aspects. From a civil law perspective, this could lead to suboptimal finance structures in companies. The prioritizing of tax aspects in the choice of how to finance companies' activities finds its origin in the completely different tax treatment of (the costs of) debt and equity in practically all Member States of the European Union (EU). In relation to equity financing within a group of companies, generally the remuneration paid to the parent company by the subsidiary for the disposal of equity - dividend - is not deductible in the determination of the taxable profit of this subsidiary. As a rule, the dividend received by the parent company will be exempt from corporate income tax because of a participation exemption in the national corporate income tax preventing economic double taxation within a group. In most cases, because of this participation exemption, capital gains with respect to the participation in this subsidiary will also be tax exempt. As a result, the tax burden related to financing through equity falls on the subsidiary. Conversely, if the activities of the subsidiaries are financed through a loan from the parent, the subsidiary can, in general, deduct the interest paid as a business expense by calculating its taxable profit. However, the parent-creditor will be taxed with corporate income tax on the interest received on this loan. Possible decreases in the value of the loan can, in principle, be deducted by the parent. This means that the tax burden resulting from debt financing lies with the parent-creditor.

This diametrically opposite tax treatment of (the costs of) debt and equity within a group of companies, combined with the fact that within such a group it is quite easy to change financing from debt to equity (or vice versa), means that from a tax perspective financing through debt will be preferred if the subsidiary-debtor is situated in a high tax rate country, since the interest costs diminish the highly taxed profits in that country. If the parent-creditor is situated in a low tax rate country, a considerable saving of finance costs within an international concern can be achieved. This is even more attractive if a so-called hybrid financial instrument is at stake: then, in the country of the subsidiary, the interest paid is considered to be a business cost, and in the country of the parent to be a tax-exempt dividend.

If the parent is situated in a high tax rate country and the subsidiary in a low tax rate country, financing the activities of the foreign subsidiary through equity could have priority. The parent may also be able to take a loan from a bank to finance these expenses.[1]

The opposite tax treatment of debt and equity leads to tax planning structures and explains why in high tax rate countries a strong tendency exists to finance the activities of subsidiaries in these countries through debt. Since many of these financing arrangements have certain characteristics of equity finance (e.g., no or a very long redemption period, no or insufficient security, profit-dependable interest and so forth) most of these countries apply general anti-abuse measures such as *fraus legis* and specific anti-abuse measures such as 'thin capitalization' rules prescribing maximum debt-equity relations. On the one hand, many of these measures cause 'overkill' (e.g., if rigid debt-equity ratios have been prescribed or if the interest deduction is denied in the debtor's country and the received interest is taxed in the creditor's country), but on the other hand, specific anti-abuse measures are often not always suited to tackling tax abuse because they may contain various escape clauses.

§1.02 FUNDAMENTAL SOLUTIONS FOR ACHIEVING A MORE EQUAL TAX TREATMENT OF DEBT AND EQUITY

Instead of applying and introducing general and specific anti-abuse measures, a better approach would be to introduce measures that lead to a more sustainable (durable) equal tax treatment of debt and equity. In principle, there are three ways to achieve this: (1) limiting the interest deduction by introducing a 'Comprehensive Business Income Tax' (CBIT); (2) introducing an 'Allowance for Corporate Equity' (ACE); or (3) taxing income from debt and equity effectively in the same way.

1. P.H.J. Essers, et al., (eds.), *Reforming the Law of Business Organizations (Back to Basics in Business Law and Tax Law)*, Eleven International Publishing, The Hague, 2011, pp. 141-149. *See also* S.A. Stevens, *De toekomst van de renteaftrek in de vennootschapsbelasting*, Tijdschrift Fiscaal Ondernemingsrecht 2017/150, pp. 66-75.

[A] Comprehensive Business Income Tax

With a CBIT, the compensation for debt is not tax-deductible. In this system, the company is not considered to have its own ability to pay. All income is considered to be at the disposal of the shareholders. Introducing a CBIT leads to a higher tax base. As a result, national corporate income tax rates can be reduced to realize the same tax receipt. The tax burden shifts from projects financed with equity to projects financed with debt. To avoid economic double taxation (no deduction of the paid interest at the level of the debtor in one country, taxation of the interest received at the level of the creditor in another country), a CBIT cannot be introduced without coordination at an international level.

[B] Allowance for Corporate Equity

An alternative system would be the introduction of an ACE. This allowance is granted on the basis of the book value used for tax purposes minus the value used for tax purposes of participations. If the equity is negative, ACE might lead to an addition to the taxable result. The allowance is based on a risk-free equity yield (this could also be the returns on state bonds). As a result, the corporate income tax will become a rent tax, because only the returns exceeding the 'normal' returns will be taxed. A disadvantage of ACE is that it does not fully eliminate the different tax treatment of debt and equity since interests will still be deductible for their full real amount, whereas ACE is connected to a fixed percentage. This means that anti-abuse measures preventing excessive interest deductions will still be necessary. Another disadvantage is that ACE will lead to a lower tax base for the corporate income tax. To achieve the same tax proceeds, states should increase their national corporate income tax rates, but this is considered to be detrimental to the competitive position of these states.[2]

[C] Equal Taxation of Income from Debt and from Equity

One could reason that the real problem of the unequal tax treatment of debt and equity is not related to the deduction of interest by the debtor company, but to the fact that the received interest is not taxed or taxed at a lower rate in the country of the creditor company. This could be prevented by giving priority to a system of international income allocation based on the principle of origin. In this approach, the solution to the problem is not found in the denial of the interest deduction at the level of the debtor/subsidiary, but in the attribution of taxing power on the interest received by the creditor/parent to the state of origin, being the state where the value is created. With this system, the interest received by the creditor/parent is taxed at the same corporate income tax rate as the rate applicable to the interest deducted by the debtor/subsidiary.

2. Ruud A. de Mooij and Michael P. Devereux, *An Applied Analysis of ACE and CBIT Reforms in the EU*, International Tax and Public Finance, (2011) Vol. 18, no. 93, pp. 93-120.

As a result, tax arbitrage does not make sense anymore.[3] In the future, it might be difficult, however, to determine the state of origin as, due to the development of artificial intelligence, it will be very difficult to pinpoint the human factor that is causing the creation of added value.

§1.03 ALTERNATIVE SOLUTIONS PROPOSED BY THE OECD AND THE EU

In Action Report 4, the Organisation for Economic Co-operation and Development (OECD) discusses two alternative solutions in the framework to tackle Base Erosion and Profit Shifting (BEPS): thin capitalization rules and earnings stripping rules. In the Anti-Tax Avoidance Directive 1 (ATAD1), the EU has opted for an earnings stripping rule.[4]

[A] Thin Capitalization Rules

In principle, thin capitalization rules limit the deduction of interest if a company's debt-equity ratio exceeds a certain norm. These rules encounter a good deal of criticism. First of all, they restrict the company's freedom in achieving an optimal allocation of debt and equity, mainly because the fixed debt-equity norm is very general and arbitrary. These rules also contain an incentive to finance the company's activities as much as possible through debt as long as the maximum debt-equity ratio is not reached. In case a group-escape possibility exists (meaning that if the company's debt-equity ratio is lower than the group's debt-equity ratio, the latter will apply), this exception does not take into account that the activities of the group and the company at stake may differ, as a result of which other financing relationships may be justified. A serious point of criticism is also that thin capitalization rules may lead to double taxation (interest paid is non-deductible, the interest received is taxed). Besides, excessive interest deduction will still be possible if interest is paid to companies who are linked to each other but do not qualify as associated companies. Moreover, because reference dates are decisive for the measurement of the debt-equity ratios, manipulation is possible. Last but not least, there have always been many debates on the compatibility of thin capitalization rules with EU law and existing tax treaties.

3. E.C.C.M. Kemmeren, *Source of Income in Globalizing Economies: Overview of the Issues and a Plea for an Origin-Based Approach*, Bulletin for International Taxation, (2006) Vol. 11. *See also* P.H.J. Essers, et al., (eds.), *Reforming the Law on Business Organizations (Back to Basics in Business Law and Tax Law)*, Eleven International Publishing, The Hague, 2011, pp. 71-75.
4. The first ATAD (ATAD1), Council Directive (EU) 2016/1164, dates from 12 July 2016. ATAD2, Council Directive (EU) 2017/952, dates from 29 May 2017 and contains the final text of the ATAD Directive.

[B] Earnings Stripping Rules

The ATAD contains no structural proposals to reduce, as much as possible, the inequality between financing through debt and equity. Only some consequences of this unequal treatment are restricted. In principle, the Directive accepts the deduction of interest paid, for example by a subsidiary to its parent. However, as a follow-up of Action 4 BEPS,[5] Article 4 ATAD1 contains an earnings stripping rule. This rule means that, in principle, financing costs included in the tax base can only be offset against financing benefits. However, if the interest paid exceeds the interest received, this surplus is deductible provided it is no more than 30% of the *EBITDA* (Earnings Before Interest, Tax, Depreciation and Amortisation). A lower percentage is also allowed. Tax-exempt income is excluded from *EBITDA*. Member States have several options while implementing the ATAD1. They can:

(1) decide to apply the *EBITDA* rule to groups of companies;
(2) deduct exceeding borrowing costs up to EUR 3 million;
(3) decide to offer a full deduction of exceeding borrowing costs if the taxpayer is a 'stand-alone entity' (an entity that is not part of a group and does not have an associated company or permanent establishment (PE));
(4) exclude loans which were concluded before 17 June 2016 from the determination of the exceeding borrowing costs (this exclusion is not applicable to any subsequent modifications of such loans);
(5) exclude loans used to fund a long-term public infrastructure project from the determination of the exceeding borrowing costs;
(6) introduce two group escapes in the case of consolidated groups:
    (i) An 'equity/total assets ratio escape': full interest deduction is allowed if the taxpayer's ratio is equal to (a deviation of 2% is allowed) or higher than the equivalent ratio of the group.
    (ii) An '*EBITDA* group ratio escape': first the group ratio is determined: the exceeding borrowing costs of the group vis-à-vis third parties divided by the *EBITDA* of the group. This ratio is applied to the taxpayer's *EBITDA*. The calculated amount is taken into account provided it is higher than the calculated amount based on the 30% main *EBITDA* rule.
(7) opt for temporizing the borrowing cost surplus or the amount of *EBITDA* that has not been used:
    (i) unlimited carry-forward offset of exceeding borrowing costs; or
    (ii) unlimited carry-forward offset of borrowing cost surplus and carry-back offset of not more than three years; or
    (iii) unlimited carry-forward offset of borrowing cost surplus and not more than five years carry-forward offset of unused *EBITDA*.

5. *See*: James Gadwood and Paul Morton, *Interest Deductibility: The Implementation of BEPS Action 4*, Cahiers de droit Fiscal International, (2019) Vol. 104a, IFA, pp. 15-46 and Adam Zalasiński, *Interest Deductibility: The Implementation of BEPS Action 4, EU Report*, Cahiers de droit Fiscal International, (2019) Vol. 104a, IFA, 2019, pp. 49-64.

There is also a general anti-avoidance regulation (Article 6 ATAD1).

The greatest disadvantage of this earnings stripping rule is that it also affects interest paid to third parties (real business costs). An advantage is that earnings stripping rules are relatively easy to apply, provided a generous exemption is applicable for interest that can always be deducted. However, group-escape clauses can be very complicated and to make the rules effective a broad definition of the term interest is required. An advantage of earnings stripping rules is also that they link up directly with the problem of excessive interest deductions. Interest payments or payments that are economically comparable to interest payments can be identified easier than obligations which, from a substance point of view, are comparable to debt. Tax-exempt income such as dividends received from a subsidiary and income to be allocated to a PE can be eliminated from *EBITDA*; as a result, arbitrage between interest deduction and tax-exempt income is avoided. In the case of thin capitalization rules, this is more complicated because these rules require an allocation of debts to assets that generate tax-exempt income. Another advantage of earnings stripping rules is that there is no risk of manipulation because of reference dates. However, earnings stripping rules do not take into account that companies with the same debt-equity ratios could have different interest percentages. A disadvantage of earnings stripping rules is also that they are procyclical. Companies in trouble can deduct less interest because of the lower *EBITDA*. The extra tax burden this causes leads them into deeper problems. This effect can be mitigated by allowing carry-forward of interest that could not be deducted or of unused *EBITDA*. Another consequence of earnings stripping rules is that because of the elimination of depreciations from *EBITDA*, companies with many fixed assets are privileged because they have more space for interest deductions. Because *EBITDA* is, in general, more volatile than debt-equity ratios, earnings stripping rules lead to greater unpredictability of the deductible interest. In Germany, earnings stripping rules might be considered unconstitutional because the denial of the deduction of interest paid to third parties is in conflict with the ability to pay principle. An advantage of earnings stripping rules is that they do not require the valuation of assets. In particular, the valuation of intangibles causes many problems. However, earnings stripping rules can lead to double taxation (the interest paid is non-deductible, the interest received is taxed).[6]

With respect to hybrid mismatches (for a definition, *see* Article 2 section 9 ATAD1), Article 9 requires interest deduction by the subsidiary to be allowed only if there is a corresponding inclusion of the same payment in the state of the creditor. These are so-called linking rules. As a consequence, the tax treatment of interest in the state of the debtor is made dependent on the tax system of the creditor state. Clearly, this is not a fundamental solution, but an approach inspired purely by the desire to prevent the avoidance of taxation: deduction at the level of the subsidiary, no corresponding inclusion at the level of the parent or double deduction. If the deduction is not refused in the payer's state, the amount of this payment should be included in the

6. F.J. Elsweier, *Een rechtsvergelijking tussen de Nederlandse en Duitse winstbelasting van lichamen*, FM nr. 153, Wolters Kluwer, Deventer, 2018, pp. 243-247; S.A. Stevens, *Implementatie van de earningsstrippingmaatregel*, Tijdschrift Fiscaal Ondernemingsrecht 2019/161.2.

profit in the recipient's state. Apparently, the only goal of these rules is to tax at least once: the so-called single tax principle. Undoubtedly, the European Commission, following the OECD, is not interested in avoiding the risk of double taxation as a result of mismatches or in the real causes of these mismatches.[7]

§1.04 SOLUTIONS BASED ON THE DEPENDENT ENTITY MODEL

The alternatives presented in section §1.03 of this Introduction all fit into the so-called *independent entity model*, based on the fiction that within a group a subsidiary should be treated as an independent entity. Then, in principle, intra-group payments are tax-deductible. This, however, does not reflect reality given that most subsidiaries are completely dependent on the directives of their parent company. In a dependent entity model, the subsidiary is considered to be fully dependent on its parent, meaning that intra-group payments accepted for private law purposes are not necessarily also accepted for tax purposes.

[A] Common Consolidated Corporate Tax Base (CCCTB)

The most far-reaching proposal based on the *dependent entity model* is the European Commission's plan to implement the Common Consolidated Corporate Tax Base (CCCTB), a cross-border fiscal unity, leading to the consolidation of all the profits of the various parts of this unity determined on the basis of the same EU rules.[8] On the basis of the sales, labour and assets allocation criteria, this consolidated profit is allocated to the different EU Member States where the members of this fiscal unity are present (*formulary apportionment*).[9] Accordingly, the profits allocated will be taxed in these states at the national corporate income tax rates. In such a fiscal unity, it makes no difference anymore whether group activities are financed through debt or equity. Article 11 of the related CCTB Directive proposal[10] contains an 'Allowance for Growth and Investment' (AGI), which is meant to stimulate economic growth and also address the 'debt-equity bias' in corporate income taxes. This AGI does not offer a full ACE – a deduction on the full equity stock – but a deduction on the new equity, the increase of equity in a year. This 'incremental' ACE leads to a deduction in the case of an increase of equity and an increase in the case of a decrease in equity, based on a notional interest percentage.

7. *See* G.K. Fibbe, *EC Law Aspects of Hybrid Entities*, Vol. 15, Doctoral Series IBFD, Amsterdam, 2009 and L. Parada, *Double Non-taxation and the Use of Hybrid Entities*, Vol. 66, Series on International Taxation, Kluwer Law International, Alphen aan den Rijn, 2018.
8. Council Directive on a Common Consolidated Corporate Tax Base, Com(2016) 683 (final) and Council Directive on a Common Corporate Tax Base, COM(2016) 685 (final).
9. *See also* R.S. Avi-Yonah, *The Rise and Fall of Arm's Length: A Study in the Evolution of U.S. International Taxation*, University of Michigan Law School, Public Law and Legal Theory Working Paper Series, Working Paper no. 92, September 2007, John M. Olin Center for Law & Economics, Working Paper no. 07-017.
10. The *Common Corporate Tax Base* (CCTB) proposal: *COM(2016) 685 final.*

Although CCCTB solves many problems, one of the major obstacles for implementing this proposal is to find suitable allocation criteria. Until now, the criteria proposed do not take services and digital enterprises into sufficient account. A possible solution to overcome this obstacle could be to opt only for 'sales' as allocation criterion and not (or to a lesser degree) to labour and assets, but disadvantages are linked to this solution as well.[11] Recently, European Parliament proposals have been made to also include data (*collected personal data and exploited personal data*) in the allocation criteria.[12] Considering the actual political disagreement between Member States, it is clear that the introduction of CCCTB is still very uncertain.

[B] Affiliated Corporation Permanent Establishment

Another approach based on the *dependent entity model* which, in the author's opinion,[13] deserves more attention, considers a foreign subsidiary primarily as an extension of the parent/head office as if it were a PE. In that case, there is a so-called *Affiliated Corporation Permanent Establishment*. For tax purposes, transactions and payments between such a subsidiary/PE and its parent/head office are only recognized if they comply with the at arm's-length principle in combination with the aforementioned *Significant People Functions Test* (in the case of PEs) and *Delineation Test* (in the case of subsidiaries). In my opinion, the current *Significant People Functions* and *Delineation Tests* offer sufficient possibilities to eliminate, as far as possible, many of the persisting differences between a subsidiary and a PE. On the basis of the *Delineation Test*, a subsidiary can be treated according to its (in)dependence of the parent company. For this purpose, the assets, functions and risks which can realistically be allocated to this subsidiary can also be considered for tax purposes. The same is true for a PE. To the extent that this PE can be considered to be independent from its head office, the *Significant People Functions Test* ensures that this will have corresponding tax effects (e.g., by allowing the deduction of royalties paid to the head office for the real use a PE makes of the head office's knowledge).

In the case of intra-group loans, however, the dependence of the head office/parent of the PE/subsidiary on this internal loan arrangement can be expected to be very predominant and to contain a high risk of primarily tax-driven motives. Because it is very difficult to establish a standard debt-equity ratio for these situations, with this system, no tax deduction of interest paid to the head office/parent will, in

11. *See* M.F. de Wilde, *Sharing the Pie, Taxing Multinationals in a Global Market*, IBFD, Amsterdam, 2015.
12. European Parliament, *Report on the proposal for a Council directive on a Common Consolidated Corporate Tax Base (CCCTB), Committee on Economic and Monetary Affairs*, 1 March 2018, A8-0051/2018. *See also* the Council Directive laying down rules relating to the corporate taxation of a significant digital presence, COM (2018) 147 final, and Council Directive on a common system of a digital service tax on revenues resulting from the provisions of certain digital services (COM (2018) 148 final). *See*: *Special Issue on Digital Taxation*, Intertax, (June/July 2018) Vol. 46, nos 6-7.
13. The following is based on my contribution to the *Liber Amicorum in Honour of Bertil Wiman, International Taxation in a Changing Landscape* (edited by Jérôme Monsenego and Jan Bjuvberg), Kluwer Law International, Alphen aan den Rijn, 2019, pp. 79-81.

general, be possible, as in the alternative to the CBIT, described in section §1.02[A]. Only under exceptional circumstances can interest deductions be allowed, as in a situation in which the subsidiary/PE performs a treasury function or in the event of internal deliveries of goods and services with the postponement of payment. In this way, a balanced synthesis can be achieved between the *dependent* and *independent legal entity model* and justice will be done to economic reality. An important advantage is that thin capitalization and earnings stripping rules will not be necessary anymore, provided of course that all countries are willing to apply the same system (to avoid mismatches and double taxation). As a result of the broadening of the tax base, the tax rates for business profits can be lowered.

Despite the current *independent entity* fiction, under actual international tax law, an *Affiliated Corporation Permanent Establishment* is actually possible, albeit only in exceptional circumstances. Article 5(7) OECD Model Treaty states that the fact that a company which is a resident of a Contracting State controls or is controlled by a company which is a resident of the other Contracting State, or which carries on business in that other State (whether through a PE or otherwise), shall not of itself constitute either company a PE of the other. This means that the fact that a parent company which is a resident of one of the Contracting States and which controls a subsidiary that is a resident of the other Contracting State does not qualify this subsidiary *of itself* as a PE of that parent. An exception to the rule that a foreign subsidiary cannot be qualified as a PE of the parent arises if this subsidiary can be qualified as a dependent agent of the parent, the so-called *Agency-PE*;[14] *see* Article 5(5) OECD Model Treaty. Mostly, however, a foreign subsidiary does not conclude contracts in the name of and on behalf of its parent company. Because of the addition of the words 'of itself' in Article 5(7) OECD Model Treaty, it is not impossible for a subsidiary to be qualified as a PE of its parent, but then it has to be very clear that there is extreme interference of the parent in the business of its subsidiary (and the other requirements for a PE must also have been fulfilled).[15] According to Le Gall,[16] the tax authorities have the right to qualify a subsidiary as a PE if they can prove the *subsidiary's excessive*

14. R. Vann, *Tax Treaties: The Secret Agent's Secrets*, British Tax Review (2006) no. 3, p. 359.
15. This could also mean that the parent has a PE next to the enterprise of the subsidiary. *See* M. Milet, *Permanent Establishments Through Related Corporations under the OECD Model Treaty*, Canadian Tax Journal (2007) Vol. 55, no. 2, pp. 300 and 318.
16. J.P. Le Gall, *Can a Subsidiary Be a Permanent Establishment of Its Foreign Parent?, Commentary on Article 5, par. 7 of the OECD Model Tax Convention*, The David R. Tillinghast Lecture (2006), N.Y.U. Tax Law Review (2006) Vol. 60, p. 212. *See also* p. 206: 'Conversely, it appears that the dependent subsidiary performs all or some of the parent company's functions, all or part of the profit generated by the parent company shall be allocated to the subsidiary. This typically would be the case for a subsidiary, where it acts as toller or contract manufacturer for its parent company, which pays it on a cost-plus basis for this work. It appears that the parent company acts exclusively under the cover of the subsidiary, all or part of the profit generated from manufacturing would be attributed to this subsidiary, which would constitute a branch of the parent company. The parent company would only be taxed on a residual profit corresponding to the activities that it continued to perform at the headquarters.'

dependence. In several countries, examples can be found in case law where this reasoning has been followed.[17]

It might be worthwhile considering making a rule instead of an exception out of the presumption that a foreign subsidiary is to be regarded as an *Affiliated Corporation Permanent Establishment* of its parent. This is less exotic than it appears in the first instance.[18] In the 1920s and 1930s, this was already the rule. In these times, subsidiaries were regarded as PEs of their parents. In the first draft of the Model Treaty of the League of Nations of 1927, in Article 5, associated corporations were considered to be PEs and aligned with branches, factories, offices, warehouses and the like. Apparently, the legal personality of these corporations was no obstacle to qualifying them as permanent establishments.[19] However, this situation did not last for long; in the draft Model Treaty of 1928, there was no longer any reference to associated corporations as PEs.

Nevertheless, in this period several tax treaties contained an identification of subsidiaries as PEs.[20] Under German law, until 1934, a subsidiary was automatically regarded as a PE. A spectacular case at that time was, for example, the so-called *Shell Urteil* of 1930,[21] in which the German *Reichsfinanzhof* ruled that the dominant role played by the top management of Shell with respect to its German subsidiaries through the identification of these subsidiaries as PEs meant that the top management of Shell was liable for tax in Germany. This situation lasted until the end of the 1930s. As of that moment, the aforementioned text of the present Article 5(7) OECD Model Treaty became the standard.[22] The driving force behind this development was the famous United States lawyer Mitchell B. Carroll. At the request of the League of Nations, he wrote a report on the allocation of business profits.[23] This report had a major impact on the evolution of the model treaty, including the provisions on the PE. In Carroll's opinion, subsidiaries had to be treated as independent entities, which meant that according to him the concept of the *Affiliated Corporation PE* should be banned.[24]

17. *See* J.P. Le Gall, *Can a Subsidiary Be a Permanent Establishment of Its Foreign Parent?, Commentary on Article 5, par. 7 of the OECD Model Tax Convention*, The David R. Tillinghast Lecture (2006), N.Y.U. Tax Law Review (2006) Vol. 60, p. 181 and M. Milet, *Permanent Establishments Through Related Corporations under the OECD Model Treaty*, Canadian Tax Journal (2007) Vol. 55, no. 2, pp. 324 ff.
18. *See* R. Petruzzi, *The Arm's Length Principle: Between Legal Fiction and Economic Reality*, in: M. Lang, A. Storck and R. Petruzzi (eds.), *Transfer Pricing in a Post-BEPS World*, Eucotax Series on European Taxation, Kluwer Law International, Alphen aan den Rijn, 2016.
19. *See* R. Vann, *Tax Treaties: The Secret Agent's Secrets*, British Tax Review, no. 3, p. 381; M. Milet, *Permanent Establishments Through Related Corporations under the OECD Model Treaty*, Canadian Tax Journal (2007) Vol. 55, no. 2, p. 296.
20. *See* C.A. Natwar, G. Thakrar and C.A. Harshal Bhuta, *Subsidiary as Permanent Establishment*, in: Chamber of Tax Consultants on International Taxation, *International Taxation – A Compendium*, 3rd edn, March 2013, Chapter 26, p. I-710.
21. *Reichsfinanzhof* 30 January 1930, Reichssteuerblatt 1930, p. 148.
22. *See* J.P. Le Gall, *Can a Subsidiary Be a Permanent Establishment of Its Foreign Parent?, Commentary on Article 5, par. 7 of the OECD Model Tax Convention*, The David R. Tillinghast Lecture (2006), N.Y.U. Tax Law Review (2006) Vol. 60, p. 180.
23. Draft of a Bilateral Convention for the Prevention of Double Taxation, in: League of Nations, Double Taxation and Tax Evasion, League of Nations doc. C.216.M.85.1927.II.
24. *See*: M. Milet, *Permanent Establishments Through Related Corporations under the OECD Model Treaty*, Canadian Tax Journal (2007) Vol. 55, no. 2, pp. 296-299.

However, Carroll did recognize this could lead to artificial profit shifting, resulting in a situation in which the really relevant activities leading to value creation could not be taxed anymore. In his view, this phenomenon should be tackled with adjustments to the transfer pricing rules based on the at arm's-length principle.[25]

Under Carroll's influence, in the 1933 Model Treaty of the League of Nations, an article was included explicitly stating that a PE 'does not include a subsidiary company'. As from 1946, in later versions of model treaties, the text also stated that 'the mere fact that a non-resident is in a control relationship with a company resident or (carrying on business) in another treaty country does not of itself give rise to a permanent establishment in that country'. This text corresponds to the actual Article 5(7) OECD Model Treaty.

§1.05 CONCLUDING REMARKS

The problems caused by the diametrically opposite tax treatment of (the costs) debt and equity within a group of companies, in combination with the fact that within such a group it is quite easy to change financing from debt to equity (or vice versa), should be solved by introducing sustainable (durable) solutions. The BEPS and EU approaches, such as the earnings stripping rules, only look at short-term effects and are not concerned, for instance, with the prevention of double taxation. In the author's opinion, more sustainable solutions would be the introduction of an 'ACE', or, even better, a 'CBIT', in combination with a system based on the *dependent entity model* that considers a foreign subsidiary primarily to be an extension of its parent/head office as if it were a PE (a so-called *Affiliated Corporation Permanent Establishment*) as explained in section §1.04[B] of this contribution. In the case of intra-group loans, the dependence of the head office/parent of the permanent establishment/subsidiary on this internal loan arrangement can be expected to be predominant and to contain a high risk of primarily tax-driven motives. Since it is very difficult to establish a standard debt-equity ratio for these situations, with this system, no tax deduction on interest paid to the head office/parent will, in general, be possible, as in the alternative of the CBIT. For intra-group payments other than interest costs, the at arm's-length principle in combination with the *Significant People Functions Test* (in the case of permanent establishments) and the *Delineation Test* (in the case of subsidiaries) can be applied to verify their deductibility as business costs.

25. *See also* J.P. Le Gall, *Can a Subsidiary Be a Permanent Establishment of Its Foreign Parent?, Commentary on Article 5, par. 7 of the OECD Model Tax Convention*, The David R. Tillinghast Lecture (2006), N.Y.U. Tax Law Review (2006) Vol. 60, pp. 199 ff.

CHAPTER 2

The Preference of Debt over Equity for Tax Purposes

Jakob Bundgaard & Michael Tell

§2.01 SCOPE AND OUTLINE

The purpose of this introductory chapter is to shed light on the overall distinction between debt and equity from the perspective of corporate tax law.[1] A general description is provided of the difference between debt and equity, which is followed by a presentation of the tax implications arising from the use of debt and equity. Finally, the chapter concludes with a brief overview of the tax policy discussions which have evolved around the topic.

§2.02 INTRODUCTION

Essentially, companies can be financed by issuing debt or share capital (balance sheet) or by earnings (profits and losses). In addition, several other financing techniques are available, including leasing, securitization[2] and debt workouts. "Debt" and "equity" are labels for the two ends of a spectrum, between which lies an infinite number of instruments, each differing from its closest neighbors in barely perceptible ways.[3] These include hybrid financial instruments, combining debt as well as equity features.

1. The chapter is largely based on the monograph *Bundgaard*: Hybrid Financial Instruments, Kluwer, 2017.
2. *See Humphreys & Merali*: Tax Treatment of Structured Finance Transactions in PLI Tax Strategies for Corporate Acquisitions, Dispositions, Spin-Offs, Joint Ventures, Financings, Reorganizations & Restructurings, 2006, pp. 831 et seq.
3. For this description *see Bittker & Eustice*: Federal Taxation of Corporations and Shareholders, 2002, pp. 4-12.

The sources of corporate financing may be exemplified by a continuum, as illustrated in Figure 2.1.

Figure 2.1 The Debt-Equity Continuum

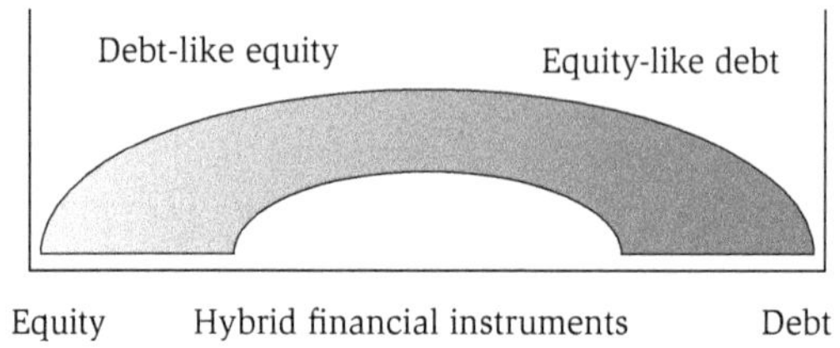

Within the world of financing, a vast array of different types of instruments exist, and more and more variations are being developed. A commonly adopted method of providing an overview is through the use of a so-called classification tree, as presented in Figure 2.2.

Figure 2.2 Classification Tree

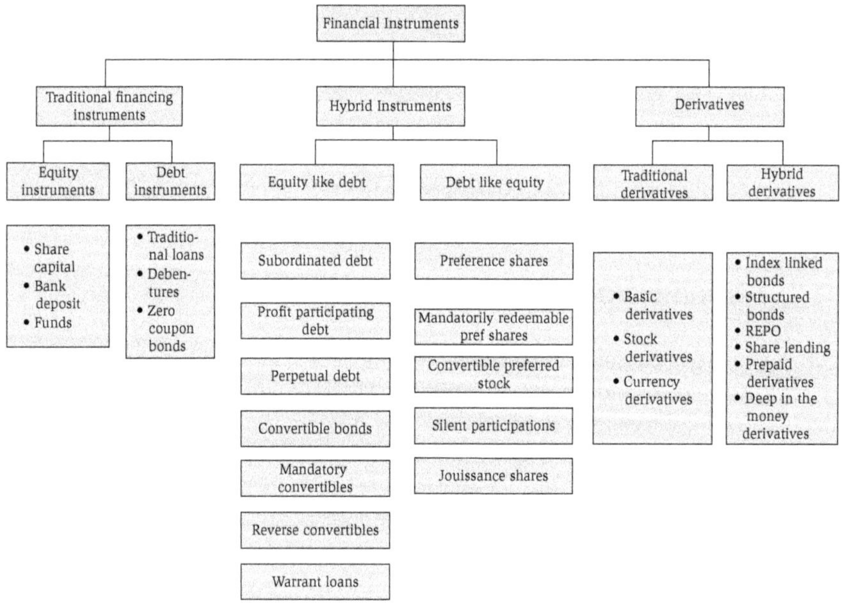

Several legal and economic differences between debt and equity instruments can be pointed out.[4] First, the legal differences are the following (Table 2.1).[5]

Table 2.1 Legal Differences Between Debt and Equity

Equity	*Debt*
The owner of shares is normally entitled to a proportion of the profits of the company. The owner is not normally entitled to recover the original investment except on the dissolution of the company. The risks that the owner undertakes are normally limited to the amount of equity capital that the owner has subscribed or has undertaken to subscribe. However, the owner would usually be able to sell the shares and thus recover the current value of the investment, which might be more or less than the amount originally invested.	The provider of loan capital is normally entitled to a periodical amount of fixed interest on the amount lent, regardless of the profit, if any, made by the company. The lender is normally entitled to recover the investment after a certain period. Like a shareowner, the lender risks losing the entire investment. The lender may in some circumstances be able to make an earlier sale of the rights to another person, at which point the lender may recover either more or less than the original investment, although the factors affecting the sale value of a bond may well be different from those affecting the value of a share.

Second, the *economic difference* is said to be that a lender (loan creditor) will look to a periodic fixed remuneration for the use of their loan capital, and to the return of the loan capital itself at the end of the loan period, while a shareholder must wait for an (additional) upside to manifest itself before the directors of the company decide that profits can be spared for distribution rather than reinvestment.[6] Debt is traditionally described as providing an investor with cash flow rights that are certain as far as the amount invested is concerned. In contrast, dividends and ordinary shares are examples where there are no rights to a cash flow as a result of the transaction.[7] There are financial risks for investors in both debt and equity, but the financial risk for equity holders is usually considered higher,[8] but also entails an infinite economic upside. As such, distinction between equity and debt is made by reference to the degree of

4. Emphasized by the *OECD* Fiscal Committee on Thin Capitalisation, Issues in International Taxation, 1987, pp. 8 et seq.
5. *See* for example the *OECD* report: Thin Capitalisation adopted by the OECD Council on November 26, 1986, legal and economic differences are pointed out in paras. 3-5. *See also Ferran*: Company Law and Corporate Finance, 1999, pp. 47 et seq., characterizing equity by the following factors: dividends, capital growth (capital gains and risk) and voting rights. *See*, moreover, *Mattsson*: Aktiebolagens finansieringsformer, 1977, pp. 9 et seq.
6. *See OECD* Fiscal Committee on Thin Capitalisation, Issues in International Taxation, 1987, pp. 8 et seq. *See also Coyle*: Hybrid Financial Instruments, 2002, pp. 2 et seq. for an overview of the economic differences between debt and equity.
7. *Id.*
8. *See Coyle*: Hybrid Financial Instruments, 2002, pp. 2 et seq. for an overview of the economic differences between debt and equity, p. 4 and *McCormick & Creamer (eds.)*: Hybrid Corporate Securities: International Legal Aspects, 1987, pp. 2-3.

certainty attached to the direction, timing and amount of cash flows.[9] In essence, debt is a resource that does not belong to the company (loan capital), while equity is part of the company's own resources.[10] Consequently, a company which is financed primarily by equity may operate in a very different way to a company mainly financed by debt.

Furthermore, in terms of corporate governance, the holders of equity are entitled to make decisions on the part of the company, while holders of debt are relegated to the sidelines. Traditional debt holders can take no part in the management of the borrowing entity, and the borrowing entity owes them no explanation for their actions.[11]

As an overview of the core elements of debt and equity, the following can be pointed out:

- Equity has no maturity, no ongoing payments that could trigger a default if unpaid, and loss absorption benefiting all creditors.[12] Debt, in contrast, usually has fixed payments and a stated maturity.
- Nonpayment of principal or interest constitutes default. Whereas shareholders are the last class of security holders to receive distributions in liquidation, debt holders, by contrast, have a right to receive payments before equity holders.[13] Equity holders may be entitled to a dividend, subject to declaration by the issuer, and equity instruments may entitle the holder to some voting rights. Dividend payments may be cumulative or noncumulative.[14]

The legal and economic differences between debt and equity also give rise to different tax treatments of debt and equity as described in the section below.

§2.03 TAX RAMIFICATIONS OF THE DEBT-EQUITY DISTINCTION

[A] General Overview

The distinction between debt and equity is considered to be one of the fundamental and yet unsolved issues of international tax law. In most jurisdictions, the distinction remains relevant to ensure the correct *classification* and the corresponding *tax treatment* of the yield from debt or equity.

9. *See OECD*: Innovative Financial Transactions: Tax Policy Implications, 2001, pp. 21-22.
10. *See Brown* in Cahiers, vol. 97b, The Debt-Equity Conundrum, 2012, p. 40.
11. *See Poindexter* in Berkeley Business Law Review, 2005, p. 253, explaining that the basis for the distinction evolves from contract theory: "While the underlying duty of the firm to its equity holders is fiduciary, the duty to its creditors is contractual. Thus, in the authors mind to determine whether an investment is debt or equity, we should ask whether the duty of the firm to investors is fiduciary or contractual." As stated in *McCormick & Creamer (eds.)*, in Berkeley Business Law Review, 2005, p. 2, these distinctions may have little economic significance in relation to HFIs, but they are of fundamental importance in determining the legal nature of the HFI.
12. *See Eiger, Green, Humphreys and Jennings & Mares*: Hybrid Securities: An Overview, Practical Law, Multi-Jurisdictional Guide 2015/16, Capital Markets, pp. 1 et seq.
13. *Id.*, p. 2.
14. *Id.*

In simple terms, the core tax issue of corporate finance is the difference in the tax treatment of the remuneration on debt and equity. If tax laws were neutral, it would be irrelevant from a taxation perspective whether corporations were financed through debt or equity, whereas the lack of neutrality makes it crucial to be able to distinguish between equity/dividends and debt/interest.[15] As a general rule, the tax treatment of equity financing and debt financing follows the same basic principles around the world[16] but entails a preference of debt over equity as explained in further detail below. The debt bias is well documented.[17]

The debt-equity conundrum has been dealt with in various ways in different jurisdictions. A global trend has emerged over a longer period of time which has gained speed most recently with the aim of neutralizing the treatment of debt and equity.[18]

Relevant measures include means of reducing the appeal for debt financing by restricting interest deductibility or reclassifying debt into equity.[19] As of 2021, interest limitation rules are mandatory in all European Union (EU) Member States and recommended by the Organisation for Economic Co-operation and Development (OECD)/G20 in the Base Erosion and Profit Shifting Project (BEPS).[20]

Alternative approaches to the above interest restrictions include allowance for equity or deductible dividends. Such approaches stimulate equity investments positively rather than (negatively) restricting debt financing. In recent years, several countries have followed this approach and countries such as Belgium, Brazil, Liechtenstein and Italy have all introduced rules which allow companies a deduction for notional interest on equity. Other countries have considered introducing similar regimes, and even the EU commission included an Allowance for the Cost of Equity (ACE) system in its proposals for a Common (Consolidated) Corporate Tax Base.

---

15. *See Helminen* in Kluwer Law International: The Dividend Concept in International Tax Law: Dividend Payments Between Corporate Entities, 1999, p. 12.
16. *See Piltz* in Cahiers, vol. LXXXIa, Permanent Establishments of Banks, Insurance Companies and Other Financial Institutions, 1996, pp. 87 et seq.; *OECD,* Thin Capitalisation, 1986, paras. 7 et seq., *Burmeister*: Unternehmensfinanzierung im Internationalen Steuerrecht, 2003, pp. 36 et seq.
17. *See also* the Final Report from the European Commission written by the *Centre for European Economic Research (ZEW) GmbH* in Taxation paper No 65: The Effects of Tax Reforms to Address the Debt-Equity Bias on the Cost of Capital and on Effective Tax Rates, dated October 25, 2016, Chapter 5, which stated that a debt bias is found in most tax systems in the EU Member States.
18. *See,* for a recent analysis, for example *de Mooij*: Tax Biases to Debt Finance: Assessing the Problem, Finding Solutions, IMF Staff Discussion Note, 2011.
19. *Id.* and *Blessing* in Bulletin 2012, pp. 209 et seq. *See also Schön* in Bulletin 2012, pp. 490 et seq.
20. *See* Council Directive (EU) 2016/1164 of July 12, 2016, laying down rules against tax avoidance practices that directly affect the functioning of the internal market and OECD/G20 Base Erosion and Profit Shifting Project on Limiting Base Erosion Involving Interest Deductions and Other Financial Payments, Action 4 (Final Report dated October 2015 and Updated Report dated December 2016).

Despite the efforts to reduce the preference of debt over equity, as shown in this chapter, there still seems to be a preference of debt over equity for tax purposes, as it appears that more fundamental tax reforms are needed to overcome the debt bias.[21]

[B] Tax Framework Regarding Debt and Equity

The distinction between debt and equity has been established in the context of civil law, in particular contract law, corporate law and insolvency law.[22] Debt and equity serve as categories for particular combinations of financial risk and rewards, voting and control rights under a contract providing funds for a business as stated above.[23] From this starting point, the distinction between debt and equity has found its way into domestic tax law, while no specific international tax law regime exists regarding corporate financing.[24]

Clearly, a distinction between debt and equity is relevant in most countries, while in reality, the debt versus equity distinction is often mostly concerned with the interest versus dividend distinction rather than the actual debt versus equity distinction in itself, as the actual discrimination or preference for tax purposes is caused by:

- interest being deductible while dividends generally are not;[25]
- interest is taxable while some dividends often obtain a more favorable tax treatment;
- interest withholding tax and dividend withholding tax rates often differ, with interest generally being subject to lower rates or exemption;
- interest may accrue for tax purposes, but dividends are generally taxed on distribution.

Below the principles governing the taxation of cash flows from debt and equity instruments are described in general terms. The purpose of this general description is to illustrate the different tax treatment of remuneration from debt and equity.

[1] Tax Treatment of an Equity Issuer

Generally, corporate earnings from equity are subject to corporation tax in the country of residence of the issuing company. As a main rule, remuneration on equity (dividends) is nondeductible in the calculation of taxable profits.[26] As such, dividends are

21. *See also* Final Report from the European Commission written by the *Centre for European Economic Research (ZEW) GmbH* in Taxation paper No 65: The Effects of Tax Reforms to Address the Debt-Equity Bias on the Cost of Capital and on Effective Tax Rates, dated October 25, 2016, p. 9.
22. *See*, for example, *Schön* et al. in Competition and Tax Law Research Paper Series No. 09-09, 2009: Debt and Equity: What's the Difference? A Comparative View, Max Planck Institute for Intellectual Property, p. 2.
23. *Id.*
24. *See also Brown* in Cahiers, vol. 97b, The Debt-Equity Conundrum, 2012, p. 32.
25. *Id.*, p. 21.
26. *See*, for example, *Brown* in Cahiers, vol. 97b: The Debt-Equity Conundrum, 2012, p. 21.

paid out of taxed earnings. Exceptions to this rule do, however, exist in certain jurisdictions.[27]

[2] Tax Treatment of an Equity Investor

In the shareholder's country of residence, dividends are in principle taxable, possibly with a credit for the withholding tax and/or corporate income tax (CIT) levied at the level of the paying corporation. Presupposing the existence of an international affiliation privilege or participation exemption, the dividends are tax-exempt if the requirements are fulfilled.

In the country of source of the dividend, the shareholder may, in addition, be subject to a withholding tax on the shareholder's account, which is, however, reduced or eliminated in many instances as a result of double tax treaties or the EU Parent-/Subsidiary Directive (PSD).[28]

The state of residence of the dividend recipient has the right to tax according to Article 10(1) of the OECD Model Convention, while such dividends may also be taxed in the source state of the paying company, according to Article 10(2). The latter taxing right is limited under the OECD Model Convention, whereby the tax so charged shall not exceed 5% if paid to parent companies owning more than 25% of the capital of the company paying the dividends or 15% in all other cases. Double taxation arising from the imposition of withholding tax in the source state on a dividend received may be reduced by the application of the credit method under Article 23A(2) or Article 23B of the OECD Model Convention.

Dividends paid between companies in EU Member States are, in principle, covered by the PSD. The PSD requires double taxation to be avoided by either exempting the dividends or granting a tax credit equivalent to the tax already paid on the distributed profits. Dividends not covered by the PSD may be subject to (temporary or permanent) double taxation since no obligation to abolish such double taxation exists according to EU law. The PSD applies to distributions of profits between associated companies from different EU Member States. The companies involved must be subject to CIT in their respective Member State(s).[29] Both the payer and the recipient must be organized in a legal form listed in the annex to the directive. The profit

27. An example of an exception can be found, for example, in the Brazilian JCP-regime, which allows for deductible dividend distributions. *See* further details on ACE regimes in Working Paper No. 72 2018 from the European Commission written by *Nicola Branzoli and Antonella Caiumi:* How Effective Is an Incremental ACE in Addressing the Debt Bias? Evidence from Corporate Tax Returns, dated June 27, 2018.
28. *See also Burmeister*: Unternehmensfinanzierung im Internationalen Steuerrecht, 2003, pp. 36 et seq.
29. It should be noted that the ECJ has stated in the *Beneficial owner* cases (joined ECJ cases on dividends (PSD) C-116/16 and C-117/16 and the joined cases on interests (IRD) C-115/16, C-118/16, C-119/16, C-299/16) that there is, in EU law, a general legal principle that EU law, including the PSD, cannot be relied on for abusive or fraudulent ends and that a Member State *must* refuse to grant the benefit of the provisions of EU law, including the PSD, where they are relied upon in the aim of benefiting from an advantage in EU law, even if the conditions for benefiting from that advantage are fulfilled only formally, and despite the absence of provisions of national law providing for such a refusal.

distributions must be made to associated companies with a direct holding of 10% in the capital of the companies paying the dividends.[30]

[3] Tax Treatment of a Debt Issuer

Remuneration of debt (interest) is generally considered a deductible (business) expense in the calculation of taxable profits in the country of residence of the debtor/issuer.[31] As such interests are effectively free of CIT, whereas the creditor/lender in both the national and international contexts is the only person likely to suffer tax on interest payments.[32]

However, domestic restrictions on interest deductibility may impose limitations on the deductibility of the issuer.[33] Historically, rules on thin capitalization with a focus on solvency have been the predominant rules on limitations on the deductibility of interest,[34] while more general interest limitation rules based on the earnings of the issuer seem to be the new way forward, sometimes supported by more targeted rules such as rules on thin capitalization.[35]

All EU Member States are, as a minimum, obliged to transpose the earning-based limitation rule in the Anti-Tax Avoidance Directive (ATAD) Article 4, which is an implementation of OECD BEPS Action 4 approach. Other domestic and diverse restrictions targeting specific situations may also apply.[36] As such, exceeding borrowing costs (net financing cost) are not deductible if they exceed 30% of the company's or the group's earnings before interest, tax, depreciation and amortization (EBITDA), which is also the recommended approach in OECD BEPS Action 4. Even stricter general or targeted local interest limitation rules may also apply. In most non-EU Member States, more classic thin capitalization rules and local specific anti-tax avoidance rules still seem to be more predominant than the recommended approach in OECD BEPS Action 4.[37]

See also the ECJ's answers to question 5 in paras. 143-156 in C-118/16 on the application of the PSD on a Luxembourgish "Société en Commandite par Actions" (SCA) also classified as a "Société d'Investissement en Capital à Risqué" (SICAR).

30. *See also* paras. 70, 72 and 76 in the joined ECJ cases C-116/16 and C-117/16.
31. *See OECD*: Thin Capitalisation, 1986, para. 8, *Piltz* in Cahiers, vol. LXXXIa, Permanent Establishments of Banks, Insurance Companies and Other Financial Institutions, 1996, p. 92 and *Burmeister*: Unternehmensfinanzierung im Internationalen Steuerrecht, 2003, pp. 36 et seq.
32. *See OECD*: Thin Capitalisation, 1986, para. 8 and *Piltz* in Cahiers, vol. LXXXIa, Permanent Establishments of Banks, Insurance Companies and Other Financial Institutions, 1996, p. 92.
33. *See*, for example, *Brown* in Cahiers, vol. 97b, The Debt-Equity Conundrum, 2012, pp. 35 et seq.
34. *See Hinny* in Cahiers, vol. 93b: New Tendencies in Tax Treatment of Cross-Border Interest of Corporations, 2008, p. 23.
35. *See*, more in relation to the EU Member States, the Final Report from the European Commission written by the *Centre for European Economic Research (ZEW) GmbH* in Taxation paper No 65: The Effects of Tax Reforms to Address the Debt-Equity Bias on the Cost of Capital and on Effective Tax Rates, dated October 25, 2016, Chapter 6.
36. *Id.*
37. Countries such as Australia, Brazil, Canada, China, Japan, New Zealand and South Africa still apply more traditionally based thin capitalization rules, while the US has recently adopted the earning-based approach as recommended in OECD BEPS Action 4.

[4] Tax Treatment of a Debt Investor

Generally speaking, interests received are as a main rule taxable in the hands of the investor/lender according to the domestic legislation of the country of residence.[38] However, this conclusion does not always include companies resident in tax havens which are either not subject to CIT at all or subject to very limited taxation.

The lender is usually liable to tax on the interest received but may claim credit for the withholding tax levied by the source state. Interest is not usually subject to withholding tax or at least to a withholding tax that is lower than a withholding tax on dividends. Withholding taxes on interest are often reduced or eliminated in the source state according to tax treaties or the Interest-/Royalty directive (IRD).

According to Article 11 of the OECD Model Convention, the right to tax interest income is allocated to the recipient's state of residence. However, according to Article 11, paragraph 2 of the OECD Model Convention, the interest income may also be taxed in the source state, but limited to 10% of the gross amount of the interest. According to tax treaties, double taxation arising from the imposition of withholding tax in the source state on a dividend received may be reduced by the application of the credit method as stated in Article 23A, paragraph 2 or Article 23B of the OECD Model.

Interest payments between associated companies within the EU may avoid withholding tax (but not income tax) according to the IRD. In Article 1, paragraph 1 IRD, it is stated that interest payments arising in a Member State shall be relieved from any form of tax in the source state on condition that the beneficial owner of the interest is a company or a permanent resident in another Member State belonging to a company in a Member State. Under the IRD, it is required that both the borrowing company and the lending company fall under the definition of a "company of a Member State," that is mentioned in the annex, a taxable entity resident in a Member State. Another important requirement is the association between the companies as defined in Article 3, paragraph 1(b). A company is considered to be associated with another company if it: (i) directly owns at least 25% of the capital of the other company, (ii) if the other company directly owns at least 25% of the capital of the first company or (iii) if a third company directly owns at least 25% of the capital of both the paying company and the receiving company.[39]

38. *See OECD*: Thin Capitalisation, 1986, para. 8 and *Piltz* in Cahiers, vol. LXXXIa, Permanent Establishments of Banks, Insurance Companies and Other Financial Institutions, 1996, p. 92 *see also Burmeister*: Unternehmensfinanzierung im Internationalen Steuerrecht, 2003, pp. 36 et seq. and *Brown* in Cahiers, vol. 97b, The Debt-Equity Conundrum, 2012, p. 28.

39. It should be noted that the ECJ has stated in the *Beneficial owner* cases (joined ECJ cases on dividends (PSD) C-116/16 and C-117/16 and the joined cases on interests (IRD) C-115/16, C-118/16, C-119/16, C-299/16) that there is, in EU law, a general legal principle that EU law, including the IRD, cannot be relied on for abusive or fraudulent ends and that a Member State *must* in just instances refuse to grant the benefit of the provisions of EU law, including the IRD, despite the absence of provisions of national law providing for such a refusal.

[5] *Overview of Tax Consequences*

The distinction between debt and equity is still essential in international tax law. Table 2.2 summarizes the tax consequences associated with the debt-equity distinction in general terms not taking into consideration any details of domestic law.

Table 2.2 Tax Consequences Associated with Debt and Equity

Financing	*Taxpayer*	
	Issuer	*Investor*
Equity	Dividends are not deductible. *Modification*: Allowance for Corporate Equity regimes or actual deduction for dividends.	Dividends are taxable income in the hands of the shareholder, regardless of whether they arise from ordinary dividends. Withholding tax in the source state is levied in the hands of the investor. *Modification*: affiliation privilege /participation exemption.
Debt	Interest payments are deductible in the income tax calculation. *Modification*: Limitations on deductibility (thin capitalization, EBITDA rules, etc.)	Interest is taxable income in the hands of the creditor. *Modification*: International tax havens and special tax regimes.

As seen above, debt financing often reduces the tax base of the issuer, while increasing the tax base of the investor. Equity financing, however, often does not reduce the tax base of the issuer nor does it increase the tax base of the investor. Hence, a system of *one level of tax* seems to be pursued, a tax either at the level of the issuer (equity) or at the level of investor (debt).[40] As such, purely from a tax perspective debt is preferred over equity if the taxation of the issuer is higher than the taxation of the investor (including withholding taxes). This conclusion is of course simplified.

Jacobs has carried out a comprehensive study on the difference between a German parent corporation opting for either debt or equity financing of a domestic, French, Japanese and United Kingdom subsidiary.[41] Jacobs concluded that it is not possible in general to say whether debt or equity financing should be preferred (a conclusion which remains valid today). The conclusion rests on a multitude of factors, which may dramatically affect the benefit of the financing alternatives. Such factors include the following:

40. *See also Brown* in Cahiers, vol. 97b, The Debt-Equity Conundrum, 2012, p. 20.
41. *See Jacobs* in StuW 1996/1: Steuerliche Vorteilhaftigkeit des Einsatzes von Eigen- oder Fremdkapital bei der international Konzernfinanzierung pp. 26 et seq.

- Which taxes are included: taxes in the country of the foreign subsidiary, withholding taxes and shareholder taxation?
- The actual situation of the foreign subsidiary in terms of taxes, in other words is the subsidiary profitable or lossmaking?
- Whether the actual form of financing is classical debt, equity or hybrid financing?
- Are there any foreign limitations according to thin capitalization rules?
- Is a foreign financing corporation interposed?
- How is the double taxation of dividends and interests relieved, by way of exemption, indirect credit or fictitious credit?

Even if the conclusion rests on a multitude of factors, the mere complexity of the debt versus equity distinction and the unequal treatment in itself give rise to some tax policy considerations in relation to maintaining a tax distinction of the debt versus equity.

§2.04 TAX POLICY CONSIDERATIONS

[A] Is a Distinction Between Debt and Equity Needed?

The debt versus equity distinction is well established in many countries even though it has little underlying theoretical basis. Most tax law commentary has argued that equity and debt fulfill the same economic function and thus should not be taxed differently.[42]

This issue has been analyzed from a tax policy perspective by Emmerich in United States (US) Law, which also seems relevant in the context of other jurisdictions.[43] The analysis shows that the attempts by the US Courts and the Treasury to enforce the debt versus equity distinction have failed because the traditional rationale for the distinction is both impracticable and based upon factually incorrect premises.

The classical distinction in US Tax Law between shareholders and creditors (lenders) and, therefore, between dividends and interest, was drawn by the Second Circuit in *Commissioner v. O.P.P. Holding Corp.* (76 F.2d 11 (2d Cir. 1935). In this often-quoted distinction the Court stated that:

> [t]he shareholder is an adventurer in the corporate business; he takes the risk, and profits from success. The creditor, in compensation for not sharing the profits, is to be paid independently of the risk of success, and gets a right to dip into the capital when the payment date arrives … .

42. *See Mackenzie* in JAFRA vol. 1, issue no. 1, 2006, pp. 31 et seq. *Rumble & Wood* have argued in an Australian context that there should be no difference in the way debt and equity instruments are taxed. *See Rumble & Wood* in Intertax, vol. 31, 2003, pp. 409 et seq. Hariton has argued in the following way: "The task of drawing a line between equity and debt might be simpler if there were a more palpable reason for treating them in a different way. After all, equity and debt are both claims upon the assets of a corporation, and both are acquired in exchange for capital. The only economic distinction between them is the variability of their returns … ." *See* Tax Law Review 1988, p. 775.
43. *See Emmerich* in University of Chicago Law Review, Hybrid Instruments and the Debt-Equity Distinction in Corporate Taxation, vol. 52, 1985, pp. 118 et seq.

Emmerich states that this view is based on the notion that, because the shareholder benefits from investing through the corporate form, he should not be allowed to extract his profits until after they have been taxed at the corporate level.[44] Conversely, it is stated that the cost of borrowing money (interest) is seen as an ordinary and necessary cost of doing business that should no more be met out of after-tax dollars than should workers' salaries or the cost of raw material.[45] The author finds no better explanation stated by the Congress and concludes that the deductibility of interest is apparently so intuitively that Congress has deemed it unnecessary to explain Internal Revenue Code (IRC) § 163(a) or its predecessors.[46]

Despite the intuitive appeal and the actual use of the distinction as often based on the O.P.P. case and the like, it may be stated that the Court's reasoning does not successfully draw a principled distinction between debt and equity.[47] In conclusion, it is held that the O.P.P. Holding standard has proven to be essentially empty which has resulted in a lack of consistency and clarity.[48]

Emmerich then turns to financing theory in order to see whether the discipline provides a principled distinction between debt and equity. Based on the propositions by Modigliani & Miller, it is concluded that finance theory does not support a principled distinction between debt and equity. Any attempt to classify instruments as either debt or equity in a principled fashion is likely to be arbitrary in practice and will encourage wasteful efforts by tax planners to create instruments that take advantage of whatever line is drawn.[49]

Nevertheless, the history of debt and equity taxation in many countries shows that debt and equity have actually been treated differently for tax purposes.[50] A difference between the two forms of financing does currently exist and is highly

44. *Id.*, p. 122.
45. *Id.*, p. 122.
46. *Id.* fn. 23.
47. *Id.*, p. 122, stating: "... The distinction fails because the difference between creditor and shareholder is, in an important sense, one of degree only. Both shareholders and creditors contribute capital to the corporation in the expectation that the corporation will be able to use this capital productively and return it to them along with a share of the resulting gain. Furthermore, it is inaccurate to characterize all shareholders as necessarily bearing more risk than all creditors. The degree of risk to which an investor is exposed, and the potential payoff that he can expect, can vary more between the bond of one company and the bond of another than between the debt and stock of the same company ... ."
48. *Id.*, p. 128.
49. The author's rationale is seemingly based on fairness arguments. It is stated: "Accordingly, the market will always respond with new instruments to take advantage of any line drawn by the Service. Such a response tends to be especially strong from large, publicly held corporations that constantly raise new capital, employing professional advisors to aid them in doing so. Investment banker and tax lawyers monitor the latest tax regulations and develop instruments having the desired tax and financial characteristics, thus obtaining large tax savings for their clients. As a result, those corporations that invest in intensive tax planning enjoy an advantage over those that do not."
50. An exception would be a Comprehensive Business Income Tax (CBIT) or a Cost of Capital Allowance (COCA) tax system as mentioned below in section §2.04[D]. *See also*, for example, Final Report from the European Commission written by the *Centre for European Economic Research (ZEW) GmbH* in Taxation paper No 65: The Effects of Tax Reforms to Address the Debt-Equity Bias on the Cost of Capital and on Effective Tax Rates, dated October 25, 2016, Chapter 7.

unlikely to change in the near future.[51] The question remains about what should be done with the distinction: should it be abolished or preserved?

[B] Proposals to Improve the "Line-Drawing"

It has been argued that any line drawn between debt and equity is inherently arbitrary and that a clear line is, therefore, essential if a tax system is to be built around that line. Such a tax system can include measures imposing a maximum debt/equity ratio, earning-based limitations and/or a deduction with respect to notional interest on equity. Issuers and investors can then develop products *with no bells and whistles* that accurately reflect the desired risk/reward trade-off and are intended to ensure that the instrument receives the desired tax treatment.[52]

A number of scholars have developed proposals with the aim of improving the line-drawing. One of the simplest proposals is presented by Emmerich.[53] On the basis of a foregoing analysis, Emmerich proposes a test to govern the classification of debt and equity for instruments issued in arm's-length transactions by large, publicly held corporations. Under the proposed test, financial instruments that *closely resemble straight debt* (based on a classic notion of debt) would be treated as debt unless they were sold as packages of separately salable debt and equity instruments. In other words, the author simply suggests that debt treatment should only be granted to debt instrument which carries the primary characteristics of debt. In the words of the author, this is not to untie the Gordian knot but simply to cut it.[54]

Another attempt to improve the line-drawing is the bright-line test suggested by Thompson.[55] In general terms, Thompson finds that such rules would have the effect of only treating those instruments that are clearly debt as debt for income tax purposes and, thus, only they would curtail the erosion of the corporate tax base.[56]

Schön argues that the debt-equity distinction should endure. According to the author, the debt-equity distinction has not broken down, but in (urgent) need of repair and a common understanding of its underlying policy options.[57] Schön demonstrates that the debt-equity divide cannot easily be dismissed and that equity treatment, as

51. See *Mackenzie* in Journal of Applied Research in Accounting and Finance, Taxation as a Driver for Designing Hybrid Securities, vol. 1, issue no. 1, 2006, p. 35.
52. *See also Brown* in Cahiers vol. 97b, The Debt-Equity Conundrum, 2012, p. 42.
53. *See Emmerich* in University of Chicago Law Review, Hybrid Instruments and the Debt-Equity Distinction in Corporate Taxation, vol. 52, 1985, pp. 118 et seq. (p. 120).
54. *Id.*, p. 148.
55. *See* Thompson *in Tax Notes; A Suggested Approach to Debt/Equity Issues and Leveraged Acquisitions, January 23, vol. 42, 1989, pp. 483 et seq.*
56. *Id.*, p. 485.
57. *See Schön*, in Bulletin for International Taxation: The Distinct Equity of the Debt-Equity Distinction, vol. 66, 2012, p. 502. *See*, moreover, *Schön* et al.: Debt and Equity: What's the Difference? A Comparative View, Max Planck Institute for Intellectual Property, Competition and Tax Law Research Paper Series No. 09-09. *See also Schön* et al. in British Tax Review (BTR), No. 2, Debt and Equity in Domestic and International Tax Law—A Comparative Policy Analysis, 2014, pp. 146–217.

opposed to debt treatment, should refer to the power of the company to decide on the distribution of funds.[58]

Bärsch has also developed a number of different reform options and has identified two coordinated domestic tax law classification approaches. These proposals share the idea that the coordinated domestic tax classifications of the remuneration of equity or debt should be based solely on genuine tax rules since reference to domestic company law classification increases complexity.[59] Bärsch argues that two alternatives are available.[60]

The first being that the classification should rely on the distinctive characteristics of the instrument and that it seems advisable that instruments should be classified as debt only if: (1) the capital borrower is both noncontingently obliged to provide a noncontingently determined repayment amount and the corresponding repayment date is effectively not longer than thirty years after the issuance and (2) this repayment amount is not subordinated to all other creditors of the capital borrower. Finally, it is concluded that the tax classification shall disregard the remuneration as a decisive characteristic.

As a second nonharmonized domestic classification approach, Bärsch argues that this should avoid an entirely new set of decisive characteristics by making reference to the foreign domestic tax classification. In this context, the author prefers an approach where reference is made to the domestic tax classification of the source country either in a harmonized way or by means of tiebreaker rules.[61]

Lastly, as another approach, Bärsch introduces options that depart from the coexistence of source-based and residence-based taxation, but which in principle do not depart from the debt-equity dichotomy. Here different suggestions are developed such as introducing withholding taxes on interest payments and restrictions on deductibility. The author recommends introducing tax exemption for interest payments as well as dividend payments in the case of an effective corporate income taxation in the source country.[62]

[C] Proposals Eliminating the Effects of the Current Debt-Equity Distinction

Plumb has argued a need for legislative reappraisal under the assumption that there is nothing more complex than trying to draw a line, which does not exist.[63] Plumb stated:

> that it is time for Congress to reexamine the purposes, if any, served by distinguishing debt from equity and, to bring that fruitless exercise to an end ... .[64]

58. *See Schön*: The Distinct Equity of the Debt-Equity Distinction, in Bulletin 2012, p. 502.
59. *See Bärsch*: Taxation of Hybrid Financial Instruments and the Remuneration Derived Therefrom in an International and Cross-border Context—Issues and Option for Reform, 2012, p. 306.
60. *Id.*, p. 323.
61. *Id.*, pp. 323 et seq.
62. *Id.*, p. 324.
63. *See Plumb* in Tax Law Review: The Federal Income Tax Significance of Corporate Debt. A Critical Analysis and a Proposal, vol. 26, issue no. 3, 1971, pp. 619 et seq.
64. *Id.*, p. 620.

And further that:

> The truly pertinent questions, relevant to the soundness of the tax system, are whether the tax laws should discriminate against equity capital and discourage the formation of new and risky enterprises [...], whether the tax laws should compel corporations, if they are to remain competitive, to make the maximum possible use of debt financing, even to an extent that may be unhealthy in the case of outside debt and unrealistic in the case of debt to shareholders, or whether the tax laws should be as neutral as possible in their effect upon such business judgements, and finally, whether an equitable and efficient tax system can longer tolerate a self-selected tax burden, permitting a taxpayer, by exercising his admittedly free right to choose a capital structure, to determine for himself how large a tax shall be borne for the privilege of doing business in corporate form.[65]

Plumb evaluates different possible solutions to the problem. One method is by making interest a nondeductible expense for CIT purposes. This possibility is rejected since such a proposal in Plumb's view would resolve the problem, but only shift the focus of the tax minimization problem, by encouraging such alternatives to borrowing (or to credit purchases) as the leasing or licensing of property, as well as the sale and leaseback of property the corporation already holds.[66] Another possibility is to allow a deduction for dividends paid. Yet another proposal is to introduce debt-to-equity ratios in general.

Hariton has tried to develop a more structural understanding by introducing the alternative structural approach stating:

> Perhaps I should admit at this point that I feel rather silly listing attributes as separate characteristics and piling them up on a scale, all to support my position that an instrument should be respected as debt for tax purposes.

The real question, to the author's mind, is not how many debt characteristics an instrument possesses, but rather to what extent the instrument insulates the investor from the risk and rewards of the issuer's business. This question only has meaning in the context of the relationships between different classes of investors in the corporation.[67] Equity confers more business risk than does debt in the same corporation. Therefore, according to Hariton, to answer the question one must consider the rights conferred by other investments in the capital of the issuer, what other capital exists to support the rights conferred by other investments in the capital of the issuer and what other obligations must first be met by the issuer.[68] Accordingly, it is not possible to characterize an instrument as equity or debt by reference to a checklist of abstract attributes that equity and debt supposedly possess. The relationship between the different classes of investors in the corporation is not on the checklist of factors

65. *Id.*, pp. 620-621.
66. *Id.*, p. 626.
67. *See Hariton* in Tax Law Review, vol. 43, The Taxation of Complex Financial Instruments, 1988, p. 522.
68. *Id.*

presented above. The specific questions of interest according to Hariton are the following:[69]

(1) How much equity capital supports the investor's rights?
(2) How much debt capital is senior to it?
(3) To what extent will the investor participate in the issuer's profits?
(4) What rights, if any, will the equity still have if the lender loses money?

The traditional factors are only useful insofar as they refer to these questions.[70] By way of an example, Hariton mentions the traditional factors regarding subordination and thin capitalization, which are not yes-no questions but rather concern how much equity exists to support the issuer's promises and what other promises the issuer has made that have priority.

[D] Proposals Eliminating the Debt-Equity Distinction Itself

It has also been suggested that the distinction between debt and equity be eliminated for purposes of characterizing taxable income (or deductible expenses). This approach includes scenarios where deductibility is not allowed for yield on debt as well as equity. Another well-known proposal is the introduction of the so-called ACE regimes (Allowance for Corporate Equity).

Kleinbard suggests a "Cost of Capital Allowance" system (COCA), where the allowance of the issuing corporation would equal a set rate multiplied by its invested capital.[71] Under the COCA proposal, every business enterprise would receive an annual allowance for the cost of the capital deployed in its business. That allowance would be uniform regardless of the form the capital took and regardless of the actual creditworthiness of the issuer.[72] The COCA rate would be applied to the issuer's total capital to determine the issuer's annual COCA.[73]

Andrews suggested granting issuing corporations a statutory allowance on qualified capital contributions. Andrews would, however, restrict the deduction to

69. *Id.*
70. *Id.*
71. *See Kleinbard* in Tax Notes, vol. 106, The Business Enterprise Income Tax. A Prospectus, 2005, pp. 101 et seq., and *Kleinbard* in Taxes, Beyond Good and Evil Debt: A Cost of Capital Allowance System, vol. 67, 1989, pp. 943 et seq.
72. In a recent Swedish reform proposal, a modified CBIT model was proposed (cf. SOU 2014:80) and (for the commentary *see Lodin* in Nordic Tax Journal: An Overview of the Proposal of the Swedish Government Committee on Corporate Taxation, issue 2, 2014, pp. 43 et seq. The model would disallow deduction for cases in which financial costs exceed the financial income of a company, while also lowering the effective corporate tax rate from 22% to 16.5%. *See also* Final Report from the European Commission written by the *Centre for European Economic Research (ZEW) GmbH* in Taxation paper No 65: The Effects of Tax Reforms to Address the Debt-Equity Bias on the Cost of Capital and on Effective Tax Rates, dated October 25, 2016, Chapter 7.
73. A system based on COCA has been found to be too radical by Kau. *See Kau* in Taxes, Carving Up Assets and Liabilities-Integration or Bifurcation of Financial Products, vol. 86, 1990, pp. 1003 et seq. (p. 1005).

newly contributed equity capital to avoid a tax windfall to current equity holders who did not expect a tax benefit when they purchased their shares.

The COCA deduction would appear to reduce the debt-equity distinction, although it only focusses on the corporate-level consequences of the proposal. Taking into account the investor-level consequences, the COCA deduction proposal would, in the view of Kau, invert the bias toward the issuing of debt, creating a new bias in favor of issuing equity.[74]

Economic theory has developed different solutions with the objective of neutralizing the tax treatment of debt and equity. The model proposed to obtain full neutrality is referred to as a Comprehensive Business Income Tax (CBIT), which denies deductibility by firms and treats debt as the current CIT treats equity.[75] There are, however, currently no real-world examples of CBIT.[76]

ACE has been on and off tax reformers' agendas since the 1980s.[77] Since then, proponents have repeatedly argued in favor of such a tax. The ACE has a number of interesting features.[78] The idea of an ACE is to address the difference in the treatment of debt and equity by allowing firms to deduct a notional interest rate on their equity as well. As a consequence, the ACE reduces the debt financing bias and reduces the tax motivations for leverage and, consequently, reduces the need for specific anti-avoidance and anti-arbitrage legislation. However, ACE systems may also be seen as a means to stimulate equity investment in the corporate sector of the country in question. In the present economic environment, ACE may be seen as a way to increase the attractiveness of a capital importing country.

In theory, the allowance for corporate capital (ACC) is even more neutral. Under the ACC, the interest deduction is abolished and replaced by a deduction for the notional risk-free return on all capital, irrespective of whether it is financed by debt or equity.[79]

74. *Id.*, p. 1141.
75. *See also* Final Report from the European Commission written by the *Centre for European Economic Research (ZEW) GmbH* in Taxation paper No 65: The Effects of Tax Reforms to Address the Debt-Equity Bias on the Cost of Capital and on Effective Tax Rates, dated October 25, 2016, Chapter 7.
76. *See de Mooij*: Tax Biases to Debt Finance: Assessing the Problem, Finding Solutions, IMF Staff Discussion Note, 2011, p. 16.
77. *See Klemm*: Allowances for Corporate Equity in Practice, IMF Working Paper WP/06/259, 2006, p. 3. A firmer reform proposal was presented by the Institute for Fiscal Studies in 1991: *Deveraux & Freeman:* A General Neutral Profits Tax, Fiscal Studies vol. 12, 1991, pp. 1-15 and *Gammie* in European Taxation, Corporate Tax Harmonization: An Ace Proposal, vol. 31, 1991, pp. 238 et seq. *See also* the Institute for Fiscal Studies, Miirlees Review, Reforming the Tax System for the 21st Century, Tax by Design, pp. 421-425 and *Blessing* in Bulletin for International Taxation: The Debt-Equity Conundrum - A Prequel, vol. 66, 2012, p. 212.
78. *Id.*, pp. 4 et seq.
79. *Id.*, p. 211. *See also* the Final Report from the European Commission written by the *Centre for European Economic Research (ZEW) GmbH* in Taxation paper No 65: The Effects of Tax Reforms to Address the Debt-Equity Bias on the Cost of Capital and on Effective Tax Rates, dated October 25, 2016, Chapter 7.

§2.05 CONCLUSION

The distinction between debt and equity is considered to be one of the fundamental and yet unsolved issues in international tax law. It cannot be denied that the debt-equity distinction has caused and continues to cause some concern in the area of international tax law. The primary concern among policy makers involves tax-motivated excessive leveraged financing and tax arbitrage. From a business perspective, the distinction causes uncertainty and potential double taxation. Consequently, the distinction does not seem fully capable of meeting the challenges and needs of the twenty-first century. Some degree of improvement seems to be in place. But which solutions should be adopted and is there one solution to fit all?

Many possible solutions have been presented above, yet no single approach is globally predominant. It seems that many of the responses in recent times aim at the symptoms of the problems rather than their root causes. This is demonstrated by the increase in interest limitation rules as well as linking rules. The current trends following the OECD/G20 BEPS project, the EU and US initiatives do not solve all the problems, but merely ensure that certain mismatches are less likely to occur in the future international tax landscape. A more solid solution would require fundamental tax reform, either through unilateral neutralization efforts such as the introduction of ACE regimes or by harmonizing the classification on a global scale, although such a solution would obviously be less feasible.

CHAPTER 3

The Interest Limitation Rule in the ATAD

Mario Grandinetti

§3.01 INTRODUCTION

In 2013, the Organisation for Economic Co-operation and Development (OECD) launched the project on Base Erosion and Profit Shifting (BEPS) with the support of G20 countries. The project is intended to be an answer to the increased perception that large multinational enterprises deliberately avoid paying their 'fair amount of taxes' by exploiting the loopholes and mismatches between different domestic tax systems.

The idea behind the BEPS Project is to create wide international consensus around a set of rules aimed at tackling international tax avoidance and to establish the conditions to be able to constantly monitor the progress in this field.

The project is articulated in fifteen Actions, and Action 4[1] is dedicated entirely to the improper deduction of interest by multinational enterprises.

The Final Action 4 Report recommends the adoption of a fixed ratio rule limiting the deductibility of interest from 10% to 30% of the company's EBITDA (earnings before interest, taxes, depreciation and amortization), or, alternatively, to a *ratio* calculated at group level, which may allow an entity to deduct more interest expenses depending on the relative net interest/EBITDA ratio of the whole group.

The European Union (EU) also plays a key role in the fight against international tax evasion and avoidance. Already in December 2012, the European Commission

1. OECD, *Limiting Base Erosion Involving Interest Deductions and Other Financial Payments, Action 4 – 2016 Update.*

promoted an Action Plan[2] to combat those practices. Subsequently, it strongly reaffirmed the work of the OECD on BEPS and has always been one of the first-movers in the implementation of the BEPS package.

In this context, on 28 January 2016, the Commission released a proposal for an Anti-Tax-Avoidance Directive (ATAD) that mandates Member States to transpose in their domestic legislation or, where necessary, to adapt their national law to one general and four specific anti-avoidance rules. The ATAD is one of the most important acts of the EU aimed at implementing the OECD recommendations contained in the BEPS package.[3]

The Directive was adopted on 12 July 2016,[4] and it is interesting to mention that it includes a number of anti-tax avoidance measures previously included in the proposal for a common consolidated corporate tax base (CCCTB)[5] of 2011.[6] At that time, Member States were not able to reach a political agreement on that proposal, while in the case of the ATAD it is commonly perceived that the BEPS has contributed significantly to the creation of a favourable 'political environment' for such an agreement.[7]

The final version of the ATAD adopted by the Council varies considerably compared to the first proposal because it was the object of intense technical discussion at several meetings held between EU Ministers of Finance and the European Commission. It contains a general anti-avoidance rule (GAAR) and three specific anti-avoidance rules: (i) an interest limitation rule, which is the topic of this chapter; (ii) a CFC rule; and (iii) anti-hybrid mismatch rules.[8]

Moreover, soon after the adoption of the ATAD, a number of Member States started to claim that the scope of the anti-hybrid mismatch rule was too narrow in the light of the BEPS recommendations. That claim led to the release, on 25 October 2016, of a proposal for a follow-up Directive,[9] often referred to as 'ATAD 2', aimed

2. Communication from the Commission to the European Parliament and the Council – An Action Plan to strengthen the fight against tax fraud and tax evasion, Brussels, 6 December 2012, COM(2012)722 final.
3. On this point, *see also* R. Iaia, *La 'Interest Limitation Rule' della direttiva 'antielusione' (ATAD)*, in Dir. prat. trib., 6/2018, p. 2455.
4. Council Directive (EU) 2016/1164 of 12 July 2016 laying down rules against tax avoidance practices that directly affect the functioning of the internal market (*see* W. Haslehner, Chapter 12 in this volume).
5. Proposal for a Council Directive on a Common Consolidated Corporate Tax Base (CCCTB), 2 December 2015, No. 14544/15.
6. On this point, *see also* J. C. Lobita, *The ATAD's Interest Limitation Rule – A Step Backwards?*, in 59 Eur. Taxn. 2/3 (2019).
7. P. J. Wattel, O. Marres, H. Vermulen, *Terra/Wattel – European Tax Law*, Wolters Kluwer, AH Alphen aan den Rijn, 7th Edition, p. 246.
8. For a general overview, *see also* S. Govind, S. Zolles, *The Anti-Tax Avoidance Directive*, in M. Lang et al., *Introduction to European Tax Law on Direct Taxation*, 5th Edition, Linde, Wien, 2018, p. 217.
9. Proposal for a Council Directive amending Directive (EU) 2016/1164 as regards hybrid mismatches with third countries, 25 October 2016, COM(2016)687 final.

specifically at expanding the anti-avoidance rule on hybrid mismatches.[10] It was eventually adopted on 29 May 2017.

The present chapter starts with a general analysis of the interest limitation rules, the purpose of which is to identify both the main features that are common to those rules, regardless of the jurisdiction, and the legal issues that they raise.

Then, the focus is shifted to the interest limitation rule contained in the ATAD (the 'ATAD EBITDA Rule') and all its elements are reviewed individually, that is the scope and its functioning (section §4.02[A]), the so-called *de minimis rule*, the stand-alone provision and the exceptions (section §4.03[B] by Alessandro Vicini Ronchetti).

§3.02 INTEREST LIMITATION RULES IN GENERAL

In general, most tax systems allow the deduction of interest expenses where they are incurred to earn income that is subject to tax in that jurisdiction. In the light of this, multinational enterprises frequently take advantage of this possibility and use the deduction of interest expenditure within their strategies of international tax optimization.[11]

In particular, intra-group debt financing has often been used to disconnect business profits from the place where they are effectively generated and relocate them in jurisdictions where it is possible for the group to exploit and take advantage of a tax rate differential.[12]

Unlike several other tax strategies addressed by the OECD in the BEPS Project, the generation of interest expenditure is not something that has appeared on the scene in recent times. To put it in a very simple way, tax optimization strategies based on the deductibility of interest involve the use of debt financing to generate deductible expenditures and reduce the taxable base. Instead of raising capital through the sale of shares, which remunerate the invested capital with non-deductible dividends, a company can opt to sell debt instruments to investors, so as to obtain capital in return for which the creditor receives the payment of a (deductible) interest.

With regard to cross-border scenarios, the deductibility of interest is at the basis of three 'main types' of tax optimization strategies:[13]

(1) the deduction of excessive interest paid to non-residents;

10. Council Directive (EU) 2017/952 of 29 May 2017 amending Directive (EU) 2016/1164 as regards hybrid mismatches with third countries. As a consequence of the adoption of this Directive, the anti-hybrid mismatch rule under ATAD 2 fully replaced the anti-hybrid mismatch rule under 'ATAD 1'.
11. *See*, among others, *Tax Grouping in an EU Context: All Roads Lead to Brussels*, in 58 Eur. Taxn. 7 (2018); and M. Tell, *Interest Limitation Rules in the Post-BEPS Era*, in 45 Intertax, 11, p. 750 (2017).
12. *See*, among others, J. Hey, *Base Erosion and Profit Shifting and Interest Expenditure*, in 68 Bull. Intl. Taxn. 6/7 (2014).
13. On this point, *see also* B. J. Arnold, *Restrictions on Interest Deductions and Tax Treaties*, in 73 Bull. Intl. Taxn. 4 (2019).

(2) the deduction of interest by residents in connection with exempt or preferentially taxed foreign-sourced income;
(3) the deduction of interest by non-residents in connection with domestic-sourced income.

If adopted within the dynamics of multinational groups, these strategies can result, for example, in debt instruments sold to other members of the same group, with the consequence that the payment of interest will result in the creation of a deductible expenditure for the payer and the receipt of active interest for the payee. This makes it possible to arbitrarily erode the taxable base of group members located in high tax jurisdictions and shift group profits to low tax jurisdictions.[14]

Other ways of allocating group profits to low tax jurisdictions and expenditures to high tax jurisdictions are through 'external' debt financing for cross-border acquisitions and through equity contributions that result in debt allocated to jurisdictions with a high level of taxation (that finance tax exempt of deferred dividends).[15]

A factor that contributes significantly to the spread of these kinds of transactions is that they are perfectly legal from a contract law perspective and can be carried out with very low transaction costs.[16]

There has been a long tradition of anti-avoidance legislation in this field to tackle this type of conduct, which is not only negative from a tax perspective but, more in general, also because it leads to an economic environment where companies are over-indebted.[17]

In theory, the strategies of tax optimization described above require different solutions. Indeed, 'pure internal' intra-group financing has its ultimate root in the different tax treatment of debt and equity, which are almost fully interchangeable from a management perspective but result in a very different tax treatment.

Rules restricting the deductibility of interest may take various names according to the context but are in general divided into two main categories: 'thin capitalization rules' and 'earnings-stripping rules'.[18]

---

14. For some examples with explanations *see*, among others, T. Edgar, J. Farrar, A. Mawani, *Foreign Direct Investment, Thin Capitalization, and the Interest Expense Deduction: A Policy Analysis*, 56 Can. Tax J. 4, pp. 815-821 (2008).
15. With regard to this point, *see also*, among others, the research paper authored by J. R. Hines Jr., *The Tax Treatment of Expenses Incurred to Earn Foreign Source Business Income: Principles, Policies, and Options*, August 2008, prepared for the Advisory Panel on Canada's System of International Taxation.
16. J. Hey, *supra* at 12.
17. With regard to this point *see*, among others, J. Owens, *The Taxation of Multinational Enterprises: An Elusive Balance*, in 67 Bull. Intl. Taxn. 8 (2013) and J. Hey, *supra* at 12.
18. *See also* B. J. Arnold, *supra* at 13 (p. 2) who states that: 'it should be noted that the terms "thin capitalization rules" and "earning-stripping rules" are often used indiscriminately to refer to restrictions on the deduction of interest that are based on a debt: equity ratio and the ratio of interest to a financial measure of earnings, respectively. [...] Earnings-stripping rules are fundamentally similar to thin capitalization rules, except that excessive interest is determined by reference to a resident company's interest expenses relative to its earnings rather than its debt relative to its equity'.

In the traditional sense, the expression 'thin capitalization rules' refers to a limitation in the deductibility of interest if a company's debt-equity ratio exceeds a certain level. On the other hand, 'earnings-stripping rules', which are the type of rule contained in the ATAD, determine excessive interest with reference to a resident taxpayer's interest expense in relation to its earnings, rather than on the basis of its debt in relation to equity.[19]

Moreover, it is also noteworthy that, in general, the category of 'thin capitalization rules' gathers the rules applicable to interest paid to non-residents or non-resident shareholders of a resident company, while 'earnings-stripping rules' are those applicable to interest paid to both residents and non-residents.[20]

Both types of interest limitation rule attract a significant amount of criticism. In particular, thin capitalization rules are often criticized on the grounds that due to their inflexibility and arbitrariness they may discourage an efficient debt/equity allocation by stimulating the company's financing with debt until the set threshold is reached.

On the other hand, the earnings-stripping rules are often criticized as they affect the interest paid to third parties (real business cost).[21]

Nowadays, a high number of jurisdictions have what is known as 'interest limitation rules[22]' in place, namely a set of rules that renders it inconvenient to deduct interest over a certain threshold by preventing its deductibility for tax purposes. These thresholds can be calculated in three ways:

(1) by relying on a general arm's-length approach (mention is made of the relationship between interest deductibility and transfer pricing later on in this short introduction);[23]
(2) by using a fixed equity/ratio approach. In this case, interest is not deductible to the extent that the taxpayer's interest expense exceeds a fixed percentage of a financial measure of its earnings, such as the EBITDA or the EBIT (*earnings before interest and taxes*);
(3) by using an approach combining the previous two (e.g., a fixed equity/debt ratio that can be disregarded where the taxpayer is able to prove that its debt does not exceed an 'arm's length amount').

Interest limitation rules take different forms according to the characteristics and the traditions of each jurisdiction. For example, while in the United States they are widely set out in case law, in most other jurisdictions they are mostly enshrined in statutes.[24]

19. *See* P. Essers, Chapter 1 in this volume.
20. On this aspect, *see also*, among others, D. J. Piltz, *General Report*, in *International Aspects of Thin Capitalization* (IFA Cahiers vol. 81b, IBFD 1996), Online Books IBFD.
21. *See* P. Essers, Chapter 1 in this volume.
22. Some countries, such as Canada, for example, adopted thin capitalization rules as early as the 1970s.
23. On this point, *see also*, among others, P. Hinny, *General Report*, in *New Tendencies in Cross-Border Treatment of Interest of Corporations* sec. 3.3 (IFA Cahiers vol. 93b, IBFD 2008), Online Books IBFD.
24. B. J. Arnold, *supra* at 13.

Moreover, despite the common features shared by these rules in various jurisdictions, it is possible to affirm that historically they did not reach an appreciable level of coordination at world level and can still be distinguished from each other on the basis of underlying concepts and the way in which they are designed.[25]

Already in 1998, the OECD focused on the possible negative consequences of thin capitalization in its milestone report on 'Harmful Tax Competition - An Emerging Global Issue',[26] where it ascertained that a large number of OECD countries 'apply general or specific legislative rules to address cases of base erosion attributable to the thin capitalization of resident companies to non-residents' and expressed its will to 'explore whether it should recommend to Member countries that do not have such rules that they consider their introduction [...]'.

In theory, these kinds of rules can be gathered under four different groups:

(1) limits to thin capitalization in respect of intra-group financing, thus somehow limited in scope to related-party debt;
(2) limits to thin capitalization with regard to both infra-group financing and third-party financing (or both 'internal' and 'external' debt);
(3) the non-deductibility of interest related to tax-exempt dividends only;
(4) the application of withholding taxes on interest, which can be structured in order to be levied with regard to foreign investors, internal investors or various combinations of the same.

The BEPS Project, and as a consequence also the ATAD, is having a huge impact on this field of taxation because it is contributing significantly to the convergence of a number of domestic rules that have historically been quite uncoordinated. And, although there is no unanimity among scholars on the practical outcomes that may legitimately be expected, it seems to be generally accepted that a higher level of coordination would, in itself, constitute a notable advance in tackling harmful tax practices.

Indeed, a consistent legal framework at world level in this field is expected to enable solutions to be found that coordinate the taxation of profits and the deduction of expenditures, thus leading to scenarios in which every jurisdiction involved is able to obtain a fair share of revenue (internation equity argument).[27]

Returning to the distinction drawn at the beginning of this paragraph, it has to be noted that the Final Report on BEPS Action 4 concludes, among others, that in this realm earnings-stripping rules are preferable to thin capitalization rules in the strict sense for at least three reasons:[28]

25. *See also* J. Owens, *supra* at 17.
26. OECD, *Harmful Tax Competition – An Emerging Global Issue*, p. 62 (1998).
27. On this point, *see also* W. Schön, *International Tax Coordination for a Second-Best World (Part II)*, in 2 WTJ 1, sec. 4.5 (2010).
28. For a comment, *see also* B. J. Arnold, *supra* at 13.

(1) the earnings of the company provide a better indication of its ability to carry and service debt than its debt/equity ratio;
(2) thin capitalization rules do not take prevailing interest into account, and a company can carry more or less debt depending on prevailing interest rates;
(3) thin capitalization rules can easily be avoided by stuffing equity into a company just prior to the measurement of the equity/debt ratio.

As a conclusion of the Final Report, the OECD recommends limiting the deductibility of net interest, namely of the interest expenses less interest income, from 10% to 30% of its EBITDA or EBIT determined in accordance with tax rules. It also states that an optional higher deductibility should be allowed to entities belonging to a group that at worldwide level has a higher interest/EBITDA ratio (computed in accordance with financial accounting information).

Moreover, the non-used portions of interest deductibility capacity should be 'usable flexibly', and it should be possible to carry back and forward any non-deductible interest for a year and allocate it to any such non-used capacity.

The OECD report also raises a red flag with regard to the fact that the structures tackled by interest deductibility limitation rules make them widely overlap with other areas of the BEPS Project:

- Action 2, Hybrid Mismatches Arrangements: the extensive possibilities for creating and designing financial instruments makes it possible to exploit conflicts of qualification through hybrid financial instruments. In particular, debt structures can be used to create the so-called double-dip structures, namely arrangements under which the taxpayer claims deductions in multiple jurisdictions vis-à-vis a 'single interest flaw'.
- Action 3, CFC Rules: 'aggressive' group financing companies can also be countered, to a certain extent, by CFC Rules, with the consequence that, where they are in place, any interest limitation rule has to be coordinated with them.[29]
- Action 5, Harmful Tax Competition: interest limitation rules can be analysed in the light of this Action too, because harmful tax competition can also be achieved through 'intentional loopholes' and 'generous domestic rules' on interest deductibility.
- Transfer Pricing Rules: some jurisdictions, like the United Kingdom, for example, historically used transfer pricing rules to identify excessive debt. This area is also addressed by Actions 9, 10 and 11 of the BEPS Project and,

29. For example, already back in 2014, Hey stated that: 'Unfortunately, the ECJ in *Cadbury Schweppes* (Case C-196/04) limited the scope of application of CFC rules in line with the standard concept of abuse to wholly artificial arrangements, and not much is required to demonstrate "real" financing activities. Consequently, it may be necessary to provide additional safeguards by specific interest-related anti-avoidance rules that must also satisfy the constraints of the fundamental freedoms as perceived by the ECJ.'

although the OECD rejected the arm's-length approach for infra-group financing,[30] it still coexists with Action 4 and is heavily debated among scholars. Indeed, while Action 4 sets a cap above which interest cannot be deducted, nothing is explicitly established with regard to the ways in which infra-group financing shall be managed nor at which interest rate. The point is that, at least in theory, a cap set at 30% is still relatively high and leaves some leeway for BEPS conducts. The reliance on arm's length in this field too would, on the one hand, give greater possibility to tackle this conduct effectively regardless of the specificities of the financial structure, but, on the other hand, it has to be acknowledged that intra-group financing is so remote from the value-creation chain that seems to be arguable whether a reliable 'arm's length' can be identified.[31]

With a more specific focus on the ATAD, the fact that action is taken at EU level is a development in the sense that it makes it possible to overcome, or at least significantly reduce, the potential clashes that have always affected the relationship between interest limitation rules and EU law.[32]

In particular, as the Member States still have a wide margin regarding how they shape their domestic tax rules, it is of crucial importance that interest limitation rules as transposed from the Directive guarantee the protection of EU fundamental freedoms under the Treaty on the Functioning of the EU (TFEU).[33] They must, therefore, be structured in a way that does not create any unjustified restriction on cross-border (EU) arrangements.

The European Court of Justice (ECJ) has dealt several times with the legitimacy of domestic anti-avoidance provisions, with the conclusion that they are acceptable under EU law, for example: (i) where they are applicable only to wholly or partly artificial arrangements; (ii) where the taxpayer is given the opportunity to prove the genuineness of its arrangement; and (iii) where it complies with the principle of legal certainty.

With more specific regard to the topic of this contribution, it is noteworthy that almost two decades ago the ECJ in the Case C-324/00, *Lankhorst-Hohorst*,[34] held that a different tax treatment of the interest deductions operated by a domestic entity with respect to the fact that interest is paid to a non-resident shareholder or to a company incorporated and governed under the German law which is exempted from corporation tax (because it is non-profitable) amounts to an unjustifiable restriction of fundamental

30. OECD, BEPS Action 4, para 15: '[arm's length rules alone] are not considered to be best practices in tackling base erosion and profit shifting involving interest and payments economically equivalent to interest'.
31. For a detailed analysis of this aspect and of the scholarly debate around it, *see also* C. Burnett, *Interest Deductibility: Implementation of Action 4 of the OECD/G20 Base Erosion and Profit Shifting Project and the Future of Transfer Pricing of Intra-Group Finance,* in 73 Bull. Intl. Taxn. 6/7 (2019).
32. On this interaction, *see also,* among others, S. Douma, *Limitations on Interest Deduction: An EU Law Perspective,* in 3 BTR (2015), 364.
33. *See also,* among others, A. P. Dourado, *The EU Anti Tax Avoidance Package: Moving Ahead of BEPS?,* in 44 Intertax 6 & 7 (2016), 440 and G. Bizioli, Chapter 5, in this volume.
34. CJEU, Case C-324/00 of 12 December 2002, *Lankhorst-Hohorst,* ECLI:EU:C:2002:749.

freedoms. In particular, the judges stated that the German tax legislation in force at that time made it less attractive for companies established in other Member States to acquire, create or maintain a subsidiary in Germany, thus violating the freedom of establishment laid down in Article 49 TFEU.[35]

The Court also rejected the argument according to which different tax treatment was justifiable in the light of the risk of tax evasion because the legislation was not specifically targeted at tax evasion or avoidance.[36]

All the findings mentioned have been applied in several circumstances and are applicable also to interest deductibility rules deriving from the ATAD, with the consequence that, put in very simple terms, they must be applicable without distinction between domestic and cross-border situations or target wholly/partly artificial arrangements.

However, it has also to be taken into consideration that, because interest limitation rules are an exception to the net income taxation principle, in many jurisdictions they are likely to raise constitutional issues.[37]

The net income taxation principle is generally considered to derive from the ability-to-pay-principle. Just to briefly mention a couple of examples that will be developed later in the following chapters of this book, in the Italian legal system,[38] the ability-to-pay principle is enshrined in Article 53 of the Constitution and its consequence in this field is that a total or partial non-deductibility of interest can be justified only vis-à-vis a non-participation of the expense in the generation of the income.[39]

In this perspective, a rule limiting the deductibility of interest could be justifiable for tax anti-avoidance purposes where its ultimate goal is to calculate any increase in the taxable wealth accurately.

The Italian interest limitation rule is based on a fixed debt/equity ratio. It is contained in Article 96 of the Tax Code[40] and was amended at the beginning of 2019. Italian scholars have traditionally questioned its constitutionality putting forward two main arguments that deserve to be taken into consideration even beyond the Italian

35. *See* para. 32 of the judgment.
36. *See* paras 37–38 of the judgment. For a comment *see*, among others, A. P. Dourado, *The Interest Limitation Rule in the Anti-Tax Avoidance Directive (ATAD) and the Net Taxation Principle*, in EC Tax Rev., 3 (2017), 112 ss.
37. A. P. Dourado, *supra* at 33, states: 'Net income taxation in each sovereign State is a manifestation of the ability-to-pay principle and was designed under a symmetric condition. This symmetric condition means that tax deduction of expenses and losses is allowed to the extent that the jurisdiction expects that an investment will be successful and that it will share the success by means of taxing revenue, in an overall cost-benefit analysis. [...] Because interest limitation rules are an exception to the principle of net taxation, there may be issues of unconstitutionality in some Member States.'
38. *See* G. Vanz, Chapter 7, in this volume.
39. For a general overview *see*, among others, G. Falsitta, *Giustizia tributaria e tirannia fiscale*, 403 (Giuffrè, Milan, 2008); D. Stevanato, *Prime considerazioni sui limiti generalizzati alla deducibilità degli interessi passivi introdotta dalla manovra finanziaria 2008 – L'indeducibilità degli interessi passivi tra utilizzo extrafiscale dell'imposta ed esigenze di misurazione della capacità economica individuale*, in Dialoghi tributari, p. 1022 (2007); and G. Escalar, *Dubbi di costituzionalità sul regime degli interessi passivi per banche ed assicurazioni*, in Corr. trib., 1238 ss. (2009).
40. IT Presidential Decree No. 917 of 22 December 1986, Article 96. National Legislation IBFD.

legal and tax system.[41] First, because a single limit is applicable to all companies regardless of their specific features, it seems unreasonable to state that they are always able to reflect the business reality of every sector, industry, business and so on.

Second, they are very 'mechanical' and do not allow for the submission of evidence.[42]

On the same note,[43] in a judgment delivered on October 2015,[44] the German Federal Fiscal Court declared the German rule on the limitation of interest deductibility unconstitutional[45] and referred it for constitutional review on the grounds that it violated the principle of equality enshrined in Article 3(1) of the Constitution.[46] In particular, the judges held that it violated the legislator's fundamental, systematic decision to apply the objective net principle and no valid justification could be found for it, for example the purpose of controlling the economic policy, the coverage of the state's financing needs, the fight against abuse and so on.[47]

§3.03 THE ATAD EBITDA RULE

[A] Scope

Article 1 of the ATAD mandates that the Directive is applicable to all taxpayers subject to corporate tax in one or more Member States or that are resident for tax purposes outside the Union but have a permanent establishment in one or more Member States.

Departing partially from what was recommended by the OECD in the BEPS, the EU decided not to extend the scope of the ATAD to types of entities which are not subject to corporate tax in a Member State, like transparent entities such as partnerships, for example. This approach is justified by the fact that a wider scope would result in the undesirable need to cover a broader range of national taxes, which would make the functioning of the whole system far more complex.[48]

The interest limitation rule set out in Article 4 of the ATAD mandates that borrowing expenses in excess are deductible in the tax year in which they occurred up

41. *See*, among others, G. Zizzo, *Abuso di regole volte al 'gonfiamento' della base imponibile ed effetto confiscatorio del prelievo*, in Rass. trib., para. 6 (2010); and A. E. La Scala, *Gli interessi passive nella determinazione del reddito d'impresa*, 393 ss. (Aracne, Rome, 2016).
42. For a detailed analysis of this issue within the Italian legal system, *see* in particular G. Vanz, *The Italian Interest Limitation Rule: Constitutional Issues*, in Eur. Taxn. 173 (April 2018). He states *inter alia*: 'This technique is based on the presumption of law principle. [...] According to Article 53 of the Italian constitution, presumptions of law are allowed on two conditions. The first is that the presumption is reasonable: it has to correctly correspond to what normally happens in reality. The second is that the presumption must be a rebuttable presumption.'
43. *See* D. Reich, Chapter 6, in this volume.
44. DE: Federal Fiscal Court (*Bundesfinanzhof*), 14 October 2015, I R 20/15.
45. For an historical perspective of the German legislation in this field, *see also* N. Herzig, et al., *Impact Study of the New German Interest Capping Rule*, in 36 Intertax, 12, p. 577 (2008).
46. *See also* L. Hillmann, R. Hoehl, *Interest Limitation Rules: At a Crossroads Between National Sovereignty and Harmonization*, in 58 Eur. Taxn. 4 (2018).
47. For a detailed analysis *see also* S. Lampert, *Article 4 of the EU Anti-Tax Avoidance Directive in Light of the Questionable Constitutionality of the German 'Interest Barrier' Rule*, in 56 Eur. Taxn. 8 (2016).
48. *See* 'whereas' n. 6 of the Directive.

to 30% of the taxpayer's EBITDA or at a fixed maximum amount of EUR 3 million for each entity of the group of which it is part.

Tax-exempt income is excluded from the calculation of the taxpayer's EBITDA, with the consequence that where present it decreases the amount of deductible interest. In addition to that, Member States are also permitted to either keep or pass targeted rules against intra-group debt financing, in particular thin capitalization rules.[49]

Where the taxpayer belongs to a group which submits consolidated account, the indebtedness of the overall group at worldwide level may be considered for the purpose of granting taxpayers entitlement to deduct higher amounts of exceeding borrowing costs. In the preamble to the ATAD, it is also specified that the interest limitation rule under analysis should apply in relation to a taxpayer's exceeding borrowing costs without distinction of whether the costs originate in from debt taken out nationally, from cross-border lending within the Union or with a third country, or whether they originate from third parties, associated parties or intra-group.[50]

In order to reduce the administrative burden caused by interest limitation without harming its tax effect, the preamble to the ATAD also considers the possibility for Member States to provide a safe-harbour clause, under which net interest is always deductible up to a fixed amount, even when this leads to a higher deduction than the EBITDA-based ratio.[51]

The interest limitation rule set out in Article 4 of the ATAD is applicable to every taxpayer within the scope of the Directive, but with three optional variations:

(1) under Article 4(1), Member States may also treat as a taxpayer: (i) an entity that is either permitted or required to apply the rules on behalf of a group, as defined by domestic tax law; (ii) an entity within a group, as defined by domestic law, which does not consolidate the results of its member for tax purposes. As a consequence of the application of this variation, exceeding interest expenses and EBITDA are calculated at group level and take into consideration the situation of all its members;
(2) under Article 4(3)(b), stand-alone entities may be given the right to fully deduct exceeding borrowing costs. The definition of *standalone* is to be found in the last sentence of Article 4(3): 'For the purposes of point (b) of the first subparagraph, a standalone entity means a taxpayer that is not part of a consolidated group for financial accounting purposes and has no associated enterprise or permanent establishment';[52]

49. *Ibidem.*
50. *See* 'whereas' n. 7 of the Directive.
51. *See* 'whereas' n. 8 of the Directive.
52. In addition to that, Article 2(4) of the ATAD states that 'associated enterprise' means: (i) an entity in which the taxpayer holds directly or indirectly a participation in terms of voting rights or capital ownership of 25% or more or it is entitled to receive 25% or more of the profits of that entity; (ii) an individual or entity which holds directly or indirectly a participation in terms of voting rights or capital ownership of 25% or more in a taxpayer or is entitled to receive 25% or more of the profits of the taxpayer. Finally, the same piece of legislation also clarifies that: 'If an individual or an entity holds directly or indirectly a participation of 25% or more in a taxpayer

(3) under Article 4(7), Member States may exclude financial undertakings from the scope of the interest limitation rule, including those cases in which, for financial account purposes, they are part of consolidated groups.[53] The ultimate rationale underlying this option is to be found in the fact that these companies would fall outside of the scope of the rule anyway due to the fact that the amount of active interest that they earn is almost always higher than their borrowing costs[54] and that they operate in a highly regulated sector which leaves them very limited leeway for BEPS practices through interest deduction.[55]

By giving a definition of what a 'financial entity' is, Article 2(5) of the Directive narrows the scope of applicability of the last variants to a certain number of different entities, including, for example, 'investment firms', which here means any legal person whose regular occupation or business is the provision of one or more investment services to third parties and/or the performance of one or more investment activities on a professional basis; 'insurance undertakings', which here means a direct life or non-life insurance undertaking which has received authorization, etc.

Nevertheless, this shall be applicable directly to the company benefiting from the exclusion. For example, the head of a tax group cannot be considered as a financial undertaking simply because the other members of the group are financial undertakings.

[B] The General Rule

The interest deductibility limitation rules contained in the ATAD function in a 'quite mechanical way'. It fixes a ratio for deductibility of interest expenses based on the EBITDA, which consists of the imposition of a cap of 30% on the deductibility of the exceeding borrowing costs incurred by the taxpayers during the tax year. Under Article 4(1) 'Exceeding borrowing costs shall be deductible in the tax period in which they are incurred only up to 30 percent of the taxpayer's earnings before interest, tax, depreciation and amortisation (EBITDA).'

The ATAD EBITDA Rule sets a minimum standard, with the consequence that Member States are entitled to implement stricter rules and are prevented from putting

and one or more entities, all the entities concerned, including the taxpayer, shall also be regarded as associated enterprises.'

53. The exact wording of the norm is as follows: 'Member States may exclude financial undertakings from the scope of paragraphs 1 to 6, including where such financial undertakings are part of a consolidated group for financial accounting purposes.'
54. *See also* P. J. Wattel, O. Marres, H. Vermulen, *supra* at 7, p. 251.
55. *See also* A. Zalasiński, IFA Cahiers, *Interest Deductibility: The Implementation of BEPS Action 4 - EU Report*, London Congress 104 (2019) 55.

on place more lenient ones: for example, they may lower the cap, but not raise it above 30%.[56,57]

This rule does not explicitly address whether its content should be applicable only to interest paid to related parties or also to unrelated ones; insofar as the transposition outcome is in line with the Directive, it seems that both solutions are acceptable.

What shall always be taken into due consideration is the compatibility of the domestic rule with EU law, and in particular with fundamental freedoms that prohibit any discrimination between domestic and cross-border (European) arrangements.

Article 2(1) of the ATAD refers partially to the domestic law of Member States and 'borrowing costs' as interest expenses on all forms of debt, other costs economically equivalent to interest and expenses incurred in connection with the raising of finance as defined in domestic law.[58]

The following 2(2) defines 'exceeding borrowing costs' as 'the amount by which the deductible borrowing costs of a taxpayer exceed taxable interest revenues and other economically equivalent taxable revenues that the taxpayer receives according to national law'.

Under Article 4(2), the EBITDA for interest limitation purposes has to be calculated by adding back to the income subject to corporate tax in the taxpayer's Member State the tax-adjusted amounts for exceeding borrowing costs as well as the tax-adjusted amounts for depreciation and amortization. Tax-exempt income shall be excluded from the EBITDA of a taxpayer.

The aforementioned definition of EBITDA is very general and leaves scope for a partially differentiated application at domestic level. In the light of this, it also seems reasonable to claim that the different ways in which the domestic laws of Member States may categorize economic facts are also likely to have an impact on the result of the EBITDA calculation.[59]

---

56. According to Recital (6) of the ATAD, for example, Member States may adopt an alternative measure referring to a taxpayer's earnings before interest and tax (EBIT) and fixed in a way that it is equivalent to the EBITDA-based ratio.
57. Finland and Norway, for example, have adopted a 25% cap.
58. The Directive provides a very detailed definition of this item and its exact wording is as follows: '[...] interest expenses on all forms of debt, other costs economically equivalent to interest and expenses incurred in connection with the raising of finance as defined in national law, including, without being limited to, payments under profit participating loans, imputed interest on instruments such as convertible bonds and zero coupon bonds, amounts under alternative financing arrangements, such as Islamic finance, the finance cost element of finance lease payments, capitalised interest included in the balance sheet value of a related asset, or the amortisation of capitalised interest, amounts measured by reference to a financing return under transfer pricing rules where applicable, notional interest amounts under derivative instruments or hedging arrangements related to an entity's borrowings, certain foreign exchange gains and losses on borrowings and instruments connected with the raising of finance, guarantee fees for financing arrangements, arrangement fees and similar costs related to the borrowing of funds'.
59. In this regard, A. Zalasiński, IFA Cahiers, *supra* at 55, p. 65, offers five remarks in this respect:
    (a) in principle, all income items subject to corporate income tax should be included in the EBITDA. There may be issues, for example, with the inclusion of fair value gains and losses on derivatives;

The mechanical functioning of this rule has also raised doubts with regard to its compatibility with the principle of proportionality. Indeed, as the EU law requires that any measure taken at EU level must not go beyond what is necessary to pursue the intended purposes, it seems legitimate to wonder whether the ATAD EBITDA Rule meets such a proportionality standard.

Proportionality can theoretically be divided into two components: first, the 'suitability' of the measure to reach the goal for which it has been put in place; second, the 'need' for the measure to reach that goal.

In this perspective, before implementing a measure, it is necessary to carry out research in order to identify the measures suitable for the specific purpose, and then the less invasive one for the affected subjects must be chosen from among them.

If applied to the ATAD EBITDA Rule, the above-mentioned analysis may lead to the conclusion that it goes far beyond the 'sole' anti-avoidance purpose for which it has theoretically been implemented, on the grounds that by introducing a predetermined and statutory binding evaluation of what is an appropriate level of deductible interest, it actually encourages the capitalization of companies in Europe.

Moreover, by making it extremely easy for national tax administrations to base tax assessments on solid grounds, especially in the case of complex intra-group financing arrangements, it seems to contradict the ECJ findings in the case *Leur-Bloem*,[60] where the judges state that under the principle of proportionality '[in order to determine whether the planned operation has such an objective,] the competent national authorities cannot confine themselves to applying predetermined general criteria but must subject each particular case to a general examination. According to established case-law, such an examination must be open to judicial review' (paragraph 41).

Simply put, it seems questionable whether the fact of passing such a purely quantitative limit per se can be considered suitable for proving tax avoidance or evasion. Indeed, there are stages in the life of a company, for example start-up or renovation, where a high level of debt is acceptable from a business perspective and in the long-term positive for the whole economic system.

In order to avoid these potential incompatibilities, it has been suggested that the focus should rather be on the development of a suitable version of the arm's-length principle.[61] This would allow the implementation of a solution which is much more flexible and adaptable to each specific situation, thus avoiding potential clashes with

(b) the carry-back/carry-forward as regulated by each jurisdiction may affect the calculation of the EBITDA. In principle, tax-adjusted EBITDA should be calculated on a current year basis, without including losses incurred in other tax years;
(c) as only corporate taxes are relevant for ATAD purposes, the tax EBITA should not include the tax base of other taxes, such as the capital gains tax);
(d) according to the wording of the rule, any amount that benefited from double taxation relief should be excluded from EBITDA;
(e) it is worth nothing that certain areas, such as the treatment of CFC charges, remain to be regulated in more detail by domestic legislation.

60. ECJ, Case C-28/95, *Leur-Bloem*, ECLI:EU:C:1997:369.
61. *See*, in particular, P. van Os, *Interest Limitation under the Adopted Anti-tax Avoidance Directive and Proportionality*, in 6 EC Tax Rev. pp. 184 ss (2016).

EU law that are generated by the mechanical functioning of the current structure of the rule.

At the end of the day, although the OECD explicitly rules out the approach to interest limitation based on the arm's length, nothing prevents the specificities and the founding principles of the EU legal system from calling for solutions that are more in line with the European context.

CHAPTER 4

ATAD Interest Expenses Exclusion Clauses

Alessandro Vicini Ronchetti

§4.01 PREMISE

In addition to the rules analyzed in the other chapters of the book, Article 4 of the Directive provides[1] specific clauses in which the interest expenses limitation is not applied as stated by said Article 4, when certain circumstances are met.[2]

In particular, in the present chapter, paragraphs 4, 5, 6, 7 of Article 4 will be scrutinized.[3]

As already stated in other chapters, interest expenses limitation deduction provided by the European Union (EU) Directive includes several rules already introduced by the Organisation for Economic Co-operation and Development (OECD) through Base Erosion and Profit Shifting (BEPS) Action 4 Report.[4] The scope of Article 4 of the ATAD is, in fact, largely inspired by Action 4[5] which aims at preventing base erosion through the use of interest expenses.[6] Consequently, our interpretation of the

1. For a general overview and comparative analysis *see* D. GUTMANN, et al., *The Impact of the ATAD on Domestic Systems: A Comparative Survey*, in *European Union*, 2017, 2 et seq.
2. Exclusion clauses that are similar to those already provided by German tax legislation. *See* N. HERZIG, *Impact Study of the New German Interest Capping Rule*, in *Intertax*, 2008, 579 et seq.
3. In particular, with reference to the clauses regarding fixed ratio, *de minimis* rule and volatility of revenues, *see* C. STENBERG, *Implementation of an Interest Deduction Rule. Threshold for Application*, in E. Pinetz and E. Schaffer, *Limiting Base Erosion*, Linde, 2017, 349 et seq.
4. With regard to the "historical well-known" attention paid by Governments in order to prevent interest expenses on intragroup loans from being charged with abuse for tax law reasons, *see* P. HINNY, *General Report*, 2008 IFA Congress.
5. On BEPS Action 4 *see* J. HEY, *Base Erosion and Profit Splitting and Interest Expenditure*, in *Bulletin for International Taxation*, June-July 2014, 332 et seq.; C. BURNETT, *Interest Deductibility: Implementation of Action 4 of the OECD/G20 Base Erosion and Profit Shifting Project and the Future of Transfer Pricing of Intra-Group Finance*, in *Bulletin for International Taxation*, 2019.
6. D. LEDURE, J. C. PAQUOT, M. VAN DER VELDEN, *The Implementation of the 30% EBITDA Rule in Belgium: An Angle with a Twist*, in *International Transfer Pricing Journal*, May-June, 2018, 230.

aforementioned paragraphs cannot ignore what the OECD affirms on the topic in the relevant Report.[7]

§4.02 TAX DEDUCTION OF INTEREST EXPENSES UP TO EUR 3 MILLION (THE SO CALLED "*DE MINIMIS*" CLAUSE) AND THE STAND-ALONE CLAUSE

[A] *De Minimis* Clause

As stated in point 8 of the Directive Recitals, in order to reduce the administrative and compliance burden of the rules without significantly diminishing their tax effect, it is appropriate to provide for a safe harbor rule so that net interest is always deductible up to a fixed amount, when this leads to a higher deduction than the EBITDA-based ratio (Earning Before Interest Depreciation and Amortization). The above objectives have been stated in paragraph 3, let. (a), Article 4 of the ATAD.

I have to point out that similar considerations have been stated by the OECD in the paper dedicated to base erosion potentially carried out through intragroup charging of interest expenses. Paragraph 36 of Action 4, states: "In order to remove entities which pose the lowest risk from the scope of a general interest limitation rule, a country may apply a *de minimis* threshold based on a monetary value of net interest expense." Coherently, the EU Directive provides for the possibility to deduct interest expenses for tax purposes up to EUR 3 million. If the taxpayer is a group entity, this limitation has to be considered for the entire group. The latter provision is also stated in Action 4 where the Report affirms: "It is recommended that such a threshold should be based on the total net interest expense of all entities in the local group."[8]

The rule is interpretable, in our opinion and according to the wording of the paragraph, assuming that the first EUR 3 million of interest expenses will be integrally deductible without considering the limitation rule, while the exceeding amount will be deductible according to the "EBITDA criteria."

The choice of considering "group" threshold as relevant instead of a separate legal entity amount is due to the need to prevent group structures from establishing multiple entities, each of which falls below the threshold. The need to prevent possible fragmentation through the incorporation of multiple entities is also affirmed in Action 4 as well as emphasized by several authors.[9]

On the limitation rule and its interaction with anti-hybrid rules as regards hybrid entities, *see* L. Parada, *Double Non-taxation and the Use of Hybrid Entities*, Wolters Kluwer, 2018, 343.

7. As affirmed: "Because the adopted rule is based on the OECD's recommended approach, relevant OECD considerations or recommendations are provided for purposes of clarifying the three elements of the rule." *See* P. Van Os, *Interest Limitation under the Adopted Anti-tax Avoidance Directive and Proportionality*, in *EC Tax Review*, 2016, 190.
8. *See* point n. 55, of Action 4 Report.
9. Stenberg 355. For completeness it should be noted that part of the doctrine does not agree with the possibility that "the minimum clause" will exclude possible abusive behavior, *see* P. Van Os, *Interest Limitation under the Adopted Anti-tax Avoidance Directive and Proportionality*, in *EC Tax Review*, 2016, 191.

The amount of threshold up to which interest expenses are fully deductible raises a doubt with regard to the application of the rule in the case of value that exceeds the EUR 3 million limit. The question in such a case is whether the entire amount of interest expenses is subject to the EBITDA "test" or only the exceeding amount is subject to the specific rule limitation, admitting, as a consequence, a tax deduction of the entire amount up to EUR 3 million. In this regard, it is reasonable to interpret such a clause assuming that the EBITDA limitation rule is applicable only to exceeding interest expenses. The proposed interpretation is coherent with the need to prevent taxpayers with interest expenses exceeding the EUR 3 million barrier by just a few euros from being subject to an inequitable tax burden with respect to taxpayers that incur exceeding borrowing cost equal to EUR 3 million.

[B] Stand-Alone Clause

The following let. (b) of paragraph 3 affirms a second clause which allows the deduction of interest expenses without any limitation. It states the possibility "to fully deduct exceeding borrowing costs if the taxpayer is a stand-alone entity." The Directive affirms that a "stand-alone entity" is a taxpayer that is not "part of a consolidated group for financial purposes and has no associated enterprises or permanent establishments."

The notion of associated enterprise is stated in paragraph 4, Article 2 in which it is affirmed that it refers to "an entity in which the taxpayer holds directly or indirectly a participation in terms of voting rights or capital ownership of 25 percent or more or is entitled to receive 25 percent or more of the profits of that entity." On the contrary, the Directive does not provide for an explicit definition of permanent establishment but, incidentally, in paragraph 8, Article 2, with regard to the transfer of business carried on by a permanent establishment it affirms that such a transfer occurs when "... a taxpayer ceases to have a taxable presence in a Member State ... ." In the absence of any other indication by the ATAD, I believe permanent establishment can be reasonably interpreted according to the notion of business presence of a foreign company in a foreign jurisdiction provided in each Member State.[10]

The aforementioned rule confirms the *ratio* of the Directive which is no tax deduction of interest expenses if such costs are charged in the aim of reducing the group tax burden abusively. Such a conclusion is confirmed by the Action 4 Report which affirms that the fact that a stand-alone entity is not part of a group means that the nature and level of BEPS risk that a stand-alone entity poses is often different to that posed by entities in a group. In many cases, stand-alone entities are small entities, owned directly by an individual, where there are no other entities under common control. In these cases, due to the entity's small size and lack of related parties, the risk of BEPS involving interest is likely to be relatively low. However, in other cases, stand-alone entities may be large entities held under complex holding structures

10. It can be reasonably affirmed that the notion should coincide with what is stated by the OECD model and its commentary.

involving trusts or partnerships, where there are a number of entities under the control of the same investors.

In these cases, the level of BEPS risk may be similar to that posed by a group structure. In both scenarios, where BEPS involving interest occur, it will arise as a result of payments to related parties and third parties.

[C] A Few Remarks on the "Stand-Alone" and *De Minimis* Clause

As stated above, the possibility of not applying the deduction barrier for companies which are not members of a group or, alternatively, have sustained interest expenses under certain amounts is, in our opinion, acceptable. At the same time, such specific rules demonstrate that the EU legislator takes into consideration the potential obstacles represented by administrative duties that Article 4 of the Directive implies.

At the same time, the "stand-alone" clause confirms the nature of the Directive that is aimed at contrasting tax avoidance behavior and, as a consequence, since such a possibility cannot be put into practice in the case of loans to third parties, legal entities that cannot stipulate intragroup loans may be excluded from the application of Article 4.

I believe that the ATAD provides no binding rule for each Member State in this regard but only suggests that Member States should provide the domestic law with such a provision.

Since the scope of the entire Directive is to avoid potential abuse of the law which could lead to taxable base erosion or profit shifting,[11] it is difficult to understand why the European legislator did not provide for a binding legislative provision but only recommended that each Member State adopt such a rule.

Nevertheless, it has to be pointed out that even if the possibility of applying the stand-alone clause exclusion is not strictly considered a binding rule by the Directive, it could be sustained that such a clause should be applicable in any case. The above may be assumed in view of the fact that the missing provision of the clause will lead to a violation of the proportionality principle.[12]

---

11. Recital N. 5 of the ATAD premise affirms: "It is necessary to lay down rules against the erosion of tax bases in the internal market and the shifting of profits out of the internal market. Rules in the following areas are necessary in order to contribute to achieving that objective: limitations to the deductibility of interest, exit taxation, a general anti-abuse rule, controlled foreign company rules and rules to tackle hybrid mismatches. Where the application of those rules gives rise to double taxation, taxpayers should receive relief through a deduction for the tax paid in another Member State or third country, as the case may be. Thus, the rules should not only aim to counter tax avoidance practices but also avoid creating other obstacles to the market, such as double taxation."
12. *See* Chapter 7, 101 in which, with regard to the introduction of the ATAD Directive by the Italian State (the latter does not expressly introduce a stand-alone clause) G. Vanz affirms the violation of the proportionality principle. With regard to the potential infringement of proportionality, *see also* R. Iaia, *"La interest limitation rule" nella direttiva "Antielusione" ("Atad")*, in *Dir. prat. trib.*, I, 2018, 2455. Along the same lines, *see* A. Navarro, L. Parada, P. Schwarz, *The Proposal for an EU Anti-avoidance Directive: Some Preliminary Thoughts*, in *EC Tax Review*, 2016, 118, 119; J. Camona Lobita, *European Union—The ATAD's Interest Limitation Rule—A Step Backwards?*, in *European Taxation*, 2019, 60 et seq.

In addition, and again with regard to other potential missing clauses, it seems that also the lack of specific exclusion for domestic groups applying for a tax consolidation regime at Member State level may be criticized. In fact, in this case too, it seems that the requirements provided for by Action 4[13] and by the ATAD[14]—the possibility to reduce the taxable base through international intragroup loans and connected related interest expense charges—are not present.[15]

§4.03 GRANDFATHER CLAUSE

Letter (a), paragraph 4, of Article 4 of the Directive provides for a grandfather clause. It states that new rules introduced by the ATAD will not be applicable to loans concluded before June 17, 2016. The same let. (a) specifies that the aforementioned clause is not applicable in the case of loans which, although concluded prior to that date, are subject to modification.

First of all, in our opinion, the chosen date warrants a few comments. Even though not expressly confirmed by the EU legislator, the date, June 17, 2016, should be connected to the issue which occurred on June 17, 2015—involving the "Communication from the Commission to the European Parliament and the Council—A Fair and Efficient Corporate Tax System in the European Union: 5 Key Areas for Action" in which five key areas are proposed where the coordination of corporate taxation should be improved.[16]

---

13. The Action 4 executive summary affirms: "Thus, multinational groups may achieve favourable tax results by adjusting the amount of debt in a group entity. The influence of tax rules on the location of debt within multinational groups has been established in a number of academic studies and it is well known that groups can easily multiply the level of debt at the level of individual group entities via intra-group financing. Financial instruments can also be used to make payments which are economically equivalent to interest but have a different legal form, therefore escaping restrictions on the deductibility of interest. Base Erosion and Profit Shifting (BEPS) risks in this area may arise in three basic scenarios:

    - Groups placing higher levels of third party debt in high tax countries.
    - Groups using intragroup loans to generate interest deductions in excess of the group's actual third party interest expense.
    - Groups using third party or intragroup financing to fund the generation of tax exempt income."

14. It is stated that the Directive aims to affirm taxation in the jurisdiction where the value is created and, in addition, "It is thus imperative to restore trust in the fairness of tax systems and allow governments to effectively exercise their tax sovereignty."
15. Point 3 of the introduction to Action 4 affirms: "In the cross-border context, the main tax policy concerns surrounding interest deductions related to the debt funding of outbound and inbound investment by groups. Parent companies are typically able to claim relief for their interest expense while the return on equity holdings is taxed on a preferential basis, benefiting from a participation exemption, preferential tax rate or taxation only on distribution. On the other hand, subsidiary entities may be heavily debt financed, using excessive deductions on intragroup loans to shelter local profits from tax. Taken together, these opportunities surrounding inbound and outbound investment potentially create competitive distortions between groups operating internationally and those operating in the domestic market."
16. On this matter, it should be noted that the said document does not include any provision or any recommendation with regard to the interest expenses regime.

Let us consider the kind of loan agreement changes that are included in the clause. In particular, new rules will be applied to loans even if they are concluded before June 17, 2016, if the amount or duration of the loan increases. In such a case, the new ATAD rules will not be applicable to the original terms of the loan but only to the new amount/duration agreed.

The grandfather rule, as stated by Recital 8 of the ATAD, is aimed at facilitating the transition to the new interest expenses limitation legislation.

It has to be clarified, in addition, that it is left open to Member States to decide whether to introduce the clause or not when implementing the ATAD in the national legislation.

For an in-depth investigation into the matter, it should be pointed out that a potential grandfather clause is mentioned in the Action 4 Report where the justification is described as follows: "A country may exclude interest on existing loans from the scope of rules, either for a fixed period or indefinitely. This may be particularly relevant for third party loans which form part of a group's regulatory capital, as these loans are often long-dated and there may be substantial penalties if they are repaid early. In any case, these 'grandfathering' rules should only apply to loans entered into force before interest limitation rules are announced, and should cease to apply if a loan is subsequently re-financed or if the terms of the loan are significantly modified, to the extent that this results in an increase to the tenor of the loan, the principal of the loan or to the rate of interest that applies."[17]

An interesting matter of interpretation is connected to the above clause. It is not clear whether any kind of modification would lead immediately to the revocation of the grandfather benefit or whether such modification should be significant, as affirmed by the OECD. If the second interpretation, which, quite honestly, seems to be the more reasonable is confirmed, it will, in any case, confer wide discretionary powers on each Tax Judge in each Member State. This latter consequence will lead not only to an increase in different behaviors within the EU but, as will be more adequately described at the end of the present section, also to an unacceptable lack of harmonization which, on the contrary, should be achieved between Member States through the legislative instrument called "directive."[18]

§4.04 GROUP RATIO ESCAPE CLAUSE

It has to be noted that the EBITDA interest barrier that is not applicable to stand-alone entities is independent from market interest conditions. Therefore, it may involve potential disadvantages for enterprises that carry out a business in capital intensive sectors. In order to avoid a potential and unjustified "tax cost" for taxpayers who are in the latter situation, paragraph 5, of Article 4, provides for a "group ratio escape rule." In fact, there may be companies that carry on an activity in a business where it is very

17. Action 4 Report, 190.

18. *See* G. Ginevra, *The EU Anti-Tax Avoidance Directive and the Base Erosion and Profit Shifting (BEPS) Action Plan: Necessity and Adequacy of the Measures at EU Level*, in *Intertax*, 2017; A.P. Dourado, *The EU Anti-tax Avoidance Package: Moving Ahead of BEPS?*, in *Intertax*, 2016, 443.

difficult to maintain a balanced or a profitable economical and financial trend unless they have large dimension from equity or assets point of view.[19]

In particular, in paragraph 5 mentioned above, two different potential limitation regimes are provided.

The two regimes provide for the possibility of combining the fixed *ratio* calculated by the legal entity with a *ratio* calculated in accordance with group items. As already mentioned above, a fixed *ratio* rule does not take into consideration the fact that groups in different sectors may be leveraged differently and, even without a sector bias, some groups are simply more highly leveraged. As a consequence, in the case of application of a single fixed ratio rule, groups which have a net third-party interest/EBITDA ratio above the benchmark would be unable to deduct all of their net third-party interest expenses.

Therefore, in order to reduce the impact on more highly leveraged groups, the EU Directive provides for a combination of legal entity and group ratios. This allows an entity in a highly leveraged group to deduct net interest expense in excess of the amount permitted under the fixed ratio rule, based on a relevant financial ratio of the worldwide group.

Group ratios for the deduction of interest expenses are also provided by Action 4 Report. The ATAD offers Member States two alternative methods which allow an entity to deduct additional interest expenses if certain group requirements are met. Such requirements can be based on the amount, at group level, of assets or EBITDA.

The first "escape rule" is based on the value of group assets and allows, for tax purposes, for the entire deduction of exceeding interest expenses in those cases in which the taxpayer (single legal entity) can demonstrate that the ratio of its equity over its total assets is equal to or higher than the equivalent ratio of the group and subject to the following conditions: (i) the ratio of the taxpayer's equity over its total assets is considered to be equal to the equivalent ratio of the group if the ratio of the taxpayer's equity over its total assets is lower by up to two percentage points; and (ii) all assets and liabilities are valued using the same method as in the consolidated financial statements.[20]

If the legal entity, which is a member of a group, meets the requested ratios, entire exceeding borrowing expenses become tax-deductible; on the contrary, the default interest limitation rules are applicable. As stated, the effect of the clause is that the "interest limitation rule will, on balance, particularly hit entities that, from the perspective of the entire group, are excessively leveraged. At the same time, this implies that if the group as a whole is heavily leveraged as well, the taxpayer would be expected to pass the equity escape."[21]

According to the second "escape rule" option, the taxpayer can deduct exceeding borrowing costs at an amount in excess of what it would be entitled to deduct according to the fixed ratio on a legal entity base.

19. In this regard, *see* J. M. Almudi Cid, J. A. Ferreras Gutiérrez, P. A. Hernàndez Gonzàlez-Barreda, *Combating Tax Avoidance in the EU*, 2019, Walters Kluwer, 155 et seq.
20. Equity taxpayer/Total assets taxpayer ≥ Equity group/Total assets group.
21. P. J. Wattel, O. Marres, H. Vermuelen, *European Tax Law*, vol. I, Walters Kluwer, 2018, 254.

This higher limit to the deductibility of exceeding borrowing costs shall refer to the consolidated group for financial accounting purposes in which the taxpayer is a member and be calculated in two steps:

(i) the group ratio is determined by dividing the exceeding borrowing costs of the group vis-à-vis third parties over the EBITDA of the group; and
(ii) the group ratio is multiplied by the EBITDA of the taxpayer.[22]

Basically, the second "escape rule" considers the extent to which the taxpayer's EBITDA contributes to the group EBITDA, and on the basis of this ratio, exceeding borrowing cost of the entire group vis-à-vis third party are subsequently allocated to the taxpayer.

[A] Remarks on the Group Ratio "Escape Rule"

The above "group ratio" determination implies that the items used must be recorded according to homogeneous accounting criteria, and this rule is expressly provided only for values described under let. (a). I believe, however, that such a conclusion should also be applied to figures referred to under let. (b) ratio.

In addition, with regard in particular to the group ratio which concerns (?) assets/equity values, that is let. (a), I believe that a recapture clause is missing. More specifically, in the absence of any specific anti-abuse rule, it may be possible to increase the equity of the group just a few days before the closing date of the financial statement; this allows the deduction of interest expenses to be increased. On this particular matter, in Germany where the same group *ratio* rule is in force, a detailed anti-abuse rule is applicable. However, it has to be taken into account that the potential abuse of the clause described may be challenged by the tax authority according to Article 6 of ATAD (General anti-abuse rule).

Finally, the group ratio "escape rules" provided by the Directive do not specify the kind of items that have to be taken into account. In the paragraph of Article 4 describing the calculation of EBITDA, it is expressly stated that items are relevant according to tax law that may not coincide with the book value. On the contrary, paragraph 5 of Article 4, in which the value of equity and assets are mentioned, does not provide any specific details in order to clarify whether such values are relevant according to tax value or financial statement value. The missing detail may allow the rule to be interpreted differently; in other words for this specific clause an item could be relevant for book purposes and such a conclusion would be coherent with the "Roman law rule" *ubi lex voluit dixit, ubit lex noluit tacuit*. Despite the heterogeneity of the items described above, a coherent calculation of the interest expenses deduction limitation is not guaranteed.

22. Exceeding borrowing costs of the group vis-à-vis third parties/Group EBITDA x Taxpayer EBITDA.

§4.05 LONG-TERM PUBLIC INFRASTRUCTURE EXCLUSION

Paragraph 4, let. (b) of the ATAD allows the interest expenses limitation not to be applied in the case of specific infrastructure investments. In particular, it is stated that such a possibility may be applied in the case of "loans used to fund a long-term public infrastructure project where the project operator, borrowing costs, assets and income are all in the Union." The Directive specifies that a long-term public infrastructure project means a project to provide, upgrade, operate and/or maintain a large-scale asset that is considered to be in the general interest of the public by a Member State.

In addition, as a logical consequence, incomes arising from the infrastructure project will not be included in the EBITDA value relevant for the interest expenses deduction limit, while any excluded exceeding borrowing cost shall not be included in the exceeding borrowing costs of the group vis-à-vis third parties referred to in point (b) of paragraph 5.

Regarding the notion of "public" used by the EU legislator, for the sake of coherency, I believe that the Action 4 Report interpretation should be adopted which provides the following statement: "A public benefit entity will typically be an entity whose primary objective is to provide goods or services for the general public, community or social benefit and where any equity is provided with a view to supporting the entity's primary objectives rather than to provide a financial return to equity holders. The definition of a public benefit entity used by a country may be contained in law or a relevant applicable accounting standard."[23]

The justification for the exclusion referred to above can be found in the content of Action 4, in which on page 43, the OECD affirms that "In some countries, privately-owned public-benefit assets may be large-scale assets financed using a high proportion of debt. However, because of the nature of the assets and the close connection with the public sector, some such financing arrangements present little or no base erosion or profit-shifting risk."

§4.06 THE POSSIBILITY TO CARRY FORWARD OR CARRY BACK NONDEDUCTIBLE EXCEEDING BORROWING COSTS AND THE UNUSED INTEREST CAPACITY

Paragraph 6 of the ATAD provides rules which, on the contrary, allow the deduction of interest expenses in following or previous fiscal years. Therefore, potential tax benefits may be reached assuming that the EBITDA items meet the values requested by law.

The aforementioned rule aims, like the rules regarding "group ratio," at preventing the volatility of revenues, which reflects on the EBITDA value and the potential interest expenses and revenues mismatch, from precluding the deduction of interest, taking into account that, theoretically, in the following fiscal year an exceeding capacity of EBITDA may occur.

23. OECD Action 4 Report, note 2, p. 45.

It may be affirmed that, except in cases where an entity's interest capacity precisely matches its net interest expense, the application of the EBITDA rule will result in an entity either incurring an interest disallowance, that is where its net interest expense exceeds the maximum permitted limit, or having unused interest capacity where its net interest expense is below the maximum permitted limit. Enabling disallowed interest expense and unused interest capacity to be used in other periods through carryforward or carryback provisions would have clear benefits for entities, reducing the risk of a permanent disallowance of interest expense where interest expense and EBITDA arise in different periods.

According to the Action 4 Report, from a country's perspective, "this could also support a policy that the level of an entity's net interest deductions should be linked to its level of earnings over time."

A preliminary consideration can be made. The rule described above seems to confirm that the entire ATAD legislation does not seem to be a strict anti-abuse juridical instrument with regard to interest expenses, but, if anything, it appears to be more a provision aimed at countering the deduction of interest expenses in the absence of congruous positive revenues.

In particular, paragraph 6 of Article 4 allows Member States to introduce the possibility to:

(a) carry forward, without a time limitation, exceeding borrowing costs which cannot be deducted in the current tax period;
(b) carry forward without a time limitation, and back for a maximum of three years, exceeding borrowing costs which cannot be deducted in the current tax period under paragraphs 1-5;
(c) carry forward exceeding borrowing costs without a time limitation and, for a maximum of five years, unused interest capacity which cannot be deducted in the current tax period.

The above treatment may be applied where the amount of interest expense in an entity exceeds that which is allowable merely as a result of a timing mismatch which will be corrected in the future. This may arise, for example, where an entity incurs interest expense to fund a project or investment that will give rise to earnings in a future period. There may also be cases where an entity's EBITDA fluctuates for reasons beyond its control, for example as a result of changing market conditions that increase or reduce the amount of net interest expense it may deduct for tax purposes. In addition, under the group ratio rule, the amount of net interest expense that an entity can deduct may be affected by volatility in the EBITDA elsewhere in the group. In these cases, as also stated in the Action 4 Report, a permanent disallowance of interest expense would introduce a level of uncertainty for groups which could make long-term planning difficult and which a country may view as undesirable.

Let us look in detail at the consequences of the abovementioned allowances and the reasons for certain limitations provided for by the EU legislator, and, finally, let us make a brief comparison with what is stated on this matter in the Action 4 Report.

Paragraph 6 of the ATAD attributes a different "role" to the two potential benefits that are allowed to the taxpayer.

The possibility to "use" exceeding interest expenses is treated more favorably than the "unused interest capacity." In fact, according to the options proposed to Member States by the Directive, they may be a carryforward without a time limitation or a carryback for a maximum of three years. However, the possibility regarding "unused interest capacity" is limited only in case c), paragraph 6 where it can only be carried forward (never carried back) for a maximum of five years.

In particular, the possibility to carry forward the "unused interest capacity" for a long time could give rise to a sizeable tax asset which can only be realized either by increasing the level of interest expenses sustained by the company or by reducing the level of EBITDA in future fiscal years. As observed in the Action 4 Report, "... neither of which should be incentivized by a rule to tackle base erosion and profit-shifting."[24]

In addition, it should be observed that also the possibility to carry forward exceeding interest expenses could lead an entity to increase such costs over the maximum allowed by the EBITDA rule—considering that, in any case, they will be deductible in the future, although such a possibility is, of course, judged to be less significant since the carrying back of nondeductible interest expenses and the carrying forward of unused capacity will involve an immediate cash benefit.

However, according to the suggestions made in Action 4 on the matter, many potential alternatives have been proposed. In particular, the report suggested that countries impose limits in terms of time and/or value according to different rules that take into consideration: (i) the number of years in which disallowed interest expense or unused interest capacity may be carried forward or disallowed interest expense may be carried back; (ii) the value of carryforward likely to decrease over time (10% per year); (iii) a monetary fixed amount cap to be imposed on the value of carryforward or carryback; (iv) the amount of a carryforward or a carryback that may be used in a single year could be limited, for example, providing that no more than a percentage of current net interest expense may be set off against unused interest capacity carried forward from previous years; (v) to preclude a carryforward in the case of "typical" abusive behavior, for example, where a company changes ownership and also changes the nature of its economic activity.[25]

24. OECD Action 4 Report, 73. By the way, the same conclusions may be applied with respect to carrybacks of disallowed interest expenses.

25. It also has to be considered that a rule providing for different limits, depending upon whether interest expense is disallowed under the fixed ratio rule or under the group ratio rule, may be introduced but it could be more complex to apply and administer.

§4.07 FINAL REMARKS ON CLAUSES NOT ALLOWING THE APPLICATION OF THE INTEREST LIMITATION RULE

To conclude, a few considerations can be summarized from a general perspective on the several rules which provide for the deduction of borrowing expenses without the EBITDA limit rule application.

I have seen that with regard to the rules above, the ATAD does not bind the Member States to introduce the benefit, but allows each government to decide whether to apply them or not in domestic legislation.

The considerable discretion granted by the EU to Member States may involve not only difficulties for achieving a more harmonized regime but also potential hidden incentives for attracting foreign investments and therefore undesired competition.[26]

The clauses analyzed in the chapter may lead to a potential infringement of the proportionality principle due to the fact that domestic groups are not included in the cases in which the interest barrier limitation is not applicable. As described, there are other circumstances in which it seems that the EU Directive has introduced clauses that could lead to discriminatory consequences. I believe that a general escape rule would be appropriate instead of the analytical and limited derogation regime clauses provided in paragraphs 3-6.[27]

The above could also imply less conflict between rules adopted by each Member State that may theoretically lead to a significantly different tax treatment of interest expenses in EU jurisdictions.

In addition, no exceptions from the application of the rule are provided in order to exclude possible double taxation (in the case of nondeduction of interest expenses and, at the same time, taxation of interest income earned by a company of the group). Such a consequence is clearly in contradiction with Recital 5 of the ATAD which affirms that the Directive "should not only aim to counter tax avoidance practices but also avoid creating other obstacles to the market, such as double taxation."[28] Finally, the heterogeneous (and nonbinding) kind of exclusion from the ordinary rule allows us to conclude that the ATAD may not be seen in its entirety as a systematic and coherent legislation aimed at contrasting tax avoidance. The analysis of the law suggests that it

---

26. "The current wording of article 4 provides Member States with the option to transpose less restrictive and more attractive rules, acting as favourable entry points for capital in the EU internal market that can later circulate freely due to the fundamental freedoms." *See* J. Carmona Lobita, *European Union—The ATAD's Interest Limitation Rule—A Step Backwards?*, in *European Taxation*, 2019, para. 2. The author points out that "... Member States have an enormous number of options that can be combined in multiple ways." He has exhaustively mapped the rules reaching a total of 288 potential ways of adopting the ATAD. As a consequence, this generates a complex scenario for the tax authority, taxpayers and, finally, tax judges.
27. I agree with Giuseppe Vanz's conclusion described in Chapter 7, section §7.10, *see also* S. Douma, *Limitations on Interest Deduction: An EU Law Perspective*, in *British Tax Review*, 2015., 370 et. seq.
28. For more detailed remarks on the matter *see* Giuseppe Vanz as referred to above.

resembles more a law for the purpose of increasing the taxable income of corporations/groups in order to increase revenues for the tax authorities.[29]

29. Such considerations are implicitly confirmed by the EU Commission in the Communication from the Commission to the European Parliament and the Council, COM (2015) 302 final, 5 which states: "Despite the stability in corporate revenue, many factors suggest that corporate tax revenues should instead have increased over time. First, policies to broaden the tax base have partly offset the impact of lower rates. Second, incorporation has increased in recent years and this has increased the overall base. Lastly, relatively low interest rates in recent years have limited the interest deductibility from the corporate tax base which has also had a base broadening effect. These effects do not only explain the stability of tax revenues, they indeed raise the question why the share of corporate taxes in total revenue has not increased over time. This may be due to the fact that certain companies pay far less than the statutory tax rate, including by engaging in aggressive tax planning."

CHAPTER 5

Interest Limitation Rule and EU Law

Gianluigi Bizioli

§5.01 INTRODUCTION

In furtherance of the aims and objectives targeted by the Organisation for Economic Co-operation and Development (OECD) through the so-called *Base Erosion and Profit Shifting* (BEPS) project, the European Union (EU) moved steps ahead adopting two Directives named 'Anti-Tax Avoidance Directive'[1] (ATAD)[2] tackling many of the issues raised in the BEPS Reports. In particular, ATAD 1 considers interest deductibility as a problem for the Internal Market, other than a BEPS issue. Namely, the limitation of the deductibility of interests in intercompany financing schemes relies upon the foreword that both '*[t]he OECD and other EU institutions have flagged the following (...) measures which could help address aggressive tax planning: limiting* interest

1. A few months after the adoption of the ATAD, a new Directive was issued, so-called ATAD 2 (Council Directive of 29 May 2017 amending Directive (EU) 2016/1164 as regards hybrid mismatches with third countries) that shall be adopted by Member States within 31 December 2019 (Article 2(1) ATAD 2) and applied as of 1 January 2020. For the limited scope of this article, the interest limitation rule has been affected by ATAD 2 in two parts, namely (i) amending the rule concerning full deduction of interest for groups (Article 1(3)(a) ATAD 2 amending Article 4(5)(a) ATAD); and (ii) providing for the possibility to use consolidated financial statements prepared under accounting standards other than the IFRS or the national financial reporting system of a Member State (Article 1(3)(b) ATAD 2 amending Article 4(8) ATAD).
2. Council Directive (EU) 2016/1164 of 12 July 2016 *laying down rules against tax avoidance practices that directly affect the functioning of the internal market*, in O.J. 19 July 2016, L 193/1, hereinafter 'ATAD'.

deductions, one of the principal instruments for profit shifting [emphasis added]'[3] that might '*affect the functioning of the internal market*'.[4]

The theoretical foundation of this measure relies on the pre-assumption that a taxpayer (usually a company) resident in a high-tax jurisdiction might lower its own tax burden through the deduction of interest on loans granted by a lender that is resident, in turn, in a low-tax jurisdiction.[5] The combined effect of the reduction of the tax burden in one jurisdiction and under-taxation on interest in the other jurisdiction is addressed as (better, is likely to generate) a BEPS effect.[6]

Clearly, the objective of shifting profits from one State (the high-tax jurisdiction) to another one (the low-tax jurisdiction) makes sense to the extent that it aims at lowering the overall tax burden for the group as a whole, while it would be clearly meaningless in cases where the parties do not belong to the same group.[7]

However, the transplant of the BEPS measures in the EU context should be operated carefully, as it was suggested, from the very beginning, by the OECD and, wisely enough, by the European Commission itself. The EU legal framework differs significantly from the international tax law order, both considering the normative and institutional profiles, and the implementation requires prudence and the peculiar adaptation to features of the Union. In particular, the Interest Limitation Rule (hereinafter the 'ILR') should be assessed according to the principle of prohibition of abuse of law and the fundamental freedoms.[8] One might wonder whether these two objectives were duly achieved through the ATAD.

In this vein, this chapter focuses on the compatibility of ATAD ILR with EU law. Section §5.02 briefly introduces the general features of the provision; section §5.03 addresses the compliance with the various sources of EU law: fundamental freedoms, the Charter of Fundamental Rights and the secondary legislation.

3. European Commission, *Anti-Tax Avoidance Package: Next steps towards delivering effective taxation and greater tax transparency in the EU* (SWD(2016) 6 final), COM(2016)23 final of 28 January 2016, para. 4, p. 5.
4. European Commission, *Proposal for a Council Directive laying down rules against tax avoidance practices that directly affect the functioning of the internal market*, COM(2016)26 final, 2016/0011 (CNS), para. 1, p. 3.
5. An anti-tax avoidance measure about cross-border payment of interest is already provided for in the I&R Directive (that, in principle, has a limited scope, in terms of subjective and objective scope) which, however, precludes the application of source taxation when the Directive requirements are not met.
6. The BEPS risks in the area of interest deduction arise in three basic scenarios: groups planning high levels of third-party debt in high-tax countries; groups entering intercompany loans to generate excess interest deduction of the group's actual third-party interest expense; and groups using third-party or intragroup financing for retrieving tax-exempt income.
7. Unless, of course, the scheme is intended to achieve other BEPS targets, such as tax lowering through hybrid financing schemes or other contractual arrangements leading to the same under-taxation effects for the entity paying interest.
8. The European Commission fairly recognises that the proposed ATAD '*sets out legally binding rules to enable Member States to effectively tackle corporate tax avoidance in a way which preserves their collective competitiveness and respects the Single Market, Treaty Freedoms, the EU Charter of Fundamental Rights and EU law in general*' (European Commission, *Proposal for a Council Directive laying down rules against tax avoidance practices that directly affect the functioning of the internal market*, COM(2016)26 final, 2016/0011 (CNS), para. 1, p. 3).

§5.02 INTRODUCTION ON ARTICLE 4 ATAD

Article 4 ATAD provides that '*[e]xceeding borrowing costs shall be deductible ... only up to 30 percent of the taxpayer's earnings before interest, tax, depreciation and amortisation (EBITDA)*'.

At the outset, it is worth to underline that Article 4 ATAD applies notwithstanding any abusive scheme in which a taxpayer has been involved, whereas the mere excess of borrowing costs activates the 'interest limitation' deduction. However, upholding a teleological interpretation, sided by a systematic interpretation (as the ILR is included in the wider context of the ATAD) one could argue, from an EU perspective, that Article 4 ATAD has an anti-avoidance purpose.[9]

In addition, although it relies upon the OECD outcome of the BEPS project, the ILR is enshrined in the EU law and, as such, should lead to a uniform and autonomous approach according to the *acquis communautaire*.[10]

Despite this basic assumption, there are some features of the ILR that impact on the uniform implementation of the provision across Europe.

First, the ILR shall *not* be analysed in an isolated fashion since it interacts with the Member States' domestic tax systems.[11] Thus, according to some scholars, it can be argued that it consists 'of a starter, a main course and a dessert'.[12]

In addition, the European ILR was drafted with a 'limited' temporal scope. Namely, Article 11(6) ATAD, derogating Article 4, provides that Member States which have national '*targeted rules*'[13] '*equally effective to the interest limitation rule*' may apply these targeted rules for a limited period of time.[14]

However, from another perspective, it would be clearly incorrect to state that the ILR was intended as a *final* measure to counteract BEPS borrowing schemes, as it should be understood in the Commission Report to the Council, expected by 9 August 2020: '*in particular the impact of Article 4*' (Article 10). This highlights the Council's idea that such provision deserves due attention and, in the light of domestic implementation of such rules arguably will need some further adaptations and amendments.

9. *See* A.P. Dourado, *The Interest Limitation Rule in the Anti-Avoidance Directive (ATAD) and the Net Taxation Principle*, 45 *Intertax* 3 (2017), p. 118.
10. B. Terra and P. Wattel, *European Tax Law, Volume I General Topics and Direct Taxation* (Wolters Kluwer, Alpheen aan den Rijn, 2019) p. 247 stress that '*the objective is to ensure a uniform implementation of the BEPS-package*'.
11. L. Hiltman and R. Hoel, *Interest Limitation Rules: At a Crossroads Between National Sovereignty and Harmonization*, 58 *European Taxation* 4 (2018), para. 4 observe that '*in addition to the EBITDA-fixed ratio rule, member States can enact additional provisions to take the characteristic of their national tax system into account*'.
12. *See* B. Terra and P. Wattel, *supra* n. 10, p. 247.
13. Namely, Greece, France, Slovakia, Slovenia and Spain, the sole countries duly fulfilling the notification procedure and whose domestic tax measures were deemed to be '*equally effective*'.
14. Although an analysis of the one true meaning of the notion of 'equally effective' led to quite wide assumptions by the EU Commission (*see* European Commission Notice, *Measures considered equally effective to Article 4 of the Anti-Tax Avoidance Directive* (2018/C 441/01) in O.J. 7 December 2018, C441/1), the Commission's assumptions might be employed as a valid interpretative tool. *See, also,* suggested by A. Zalasiński, *EU Report Interest Deductibility; The Implementation of BEPS Action 4*, in IFA Cahiers, 104a (IBFD, Amsterdam, 2019), pp. 60-63.

Second, the scope of EU ILR is further narrowed by the nature of the ATAD as a 'minimum standards', implying that Member State might design implementing measures that set stricter rules than those embodied in the ATAD.[15]

Third, one further aspect to be considered is the structure of the Member States' tax systems that, as will be stressed below, might have an impact on the functioning of the rule (e.g., when considering exempt income) and when addressing the features of 'group' taxation regimes.

Fourth, there are some critical issues, affecting both the objective and subjective scopes of the ILR that might lead to a puzzling (and, in some event, inconsistent) implementation. A few preliminary takeaways are therefore necessary on the subjective and objective scope of the ATAD.

[A] Personal Scope

The ILR focuses on 'all taxpayers that are subject to corporate tax in one or more Member States, including permanent establishment in one or more Member States', whose taxable base is lowered by reason of interest payments (the borrower) and, as a natural corollary, assumes the fact-of-the-case under the domestic tax law of such taxpayer.[16] According to the literal wording of the Directive, a European based permanent establishment (PE) of a head office resident in a third State would be a 'taxpayer' even if the head office was *not* subject to corporate income tax in its home country.[17]

However, the ILR allows two main options: (i) the exclusion of financial undertakings from the scope of the ILR (Article 4(7) ATAD); (ii) the treatment of a 'standalone entity' that is defined as '*taxpayer that is not part of a consolidated group for financial accounting purposes and has no associated enterprise or permanent establishment*' (Article 3 ATAD). Such entities may be granted the right to fully deduct interests (Article 3(b) ATAD).

At the outset, it is worth to underline that the design of the subjectivity of scope of the ATAD is likely to increase (and *not* discourage) abusive practices, since ILRs

15. C. Docclo, *The European Union's Ambition to Harmonize Rules to Counter the Abuse of Member States' Disparate Tax Legislation, Bulletin for International Taxation* 7 (2017), p. 368 holding that the standards are '*not yet ready for use*'.
16. Interaction with other anti-avoidance rules is an issue, as it is fairly evident the overlap that might happen when the same one scenario affects both the interests limitation rule and, e.g., hybrid mismatches on financial instruments that might be solved only insofar the ILR takes the precedence but might overlap, again, in later periods, due to carry-forward rules. *See* A. Schnitger and I. Zavirov, *The Interest Limitation Rule,* in P. Pistone and D. Weber (eds), The Implementation of the Anti-BEPS Rules in the EU: A Comprehensive Study (IBFD, Amsterdam, 2018), pp. 267-268.
17. C. Docclo, *supra* n. 15, p. 369.

shall *not* apply to individuals.[18] Similarly, the exclusion of transparent entities might open room for abusive practices.[19]

However, as already mentioned, the ATAD provides the 'minimum standard', so that every MSs can decide whether ILR should apply to such type of entities or not.[20] Again, this conclusion might create room for discriminatory treatments insofar such rules lead to the detrimental treatment of cross-border cases if compared to merely domestic ones.

The inclusion of PEs in the subjective scope of the ATAD could be confusing as the ATAD lacks a definition of PE (and, notably, in other sources of EU secondary law in the field of direct taxation).

In depicting the personal scope, an aspect deserving due attention is the role of 'residence' in the application of the ATAD since the Directive does not provide any tiebreaker rule[21] and does *not* forbid the application of the rule in dual residence cases.

Another remarkable aspect to be considered is the actual taxation of the subject since if the taxpayer is, as a matter of fact, exempt from corporate income tax, the ILR would be meaningless. This lead some authors to consider that 'exempt' entities, although being liable to corporate income tax (and, therefore, in principle, affected by the ILR) should not be included in the scope of the ILR.[22] The conclusion could be drawn from the Court of Justice of the European Union (CJEU) decision in the *Wereldhave* case,[23] but this would entail that '*wording, aim and context*' of the two Directives at stake are fairly overlapping.[24] This conclusion may find some grounding whether one supports the opinion that the ILR shall be interpreted against the background of the *effects* it aims at achieving and the protection of States' '*revenue*' deriving from the application of the ILR.[25]

18. S. Govind and S. Zolles, *The Anti-Tax Avoidance Directive*, in M. Lang et al. (eds), Introduction to European Tax Law on Direct Taxation (Linde Verlag, 2018), m.no. 606.
19. The ATAD expresses that '*it is not desirable to extend the scope of this Directive to ... transparent entities*', deemed to be a landmark case of taxpayers that are *not* subject to corporate income tax (Whereas (4) ATAD).
20. This approach would be justified, since MSs should try to achieve a '*higher level of tax neutrality when it comes to the choice of legal forms*', against the background that such measures should act as minimum standards, as suggested by A. Schnitger and I. Zavirov, *supra* n. 16, p. 271.
21. S. Govind and S. Zolles, *supra* n. 18, m.no. 607.
22. This is the stance taken by J. Carmona Lobita, *The ATAD's Interest Limitation Rule – A Step Backwards?*, 60 *European Taxation* 2/3 (2019), p. 62 and, along the same path, B. Terra and P. Wattel, *supra* n. 10, pp. 248-249, holding that '*subjectively tax-exempt funds ... would not fall under the personal scope of the ATAD*'.
23. CJEU, Case C-448/15 *Werehalde Belgium*, 8 March 2017, para. 34 reading: '*the inclusion in national legislation of a provision whereby a specific category of companies may, in certain circumstances, be entitled to be taxed at a zero rate is tantamount to not subjecting those companies to that tax*'.
24. S. Govind and S. Zolles, *supra* n. 18, m.no. 610.
25. One of the two economic aspects to be considered in evaluating the 'equally effective' criterion. *See* European Commission Notice, *Measures considered equally effective to Article 4 of the Anti-Tax Avoidance Directive* (2018/C 441/01).

[B] Objective Scope

The objective scope of the ILR is outlined by Article 2 ATAD which tackles the definitions of (i) Borrowing Costs and (ii) Exceeding Borrowing Costs for the purposes of the Directive.

The notion of 'Borrowing Costs' means interest expenses on all forms of debt, included other costs '*economically equivalent*' to interest and expenses incurred in connection with the raising of finance as defined in national law.[26] As a corollary, the notion of 'Exceeding Borrowing Costs' means the amount by which the deductible borrowing costs of a taxpayer exceeds taxable interest (and other economically equivalent revenues) that the taxpayer receives according to domestic law (Article 2(2) ATAD).

The ILR is expressed according to the following ratio: Exceeding Borrowing Costs are deductible only up to 30% of the taxpayer's EBITDA that shall be calculated by adding back the tax-adjusted amounts for Exceeding Borrowing Costs plus the tax-adjusted amounts for depreciation and amortisation, while '*tax exempt income*'[27] shall be excluded (Article 4(1) ATAD).

The objective scope of application of the rule is supplemented by some (better, many) derogations or options.[28]

First, one shall consider those affecting '*consolidated group for financial accounting purposes*'[29] that might be applied to the ILR.[30]

The first derogation is intended to allow the taxpayer to fully deduct the Exceeding Borrowing Costs, subject to a comparative evaluation of the following two parameters: (i) the ratio of equity over total assets of the taxpayer; and (ii) the ratio of equity over total assets of the group (the 'equivalent ratio').

The second derogation is intended to allow a deduction of Exceeding Borrowing Costs (referring to the consolidated group for financial accounting purposes) in which the taxpayer is a member and shall be calculated in two steps: (i) dividing the Exceeding Borrowing Costs of the group vis-à-vis third parties over the EBITDA of the group (Art. 4(5)(b)(i) ATAD); and (ii) multiplying the group ratio to the EBITDA of the taxpayer calculated pursuant to paragraph 2 of Article 4 ATAD (Art. 4(5)(b)(ii) ATAD).

Interest and economically equivalent costs are taken into consideration, notwithstanding their nature (aside from geographical origin and identity of the

---

26. Reference to *national law* widens the scope of the provision that is further expanded through a list of cases that might be included such as, '*payments under profit participating loans, imputed interest on instruments such as convertible bonds and zero coupon bonds, amounts under alternative financing arrangements, etc.*'. *See*, Article 2(1) ATAD and B. Terra and P. Wattel, *supra* n. 10, p. 252.
27. That, for the sake of clarity, is *not* defined by Article 2 ATAD.
28. Aside a grandfathering rule, provided for in Article 4(4)(a), ATAD for existing loans that will *not* be addressed in this article.
29. Article 4(5), ATAD that shall be read in conjunction with Article 4(8) ATAD, holding that it '*consists of all entities which are fully included in consolidated financial statements drawn up in accordance with the International Financial Reporting Standards or the national financial reporting system of a Member State*'.
30. Application of the ILR to groups under national tax law is optional.

debtor/creditor).[31] This implies that, for the calculation of the ILR, one shall consider all interest, including those capitalised on qualifying assets.[32]

The ILR is intended to limit the deductibility of Exceeding Borrowing Costs, thereby allowing (without limitation) deduction of borrowing costs below such threshold. The fact that ILR is intended to be a 'minimum standard' entails States to go beyond (i.e., imposing more stringent ILR ratio) what is stated in Article 4 ATAD. In turn, this could jeopardise the market and open to group tax schemes which aim at shifting borrowing costs in Member States where the ILR is less stringent.

As set forth above, both Borrowing Costs and Exceeding Borrowing Costs are defined in the ATAD relying upon the 'national law' of the taxpayer (Articles 2 and 2(1) ATAD).[33] This provision shall be read in conjunction with Article 4 ATAD which refers: (i) to the *'corporate tax in the Member State of the taxpayer'*[34] applicable *'in a tax year'* (Article 4(1) ATAD);[35] and (ii) to *'national tax laws'* on group taxation regimes (Articles 1(1) and (2) ATAD).

Article 4(2) ATAD further clarifies that the relevant earnings before interest, tax, depreciation and amortisation (EBITDA) is not that assessed according to the 'accounting' rules but rather the EBITDA that results as the outcome of *'tax-adjusted amounts'* that shall be added. This might open the room for inconsistencies among Member States' approaches[36] and, as a matter of fact, fragmentation among domestic ILR rules.

§5.03 THE MAIN POINTS AT A STAKE IN A EU-ORIENTED APPROACH TOWARDS THE ILR

The ILR raises, substantially, three main issues: (i) the compatibility with the Charter of Fundamental Rights of the EU; (ii) the compatibility with EU freedoms and the prohibition of State Aid;[37] and (iii) the compatibility with EU secondary legislation.

31. C. Docclo, *supra* n. 15, p. 369.
32. This is the approach supported by the OECD, *Limiting Base Erosion Involving Interest Deductions and Other Financial Payments. Action 4 – 2015 Final Report* (OECD Publishing: Paris, 2015), p. 30. *Contra*, F. Mazzoleni, *Implementation of an Interest Deduction Rule: Definition of Interest and Equivalent Payments*, in E. Pintez and E. Schaffer (eds), Limiting Base Erosion (Linde Verlag, 2017), p. 329, who considers that such items of income shall not be considered for the purposes of the interest deduction rule.
33. Among others, W. Heyvaert and E. Moonen, *ATAD Implementation in Belgium: An Analysis of the New Interest Limitation Rule*, 7 *European Taxation* (2019), p. 322.
34. Article 2(2), ATAD. That shall be read as follows, income subject to 'corporate tax' in the State where the taxpayer is resident and, then, subject to unlimited tax liability. As suggested by A. Zalasiński, *supra* n. 14, p. 57 amounts taxed in other taxes (such as Capital Gains tax) should not be included in the EBITDA calculation. The same problem, as suggested by the quoted author, may arise regarding income included in the taxable base due to CFC legislation.
35. Rules on carry-forward of Exceeding Borrowing Costs are laid down in Article 4(6), ATAD.
36. *See*, e.g., the Belgian approach (reported by D. Ledure, J.C. Paquot and M. Van der Velden, *The Implementation of the 30% EBITDA Rule in Belgium: An Angle with a Twist, International Transfer Pricing Journal* 5/6 (2018), p. 322).
37. S. Douma, *Limitations on Interest Deduction: An EU Law Perspective, British Tax Review* (2015), p. 370.

[A] Impact (If Any) on EU Secondary Legislation

When it comes to EU secondary legislation, one shall first check whether the ATAD might affect (and be at the odds) the Interest and Royalties Directive ('I&R Directive').

By this token, the judgment delivered in the *Solar Technology* case[38] might be useful in excluding an overlap between the two sets of rules, addressing different type of taxpayers. Namely, while the I&R Directive is intended to prohibit the taxation of interest in the State of source paid to the lender (and for his benefit), the ATAD is intended to limit the deductibility of the same item of income on the borrower in his State of residence.[39]

[B] Compatibility with EU Freedoms

The EU Fundamental freedoms prohibit the different treatment between domestic and cross-border situations and require that measures aimed at preventing BEPS effects should not impose unjustified restrictions on cross-border dealings.

Notwithstanding the ILR aims at preventing *BEPS*, Article 4 applies alike to domestic and cross-border situations.

It should be noted that special anti-avoidance rules, which mainly apply only in cross-border situations, based on the place of residence of the lender,[40] prima facie might entail a restriction on the free movement rights.[41] Even though Article 4 ATAD does not rely on a distinction between residents and non-resident, it nonetheless may render less attractive cross-border borrowings.[42]

The domestic and cross-border cases (upon closer analysis of the relevant domestic tax system in hand) shall be treated alike, or, better, the cross-border case should *not* be treated less favourably than the domestic case.[43] As a matter of fact, treating alike domestic and cross-border cases '*[d]espite the drawback of being arbitrary, ... has the advantage of obliterating the possible risk incompatibility with the Treaties on the basis of unequal treatment*'.[44]

38. CJEU, C-397/09 *Solar Technology*, 21 July 2011.
39. This is the stance taken, among the others, by J. Hey, *Base Erosion and Profit Shifting and Interest Expenditures, Bulletin for International Taxation* (2014), p. 41 and C.H.J.I. Panayi, *The Compatibility of the OECD/G20 Base Erosion and Profit Shifting Proposal with EU Law, Bulletin for International Taxation* (2016), p. 101.
40. S. Douma, *supra* n. 37, p. 373.
41. A. Zalasiński, *supra* n. 14, p. 50 and S. Douma, *supra* n. 37, pp. 373, 375.
42. A.P. Dourado, *supra* n. 9, p. 119 holding that even if not discriminatory '*Article 4 would be disproportionate, to its aim of combating BEPS.*'
43. A. Zalasiński, *supra* n. 14, p. 50.
44. As suggested by A. Zalasiński, *supra* n. 14, pp. 51, 57. The issue of equality of treatment (and hinderance of such principle) is addressed by A.P. Dourado, *supra* n. 9, p. 120 holding that '*Article 4 of the ATAD could also be questioned in light of the principle of equal treatment, as it treats in the same manner avoidance and non-avoidance situations, domestic and cross-border situations, group companies and standalone companies, companies that need funding and those that could opt for other alternatives in the same manner,*' while some sort of relevant differences were found in the preliminary documents. For example, consider the derogation for long-term project whereas the loan should '*not exceed the value of the project asset*', as stressed by C.

According to the CJEU case law, a restriction might be justified by a specific need to prevent tax avoidance/tax abuse including where: (i) it applies to wholly (or partly) artificial situations; (ii) it is proportional to the objective pursued; and (iii) the rule is consistent with the principle of legal certainty (*see* also section §5.03[C] below).

With reference to the ILR, the CJEU has applied the aforementioned principles to cross-border interest situations, such as: (i) thin capitalisation rules (*Lankhorst-Hohorst* and *Test Claimants in the Thin Cap Group Litigation*);[45] (ii) deduction of business expenses (*SIAT*);[46] and (iii) transfer pricing rules (*SGI, Hornbach*).[47] Considering Article 4 ATAD, a key element to assess is the structure of the ILR[48] and its derogations.[49]

Some authors have argued that the (potential) non- or under-taxation of interest on the lender could not amount as a valid justification for a restriction directed to the borrower on the basis of the AG Kokott Opinion delivered in *SCA*[50] (and further supported on an analysis of the literature on case *Schempp*),[51] since it would be the result of a mere *disparity*.[52]

As interest deduction rules are based on symmetry (i.e., the item deducted by the payor should be taxed, in principle, on the recipient),[53] the CJEU has ruled out all such domestic legislations limiting the deduction of interest applied only to cross-border payments within the EU, holding that such rules were discriminatory.[54]

Both in *Bosal* and *Lankhorst-Hohorst* – once considered that the two situations were comparable[55] and that the domestic ruled entailed a discrimination – the CJEU did *not* accept the need to avoid the risk of tax avoidance or evasion as a valid argument to support the discrimination.

Docclo, *supra* n. 15, p. 371. This reasoning could be further supported with respect to the rule providing for a comparison between the single entity and the group's ratio. As stressed by G. Colombaioni, *Compatibility with EU Law of Rules Limiting the Deductibility of Interest and Other Financial Payments*, in E. Pintez and E. Schaffer (eds), Limiting Base Erosion (Linde Verlag, 2017), p. 388 '*it cannot be excluded that sound commercial reasons may support the fact that a single entity should be more leveraged than others of the group*'.

45. CJEU, Cases C-324/00 *Lankhorst-Hohorst GmbH v. Finanzamt Steifurt*, ECLI:EU:C:2002:749; Case C-524/04 *Test Claimants in the Thin Cap Group Litigation*, ECLI:EU:C:2007:161.
46. CJEU, Case C-318/10, *Société d'investissement pour l'agriculture tropicale SA (SIAT) v. État belge*, ECLI:EU:C:2012:415.
47. CJEU, Cases C-311/08 *Société de Gestion Industrielle SA (SGI)*, ECLI:EU:C:2010:26 and C-382/16, *Hornbach Baumarkt-AG v. Finanzamt Landau*, ECLI:EU:C:2018:366.
48. So that, as argued by A. Zalasiński, *supra* n. 14, p. 53 in 'loss relief' or 'profit contribution' regimes, Member States shall consider the position of each resident entity.
49. If one assumes that derogations (options left to Member States) provided for in the ILR can be used to interpret the rationale behind it, there are two options deserving attention. The option to allow taxpayers to deduct a higher amount of Exceeding Borrowing Costs comparable to the indebtedness of the group (Article 4(5)(b) ATAD) and fully deduct Exceeding Borrowing Costs by comparing Exceeding Borrowing Costs to the equity/total asset ratio of the group (Article 4(5)(a) ATAD).
50. AG Kokott, Opinion in *SCA*, joined cases C-39/13, C/40/13 and 41/13.
51. CJEU, C-403/03 *Egon Schempp v. Finanzamt München V*, Reports I-6421.
52. S. Douma, *supra* n. 37, p. 375.
53. That, as clearly put forth in A.P. Dourado, *supra* n. 9, p. 114, is, in turn, firmly linked (on the payor side) to the ability to pay principle, that is expressed by the 'net taxation' principle.
54. A.P. Dourado, *supra* n. 9, p. 115.
55. Resident paying interests domestically to resident paying interest to non-residents.

[1] *The Compatibility of the Derogations on Stand-Alone Entities and Group Taxation Regimes*

Stand-alone entities may be excluded by the scope of ILR.[56] Considering that the risk of tax avoidance should rely upon an overall (and shared) common 'tax' benefit for two entities belonging to the same group, the exclusion for stand-alone entities makes sense.[57]

However, as stressed by some author, the combined effect of considering a group as a stand-alone entity and, meanwhile, excluding stand-alone entities from the scope of ILR might lead to discriminatory results.[58] Some authors have also supported the opinion that there could be cases in which the 'standalone entities' might, nevertheless, be involved in group structures and, then, creating the risk for base erosion.[59]

Article 4 ATAD provides, as set forth above, the possibility to adapt the ILR to the features of the tax system since it considers the existence of 'grouping' regimes.

The derogation provided for in the ATAD might be challenged according to the type of derogation and the tax group regime adopted in the domestic tax system of the Member State applying the ILR.

It has been supported that the impact of the case law of the CJEU (mainly, the decision of the CJEU in the *Groupe Steria* case)[60] might be quite relevant. This would make it difficult to justify the restriction based on the argument of cohesion since it would be conditioned by the specific type of group taxation regime.[61]

In wider terms, the adaptation of some MSs' tax regimes on group consolidation (according to which the group is granted the status of 'taxpayer') to the ILR personal scope, depicted above, might lead to a discriminatory result in cases where a domestic tax group regime[62] is treated better than cross-border groups.[63] Namely, where a tax regime provides for the ILR in a cross-border context but does *not* affect borrowings within a domestic tax group, this regime could make cross-border investments less attractive.[64]

56. As suggested by A. Zalasiński, *supra* n. 14, p. 54, this is not a provision that shall be relied upon in order to assess the rationale behind the ILR since it '*is merely an optional modification of the personal scope ... It does not mean that any unrelated party interest payment is not subject to the limitation on deductibility*'.
57. B. Terra and P. Wattel, *supra* n. 10, p. 253.
58. This would be the case where the group regime is intended to apply exclusively to domestic entities. *See*, J. Carmona Lobita, *supra* n. 22, para. 2.1.
59. J. Carmona Lobita, *supra* n. 22, para. 2.3.
60. CJEU, Case C-386/15 *Groupe Steria SCA v. Ministère des Finances et des Comptes publics*, ECLI:EU:C:2015:524.
61. Z. Reijn, et al., *Tax Grouping in an EU Context: All Roads Lead to Brussels*, in 59 *European Taxation* (2018).
62. A tax regime that applies only to resident entities.
63. J Carmona Lobita, *supra* n. 22, p. 61. It is worth to underline that, as stressed by S. Govind and S. Zolles, *supra* n. 18, m.no. 619, '*[w]hile Article 4 ATAD does not provide any restrictions in terms of which entities can be considered part of a group, Recital 7 seems to support a restriction to entities of the same State*'.
64. This would be the case, under domestic tax rules investigated by A. Schnitger and I. Zavirov, *supra* n. 16, p. 269.

[2] *Potential Double Taxation Discouraging Investments in Other Member States*

ILRs are likely to pave the road to double-taxation scenario – whereas the same item of income not deducted in the State of the payor is, meanwhile, fully taxed in the State of the recipient – unless the other State provides for an adjustment.[65]

While, in general terms, double taxation could be mitigated through a carry-forward mechanism,[66] there could still be cases of (domestic rules led to) detrimental treatments for cross-border groups, if compared to purely domestic ones, since domestic group systems, as a matter of principle, do not extend to entities across the border.[67]

Focusing on carrying forward of unrelieved borrowing costs, in more general terms, it is worth to underline that Article 4 ATAD does *neither* coordinate carry-forward and carry-back of Exceeding Borrowing Costs with carry loss mechanisms employed in Member States *nor* provides any guidance on potential 'trade' of entities holding unused excess borrowing costs. As pointed out, these types of strategies might be counteracted, where applicable, through a General Anti Avoidance Rule (GAAR) under Article 6 ATAD.[68]

Payment of outbound interests might entail the application of withholding taxes in the State of the borrower. This implies that, once payment is done, the interest has been effectively taxed in the State of source and would be potentially subject to double taxation also in the other State (the State of the lender). This scenario shall be considered in the light of Recital (5) of the ATAD holding that '*[w]here the application of those rules gives rise to double taxation, taxpayers should receive relief through a deduction for the tax paid in another Member State or third country, as the case may be. Thus, the rules should not only aim to counter tax avoidance practices but also avoid creating other obstacles to the market, such as double taxation*'.

Clearly, the ATAD recognises the detrimental effects of potential double taxation (led by the ILR and other ATAD measures) and recommends that taxpayer 'should receive' a deduction for taxes paid in another MS. However, this adjustment is *not* directly provided for in the ATAD[69] and is left to the MSs to eliminate distortions that might affect investments in other MSs.

[C] Compatibility with the Charter of EU Fundamental Rights and State Aid Provisions

As hold by leading scholars when dealing with the *SIAT* case (concerning the deductibility of an item of income in one State where the recipient, in another State, is

65. N. Bravo, et al., *Implementing Key BEPS Actions: Where Do We Stand?*, 45 *Intertax* 12(2017), p. 857.
66. L. Parada, *Hybrid Entity Mismatches and the International Trend of Matching Tax Outcomes: A Critical Approach*, 46 *Intertax* 12(2018), p. 990.
67. A. Zalasiński, *supra* n. 14, p. 58.
68. *See* B. Terra and P. Wattel, *supra* n. 10, p. 253.
69. J. Carmona Lobita, *supra* n. 22, p. 62.

not subject to tax), a violation of the Charter may *itself give rise* to a restriction of EU freedom.[70]

Namely, a restriction of freedom (to provide services, in the *SIAT* case) shall meet the requirements of legal certainty (when addressing the justification and proportionality analysis), which is to be compliant with the Charter of fundamental rights. The perspective adopted by the Commission, laying down a set of rules and several derogations, could also open the room for infringement of the State Aid rules.

This is clearly recognised in the documents adopted by the Commission[71] where it is stated that lifting anti-avoidance rules only for selected taxpayers could amount to a State Aid.

By this token, taxpayers may be given the right to deduct Exceeding Borrowing Costs up to EUR 3,000,000 or – if the taxpayer is a stand-alone entity – fully deduct Exceeding Borrowing Costs. This shall equally be applied, under domestic rules, in cases where the group is deemed to be a taxpayer.[72]

One ambit in which this might happen is the exclusion concerning long-term infrastructural projects since a State shall give evidence that financing projects concerning infrastructure projects do not amount to a restrictive rule.[73]

70. S. Douma, *supra* n. 37, p. 372.
71. *See* EU Commission, *Draft Commission Notice on the notion of State aid pursuant to Article 107(1) TFEU*, Brussels, 2014, para. 184.
72. Conditional upon the application of the GAAR (under Article 6 ATAD) as anti-fragmentation rule, aimed at avoiding the use of more than one *de minimis* rule in more than one MSs. *See*, in this perspective, A. Zalasiński, *supra* n. 14, pp. 57-58.
73. C. Docclo, *supra* n. 15, p. 371.

Part II The Interest Limitation Rule in the ATAD: Issues of Implementation

CHAPTER 6

Germany

Daniel Reich

§6.01 INTRODUCTION

The interest limitation rule in Article 4 of the Anti-Tax Avoidance Directive (ATAD) very closely resembles the existing German interest limitation rule ("Zinsschranke") of section 4h Einkommensteuergesetz (Income Tax Act—EStG) in combination with section 8a Körperschaftsteuergesetz (Corporate Income Tax Act—KStG).

The first part of the following chapter will describe the German interest barrier as appropriate and give an overview of the legal development and purpose of the regulation. In the second part, the question raised by the Federal Fiscal Court (Bundesfinanzhof—BFH) as to whether the German interest barrier is compatible with the German constitution (Basic Law) will be examined. For this purpose, the decision of the BFH is first presented giving its considerations, before the author then carries out an independent assessment of the constitutional conformity of the German interest barrier. The chapter concludes with considerations on the consequences that will result from the expected decision of the Federal Constitutional Court (Bundesverfassungsgericht—BVerfG) regarding the German interest barrier and the potential need for the implementation of Article 4 ATAD.

§6.02 THE GERMAN INTEREST BARRIER

With section 4h EStG, the legislator pursues the aim of restricting the deduction of borrowing costs at the level of the interest-paying enterprise under certain conditions. In the ideal case, in which the use of the borrowing costs is carried forward, the regulation results in a restriction of the deduction of borrowing costs only for a limited period of time. Insofar as borrowing costs are incurred only on the amount of interest income, the borrowing costs continue to be fully deductible without any restriction. If the enterprise's interest balance is negative, the deductibility of the exceeding borrowing costs is limited to 30% of the taxpayer's offsettable EBITDA (earnings before interest, taxes, depreciation and amortization). Borrowing costs that are not deductible under section 4h EStG do not reduce the taxable income of the taxpayer. Technically though, this is implemented by means of a complicated, multilevel system of rules and exceptions.

In contrast to the ATAD interest barrier, it should be noted that section 4h EStG applies not only to corporations but, because of its position in the Income Tax Act, also to individual entrepreneurs and partnerships. However, the broader personal scope of application of the German interest barrier compared to ATAD is compatible with ATAD, as ATAD only defines a minimum level of protection with regard to corporate income tax subjects. For corporate income tax purposes, section 4h EStG is supplemented by section 8a KStG.

[A] Overview of Legal Development and Regulatory Purpose

The interest barrier was introduced as part of the 2008 corporate tax reform.[1] Since its entry into force, the interest barrier has already been amended three times.

The first amendment added sentence 3 to paragraph 5, which regulates the corresponding application of section 8c KStG (the so-called detrimental acquisition of shares) to the carryforward of borrowing costs.[2] The second amendment initially increased the exemption limit for a limited time.[3] The third amendment has permanently increased the exemption limit from EUR 1 million to EUR 3 million. It has also introduced an EBITDA carryforward and increased the tolerance limit in the equity ratio comparison from 1% to 2%.[4]

The interest barrier is directed against excessive debt financing of enterprises and is intended to prevent enterprises from striving for a high debt ratio for tax optimization purposes alone. Seen as an anti-abuse regulation, the interest barrier is intended to combat the undesirable transfer of profits abroad.[5] In particular, groups should not be able to transfer income generated in Germany abroad by means of cross-border intragroup debt financing. It is also intended to prevent groups from getting into debt on the capital market through their German subsidiaries and thereby reduce the tax base in Germany through the interest paid.

The interest barrier is also a counter-financing measure to lower the corporate income tax rate.[6] Furthermore, the interest barrier is intended to protect enterprises

1. Unternehmensteuerreformgesetz 2008, BGBl I 2007, 1912.
2. Jahressteuergesetz 2008, BGBl I 2007, 3150, Bundestag Printed Matter 747/07.
3. Bürgerentlastungsgesetz, BGBl I 2009, 1959.
4. Wachstumsbeschleunigungsgesetz, BGBl I 2009, 3950.
5. Bundestag Printed Matter 16/4841, 31.
6. *See* H. Weggenmann/G. Claß, *Die Zinsschrankenregelung auf dem verfassungsrechtlichen Prüfstand*, BB 2016, 1175 (1179).

against insolvency by promoting higher equity ratios.[7] And finally, it is also designed to safeguard the domestic tax base.[8]

[B] Basic Rule of the Interest Barrier, Section 4h(1) Sentence 1 EStG

According to the first sentence of the rule, borrowing costs can be deducted as business expenses up to the amount of the interest income of the same tax period. If the borrowing costs exceed the interest income, the exceeding borrowing costs can only be deducted up to the amount of 30% of a modified operating result (EBITDA).

Because of its position in the Income Tax Act, the interest barrier is in principle applicable to individual entrepreneurs and to shareholders of business partnerships. Through section 8(1) KStG, the interest barrier with the modifications of section 8a KStG is to be applied to corporations. By virtue of section 15 sentence 1 no. 3 KStG, section 4h EStG does not apply to controlled companies that are part of a consolidated group for financial accounting purposes. The parent and controlled companies are regarded as one enterprise within the meaning of section 4h EStG. Exceeding borrowing costs and the EBITDA shall be calculated at the level of the group and comprise the results of all its members when section 4h(1) EStG is applied.

[C] EBITDA Carryforward, Section 4h(1) Sentences 3 & 4 EStG

Section 4h(1) sentences 3 and 4 EStG stipulate the EBITDA carryforward. EBITDA carryforward means that in the years in which the business with its borrowing costs does not use up the deduction limit of the interest barrier, the unused amount of this deduction limit is carried forward to future fiscal years, but at most to the following five fiscal years. The EBITDA carryforward has the effect that borrowing costs that cannot be deducted after taking into account interest income and the offsettable EBITDA are deductible up to the amount of the EBITDA carried forward in subsequent years. Providing the offsettable EBITDA exceeds the borrowing costs reduced by interest income, it may be carried forward to the next five fiscal years. An EBITDA carryforward that is not used in these five years expires and is lost.[9]

An EBITDA carryforward does not occur according to section 4h(1) sentence 3, 2nd half sentence EStG in fiscal years in which the interest barrier according to paragraph 2 is not applicable. Otherwise, considerable EBITDA carryforwards could arise in years in which the borrowing costs are fully deductible. According to paragraph 1 sentence 4, nondeductible borrowing costs are deductible up to the amount of EBITDA carried forward from previous fiscal years and reduce the EBITDA carried forward in their chronological order. If nondeductible borrowing costs remain thereafter, they are to be carried forward to the following fiscal years.

7. Bundestag Printed Matter 16/4841, 31.
8. Bundestag Printed Matter 16/4841, 35.
9. This is one of the main reasons why the First Senate of the BFH considers the interest barrier to be a breach of the "objective net principle."

[D] Carryforward of Nondeducted Borrowing Costs to Subsequent Fiscal Years, Section 4h(1) Sentence 5 EStG

Borrowing costs subject to the interest barrier are generally not lost but can be carried forward to subsequent fiscal years without any time limit.[10] Logically, however, the taxpayer can only actually use the interest carryforward if the financing situation of the business changes significantly in a later fiscal year. There is no carryback of borrowing costs. Additionally, the carryforward of borrowing costs is lost when the business is transferred or abandoned.

The carryforward of borrowing costs can ultimately result in the exemption limit of EUR 3 million being exceeded, even though the interest expenses for the current fiscal year may be below this amount.[11]

[E] Exceptions to the Application of the Interest Barrier, Section 4h(2) EStG

Section 4h(2) sentence 1 lit. a-c EStG specifies three alternative exceptions to the rule, the intervention of which would invalidate the suspicion of abuse according to paragraph 1 sentence 1 and would therefore allow unrestricted deduction of operationally induced borrowing costs (current borrowing costs and any carryforwards). If taxpayers wish to claim them, they must prove that the conditions of these exceptional circumstances are met. The aim of the first restriction is to exclude small- and medium-sized enterprises from the scope of the interest barrier. The other two restrictions are intended to allow the full deduction of borrowing costs, provided that no cross-border group tax planning is carried out at the expense of the German tax base.[12]

[1] Exemption Limit of EUR 3 Million

The interest barrier does not apply if the amount of borrowing costs exceeding the amount of interest income is less than EUR 3 million.

The intention of the legislator was to ensure that small- and medium-sized enterprises are not affected by the restrictions on the deductibility of borrowing costs.[13] The amount of EUR 3 million is structured as an exemption limit. If the amount of exceeding borrowing costs is up to EUR 3 million, there is no limitation on deductibility; if the amount of exceeding borrowing costs is EUR 3 million or more, the limitation on deductibility applies to the entire borrowing costs.

10. R. Schenke in Kirchhof/Söhn/Mellinghoff, EStG Commentary, § 4h EStG, m.no. B 72 (295th update 2019).
11. C. Hick in Herrmann/Heuer/Raupach, EStG Commentary, § 4h EStG, m.no. 35 (291st update 2019).
12. R. Schenke in Kirchhof/Söhn/Mellinghoff, EStG Commentary, § 4h m.no. A 18 (295th update 2019).
13. Bundestag Printed Matter 16/4841, 48.

The amount of borrowing costs is formed by the borrowing costs incurred in the corresponding year as well as by the borrowing costs carried forward in this year because the carryforward increases the borrowing costs of this fiscal year according to paragraph 1 sentence 6.

For corporations, the exemption limit in section 8(1) KStG applies. In the case of controlled companies, the interest barrier and thus also the exemption limit do not apply. According to section 15 sentence 1 no. 3 KStG, the consolidated group for financial accounting purposes is regarded as one enterprise within the meaning of section 4h EStG. Therefore, the interest barrier is not to be applied to transactions within the fiscal unity. Rather, interest income and borrowing costs of the fiscal unity's controlled company are to be included in the controlling company's accounts. Consequently, the exemption limit of EUR 3 million applies only once for the consolidated group for financial accounting purposes.[14]

[2] No or Only Partial Group Affiliation

Section 4h paragraph 2, first sentence, letter (b) excludes from the scope of application of the interest barrier all those enterprises which—as parent enterprises or as subsidiaries—do not belong to a group or only belong to it partially (the so-called stand-alone clause). Obviously, the legislator assumes that abusive granting of loans occurs primarily within groups of companies.[15]

If the requirements of this exception are met, the borrowing costs of the business are fully tax deductible (including a possible carryforward from previous years). All companies in a fiscal unity are regarded as one enterprise (section 15 sentence 1 no. 3 sentence 2 KStG).

According to Article 4(3) letter (b) ATAD, an exemption from the interest barrier may be provided if the taxpayer is a stand-alone entity and if the taxpayer does not have an associated enterprise within the meaning of Article 2 no. 4 ATAD. In contrast, the stand-alone clause of the German interest barrier already applies if the enterprise does not or only in part belong to a group. This means that this German exemption from the application of the interest barrier is much broader than that of the ATAD and therefore remains below the minimum standard of protection of the Directive. Thus, regarding the stand-alone clause, there still remains to be a need for modification of the German interest barrier.

[3] Comparison of Equity in Companies with Group Affiliation

In the case of companies belonging to a group, the suspicion of typical abuse is considered invalidated if they are not financed with debt capital to an unusually high extent (the so-called escape clause).

14. B. Heuermann in Blümich, EStG Commentary, § 4h m.no. 53 (146th update 2019); Bundestag Printed Matter 16/4841, 77.
15. C. Seiler in Kirchhof, EStG Commentary, § 4h m.no. 34 (18th Edition 2019).

The interest barrier is, therefore, not applied as long as the business is not financed with considerably more debt capital than the group as a whole.

In these cases where the company is not financed with debt capital to a higher extent than the other affiliated companies of the same group, it is possible to conclude that the intragroup relationships are appropriate and that neither excessive shareholder debt financing nor an artificial transfer of other borrowing costs to an affiliated company is to be feared.[16]

Section 4h(2) sentence 1 letter (c) EStG stipulates an equity capital comparison as a benchmark for this, according to which the interest barrier is not to be applied if the equity capital ratio of a business is at least as high as that of the entire group (sentence 1) or in any case does not fall short of it by more than two percentage points (sentence 2).

In the case of corporations or partnerships subordinate to a corporation, there is a counter-exception to this exception found in section 8a(2), (3) KStG (in conjunction with section 4h(2) sentence 2 EStG) in the case of the so-called harmful shareholder debt financing.[17] Pursuant to section 8(3) sentence 1 KStG, the remuneration for borrowed capital of the enterprise or another legal entity belonging to the same group to a substantially involved shareholder (> 25%) outside the group or to an equivalent person may not amount to more than 10% of the borrowing costs exceeding the interest income. With this counter-exception, the legislator is attempting to counteract the possibilities for the transfer of profits which could otherwise result from external debt financing of companies by their shareholders and persons of equal standing.[18] If these conditions are met, the interest barrier remains applicable independent of group affiliation and equity comparison.

[F] Subordinated Partnerships

Section 4h(2) sentence 2 EStG contains a special provision for the case in which a partnership is directly or indirectly subordinated to a corporation. In this case, the complex exceptions to the application of stand-alone escape and equity escape found in section 8a(2) and (3) KStG apply *mutatis mutandis* to the operation of the partnership.[19] The legislator was concerned with the possibility of circumventing these provisions of the Corporation Tax Act by subordinating a partnership to a corporation, which as such is not subject to the special rules of shareholder debt financing for corporations. Therefore, the purpose of this provision is to prevent a circumvention of section 8a KStG.[20]

---

16. C. Seiler in Kirchhof, EStG Commentary, § 4h m.no. 39 (18th Edition 2019).
17. F. Loschelder in Schmidt, EStG Commentary, § 4h m.no. 18 (38th Edition 2019).
18. For further details, *see* J. Blumenberg/F. Lechner in Blumenberg/Benz, *Die Unternehmensteuerreform 2008*, 107 (168) (2007).
19. For special aspects of the interest barrier regarding partnerships, *see* I. van Lishaut/A. Schumacher/P. Heinemann, *Besonderheiten der Zinsschranke bei Personengesellschaften*, DStR 2008, 2341–2348.
20. S. Goebel/K. Eilinghoff *(Nicht-)Konformität der Zinsschranke mit dem Grundgesetz und Europarecht?*, DStZ 2010, 515.

[G] Loss of Unused EBITDA and Interest Carried Forward, Section 4h(5) EStG

Section 4h(5) EStG specifies the conditions under which EBITDA carryforward and interest carryforward are lost in full or on a partial basis. In addition to the limitation of the value of an EBITDA carryforward to the five-year time limit,[21] the usability of an EBITDA carryforward is also limited by the various circumstances described in paragraph 5.

First, an unused EBITDA carryforward and an unused interest carryforward are lost with the abandonment or transfer of the entire business (regardless of whether the business has been transferred against payment or free of charge). However, the carryforwards are not lost if just an asset or part of an enterprise has been transferred or if the participation quotas change.

Second, if a partner withdraws from a partnership, the EBITDA carryforward and the interest carryforward are proportionately reduced by the corresponding share in the partnership held by the withdrawing partner.

And finally, the corresponding application of section 8c KStG is stipulated for partnerships in which a corporation is involved as a partner. Accordingly, the interest carried forward in the event of a so-called detrimental acquisition of participation within five years is proportionately lost in the event of a share transfer of more than 25% or completely lost in the event of a share transfer of more than 50%.[22] However, this does not apply to the EBITDA carried forward.

§6.03 CONSTITUTIONALITY OF THE GERMAN INTEREST BARRIER

The First Senate of the BFH regards the interest barrier as a breach of Article 3(1) of the Basic Law, which cannot be remedied by an interpretation in conformity with the constitution or an equity measure.[23] However, the BFH does not recognize a violation of the property guarantee of Article 14(1) of the Basic Law since it negates a "strangulating effect,"[24] or of the principle of the clarity of the provision because it still considers the provision to be open to interpretation.

[A] Decision of the BFH from 14.10.2015, I R 20/15

The BFH's First Senate regards the prohibition of deduction triggered by the interest barrier as an inconsistent breach of the objective net principle, which it derives from

21. Above section §6.02[C].
22. For further details on the detrimental acquisition of participation *see* P. Brandis in Blümich, KStG Commentary, § 8c (146th update 2019).
23. BFH decision on 14.10.2015, I R 20/15, BStBl 2017 II, 1240.
24. Article 14 GG protects against a "strangulating" tax, which would make the results of the economic activity appear meaningless. *See* BVerfG decision on 8.4.1997, 1 BvR 48/94, BVerfGE 95, 267 (300).

Article 3(1) of the Basic Law.[25] This is not offset by the possibility of the interest carryforward since the interest carryforward could be definitively lost in certain cases and at least lead to liquidity disadvantages.[26]

Contrary to the Federal Ministry of Finance (Bundesministerium der Finanzen—BMF),[27] the BFH also considers what may be only a temporary prohibition of deduction to be in need of justification, since it cannot be aligned without contradiction to the principle of annuality of income tax and, to that extent, there would be an inconsistent deviation from the basic legislative decision for taxation based on assessment periods.

The BFH does not see any contradiction with its case law on minimum taxation:[28] the deviation from taxation based on assessment periods through loss carryforwards and loss carrybacks serves the principle of ability to pay, whereby the restrictions on offsetting losses as a result of minimum taxation can be justified by a qualified fiscal purpose, while the interest carryforward in the eyes of the BFH deviates from taxation based on the ability to pay principle. The BFH therefore does not transfer its reasoning from its case law concerning the minimum taxation to the interest barrier—that the timing of the inclusion of profit-reducing expenses, that is the "when" and not the "whether" of taxation, cannot be determined by means of the objective net principle.

The BFH then denies a justification for the infringement of the objective net principle on the basis of tax incentives pursued by the legislator. On the basis of the traditional criteria, the BFH examines whether the incentive purpose is supported by recognizable basic legislative decisions. It rejects the justification on the basis of the objective of strengthening the equity capital base with the argument that the interest barrier does not consistently pursue the incentive purpose, since the interest barrier with the exemption limit, group and escape clause (section 4h(2) sentence 1 letters a-c EStG) would remove the majority of enterprises from the scope of application, even if they had only a low equity capital base. In the BFH's opinion, the incentive purpose of securing the domestic tax base is also not consistently pursued by the interest barrier. This is already shown by the fact that the interest barrier also applies to purely domestic cases.

Furthermore, the BFH rejects a justification with the aim of counter-financing the reduction of the corporate income tax rate,[29] since a pure fiscal purpose does not relieve the legislator of the obligation to fundamental rights. But the BFH also does not recognize the "qualified fiscal purpose," which was coined by the BFH in its case law

25. Regarding the rooting of the objective net principle in the German Basic Law, *see* M. Lehner, *Die verfassungsrechtliche Verankerung des objektiven Nettoprinzips*, DStR 2009, 185; M. Jachmann, *Steuergerechtigkeit durch Abziehbarkeit von Erwerbsaufwendungen*, DFGT 2 (2005), 59; K.-D. Drüen, *Die Bruttobesteuerung von Einkommen als verfassungsrechtliches Vabanquespiel*, StuW 2008, 3–14.
26. C. Seiler in Kirchhof, EStG Commentary, § 4h m.no. 4 (18th Edition 2019).
27. BMF on 13.11.2014 - IV C 2 - S 2742-a/07/10001:009, BStBl I 2014, 1516.
28. BFH decision on 26.2.2014, I R 59/12, BStBl II 2014, 1016.
29. The uniform corporate income tax rate introduced in 2001 was initially 25% according to section 23(1) KStG. As a result of the 2008 Corporate Tax Reform Act, the uniform corporate income tax rate was lowered to 15% from 2008 onward.

on minimum taxation,[30] with regard to the interest barrier, since it recognizes no need for the interest barrier either to stabilize tax revenue or to avoid incalculable tax losses.

The BFH further rejects justification with the aim of preventing abuse, as the interest barrier would not meet the constitutional requirements for an anti-abuse typification. This is because the interest barrier, with its 30% EBITDA limit, also covers typical cases of the leveraged enterprises, normal bank financing and purely domestic interest payments, which, however, are not suspected of abuse.

Contrary to the Court of First Instance,[31] the BFH states that the domestic application of the interest barrier cannot be justified by European law, even though the European Court of Justice (ECJ) showed in *Cadbury Schweppes*[32] that the Member States were allowed to provide for standardized anti-abuse clauses as long as the limit of the scope of abuse under European Union (EU) law was not exceeded and as long as a possibility to prove economic reasons to the contrary was granted. According to the BFH, the interest barrier—to be considered constitutional—should only have a narrowly limited scope of application for purely artificial designs.

Finally, the BFH states that the interest barrier cannot be justified by the fact that other states provide for comparable standards and that the Organisation for Economic Co-operation and Development (OECD) recommends corresponding regulations in (Base erosion and profit shifting) BEPS Action Point 4.[33]

According to the BFH, this constitutional assessment is not affected by the possibility of deviating tax assessment or tax waiver for reasons of equity in accordance with sections 163 and 227 of the Fiscal Code. The BFH does not consider another, constitutionally compliant interpretation of the interest barrier to be possible, which is why it has appealed to the BVerfG on the question of whether the interest barrier is compliant with the constitution or not.

[B] Assessment of the Constitutionality of the German Interest Barrier

Now that the opinion of the BFH has been presented, the author will try to make an independent assessment of the interest barrier and its constitutionality.

[1] Infringement of the Objective Net Principle?

The BVerfG has so far left the question of the constitutional status of the objective net principle unanswered.[34] It assesses the objective net principle as a basic legislative decision that must be enforced in accordance with the requirement of consistency under the principle of equality. Exceptions to the consistent application of the objective

30. BFH decision on 26.4.2014 - I R 59/12, BStBl 2014 II, 1016.
31. FG München decision on 6.3.2015 - 7 K 680/12, EFG 2015, 1126.
32. ECJ decision on 12.9.2006 - Case C-196/04, ECLI:EU:C:2006:544.
33. OECD on 5.10.2015, *Limiting Base Erosion Involving Interest Deductions and Other Financial Payments, Action 4—2015 Final Report.*
34. *See*, for example, BVerfG decision of 9.12.2008, 2 BvL 1/07, BVerfGE 122, 210 (234).

net principle require a special, objectively justifying reason.[35] They must also be consistent and proportionate. The purely fiscal purpose of increasing state revenue cannot justify a breach of the net principle.[36] In addition to simplification purposes, recognized justifications include, in particular, nonfiscal incentives and steering purposes for reasons of public interest as well as anti-abuse measures.[37]

There are good reasons for doubting whether the interest barrier at large is in any way a violation of the objective net principle, as the law ultimately ensures that the borrowing costs can be claimed in other periods not only by means of the interest carryforward but also by means of the EBITDA carryforward.[38] The following question must be asked: what is the relationship between the principle of taxation according to ability to pay (realization of the objective net principle) and the principle of taxation of total profits, which is determined only for practical reasons in set time periods? Here it is necessary to look at the material scope of the periodicity principle regarding the interest barrier: after all, the objective net principle does not require a time-synchronous deduction of expenses.[39] Even though the principle of annual taxation of section 2(7) sentence 2 EStG applies as a general rule, consideration of ability to pay according to annual periods of time does not originate from the objective net principle and therefore is not required by it.[40] Consequently, it can be stated that in the vast majority of cases the interest barrier does not violate the objective net principle.

However, the BFH correctly considers the interest barrier to be a breach of the objective net principle in those constellations in which the interest carryforward is definitively lost, since in these cases the interest barrier may possibly lead to an ultimate nondeduction of borrowing costs. Only for these cases, a constitutionally recognized justification is necessary.

[2] Justification

Whether there is an unbiased and justifiable reason for this selective breach of the net principle is highly controversial in the literature on the interest barrier. While the majority of scholars and practitioners have been questioning the constitutionality of the interest barrier for years and agree with the opinion of the First Senate,[41] there are also some weighty voices on the opposing side—including tax courts of lower

35. *See*, for example, BVerfG decision of 4.12.2002, 2 BvR 400/98, BVerfGE 107, 27 (48).
36. BVerfG decision of 12.10.2010, 1 BvL 12/07, BVerfGE 127, 224.
37. For example, *see* BVerfG decision of 17.12.2014, 1 BvL 21/12, BVerfGE 138, 136 (181); J.Hey in Tipke/Lang, Steuerrecht, § 3 m.no. 132 (23. Edition, 2018).
38. B. Heuermann, *Steuerinnovation im Wandel: Einige Thesen zur Zinsschranke und ihrer Verfassungsmäßigkeit*, DStR 2013, 1 (2); R. Möhlenbrock, ISR 2014, 154 (155); BMF, 13.11.2014, BStBl. I 2014, 1516, StB 2014, 419; FG München, decision of 6.3.2015 - 7 K 680/12, EFG 2015, 1126.
39. B. Heuermann in Blümich, EStG Commentary, § 4h m.no. 25 (146th update 2019).
40. BFH decision of 5.9.2001, XI B 151/00, BStBl. II 2001, 552 (554); R. Schenke in Kirchhof/Söhn/Mellinghoff, EStG Commentary, § 4h m.no. A 185 (295th update 2019).
41. Among others: H. Weggenmann/G. Claß, *Die Zinsschrankenregelung auf dem verfassungsrechtlichen Prüfstand*, BB 2016, 1175-1180; M. Glahe, ISR 2016, 86-89; M. München/N. Mückl, *Die Vereinbarkeit der Zinsschranke mit dem Grundgesetz*, DStR 2014, 1469-1475; J. Hey in Tipke/Lang, Steuerrecht, § 11 m.no. 56 (23. Edition, 2018); C. Marquart/A. Jehlin, *Zu den*

instance[42]—that argue in favor of the constitutional justification of the interest barrier by means of a "qualified fiscal purpose."[43]

Possible justifications could be: strengthening the equity ratio of German enterprises; securing the German tax base; creating incentives for domestic investment and anti-tax avoidance. These legitimate objectives in themselves appear in principle to justify a restriction of the net principle from a public interest point of view. However, this also requires them to be supported by a recognizable and proportional legislative decision in this respect.[44] Whether or not this is the case with the interest barrier is yet to be examined.

[a] Strengthening the Equity Ratio of German Enterprises

According to the explanatory memorandum of the draft law, the interest barrier is intended to strengthen enterprises' equity capital.[45] By strengthening the equity base of German enterprises, protection against insolvency shall be increased and excessive borrowing shall be prevented. Recent history has shown that equity-financed companies are less affected by changes in the capital market environment and less exposed to the risk of loan cancellations. Since a higher equity ratio indicates greater financial stability, this legislative motive is comprehensible.

As an argument against the validity of this justification, it is often written that—due to the wide scope of the exceptions to the interest barriers—in practice the actual number of enterprises affected by the interest barrier is relatively small compared to the total number of German enterprises.[46]

However, this argument fails to recognize that the incentive effect lies precisely in the fact that the interest barrier is not intended to be fulfilled.[47] A successful "influencing rule"[48] is designed to be avoided by the influenced taxpayer and therefore should not generate much revenue. In fact, the rule is especially successful if it is rarely

---

verfassungsrechtlichen Grenzen einer "Steuerinnovation", DStR 2013, 2301–2306; C. Hick, FR 2014, 560–567; S. Goebel/K. Eilinghoff, DStZ 2010, 550–562.

42. FG Münster decision of 29.4.2013, 9 V 2400/12 K, DStRE 2014, 107; FG Berlin-Brandenburg decision of 13.10.2011, 12 V 12089/11, DStRE 2012, 555.
43. Among others: B. Heuermann, DStR 2013, 1; B. Heuermann in Blümich, EStG Commentary, § 4h m.no. 25 (146th update 2019); R. Ismer, *Verfassungsrechtliche Rechtfertigung der Zinsschranke*, FR 2014, 777–784; R. Möhlenbrock, ISR 2014, 155; A. Schmehl in Schön/Beck, *Zukunftsfragen des deutschen Steuerrechts*, 99 (116) (2009); W. Mitschke, *Zinsschranke wirklich verfassungswidrig?*, FR 2016, 412–416; W. Staats, *Zur Verfassungskonformität der Zinsschranke*, Ubg 2014, 520 (524); R. Schenke in Kirchhof/Söhn/Mellinghoff, EStG Commentary, § 4h m.no. A 188 (295th update 2019).
44. BVerfG decision of 9.12.2008, 2 BvL 1, 2/07, 2/08, BVerfGE 122, 210, m.no. 59; R. Schenke in Kirchhof/Söhn/Mellinghoff, EStG Commentary, § 4h m.no. A 170 (295th update 2019).
45. Bundestag Printed Matter 16/4841, 30.
46. BFH decision of 14.10.2015, I R 20/15, BStBl 2017 II, 1240; C. Marquart/A. Jehlin, DStR 2013, 2301 (2304).
47. R. Ismer, FR 2014, 777 (780); B. Heuermann in Blümich, EStG Commentary, § 4h m.no. 26 (146th update 2019).
48. R. Ismer, FR 2014, 777 (780); B. Heuermann in Blümich, EStG Commentary, § 4h m.no. 26 (146th update 2019).

fulfilled.[49] The German legislator has declared the improved equity base and, thus, the nonintervention of the interest barrier to be the goal. Consequently, the low revenue from the interest barrier speaks in favor of successful incentive effects.

It is true that the interest barrier does not always automatically lead to an increase in equity capital and that the far-reaching exceptions also leave room for some circumvention.[50] Small- and medium-sized enterprises in particular would sometimes have very little equity capital but are generally not covered by the interest barrier because of the high threshold of EUR 3 million regarding the exemption limit.[51] With this high threshold, the legislator deliberately wanted to exempt small- and medium-sized enterprises from the limitation on borrowing cost deductions and thus relieve and strengthen them in difficult economic times.[52] This is a secondary steering purpose that complements and does not run counter to the primary purpose—that of strengthening the equity base of large enterprises.

With this objective of the interest barrier in mind, an overall assessment makes it clear that the wording of the provision within the legislative assessment prerogatives is adequately aimed at actually improving the equity base of German companies and that the relatively small number of enterprises affected is not just a mere side effect or a reason to doubt the effectiveness of the rule. Based on this understanding, there is much to be said for the classification of the interest barrier as a successful and proportional influencing tax rule that justifies a partial breach of the objective net principle.

[b] Securing the German Tax Base

Additionally, the interest barrier is intended to secure the German tax base.[53] This purpose goes beyond simply generating revenue, which by itself would not be a valid justification.[54] This is why the idea of counter-financing the reduction of the corporate income tax rate (mentioned in the explanatory memorandum) cannot, by itself, serve as a justification.

The interest barrier, however, goes beyond purely fiscal purposes. It aims to ensure that the domestic tax base is not structurally eroded by the outflow of domestically generated income abroad.[55] The idea behind this justification is that taxes should be regarded economically as prices to be paid for the possibility of using the infrastructure provided by the State.[56]

---

49. Arguing against the empirical justification of typifying tax norms as a constitutional requirement: N. Melan, *"Empirische" Rechtfertigung typisierender Steuernormen als Verfassungsgebot?*, FR 2018, 1136–1142.
50. C. Marquart/A. Jehlin, DStR 2013, 2301 (2304).
51. BFH decision of 14.10.2015, I R 20/15, BStBl 2017 II, 1240; C. Marquart/A. Jehlin, DStR 2013, 2301 (2304).
52. Bundestag Printed Matter 17/15, 10; R. Ismer, FR 2014, 777 (780).
53. Bundestag Printed Matter 16/4841, 29, 48.
54. BVerfG decision of 9.12.2008, 2 BvL 1/07, BVerfGE 122, 210 (233).
55. B. Heuermann, DStR 2013, 1 (2).
56. R. Schenke in Kirchhof/Söhn/Mellinghoff, EStG Commentary, § 4h m.no. A 179 (295th update 2019).

In fact, the German legislator is thus making considerations reminiscent of those of the ECJ when it recognized the justification "balanced allocation of the power to impose taxes between Member States" in its *Marks & Spencer* decision.[57]

Therefore, such tax arrangements, which threaten to erode the domestic tax base in the long run, should be eliminable also according to considerations of economic fair-share theory[58] even if they may not clearly be qualified as tax avoidance. For that reason, it can be said that—because of the large legislative margin of manoeuvre to be granted on the question if a rule is really necessary to achieve the legislator's goal—the interest barrier appears to be a proportionate measure to secure the German tax base.

[c] Creating Incentives for Domestic Investment

In the basic model of the interest barrier, the nondeductible borrowing costs can be carried forward to subsequent fiscal years and be deducted there as long as the borrowing costs do not fully utilize the offsetting EBITDA. In this way, the interest barrier tries to create an incentive to relocate investments in Germany by offsetting future profits from these domestic investments against accumulated carryforwards of borrowing costs.[59] From a constitutional point of view, this incentive to attract domestic investment is in principle a legitimate regulatory objective.[60] It is questionable, however, whether the interest barrier in itself is sufficiently supported by a legislative decision with regard to the incentive aim to promote direct domestic investment. Even if the explanatory memorandum to the 2008 Corporate Tax Reform Act states this justification, the hoped-for incentive effect clearly does not derive as much from the interest barrier itself as from the reduction in the corporate income tax rate from 25% to 15% that was also a major part of the 2008 Corporate Tax Reform Act. Even though it has been shown that the interest barrier does not cause any (short-term) negative investment effects,[61] the incentive effect of promoting direct investments by means of the interest barrier does not appear to be sufficiently supported by a recognizable legislative decision and therefore cannot be used as a valid justification for the breach of the net principle.

[d] Anti-tax Avoidance

Another aim of the interest barrier is to combat tax-reducing arrangements,[62] which is, in principle, a valid justification.[63] In this respect, it is questionable, however, whether

57. ECJ decision of 13.12.2005, C-446/03 (*Marks & Spencer*).
58. C. Esser, *Internationaler Steuerwettbewerb*, 51, 86 (2005).
59. Bundestag Printed Matter 16/4841, 31, 48.
60. R. Schenke in Kirchhof/Söhn/Mellinghoff, EStG Commentary, § 4h m.no. A 177 (295th update 2019).
61. H. Buslei/M. Simmler, *The Impact of Introducing an Interest Barrier—Evidence from the German Corporation Tax Reform 2008*, DIW Discussion Papers, No. 1215, 21 (2012).
62. Bundestag Printed Matter 16/4841, 34.
63. BVerfG decision of 8.6.1993, 1 BvL 20/85, BVerfGE 89, 15 (24).

the interest barrier is sufficiently targeted at cases of abuse or if it exceeds the limits of typification.

For reasons of equal treatment, as well as for reasons of Union law, the scope of the provision also extends to purely domestic financing which is in no way suspected of "artificially shifting" the tax base. This means that the interest barrier applies equally to domestic and foreign situations. Therefore, the regulation does not violate the fundamental freedoms of the Treaty on the Functioning of the European Union. However, if one focuses solely on the purpose of preventing abuse, the interest barrier meets constitutional reservations with regard to Article 3(1) of the Basic Law for this reason, because the constitutional limits of an abuse typification may indeed have been exceeded.[64] The inclusion of domestic situations would not have been necessary in order to fight abuse because in these situations there is no potential for profit transfer, which would deprive the German tax authorities of their tax base. However, the inclusion of purely domestic matters is necessary in order to avoid an infringement of the fundamental freedoms of the EU, which would be infringed if the scope were limited to cross-border matters. For this reason, there is much to be said in favor of leaving the legislator particularly wide scope for typification in case of the interest barrier.[65]

However, the interest barrier, with its broad scope, also covers completely harmless structures and customary bank financing,[66] which is why it must ultimately be stated that the legislator has exceeded the limits of typification with regard to abuse prevention—albeit not because of the inclusion of purely domestic issues but because of the inclusion of financing methods that have nothing to do with tax avoidance. Therefore, in the case of the interest barrier, the fight against tax avoidance cannot be used as a justification for breaching the objective net principle.

With regard to the European fundamental freedoms and the case law of the ECJ, the question arises, however, as to whether more specific anti-abuse norms, which are linked solely to cross-border situations, would have been possible and justified.[67]

[3] Result: Constitutionality of the German Interest Barrier

The abovementioned explanations have shown that, in the author's opinion, if the German interest barrier is rightfully interpreted as being constitutionally compliant with the objective that the legislator had in mind, the BFH's criticism is ultimately unconvincing because the legislator can rely on legitimate justifications for the (partial)

64. BFH decision of 14.10.2015, I R 20/15, BStBl 2017 II, 1240; M. Glahe, ISR 2016, 86 (87); J. Hey, *Verletzung fundamentaler Besteuerungsprinzipien durch die Gegenfinanzierungsmaßnahmen des Unternehmensteuerreformgesetzes 2008*, BB 2007, 1303 (1305).
65. R. Schenke in Kirchhof/Söhn/Mellinghoff, EStG Commentary, § 4h m.no. A 174 (295th update 2019); W. Mitschke, *Zinsschranke wirklich verfassungswidrig?*, FR 2016, 412.
66. H. Weggenmann/G. Claß, BB 2016, 1175 (1178); R. Schenke in Kirchhof/Söhn/Mellinghoff, EStG Commentary, § 4h m.no. A 187 (295th update 2019).
67. For alternative concepts *see* R. Schenke in: Kirchhof/Söhn/Mellinghoff, EStG Commentary, § 4h m.no. A 281 (295th update 2019); A. Bohn, *Zinsschranke und Alternativmodelle zur Beschränkung des steuerlichen Zinsabzugs* (2009).

breach of the objective net principle, namely the goals of strengthening the equity of German enterprises and securing the German tax base, which are both sufficiently supported by a recognizable legislative decision.

[C] The Pending Decision of the BVerfG

It is questionable, after the coming into force of the ATAD, whether the BVerfG is prevented from interpreting the Basic Law in the pending proceedings to the effect that the interest barrier violates Article 3(1) of the Basic Law.[68] Such a possible preliminary effect on the interpretation of national constitutional law has not yet been decided on by the ECJ.[69] In the author's opinion, the entry into force of the ATAD has no legally binding effect on the pending proceeding before the BVerfG regarding the interest barrier relating to the dispute years 2008 and 2009, since the Directive can only have effect on future assessment periods.[70]

For future periods and especially with regard to corporations, however, this constitutional situation has now been overtaken by the primacy of European law[71] and therefore of the ATAD, which obliges Member States' legislators to implement such a regulation at the latest upon expiry of the implementation deadline. According to Article 11(1) ATAD, the Member States shall adopt and publish the laws, regulations and administrative provisions necessary to comply with this Directive by December 31, 2018. This period has already expired. It has to be noted, however, that according to Article 11(6) ATAD, those Member States which already have specific national rules targeted at preventing BEPS risks that are equally effective as the interest limitation rule set out in the Directive may apply these targeted rules up until the end of the first full fiscal year following the date of publication of the agreement between the OECD members on the official website on a minimum standard with regard to BEPS Action 4, but, in any case, up until January 1, 2024, at the latest.

Since sections 4h EStG and 8a KStG are practically covered by Article 4 ATAD, in principle only a minor act of transposition, regarding the stand-alone clause, is to be expected for Germany.

The ECJ has already concluded that if an EU rule is allegedly unconstitutional but its disapplication would be in contradiction to EU law, EU law would have to be granted full application.[72] In future cases, which occur after the entry into force and applicability of the ATAD, a previously unconstitutional interest barrier (depending on the BVerfG's decision) would have to be reapplied—at least regarding

68. Of this opinion: Mitschke, FR 2016, 412 (415).
69. For further details about a possible preliminary effect of directives on the interpretation of national constitutional law *see* M. Glahe, *Zur zeitlichen und inhaltlichen Begrenzung einer möglichen Vorwirkung der Anti-BEPS-Richtlinie*, FR 2016, 829–834; W. Mitschke, FR 2016, 412–416; E. Jabrayil, *Die Vorwirkung der ATAD-Richtlinie*, IStR 2019, 321–328.
70. Of the same opinion: M. Glahe, FR 2016, 829 (830); different opinion: W. Mitschke, FR 2016, 412 (415).
71. ECJ decisions of 15.7.1964, C-6/64, Slg. 1964, 1253, NJW 1964, 2371 (Costa/Enel); and of 17.12.1970, Rs. 11/70, Slg. 1970, 1125, NJW 1971, 343 (Internationale Handelsgesellschaft).
72. A. Dourado, *The Interest Limitation Rule in the Anti-Tax Avoidance Directive (ATAD) and the Net Taxation Principle*, EC Tax Review 2017, 112–121 (120).

corporations—due to the priority of the application of European law. The BVerfG would then withdraw its jurisdiction in accordance with its *Solange-II* jurisdiction[73] and reject future constitutional complaints and review procedures as inadmissible. To this extent, constitutional review will then no longer take place at the BVerfG, but at the ECJ.[74]

Regarding individual entrepreneurs and business partnerships, however, the constitutional situation described above and the concerns of the BFH persist for the time being, because Article 1 ATAD determines that this Directive applies only to all taxpayers subject to corporate tax.

Should the BVerfG assume that section 4h of the Income Tax Act is unconstitutional, the logical consequence in the light of ATAD would be to delete the provision in the Income Tax Act and to transfer it to the Corporate Income Tax Act, so that at least the application with regard to corporation tax subjects would be maintained in conformity with the ATAD.[75]

73. BVerfG decision of 22.10.1986, 2 BvR 197/83, BVerfGE 73, 339.
74. A. Dourado, EC Tax Review 2017, 112 (121); M. Glahe, ISR 2016, 86 (89).
75. Of the same opinion: E. Jabrayil, IStR 2019, 321.

CHAPTER 7
Italy

Giuseppe Vanz

§7.01 INTRODUCTION

The European Union (EU) Council Directive no. 2016/1164 of 12 April 2016 (the so-called Anti-Tax Avoidance Directive (ATAD)) has been implemented in Italy by Legislative Decree no. 142 of 29 November 2018.

With regard in particular to the 'Interest limitation rule' contained in Article 4 ATAD, it has been implemented by Article 1 of Legislative Decree 142/2018, which has entirely replaced Article 96 of Presidential Decree 917/1986 (the 'Testo unico delle imposte sui redditi', that is the Income Tax Code, hereinafter referred to as 'TUIR'), containing the guidelines for the deduction of interest expenses when determining the income of corporations and commercial entities resident in Italy for corporate income tax (IRES) purposes.

The structure of the new Article 96 TUIR follows that of former Article 96, with the amendments necessitated by the Directive.

Therefore, we are not facing an entirely new rule for Italy, but the revision of a rule introduced in Italy as from 1 January 2004.

This can be explained by the fact that the former Article 96 had been developed on the model already provided for under German law,[1] which later also constituted the reference model for Article 4 ATAD.

The new Article 96 TUIR came into force as from 1 January 2019.[2] We will examine its contents in the following paragraph and then assess its compliance with the ATAD and the existence of possible problems within the Italian legal system.

1. On this matter, *see* Circolare Assonime no. 46 of 18 November 2009, 17.
2. More specifically, it applies as from the tax period subsequent to the one in progress as of 31 December 2018. Moreover, a transitional arrangement is provided in Article 13, paras 2-5, Legislative Decree 142/2018.

§7.02 THE ESSENTIAL CORE OF THE ITALIAN LAW OF TRANSPOSITION

The main core of current Article 96 TUIR is the following:

- interest expenses and other similar charges [3] are deductible in each tax year up to the total amount: (i) of interest earnings and other similar income for the relevant tax period and (ii) of interest earnings and other similar income carried forward from previous tax periods;
- the excess is deductible up to the amount resulting from the sum of: (i) 30% of the ROL ('Risultato operativo lordo'), a balance sheet value which is equivalent with EBITDA[4] and (ii) 30% of any ROL that may have been carried forward from previous tax periods.[5]

As regards these rules, Article 96 provides the following definitions:

- the recognized interest expenses and interest earnings and similar charges and income are those qualified as such by the accounting principles adopted by the entity[6] and deriving from a transaction or from a contractual relationship with financial purposes or from a contractual relationship containing a considerable financial element;[7]
- by ROL reference is made more precisely to the difference between 'production value' and the 'costs of production' in the profit and loss account,[8] shown at the value resulting from the application of the provisions for the calculation of the business income. For those drawing up the balance sheet according to

3. Including those added to the cost of the assets, on the basis of the following rules: regarding the tangible and intangible capital assets for the operation of the undertaking, the interest expenses recorded in the financial statements, which increase the cost itself as a result of legal provisions, are included in the cost; following the same criteria, regarding the goods, in the manufacturing costs it is possible to add costs other than those directly attributable to the product; for immovable property, the production of which forms the purpose of the company's activity, the cost includes the interest expenses on loans contracted for its construction or renovation.
4. Earnings Before Interest, Taxes, Depreciation and Amortization.
5. Bearing in mind that priority must be given to the use of the 30% of the ROL for the tax period and only subsequently can the 30% of the ROL of previous tax periods be used, starting from that relevant to the least recent tax period.
6. Furthermore, it is required that such qualification be confirmed by the national law of transposition for the tax purposes of international accounting principles and, in particular, of the various provisions adopted to implement Article 1, para. 60, Law no. 244 of 24 December 2007, of Article 4, paras 7-*quater* and 7-*quinquies*, of Legislative Decree no. 38 of 28 February 2005 and of Article 13-*bis*, para. 11, of Legislative Decree no. 244 of 30 December 2016, as converted by Law no. 19 of 27 February 2017.
7. It should also be considered that: (1) the interest earnings assume relevance to the extent that they are taxable; (2) the financial income and charges become relevant as interest earnings or interest expenses, although deriving from financial instruments which are qualified as equity instruments, if they are nonetheless taxable or deductible respectively by the recipient or the lender; (3) for those entities dealing with the public administration, also the interest for late payment is considered to be relevant as interest earnings.
8. Referred to respectively under letters A) and B) of Article 2425 of the civil code. With the exclusion, however, of the depreciation of the tangible and intangible fixed assets, as well as the financial lease payments of capital goods.

international accounting principles, the corresponding entries of the profit and loss account are adopted.

The interest expenses and similar financial charges which, as a result of the aforementioned rules, prove to be non-deductible in a certain tax period are deductible when determining the income of subsequent tax periods, without a time limitation, on condition that in a subsequent period there is a 'sum' of deductibility that has not been used by the elements attributable to that period.

It is also possible to carry forward any: (i) excess interest earnings and similar financial income and (ii) excess ROL, compared with the requirements for the period (including the amounts carried forward from previous periods) as follows:

- in the case of excess interest earnings and similar financial income, such an excess may be carried forward indefinitely;
- in the case of excess ROL, such an excess may be carried forward to increase the 30% of the ROL of the subsequent five tax periods.[9]

With regard in particular to the carry-forward of any excess interest earnings of previous tax periods, it should be noted that such a possibility was not expressly provided for by the ATAD. However, it appears to be compatible with the objectives pursued by the ATAD.[10]

§7.03 EXCLUSIONS AND DEROGATIONS

The limitation rule regarding interest expense deductibility as described briefly above does not apply:

9. More specifically, para. 7 of Article 96 states, not without some ambiguity, that 'the excess amount may be used to increase the ROL of the subsequent five tax periods' (the author's translation from Italian). With a wording that would literally seem to allocate the excess amount to increase the ROL of the year (before the calculation of the 30%) instead of increasing the 30% of the ROL of the year (i.e., increasing the amount that signals one of the limits for deducting the excess interest in the tax period). However, in the author's opinion, reasons of logical coherence and the need to standardize the dimensions at play oblige the understanding as stated above in the text. In this sense, *see* the Explanatory Report of the Ministry of Economy and Finance, dated 10 August 2018, to the draft legislative decree implementing the ATAD, and, in particular, the comment to para. 5 of Article 2 of the draft.
10. On this matter, *see* the aforementioned Explanatory Report of the Ministry of Economy and Finance commenting on para. 1 of Article 2 of the draft, where it is stated that the choice made in Italy, 'is motivated by the fact that, following the choice to consider the interest expenses and earnings qualified as such according to the accounting principles adopted by the entity ..., it is necessary to take into account, with reference to the same operation, that there will be situations in which there will be a tax period characterized by excess interest earnings followed by tax periods characterized by excess interest expenses (for example, consider the case in which a bank loan is obtained with a contractual interest rate that is lower than the market interest rate and the consequent discounting of the value of the loan with the recognition of the *one day profit* – that generates excess interest earnings – and the subsequent accounting of the interest expenses at the market rate' (author's translation from Italian).

- to interest expenses and similar financial charges on loans used to fund a long-term public infrastructure project, on condition that a series of requirements provided for by Article 96 TUIR are met;
- to financial intermediaries,[11] to insurance companies and to holding companies of insurance groups whose interest expenses are deductible up to the limit of 96% of their amount.

In any case, absolute non-deductibility is provided for:

- interest expenses and similar financial charges linked to immovable property that does not constitute capital goods for the business, or goods, the production or exchange of which form the purpose of the business;
- the excess part of the fair value of the interest expenses and similar financial charges falling within the scope of application of the *transfer pricing* rule;[12]
- the part of the interest on shareholder loans of cooperative companies that exceeds the threshold set by the law.[13]

Furthermore, it should be noted that, in implementing the ATAD, the Italian legislator, by means of Article 14, paragraph 2, Legislative Decree 142/2018, had coherently arranged for the repeal of a specific rule[14] which, for companies effectively and predominantly involved in real estate activity,[15] excluded the application of the former limitation rule regarding the deductibility of interest expenses,[16] with regard to those interest expenses deriving from loans guaranteed by mortgages on property to be rented. As a consequence, these companies too would have had to apply, in their entirety, the limits of interest expense deductibility as stated in the new Article 96 TUIR.

Nevertheless, although characterized by considerable ambiguity, subsequent Article 1, paragraph 7, of Law no. 145 of 30 December 2018, would seem to have made provisional arrangements for the 'survival' of the aforementioned derogation regarding property companies, pending a general revision of the legislation on the taxation of real estate companies. According to the national legislation in force, the new Article 96 TUIR should not apply to such companies as far as interest expenses deriving from loans guaranteed by mortgages on property destined for rent are concerned.

11. A general definition of 'financial intermediaries' was introduced into the TUIR, at the same time as the new Article 96, by Article 12 of the Legislative Decree 142/2018.
12. Article 110, para. 7, TUIR.
13. In fact, Article 1, para 465, Law no. 311 of 30 December 2004, establishes that the interest on amounts paid by natural person shareholders to cooperative societies and their consortia at the conditions provided for by Article 13 of Legislative Decree no. 601 of 29 September 1973 are non-deductible on the part exceeding the amount calculated with reference to the minimum interest payable to holders of postal savings certificates, increased by 0.90%.
14. Contained in Art. 1, para. 36, of Law no. 244 of 24 Dec. 2007, as modified by Article 4, para. 4 of Legislative Decree no. 147 of 14 September 2015.
15. By this, reference is made to those companies whose asset value is constituted mainly by the fair value of the property destined for lease and at least two-thirds of whose revenue is represented by lease payments or business rents, the total value of which mainly consists of the fair value of buildings.
16. The one provided for by the previous version of Art. 96 TUIR.

However, this rule is in contrast with Article 4 ATAD, which does not provide for any derogation on the matter. Without prejudice to the comments made in the following paragraphs regarding the principle of proportionality, the Italian State could be induced to cancel such a rule even by means of an infringement procedure in accordance with Article 258 TFEU (Treaty on the Functioning of the European Union).

§7.04 THE RULES OF NATIONAL GROUP TAXATION

With reference to corporate groups, Article 4 ATAD included for Member States, under paragraphs 1, subparagraphs 2-3, and 5, a series of options that were not necessarily alternatives, insofar as they were, at least in part, cumulative.

Italy saw fit to lay down rules only for the case in which the national group taxation is operative.[17]

In this case, any non-deductible excess interest expenses and similar financial charges generated vis-à-vis an entity [18] may be deducted when determining the overall income of the group, to the extent that the other entities belonging to the group present, for the same tax period:

- an excess ROL, even if it is carried forward from previous tax periods;[19] or
- excess interest earnings or similar financial income for the tax period or deriving from previous tax periods.[20]

Particular rules are then laid down for cases in which financial intermediaries, insurance companies and holding companies of insurance groups participate in the national group taxation.

§7.05 FAILURE TO FORESEE REMEDIES FOR AVOIDING DOUBLE TAXATION

Recital no. 5 of the ATAD indicates that the rules contained therein, including the limitation rule on the deductibility of interest expenses, 'should not only aim to counter tax avoidance practices but also avoid creating other obstacles to the market, such as double taxation'.[21]

Again in recital no. 5, it is subsequently stated that 'Where the application of those rules gives rise to double taxation, taxpayers should receive relief through a deduction for the tax paid in another Member State or third country ... .' In such a

17. As provided for and regulated by Articles 117-129 TUIR.
18. Except those generated in a tax period prior to the adoption of national group taxation.
19. With the exclusion, also for these purposes, of the periods prior to the adoption of the national group taxation.
20. Also, in this case with the exclusion of the periods prior to the adoption of national group taxation.
21. On the matter, *see* the Conclusions presented on 29 July 2006 by the Advocate General L.A. Geelhoed in Case C-524/04, *Test Claimants in the Thin Cap Group Litigation*, EU:C:2006:436, point 69.

context, the term 'double taxation' should evidently be understood in the sense of the non-deductibility of interest expenses in the State of the payer and the simultaneous taxation of the same interest, as interest earnings, in the State of the recipient.

Nonetheless, we are dealing with an extremely vague indication. Furthermore, no clarification is given as to whether it concerns legal or also economic double taxation and what is the sphere of the addressees.

Most importantly though, it concerns an indication that is not reflected in any way by specific provisions in Article 4 ATAD.

In view of this circumstance, Italy has decided not to follow up the indication contained in recital no. 5 of the ATAD, and we find nothing on the matter in Article 96 TUIR.[22]

§7.06 FAILURE TO EXERCISE THE OPTIONS REGARDING THE '*DE MINIMIS*' AND 'STANDALONE' CLAUSES

Furthermore, the Italian State decided not to exercise any of the significant options expressly set out in Article 4 ATAD.

In particular, Article 96 does not provide for:

- the '*de minimis*' clause stated in Article 4, paragraph 3, subparagraph 1, let. a), ATAD, according to which the Member State could grant the taxpayer the right to deduct in any case (i.e., regardless of whether the limits set are complied with or not) the excess financial charges up to EUR 3 million;[23]
- the 'standalone' clause provided for by Article 4, paragraph 3, subparagraph 1, let. b), ATAD, according to which the Member State could grant the taxpayer the right to deduct in full the excess financial charges whenever the taxpayer was an independent entity, that is 'a taxpayer that is not part of a consolidated group for financial accounting purposes and has no associated enterprise or permanent establishment'.[24]

While failure to exercise the first option seems incontestable (at best criticizable in terms of appropriateness), failure to exercise the second option, on the contrary, raises some perplexities on a legal level.

Concerning the first option (the '*de minimis*' clause), the same ATAD, in recital no. 8, viewed it as a solution with the exclusive aim 'to reduce the administrative and compliance burden of the rules without significantly diminishing their tax effect'. Evidently, the Italian State believed that such a need did not exist in practice or,

22. *See* F. Pitrone, *Italy*, 'Branch Report', 'Cahier de Droit Fiscal International', 104, IFA 2019, digital version, paras 4.1 and 4.2.
23. As stated in recital no. 8 of the ATAD: 'To reduce the administrative and compliance burden of the rules without significantly diminishing their tax effect, it may be appropriate to provide for a safe harbour rule so that net interest is always deductible up to a fixed amount, when this leads to a higher deduction than the EBITDA-based ratio.'
24. Specification is given in subpara. 3 of the same Article 4, para. 3, ATAD. The definition of 'associated enterprise' is given in Article 2, no. 4, ATAD.

perhaps more probably, that the simplification did not justify the corresponding loss of revenue.

The tenor of the explanations contained in the ATAD with regard to the second option (the 'standalone' clause) is, however, quite different. In fact, recital no. 8 states: 'Since BEPS[25] in principle takes place through excessive interest payments among entities which are associated enterprises, it is appropriate and necessary to allow the possible exclusion of standalone entities from the scope of the interest limitation rule given the limited risks of tax avoidance.'

Consequently, the ATAD considers the introduction of the stand-alone clause to be not only appropriate but also necessary. Hence, it is quite astonishing that, in the formulation of the relevant rule (Article 4, paragraph 3, ATAD), Member States have been granted simple discretionary power.

On this matter, some doubts may arise in view of the wording of the ATAD in Italian, where it states that in the case of independent entities, as an exception to the general interest deductibility limitation rule, 'il contribuente può ottenere il diritto ... di dedurre integralmente gli oneri finanziari eccedenti'[26] (Article 4, paragraph 3, let. b). This is in contrast with other parts of the same Article 4 ATAD, where the granting of a simple discretionary power to the Member States is specified in far clearer and more precise terms using expressions such as 'gli Stati membri possono trattare come un contribuente anche ...'[27] (Article 4, paragraph 1, subparagraph 2) or 'gli Stati membri possono escludere dall'ambito di applicazione del paragrafo 1 ...'[28] (Article 4, paragraph 4, subparagraph 1).

In conjunction with the statements made in recital no. 8, the Italian wording of Article 4, paragraph 3, let. b)[29] could, hypothetically, be interpreted in the sense that the States must provide for the stand-alone clause, but may adapt it according to the subsistence of requirements which are such as to make it applicable only in very specific cases.[30]

However, this hypothetical interpretation is contradicted by the versions of the ATAD in other languages, in which the granting to Member States of the power to decide whether or not to grant the exception to independent taxpayers emerges with greater clarity.[31]

25. That is the phenomenon of 'BEPS' which is described with regard to interest expenses in 'Action 4: 2015 Final Report' drawn up by the OECD and endorsed by the G20.
26. This passage can be freely translated in English as follows: 'the taxpayer can obtain the right ... to fully deduct the excess financial charges'.
27. The ATAD English version of this passage is the following: 'Member States may also treat as a taxpayer ...'.
28. The ATAD English version of this passage is the following: 'Member States may exclude from the scope of paragraph 1 ...'.
29. The wording is also present in the same terms in para. 5 of the same Article 4 ATAD with reference to the taxpayers who are members of consolidated groups.
30. This would explain the wording 'il contribuente può ottenere il diritto' ('the taxpayer can obtain the right'), instead of 'il contribuente ha il diritto' ('the taxpayer has the right').
31. So, for example, we read in the German version: 'kann dem Steuerpflichtigen Folgendes gewährt werden', in the French version: 'le contribuable peut se voir autoriser à', in the Spanish version: 'se podrá otorgar al contribuyente el derecho a'; in the English version: 'the taxpayer may be given the right'. For the interpretation stated in the text, *see*: M. Barassi, *Le regole tributarie degli*

Despite the explicit indication given in recital no. 8 regarding the 'necessity' of the stand-alone clause, it is difficult to consider that Article 4, paragraph 3 of the ATAD, on its own can impose the introduction of such a clause on Member States.

Consequently, it is equally difficult to affirm that by omitting to provide for a stand-alone clause, Italy has thus violated the ATAD.

§7.07 STAND-ALONE CLAUSE AND THE EUROPEAN PRINCIPLE OF PROPORTIONALITY

If, followed to the letter, Article 4, paragraph 3, ATAD does not really seem to allow for an interpretation in terms of the 'necessity' of the stand-alone clause, we must, at the same time, ask ourselves whether this is legitimate on the level of European law.

The ATAD is, in fact, clear in its intention to counter 'tax avoidance practices'[32] and, in particular, with reference to interest expenses, the misuse made of them by 'corporate groups'. Apart from the passage from recital no. 8 quoted in the previous paragraph, the beginning of recital no. 6 should also be considered, where it states 'In an effort to reduce their global tax liability, groups of companies have increasingly engaged in BEPS, through excessive interest payments. The interest limitation rule is necessary to discourage such practices by limiting the deductibility of taxpayers' exceeding borrowing costs.'

Moreover, the ATAD openly states that it is an instrument for implementing the Organisation for Economic Co-operation and Development (OECD) conclusions (endorsed by the G20) on the instruments for counteracting the phenomenon of 'Base Erosion and Profit Shifting' (BEPS)[33] on the EU level. These included the conclusions reached in 'Action 4: 2015 Final Report' concerning 'Limiting Base Erosion Involving Interest Deductions and Other Financial Payments', which were mainly directed at countering the improper use of interest expenses at the level of multinational groups. Indeed, the description of the practices to be countered and the relative examples contained in 'Action 4: 2015 Final Report' refer to multinational groups.[34] And again,

interessi passivi, in 'Fiscalità della internazionalizzazione delle imprese – Studi sul D.Lgs. 14 September 2015 n. 147' (edited by A. Vicini Ronchetti), Giappichelli 2018, 289, no. 43.

32. This is the wording of the heading of the ATAD.
33. *See*, in particular, recitals nos 1, 2 and 3 of the ATAD.
34. *See*, for example, paras 1-3 of 'Action 4: 2015 Final Report'. As will be explained more precisely in the text, the aforementioned 'Action 4' provides for the possibility of also extending the interest expense deductibility threshold to national groups and to independent entities. However, it does not explain how the BEPS practices against which 'Action 4' is directed (basically by levering, as has been seen, on the different regimes present in the various States) can be implemented with regard to solely national groups or by independent entities. What is more, no examples are given. A few mentions are made in para. 52 (and, as cross-references, in paras 171-182) with reference to independent entities, but limited to hypotheses in which related parties are present. They are particular situations in which, in any case, a qualified connection exists between entities which, although it does not formally give rise to a true and proper group relationship, in substance it comes very close to being one, leading to a relationship commonly defined as an association. In other words, it concerns an entity which is not entirely (or only relatively) independent. In fact, if 'Action 4' defines the entities that do not belong to a group as 'independent' (para. 52) and then draws up separately the notion of 'related parties' in order to

from 'Action 4: 2015 Final Report' it appears that it is exclusively on the basis of statistics referring to multinational groups that the limit of 30% of 'non tax avoidance' was set and taken up by the ATAD,[35] that is the limit within which excess interest expenses are considered 'physiological' and, as such, not directed towards BEPS practices.[36]

The BEPS practices which Article 4 ATAD intended to counter, were, therefore, the ones implemented by corporate groups and, more specifically, by multinational groups.

Given this objective, the European principle of proportionality requires that the instrument of implementation be limited to whatever is necessary and sufficient for achieving such an aim.

Strictly speaking, Article 4 ATAD should have defined its scope of application to corporate groups (in particular multinationals) or at least have foreseen the introduction of a mandatory 'standalone' clause. This is why the often-mentioned recital no. 8 of the ATAD refers to such a clause as 'necessary' (although this is not then reflected in the text of Article 4).

In this respect, it is doubtful whether the way in which Article 4 ATAD has been drawn up complies with the European principle of proportionality.[37]

Moreover, it does not appear to the author that the main issues at stake have been tackled by the fact that the aforementioned 'Action 4' drawn up by the OECD, in establishing the multinational groups as subjects of the interest expense deductibility threshold, also contemplates the possibility of extending such a threshold to national groups and to independent entities.

---

justify the inclusion of such independent entities in the interest expense deductibility limitation rule (paras 51 and 171-182), the ATAD, on the contrary, for the purposes of the 'standalone' clause, defines the 'independent entity' more directly as being the entity that does not belong to a group and has no associated company (Article 4, para. 3, subpara 3, ATAD), encompassing in the definition of associated company many of the indications given in paras 175-182 of 'Action 4'.

35. As stated in section §7.02 of this chapter.
36. Paragraphs 96-97 of 'Action 4: 2015 Final Report'.
37. The following, among others, consider the violation of the European principle of proportionality in Article 4 of the ATAD from different perspectives: A.P. Dourado, *The Interest Limitation Rule in the Anti-Tax Avoidance Directive (ATAD) and the Net Taxation Principle*, 'EC Tax Review', 26(3), 2017, para. 10; A.E. La Scala, *Gli interessi passivi nella determinazione del reddito di impresa*, Aracne 2016, 661 et seq.; R. Iaia, *La 'Interest Limitation Rule' della direttiva 'antielusione' ('ATAD')*, 'Diritto e pratica tributaria', 2018, paras 7-7.5; J. Carmona Lobita, *European Union – The ATAD's Interest Limitation Rule – A Step Backwards?*, 'European Taxation', 59(2/3), 2019, paras 2.6-2.7. From a different angle, *see also* G. Bizioli, *Taking EU Fundamental Freedom Seriously: Does the Anti-tax Avoidance Directive Take Precedence over the Single Market?*, 'EC Tax Review', 26(3), 2017, 172, according to whom 'it is sufficiently clear that the ATAD overcomes the purpose of preventing tax abuse within the Single Market since it is an attempt to coordinate the different corporate income tax systems against the most common practice of aggressive tax planning. From this perspective, the Directive is unlikely to be considered proportionate to this objective, since it imposes a (minimum) common discipline for the prevention of aggressive tax planning to all the Member States before (and independently from) the introduction of a (minimum) common discipline harmonizing the Member States' corporate income taxes'.

As far as the envisaged extension to independent entities is concerned in particular,[38] the same 'Action 4' specifies (paragraph 52) that:

- in many cases the independent entities [39] are small sized entities, owned directly by natural persons and without any controlling relationship with other entities: in other words, cases in which the risks of 'BEPS', which, moreover, are undefined in 'Action 4: 2015 Final Report' with particular reference to independent entities, are relatively few in number;
- in other cases, the independent entities are large sized entities, owned by means of complex controlling structures (also involving trusts and partnerships), which also entail the control of other entities: these are cases in which the risks of BEPS are analogous to those typical of corporate groups.

As a result, it is clear that a single and indistinct rule, valid for any type of entity, whether it is at a low or high risk of BEPS, cannot help but run counter to the European principle of proportionality. It is a rule that takes 'a shot in the dark' so to speak, and as such has a high chance of (also) 'hitting' entities that are completely extraneous to the BEPS phenomena described.[40]

In addition, it is a rule that not only involves a deferment of the deduction of the excess interest expenses (with the consequent financial charge), but which can actually lead to the permanent 'loss' of such costs if the company is unable, in the future, to generate sufficient interest earnings or a sufficient ROL to be able to deduct them. This has consequent repercussions on the amount of tax liability and, therefore, effects of an economic nature which may prove to be very substantial.

From the point of view of respect for the European principle of proportionality, a problem arises concerning the invalidity of Article 4 ATAD (where it has not provided for a mandatory 'standalone' clause) and, in any case, of Article 96 TUIR (where the 'standalone' clause has not been added).

Although Italy has not implemented the 'standalone' clause in the new Article 96 TUIR, it is unquestionable that in applying European law, Italy must respect the general principles, among which the principle of proportionality features prominently (finding specific affirmation in Article 5, paragraph 4, TEU).

Accordingly, it may be claimed, by way of interpretation and in order to overcome the envisaged invalidity, that the principle of proportionality integrates the rule contained in Article 96 directly, with the further provision that it cannot be applied beyond what is strictly necessary and sufficient in order to achieve the purposes pursued by the ATAD, as in the case of independent entities.[41]

---

38. On the extension regarding 'national' groups, we will reflect more in depth later on in section §7.08 of this chapter.
39. By this reference is meant to entities that do not belong to a group, as defined more precisely *supra* n. 34.
40. On this matter, *see* the European Court of Justice, 3 October 2013, C-282/12, *Itelcar*, EU:C:2013:629, especially point 42. *See also* European Court of Justice, 12 December 2002, C-324/00, *Lankhorst-Hohorst*, EU:C:2002:749, point 37.
41. In general, *see* Iaia, *supra* n. 37, at para. 14.

This is also in consideration of the fact that such an interpretation would not counter the objectives of the ATAD to the extent that:

- the ATAD itself provides for the possibility for Member States to include the 'standalone' clause in their laws of transposition and 'warmly' advises such a move in view of the fact that in recital no. 8 it is described as 'appropriate and necessary';
- subsequent recital no. 16 of the ATAD points out that it is limited merely to what is necessary for fulfilling the objective pursued 'in accordance with the principle of proportionality'.

It goes without saying that, if this interpretation were held to be impossible, there would be no alternative but to bring the question of the invalidity of Article 4 of the ATAD for the violation of the general principle of proportionality before the EU Court of Justice.

§7.08 PRINCIPLE OF PROPORTIONALITY AND SOLELY NATIONAL CORPORATE GROUPS

We must then ask ourselves if the problem of compliance with the principle of proportionality concerns not only the independent taxpayers but also solely national corporate groups (i.e., those without any multinational elements).

The practices referred to by the anti-BEPS measures drawn up by the OECD in 'Action 4: 2015 Final Report' (as recalled in recitals nos 1, 2 and 3 of the ATAD), being based on the exploitation of the different tax rules present in the various legislations, are primarily related to multinational groups.[42] In fact, recital no. 5 of the ATAD, in summarizing the substantive provisions of the Directive, very clearly specifies, as we have already seen, that 'It is necessary to lay down rules against the erosion of tax bases in the internal market and the shifting of profits out of the internal market. Rules in the following areas are necessary in order to contribute to achieving that objective: limitations to the deductibility of interest ... .'

Therefore, based on the principle of proportionality, we do not see any reason why the interest expense deductibility limitations must necessarily be applied even in cases in which, although dealing with a corporate group, those 'tax avoidance practices' that the ATAD wishes to counter[43] cannot, even potentially, arise.

42. *See*, in particular, recitals nos 1, 2 and 3 of the ATAD.
43. Not by chance, in para. 49 of the aforementioned 'Action 4: 2015 Final Report' drawn up by the OECD, to justify a possible extension of the interest expense deductibility threshold to solely national groups (without, moreover, providing any explanation or example of the ways in which a solely national group could engage in the described practices of a supranational kind), it merely states that this: (i) could form part of a wider (and not clearly defined) approach for tackling BEPS phenomena (in which case the statement mentioned above in the text about taking 'a shot in the dark' would apply); or (ii) it could meet the purpose of achieving other political objectives, such as avoiding problems of competition between national and multinational groups, reducing taxpayers' preference for loans to the detriment of capital contributions or complying with constitutional obligations regarding the equal treatment of taxpayers

Nor does it seem helpful to the author to invoke the need for non-discrimination between national and multinational groups. If the aim really is to hit 'tax avoiders', a measure that is formulated in such a way, affecting indifferently both 'tax avoiders' and entities that are not and never can be such, certainly goes beyond what is necessary. It may even be observed that in this way, far from avoiding possible discrimination, it is extremely discriminatory insofar as it treats opposing cases ('tax avoiders' and 'non-tax avoiders') in exactly the same way.[44] It is quite doubtful whether administering medicine to healthy people entails non-discrimination of the sick.

On this matter, Article 4 ATAD is formulated in general terms (appropriate for including within its scope of application all entities subject to corporate tax without distinction), and it does not provide for any possibility of exemption for corporate groups (which, on the contrary, is provided for independent entities). Therefore, it does not seem that there is much room for an interpretation (even if prompted by the principle of proportionality) that can lead to the non-application on a national level of Article 4 and the Italian law of transposition vis-à-vis major solely national corporate groups.

As a consequence, nothing remains to be done, but to bring the question of the invalidity of Article 4 ATAD before the EU Court of Justice for the violation of the general principle of proportionality.

This conclusion also bears in mind that the EU Court of Justice case law is consistent in stating that 'national legislation, in order for it to be proportionate to the aim of preventing tax evasion or avoidance, must, on each occasion on which the existence of artificial transactions cannot be ruled out, give the taxable person an opportunity, without subjecting him to undue administrative constraints, to provide evidence of any commercial justification that there may have been for the transaction at issue'.[45]

Yet, if this is true for national legislation, even more so must it apply to a European directive, given that EU secondary legislation must first conform to the general principles of the European legal system, and all the more to the principle of proportionality, as it is expressly provided for in Article 5, paragraph 4, TEU.

(hypotheses on which we will dwell – immediately below in the text and in the following section §7.10 – but which appear even now symptomatic of an awareness on the part of the editors of 'Action 4: 2015 Final Report' of the weakness, with regard to solely national groups, of the justification based on countering BEPS phenomena). On the criticality of the extension of the interest expense limitation rule to national groups, *see* Dourado, *supra* n. 37, at 118.

44. On this matter, *see* the Conclusions presented on 29 June 2006 by the Advocate General L.A. Geelhoed in the Case C-524/04, *Test Claimants in the Thin Cap Group Litigation*, EU:C:2006:436, point 68.
45. Most recently, European Court of Justice, Grand Chamber, 26 February 2019, C-135/17, *X*, EU:C:2019:136, point 87.

§7.09 PRINCIPLE OF PROPORTIONALITY AND THE NEED FOR A GENERAL ESCAPE CLAUSE

This same frame of mind leads us to ask if the European principle of proportionality does not impose the introduction in Article 4 ATAD of a general escape clause, that is a clause which, beyond the specific '*de minimis*' and 'standalone' hypotheses, enables all taxpayers without distinction, including multinational groups, to escape from the interest limitation rule by demonstrating the inexistence in their specific case of the effects of 'BEPS' countered by the law.

The fact that, in the case of multinational groups, there is a high propensity for BEPS practices implemented by means of interest expenses may certainly justify the introduction of a law limiting the deductibility of interest.

Still, even admitting, by way of a hypothesis, that it was possible to demonstrate that 90% of multinational groups perform BEPS practices using interest expenses (which is quite unlikely), the fact remains that the application of the limitation (also) to the remaining 10% that do not put such practices into effect would not be justified.

A rule that is structured in such a way as to affect all taxpayers goes beyond what is necessary when it is only a part of them (regardless of whether they are many or few) who actually behave in the way the law wishes to prevent.

Instead, in such circumstances, a rule built on the model of rebuttable presumptions of law would respect the principle of proportionality. In other words, a rule that in principle applies to all taxpayers, but which, at the same time, allows the relevant taxpayers to demonstrate the inexistence of assumptions justifying the application against them. This would, in fact, be the case in the hypothesis of Article 4 ATAD, if a general escape clause were provided for.

So, ultimately, the question of the invalidity of Article 4 ATAD as a result of the violation of the general principle of proportionality, which may eventually be brought before the EU Court of Justice, should not be limited to the position of solely national corporate groups (and, where relevant, to independent entities) but should concern in broader terms the lack of an escape clause in Article 4 that is valid for all taxpayers.[46]

§7.10 ITALIAN PROBLEMS OF CONSTITUTIONAL LEGITIMACY: THE NEED FOR A GENERAL ESCAPE CLAUSE ALSO IN RESPECT OF ARTICLE 53 OF THE ITALIAN CONSTITUTION

If the problem that has arisen should not be solved on a European level, as it should be in the first instance, a question of the constitutional legitimacy of Article 96 TUIR[47] would be posed in Italy.

46. *See* Iaia, *supra* n. 37, at para. 14, who argues, however, that the question could be directly resolved by way of interpretation and only in a subordinate position by a preliminary ruling to the EU Court of Justice pursuant to Article 267 TFEU.

47. With reference to the former Article 96 TUIR, but also with a view to its modification pursuant to the ATAD, *see* G. Vanz, *The Italian Interest Limitation Rule: Constitutional Issues*, 'European Taxation', 58(4), 2018, 173 et seq. As is well known, in 2015, the issue of the constitutional

As it is now structured (i.e., without a general escape clause), Article 96 may ultimately lead to the non-deductibility of excess interest expenses. Indeed, any future deduction requires the corporation to produce sufficient interest earnings or a sufficient ROL. If this does not occur, which may be for reasons completely independent of the will of the corporation, the excess interest expenses are, in fact, lost.[48]

On the basis of the ability-to-pay principle in Article 53 of the Italian Constitution,[49] a total or partial disallowance of a cost deduction in determining income tax can only be justified if the cost does not contribute to the generation of the income.[50]

From this perspective, the total or partial non-deductibility of a cost for anti-avoidance or anti-evasion purposes can be justified because the goal is to be able to determine any increase in taxable wealth properly.

This frequently occurs by means of fixed limits, that is only allowing a deduction of a percentage of the cost or a deduction up to a maximum limit, as in Article 96 TUIR.

This technique is based on the presumption of law principle. For example, the legislator presumes that up to a certain limit a cost is fair, but beyond that limit it is symptomatic of tax avoidance or tax evasion, or, with regard to mixed-use goods or services, the legislator presumes that only a given percentage is used for business purposes and not the remaining percentage.

According to Article 53 of the Italian Constitution, presumptions of law are allowed only if the presumption is a rebuttable presumption.[51] It must, as such, be possible for taxpayers who do not fall within cases typically considered by the presumption to prove, for example, that the cost was not incurred for the purpose of tax

legitimacy of the German interest barrier rule, which constituted the reference model for the drafting of the ATAD, was raised before the German Constitutional Court: Federal Fiscal Court (*Bundesfinanzhof*), 14 October 2015, I R 20/15, available at http://juris.bundesfinanzhof.de/cgi-bin/rechtsprechung/druckvorschau.py?Gericht = bfh&Art = en&nr = 32731. The case is still pending. However, D. Reicht, *Germany*, section §6.03[B], Chapter 6 in this book, believes the question to be unfounded.

48. In general, *see* G. Zizzo, *Abuso di regole volte al 'gonfiamento' della base imponibile ed effetto confiscatorio del prelievo*, 'Rassegna tributaria', 2010, para. 6. *See also* F. Fichera, *Le penalizzazioni fiscali*, 'Rassegna tributaria', 2017, para. 2.4, who, in this regard, speaks of 'tax penalties' or 'negative tax expenditures'.
49. Article 53, para. 1, of the Italian Constitution provides that 'All are required to contribute to public expenditure on the basis of their ability to pay.'
50. In general, *see* G. Falsitta, *Giustizia tributaria e tirannia fiscale*, Giuffré 2008, 403. With specific reference to previous Article 96 of Legislative Decree 917/1986, *see also* D. Stevanato, *Prime considerazioni sui limiti generalizzati alla deducibilità degli interessi passivi introdotta dalla manovra finanziaria 2008 – L'indeducibilità degli interessi passivi tra utilizzo extrafiscale dell'imposta ed esigenze di misurazione della capacità economica individuale*, 'Dialoghi tributari', 2007, 1022; and G. Escalar, *Dubbi di costituzionalità sul regime degli interessi passivi per banche ed assicurazioni*, 'Corriere tributario', 2009, 1238 et seq. According to the Italian Constitutional Court, 22 April 1997, no. 111, para. 8, available at http://www.cortecostituzionale.it/actionPronuncia.do, the Court must verify, with reference to Article 53 of the Constitution, 'the internal consistency of the tax structure with its economic basis'.
51. I. Manzoni & G. Vanz, *Il diritto tributario. Profili teorici e sistematici*, 2nd ed., Giappichelli 2008, 400-405. The Italian Constitutional Court case law is not unanimous: *see*, in this regard, 15-28 July 1976, no. 200, para. 3, available at http://www.cortecostituzionale.it/actionPronuncia.do.

avoidance or tax evasion or that the goods or services were used entirely for a business purpose.[52]

The possibility to rebut the presumption is fundamental because the ability-to-pay principle applies to all taxpayers, without exception.[53] It is not a matter of statistics, but a guarantee to all individuals.

From these premises, it follows that Article 96 TUIR violates the ability-to-pay principle because it does not allow for evidence to the contrary to be presented: corporations can never prove that the excess interest expenses were not incurred for BEPS purposes.

At the same time, disallowing a cost deduction cannot be justified even for non-tax reasons (such as to favour capitalization [54]), despite the fact that these purposes are constitutionally relevant. Such purposes may, in fact, justify non-taxation, that is an exemption[55] or a lower tax rate (e.g., the Dual Income Tax)[56] but can never justify taxation in the absence of income.[57] And not allowing a cost to be deducted means taxing non-existent income.

Based on the above, Article 96 TUIR clearly does not respect the ability-to-pay principle.

§7.11 ARTICLE 4 ATAD AND ITALIAN CONSTITUTIONAL 'COUNTER-LIMITS'

The statements made above do not change simply because there is a European directive behind Article 96 TUIR.[58]

In fact, the Italian Constitutional Court has stated, since 1973, that it has the power to declare any Italian law ratifying the Union Treaties[59] – at that time the European Economic Community Treaty[60] – as unconstitutional insofar as the law of

52. This is in accordance with the principle of effectiveness: the conditions under which the taxpayer may give evidence to the contrary must not be framed so as to render the exercise of the right virtually impossible.
53. In fact, Article 53, para. 1, of the Italian Constitution refers to 'all' (nobody excluded), with regard to the ability-to-pay guarantee.
54. As specified in para. 49 of the aforementioned 'Action 4: 2015 Final Report'.
55. Or a deduction from the corporate income tax base, as currently provided for in Italy by Decree Law no. 201 of 6 December 2011, Article 1 (ACE – Aiuto alla crescita economica).
56. I. Manzoni, *Il principio della capacità contributiva nell'ordinamento costituzionale italiano*, Giappichelli 1965, 84-99.
57. *Ibid.*, 99-107.
58. To the contrary, with reference to the German law and the legislation of the German Federal Constitutional Court, *see* Reicht, *supra* n. 47, at para C.3., according to whom 'The Federal Constitutional Court would ... withdraw its jurisdiction in accordance with its Solange-II jurisdiction and reject future constitutional complaints and review procedures as inadmissible. To this extent, constitutional review will then no longer take place at the Federal Constitutional Court, but at the European Court of Justice.'
59. Treaty on the Functioning of the European Union (TFEU) of 13 December 2007 and Treaty on the European Union (TEU) of 13 December 2007.
60. Treaty Establishing the European Community of 25 March 1957.

ratification allows for the introduction of rules into the Italian system that violate the fundamental principles of the constitutional system.[61]

More recently, in 2017, the Italian Constitutional Court,[62] in the context of the so-called Taricco saga,[63] asked the EU Court of Justice, among other issues, whether it is correct that: (i) 'EU law and the judgments of the Court of Justice that clarify its meaning for the purposes of its uniform application cannot be interpreted as requiring a Member State to give up the supreme principles of its constitutional order' (paragraph 6); (ii) EU law 'is only applicable if it is compatible with the constitutional identity of the Member State' and 'it falls to the competent authorities of that State to carry out such an assessment' (paragraph 7); (iii) 'Under Italian law this may occur on the initiative of the courts which, having been called upon to apply this rule, have asked this Court [that is the Italian Constitutional Court] to assess its compatibility with the supreme principles of the constitutional order. *This Court will then be under a duty to ascertain, as the case may be, whether it is incompatible and consequently to assert that the rule cannot apply in Italy*' (paragraph 7, emphasis added). The EU Court of Justice issued its decision at the end of 2017[64] but avoided answering the above questions, which therefore remain open.

Finally, in 2018, at the end of the 'Taricco saga',[65] the Italian Constitutional Court was able to further specify, among other things, that:[66]

- 'It is the position of this Court that the application of the "Taricco rule" [that is the rule set in the first judgment of the EU Court of Justice on the matter [67]], within our system would violate Articles 25(2) and 101(2) of the Constitution, and, therefore, *may not be permitted, even in light of the primacy of EU Law*' (paragraph 5 of the Conclusions on points of law, emphasis added);
- 'The Constitutional Court ... alone is entitled to ascertain whether EU law contrasts with the supreme principles of the constitutional system ...' (paragraph 8);

61. Italian Constitutional Court, 18 December 1973, no. 183, IT:COST:1973:183, para. 9; *Id.*, 5 June 1984, no. 170, IT:COST:1984:170, para. 7; *Id.*, 21 April 1989, no. 232, IT:COST:1989:232, para. 3.1; *Id.*, 18 April 1991, no. 168, IT:COST:1991:168, para. 4; *Id.*, 13 July 2007, no. 284, IT:COST:2007:284, para. 3; *Id.*, 22 October 2014, no. 238, IT:COST:2014:238, para. 3.2, para. 3.2 (all in Italian and available at http://www.cortecostituzionale.it/actionPronuncia.do; Decision no. 238/2014 is also available in English at http://www.cortecostituzionale.it/documenti/download/doc/recent_judgments/S238_2013_en.pdf).
62. Italian Constitutional Court, 26 January 2017, no. 24, IT:COST:2017:24, which was an order for a preliminary ruling pursuant to Article 267 TFEU (available in English at http://www.cortecostituzionale.it/documenti/download/doc/recent_judgments/O_24_2017.pdf).
63. Concerning the applicability to the VAT crimes of the prescription required by Italian law.
64. EU Court of Justice, Grand Chamber, 5 December 2017, Case C-42/17, *M.A.S.*, EU:C:2017:936.
65. *See* G. Piccirilli, *The 'Taricco Saga': The Italian Constitutional Court Continues Its European Journey: Italian Constitutional Court*, Order of 23 November 2016 no. 24/2017; Judgment of 10 April 2018 no. 115/2018 ECJ 8 September 2015, Case C-105/14, *Ivo Taricco and Others;* 5 December 2017, Case C-42/17, *M.A.S. and M.B.*, 'European Constitutional Law Review', 14(4), 2018, 814-833.
66. Italian Constitutional Court, 31 May 2018, no. 115, IT:COST:2018:215, available in English at https://www.cortecostituzionale.it/documenti/download/doc/recent_judgments/S_2018_115_EN.pdf. The sentence was subsequently confirmed by the Constitutional Court, 21 December 2018, no. 243/2018, IT:COST:2018:243.
67. EU Court of Justice, Grand Chamber, 8 September 2015, Case C-105/14, *Taricco*, EU:C:2015:555. The second judgment of the EU Court of Justice on the matter is mentioned *supra* n. 64.

- '... the referring ordinary courts cannot apply the "Taricco rule" ... because it contradicts the principle of legal certainty in criminal matters enshrined in Article 25(2) of the Constitution' (paragraph 10);
- '... a choice relating to liability to punishment must be able to be independently gleaned from the legislative text to which citizens have access, and this is not the case with the "Taricco rule". While it is the exclusive competence of the Court of Justice to provide a uniform interpretation of EU law and to specify whether or not it has direct effect, it is likewise indisputable ... that an interpretive outcome that does not comply with the principle of legal certainty in criminal matters has no place in our legal system' (paragraph 12).

It is now quite clear, therefore, that the Italian Constitutional Court believes that it cannot (and should not) apply European law whenever it is in contrast with the fundamental principles of the Italian constitutional order.[68]

The principle of equality (Article 3 of the Italian Constitution) is certainly one of those fundamental principles of the Italian system and, at the same time, the ability-to-pay principle is the embodiment of the equality principle in the field of taxation.[69]

At least in this respect (equality), the ability-to-pay principle can, therefore, be considered a fundamental principle of the Italian system.

To the extent that Article 96 TUIR introduces a rule into Italy that provides, by means of the non-deductibility of interest, for a difference in the taxation of equal ability-to-pay situations or equal taxation of different ability-to-pay situations, the Italian law transposing the ATAD, together with the Italian law ratifying the aforementioned Union Treaties, should be declared unconstitutional by the Italian Constitutional Court.[70]

In fact, on the basis of Article 96 TUIR, two corporations with the same income produced, one of which has excess interest expenses (that are real and pertinent interest expenses, extraneous to BEPS phenomena), and the other does not, would find themselves being attributed with different incomes. On the contrary, two corporations with different income produced may find themselves being attributed with exactly the same income as a consequence of the non-deductibility of the excess interest expenses, even though they are real and pertinent interest expenses, extraneous to BEPS phenomena.

In this respect, an amendment to Article 4 ATAD or a declaration of its invalidity by the EU Court of Justice (with the consequent effects on Article 96 TUIR), along the lines of the need for a general escape clause, would enable the envisaged doubts

68. *See* D. Gallo, *La Corte costituzionale chiude la 'Saga Taricco': tra riserva di legge, opposizione* de facto *del controlimite e implicita negazione dell'effetto diretto*, 'European Papers', 3(2), 2018, 875 et seq. (893-894).
69. Manzoni & Vanz, *supra* n. 51, at 30-32.
70. Or, according to the aforementioned judgment 26 January 2017, no. 24, paras 6 and 7, the Court should order that Article 4 of the Directive ATAD is not applicable in Italy (and then Article 96 TUIR unconstitutional) or ask the EU Court of Justice for a further preliminary ruling on the subject pursuant to Article 267 TFEU.

regarding the constitutional legitimacy of Article 96 TUIR with respect to Articles 3 and 53 of the Italian Constitution[71] to be overcome.

71. A further doubt regarding the constitutional legitimacy would remain. However, for reasons of space, it cannot be investigated further on this occasion, but only referred to. In order for a legal presumption, like the one underlying Article 96 TUIR, to be considered compatible with the principles of tax law equality and ability-to-pay as referred to in Articles 3 and 53 of the Constitution, not only is it necessary for evidence to the contrary to be admissible (i.e., the general escape clause as referred to above) but also the presumption is required to be reasonable: it has to correspond to what normally happens in reality. But a single limit, such as in Article 96 TUIR, applicable to all corporations, regardless of their structural features or the business sector at issue, relevant both inside and outside corporate groups and applicable to both national and international corporate groups, cannot reflect what normally happens in reality: it is unreasonable (with reference to the former Article 96 TUIR, *see* Zizzo, *supra* n. 48, para. 7. *See also* La Scala, *supra* n. 37, at 399-401). Before posing the question at the level of the Italian Constitution, it should be raised, also in this regard, at the European level. Regardless of whether or not evidence can be given to the contrary, there are, in fact, a series of reasons for doubting the conformity to the European principle of proportionality, but also to the European principle of equality, of a rule with the characteristics as described above, which, objectively, is unsuited for distinguishing between the particularities of the individual cases (even only with regard to the type of case) and which, in the first instance, places all the taxpayers within its scope of application: indications in this sense, as well as with regard to the violation of the principle of proportionality, are present in the EU Court of Justice, 3 October 2013, C-282/12, *Itelcar*, EU:C:2013:629, points 41-42; *see also* EU Court of Justice, 12 December 2002, C-324/00, *Lankhorst-Hohorst*, EU:C:2002:749, point 37, as well as the Conclusions of the Advocate General J. Kokott presented on 19 January 2017 in the Case C-6/16, *Equiom*, EU:C:2017:34, point 30 and the Conclusions of the Advocate General M. Wathelet presented on 26 October 2016 in the Case C-14/16, *Euro Park Service*, EU:C:2016:806, point 45, where there are further references to the EU Court of Justice case law. On the violation of the European principle of equality (again referred to quite recently by the EU Court of Justice, 30 April 2019, C-617/17, *Repubblica italiana/Consiglio dell'Unione europea*, EU:C:2019:332, point 129), *see* Dourado, *supra* n. 37, at para. 12; Iaia, *supra* n. 37, at para. 8.

CHAPTER 8

Spain

Andrés Báez Moreno & Aitor Navarro Ibarrola

§8.01 INTRODUCTION: THE FALL OF THIN CAPITALIZATION RULES AND THE RISE OF INTEREST LIMITATION BARRIERS

The Spanish Corporate Income Tax Act (hereinafter "CITA") counted since 1991 on standard fixed ratio thin capitalization rules. Those rules showed no sign of malfunctioning until in 2004 the European Court of Justice (ECJ) declared its German equivalent in breach of the European Union (EU) fundamental freedoms.[1] The Spanish legislator, in what constituted a clear overreaction, repealed thin capitalization rules for cases in which the lender was a resident in a (nontax haven) EU Member State. In the context of previous taxpayer-friendly reforms, some taxpayers (mis)understood this partial repeal as an invitation or, at least, as an implicit statement of tolerance for aggressive financing structures within the boundaries of the EU. So, it comes as no surprise that the late 2000s witnessed a huge litigation with the tax authorities trying to challenge what they considered to be tax-motivated excessive indebtedness structures.[2] Even if the tax authorities were victorious in most of these cases resorting to the GAAR,[3] the Spanish Sham rule[4] or even other certainly exotic solutions, such as the direct application of Article 9 in Double Taxation Conventions (DTCs) to disregard the transactions,[5] the rules in force had shown clear signs of exhaustion. The final straw

1. ECJ, December 12, 2002, Case C-324/00, *Lankhorst-Hohorst GmbH v. Finanzamt Steinfurt*.
2. We have referred to some of these disputes in previous works: J.J. Zornoza Pérez & A. Báez Moreno "Chapter 33: Spain" in *GAARs—A Key Element of Tax Systems in the Post-BEPS Tax World* (M. Lang et al. eds, IBFD 2016), at 33.2. J.J. Zornoza Pérez & A. Báez Moreno 2018 "Anti-avoidance Measures of General Nature and Scope. GAAR and Other Rules" in *Cahiers de Droit Fiscal International* (vol. 103A, 2018), pp. 13-14.
3. Article 15 of the General Tax Act (*Ley 58/2003, de 17 de diciembre, General Tributaria*).
4. Article 16 of the General Tax Act.
5. Decision of the Spanish Supreme Court (TS) of July 18, 2012 (Rec. 3779/2009), commented in A. Navarro *Transactional Adjustments in Transfer Pricing* (IBFD 2017), section 2.1.6.

came perhaps when the Spanish Supreme Court (hereinafter "TS") declared thin capitalization rules in breach of the nondiscrimination provision of the DTC between Spain and Switzerland,[6] a statement clearly applicable to the whole Spanish tax treaty network.

In this context, the Spanish Government decided to repeal thin capitalization rules entirely for tax periods beginning on or after January 1, 2012, while at the same time introducing a general interest deduction barrier rule (hereinafter "IDBR") included in current Article 16 CITA and a special anti-abuse rule regarding the denial of interest deduction in leveraged acquisitions of intragroup companies (LAIC) in Article 15.h) CITA. For tax periods beginning after January 1, 2015, the legislator incorporated two additional interest deduction barriers for leveraged buyout transactions (LBOs) (Article 16.5 CITA) and hybrid instruments (Article 15.j) CITA). In short, the Spanish lawmaker decided to abandon a problematic reclassification rule to adopt several rules on the denial or restriction of the tax deduction of interest.[7]

The rest of this chapter is organized as follows: section §8.02 deals with the general interest deduction barrier (IDBR). Section §8.03 analyzes special interest deduction limitations regarding LAIC and "LBOs".[8]

§8.02 THE SPANISH GENERAL INTEREST DEDUCTION BARRIER

[A] Overview on the Enactment of the Rule and Its Purpose

The Spanish general IDBR applies on a comprehensive basis to almost all CIT taxpayers, as well as to Spanish permanent establishments of foreign individuals or entities performing business activities in Spain[9] and individual entrepreneurs.[10] It was introduced in March 2012 and has applied to tax periods starting on January 1, 2012 onward.[11] According to the preamble of the Royal Decree-Law that introduced this regime, its aim is to "indirectly favor equity financing" and was enacted according to "analog rules in comparative Law, [as well as] the current tax treatment of financial expenses in the international arena."[12] Notwithstanding, it is also important to

6. Decision of the Spanish Supreme Court (TS) of March 17, 2011 (Rec. 5871/2006).
7. E. Cencerrado Millán & M.T. Soler Roch "Limit Base Erosion via Interest Deduction and Others" (Intertax 2015, vol. 43, n. 1, pp. 58-71), p. 65.
8. Due to its specific characteristics, the anti-hybrid mismatch provision contained in Article 15.j of the CITA is not analyzed in this chapter.
9. Article 18.1 of the Non-Resident Income Tax Act (*Real Decreto Legislativo 5/2004, de 5 de marzo, por el que se aprueba el texto refundido de la Ley del Impuesto sobre la Renta de no Residentes*) determines that the taxable base of a PE of a foreign entity will be determined in accordance with rules contained in the CITA. Certain nuances that are beyond the scope of this contribution also apply.
10. Article 28.1 of the Personal Income Tax Act (*Ley 35/2006, de 28 de noviembre, del Impuesto sobre la Renta de las Personas Físicas*) contains a remission to the content of the CITA to determine the taxable base of entrepreneurial income obtained by individuals. Nuances may also be relevant, but their examination is beyond the scope of this contribution.
11. *Real Decreto-ley 12/2012, de 30 de marzo, por el que se introducen diversas medidas tributarias y administrativas dirigidas a la reducción del déficit público.*
12. *Id.*, preamble, II. The same statement was mentioned in the CITA, preamble, II.f) and III.1.d).

emphasize its revenue-collection purpose,[13] which is most probably the main reason why such a regime was introduced even before the Base Erosion and Profit Shifting (BEPS) project started.[14] It was also very significant that the instrument employed to enact the rule was a Royal Decree-Law, which is contemplated in the Spanish Constitution only for cases of overriding reasons of "extraordinary and urgent need,"[15] in which the government is authorized to enact a force-of-law set of measures. Indeed, such a mechanism is frequently used in taxation to surpass the principle of legality,[16] by which the essential elements of a tax must be enacted and/or modified through a law-like instrument and not through a decree.[17] According to such limitations, the urgency in tackling an excessive public deficit so as to comply with EU deficit restrictions has constantly been used as a ground to introduce changes in the Spanish tax system and especially in the CIT.[18] In addition, it is important to emphasize that the preamble of the CITA bluntly states that rules such as the IBDR are meant to "broaden the taxable base" to counteract the fall in the collection through the CIT.[19]

Currently, the rule is contained in Article 16 of Law 27/2014 enacting the Corporate Income Tax (CITA) and may be briefly described by means of its three main features that coincide with some of the measures contained in the Organisation for Economic Co-operation and Development (OECD) BEPS Action 4 proposed best practice:[20] (1) a fixed ratio rule: net financial expenses are deductible with a limit of 30% of the operating profit generated in a fiscal year; (2) a *de minimis* threshold: the first EUR 1 million of financial expenses are deductible, regardless of the described ratio; (3) a carryforward of disallowed interest and unused interest capacity: net financial expenses that were not deductible in a fiscal year may be carried forward without time constraints, albeit each year the described deductibility limitation will apply. Unused interest capacity may be carried forward within the next five fiscal years.

---

13. *See* E. Cencerrado Millán & E. Gil García "Spain" in *Interest Deductibility: The Implementation of BEPS Action 4* (IFA Cahiers de Droit Fiscal International 2019, vol. 104A), pp. 638-639.
14. The document that led to the whole BEPS process, *OECD 2013 Addressing Base Erosion and Profit Shifting*, was published on February 12, 2013, while the Spanish IDBR was introduced more than one year before. This rule was clearly inspired by the German IDBR contained in paragraph 4h of the Income Tax Act (*Einkommensteuergesetz*) that was introduced by the 2008 business tax reform (*Unternehmensteuerreformgesetz* 2008, BGBl I 2007, 1912).
15. Article 86 of the Spanish Constitution.
16. Envisaged in Art. 31.3 of the Spanish Constitution.
17. Decisions of the Constitutional Court 185/1995, FJ 3; 233/1999, FFJJ 7, 9, 10; 3/2003, FJ 4, and 136/2011, FJ 11.
18. This was indeed the motive brought up in Royal Decree-Law 12/2012 introducing the Spanish IDBR—among other tax measures—and Royal Decree-Law 20/2012, enacted only three months after and which modified the IDBR retroactively.
19. CITA, preamble, II.e).
20. *OECD 2015 BEPS Final Report on Action 4: Limiting Base Erosion Involving Interest Deductions and Other Financial Payments*, para. 22.

Example 1

Concept	*Amount (EUR)*
Net financial expense	900,000
Operating profit	4,000,000
30% operating profit	1,200,000
Amount to be deducted	900,000
Carry forward, net financial expense	0
Carry forward, unused interest capacity	300,000

In this case, the net financial expenses are EUR 900,000 and thus below EUR 1,000,000 and also below 30% of the operating profit, that is EUR 1,200,000. Therefore, the whole amount is deductible, and no book-to-tax adjustments are needed to be performed. Additionally, as there is unused interest capacity to the amount of EUR 300,000 resulting from the difference between the 30% of the operating profit figure and that of the net financial expense, a carryforward of the amount is possible up to five years.

For the time being, the IDBR has not been subject to litigation, therefore no court cases may be quoted to interpret it. Notwithstanding, the tax administration released two documents with relevant guidance[21] and also several public binding rulings have been issued.[22] As per the rationale behind the design of the IDBR, the only hint articulated by the lawmaker refers to its intent for the rule to be a temporal allocation of the expenses one;[23] that is, financial expenses that are not deductible in a fiscal year due to the application of the IDBR could be offset in the future, thus the unlimited carryforward of the amount that was not deductible. This, alongside the possibility to increase the limit of further fiscal years through the unused interest capacity, tries to address the fact that interest expenses and earnings often arise in different periods, and this should not penalize business sectors in which such a scenario is commonplace.[24] Therefore, economic double taxation generated by the restriction on the deductibility

21. General Directorate for Taxes, July 16, 2012, ruling on the limitation of the deductibility of financial expenses in the CIT (*Resolución de 16 de julio de 2012, de la Dirección General de Tributos, en relación con la limitación en la deducibilidad de gastos financieros en el Impuesto sobre Sociedades*) (GDT ruling of July 16, 2012 hereinafter). Spanish Tax Agency, February 3, 2015, note on the limitation of financial expenses enshrined in Article 16 of the CIT (*Agencia Estatal de la Administración Tributaria, nota relativa a la limitación de gastos financieros prevista en el artículo 16 de la Ley 27/2014 de 27 de noviembre*) (STA interpretative note of February 3, 2015, hereinafter).
22. The Spanish General Directorate for Taxes (*Dirección General de Tributos*, hereinafter "GDT") is competent for issuing interpretative, nonsecret rulings, the content of which is binding for the tax administration.
23. CITA preamble, III.1.d).
24. *OECD 2015 BEPS Final Report on Action 4: Limiting Base Erosion Involving Interest Deductions and Other Financial Payments*, para. 27.

of the rule proves to be temporary due to a time mismatch between the accrual of the interest and its deductibility from a tax perspective.[25]

The rationale of the rest of the features of the rule was not disclosed by the lawmaker, but it may be conjectured. The use of the operating profits indicator as a barrier to the deduction of net financial expenses would be justified in order to link the rule with the generation of income directly referred to the economic activity undertaken by the entity.[26] The use of a *de minimis* threshold is usually justified on the grounds that entities with net interest expenses below a certain amount—EUR 1 million in Spain—display a low-risk profile from a base erosion perspective.[27] Nevertheless, again from the declared aims of collection and neutralization of differences between equity and debt funding, such a restriction on the applicability of the fixed ratio is hard to justify. Moreover, fragmentation through the incorporation of a number of entities falling below the threshold is a risk that remains unaddressed. Also, the purported aim of reducing "both the compliance costs of these entities and the administrative costs of the tax authorities"[28] is senseless, because in any case, the calculation of the limit will have to take place in order to permit the deduction of the described *de minimis* amount.

The Spanish IDBR generally complies with the interest limitation rule contained in Article 4 of the Anti-Tax Avoidance Directive (hereinafter "ATAD").[29] In line with the possibility of safeguarding a higher level of protection for domestic corporate tax bases,[30] in certain aspects, the Spanish IDBR is stricter than the one proposed in the ATAD. For instance, among other features, it imposes a *de minimis* threshold below the one suggested—EUR 1 million versus EUR 3 million[31]—it does not include a group ratio rule[32], and it does not recognize the exclusion of stand-alone entities from the

25. E. Cencerrado Millán & M.T. Soler Roch "Limit Base Erosion via Interest Deduction and Others," fn. 7, p. 68.
26. *OECD 2015 BEPS Final Report on Action 4: Limiting Base Erosion Involving Interest Deductions and Other Financial Payments*, para. 23. *See* N. Burkhalter-Martinez "BEPS Action 4 and Its Compatibility with the Principle of Non-discrimination under Article 24(4) of the OECD Model Convention" (Intertax 2019, vol. 47, n. 1, pp. 55-65), p. 56. L. Hillmann & R. Hoehl "Interest Limitation Rules: At a Crossroads Between National Sovereignty and Harmonization" (European Taxation 2018, vol. 58, n. 4, pp.140-148), p.141.
27. *See OECD 2015 BEPS Final Report on Action 4: Limiting Base Erosion Involving Interest Deductions and Other Financial Payments*, para. 54. E. Cencerrado Millán & E. Gil García "Spain," fn. 13, p. 642.
28. *See OECD 2015 BEPS Final Report on Action 4: Limiting Base Erosion Involving Interest Deductions and Other Financial Payments*, para. 54. L. Hillmann & R. Hoehl 2018 "Interest Limitation Rules: At a Crossroads between National Sovereignty and Harmonization" (European Taxation, vol. 58, n. 4, pp. 140-148), p. 141.
29. Council Directive (EU) 2016/1164 of July 12, 2016 laying down rules against tax avoidance practices that directly affect the functioning of the internal market.
30. Article 3 ATAD. For a critical analysis on this respect, *see* João Carmona Lobita 2019 "The ATAD's Interest Limitation Rule—A Step Backwards?" (European Taxation, vol. 59, n. 2/3, pp. 60-65), p. 61.
31. Article 4.3.a) ATAD.
32. Article 4.5 ATAD. *See* S. López Ribas "Financing Activities: Hybrid Mismatches and the Tax Deductibility of Interest in Spain" (Bulletin for International Taxation 2016, vol. 70, n. 8, pp. 450-457), p. 454. Sanz Gadea has been claiming for the introduction of a group ratio rule since the IDBR was enacted, *see* E. Sanz Gadea "Restricción y limitación a la deducción de intereses en el Impuesto sobre Sociedades" (Estudios financieros. Revista de contabilidad y tributación: Comentarios, casos prácticos 2012, n. 355, pp. 47-104).

scope of the limitation.[33] As of the date on which the present chapter was submitted to the editor, there is no trace of a draft nor a preliminary law addressing the transposition of this rule into domestic law, a fact that may be partially justified by the difficulties derived from the political fragmentation that is impeding the formation of a stable government in Spain. Besides, the ATAD establishes that Member States which have national targeted rules for preventing BEPS risks as of August 8, 2016, which are equally effective to the interest limitation rule set out in this Directive, may apply these targeted rules until the end of the first full fiscal year following the date of publication of the agreement between the OECD members on the official website on a minimum standard with regard to BEPS Action 4, or January 1, 2024, at the latest. If one takes into account that the drafted OECD minimum standard does not apply for Action 4 items, it seems that the effective implementation date is that of 2024. Therefore, no changes are expected in the short-term in the Spanish IDBR.

Hereinafter, an in-depth examination will be made of the aspects referring to the scope of the rule (2), the calculation of the limit it poses on the deductibility of financial expenses, including the outcome when the limit is not reached and when the limit plays a role (3), and specificities referred to economic interest grouping (EIG), joint ventures (JVs) and the fiscal unity regime (4).

[B] Scope of the Rule

The IDBR applies to almost all CIT taxpayers, regardless of the industry sector they operate in, their reasonable debt-to-equity ratio according to activities performed or the domestic or cross-border nature of the financial payments accrued. Most probably, the Spanish lawmaker found that the easiest way to avoid conflicts with EU law or tax treaties[34] was to extend the rule to the generality of CIT taxpayers so as not to give rise to discriminatory outcomes.[35]

In accordance with Article 16.6 CITA, only certain specific entities are excluded from the scope of the IDBR.[36] First, the rule does not apply to credit institutions. According to the 2014 Law on organization, supervision and solvency of credit entities, credit institutions are authorized enterprises whose activity consists in collecting deposits or other repayable funds and in granting credits on their own account.[37] Specific stringent regulations at the level of both the EU and the Spanish domestic law are applicable to these entities, and the Bank of Spain as well as the Ministry of Economy have a broad authority over their supervision. Besides, those entities

33. Article 4.3.b) ATAD. *See* B. Parejo García "La regla de delimitación de deducibilidad de intereses" in *Grandes Tratados. La armonización de las normas contra la elusión fiscal relativas a la fiscalidad directa en la Unión Europea* (José Manuel Almudí Cid, Jorge Alberto Ferreras Gutiérrez, Pablo Andrés Hernández González-Barreda (dirs.) Aranzadi 2018, accessed through the Aranzadi-Westlaw database, reference BIB 2018\11852, last accessed on July 13, 2019), p.7.
34. *See* N. Burkhalter-Martinez "BEPS Action 4 and Its Compatibility with the Principle of Non-discrimination under Article 24(4) of the OECD Model Convention," fn. 26, pp. 63, 64.
35. *See* E. Cencerrado Millán & E. Gil García "Spain," fn. 13, p. 639.
36. Cfr. Article 4.7 ATAD.
37. *See Ley 10/2014, de 26 de junio, de ordenación, supervisión y solvencia de entidades de crédito,* Article 1.

dedicated exclusively to the issuance and placement of financial instruments in the market that exist to reinforce regulatory capital and the funding of credit institutions, the voting rights of which entirely correspond, directly or indirectly, to credit institutions, are also excluded from the scope of the IDBR. Likewise, mortgage securitization funds[38] and certain asset securitization funds[39] are not affected by the limitations posed in the IDBR either.

Second, insurance entities are also excluded from the scope of the IDBR. Here, an interpretative issue arises in order to determine whether this exclusion comprises all entities under the scope of the 2015 Law on the organization, supervision and solvency of insurance and reinsurance entities,[40] or just insurance entities defined as such in Article 6.1 of this Law, that is entities authorized to undertake—in accordance with such a Law or equivalent rules of an EU Member State—direct insurance activities. The latter interpretative option would entail leaving reinsurance or captive insurance activities out of the scope of the IDBR. The issue has not been resolved either through administrative guidelines or through Court decisions so far and the intention of the lawmaker remains unknown.

Moreover, there are no traces of the rationale that led to the exclusion of credit institutions and insurance companies from the scope of the IDBR, either in the preamble to Royal Decree Law 20/2012 that modified Article 16 to include such a rule or in the preamble or the preparatory works of the CITA. If the *raison d'être* of the IDBR is collection, as well as neutralization of the differences between debt and equity in taxation, there is no justification for the exclusion of the aforementioned entities. If, however, the rationale was to avoid introducing distortions in their decision-making process due to the business sector in which they operate, one could ask why these have preference over other sectors that will be greatly impacted by the rule.[41] Moreover, as the main source of income of these companies comes from financing, in most cases no net financial expenses will arise, as gross financial income will be higher than financial expenses; hence the IDBR will usually not limit deductions of financial payments in these sectors.[42] If one takes this fact into account, the said exclusion makes even less sense.

Third, the limitation will not be applicable in the fiscal year in which a CIT taxpayer ceases to exist. This measure is aligned with the notion of the IDBR as a

38. Their legal status is embedded in *Ley 19/1992, de 7 de julio, sobre Régimen de Sociedades y Fondos de Inversión Inmobiliaria y sobre Fondos de Titulización Hipotecaria*.
39. Those included in the fifth additional provision (disposición adicional quinta) of *Ley 3/1994, de 14 de abril, por la que se adapta la legislación española en materia de crédito a la Segunda Directiva de Coordinación Bancaria y se introducen otras modificaciones relativas al sistema financiero*.
40. *See Ley 20/2015, de 14 de julio, de ordenación, supervisión y solvencia de las entidades aseguradoras y reaseguradoras*.
41. For instance, Article 4.4.b) ATAD states that Member States may exclude from the scope of the fixed ratio rule exceeding borrowing costs incurred on loans used to fund a long-term public infrastructure project where the project operator, borrowing costs, assets and income are all in the Union.
42. *See OECD 2015 BEPS Final Report on Action 4: Limiting Base Erosion Involving Interest Deductions and Other Financial Payments*, para. 188.

temporary difference that serves to postpone the deductibility of net financial expenses, instead of posing a definitive disallowance. Nevertheless, one must emphasize that cases in which financial expenses are not fully compensated may exist, as the rule does not grant a credit for the unused amounts. Anyhow, it is also relevant to mention that, according to the interpretation provided by the Spanish Tax Authorities, the exclusion from the IDBR limit applies to all the fiscal years in which a company's liquidation process takes place and not exclusively to the fiscal year of effective termination.[43] However, if termination occurs due to a reorganization process, the IDBR limitation will indeed apply, regardless of whether such a termination in the form of a merger or a total division is covered by the neutrality regime or not.[44]

[C] Calculating the Limit

As stated, *net financial expenses* are deductible to the limit of 30% of the *operating profit* generated in the fiscal year.[45] To calculate the limit appropriately, the content of these two concepts must be defined accurately. Such a delineation will depart from the accounting standards envisaged in the General Accounting Plan (*Plan General Contable*)[46] nuanced by the content of the CITA.

[1] Definition of Adjusted "Net Financial Expenses" and "Operating Profits"

Net financial expenses comprise the compensation of financial earnings and financial expenses obtained in a specific fiscal year.[47] Both concepts are defined in the General Accounting Plan regulations.[48]

Financial earnings are envisaged in group 7 "sales and income" and comprise two accounts:

(1) 761 "income from debt securities" and
(2) 762 "income from loans."

Financial expenses may be found in group 6 "purchases and expenses" and encompass four accounts:

43. GDT ruling of May 9, 2016.
44. This regime is envisaged in Articles 76-89 CITA and grants neutrality in reorganizations consisting in mergers, divisions, partial divisions, transfers of assets and exchanges of shares by deferring the taxation of the accumulated capital gains that would otherwise be taxed due to these events. The content of this regime stems from Council Directive 2009/133/EC of October 19, 2009.
45. Cfr. Article 4.1 ATAD.
46. Where the main accounting rules are included in Spain. Even if there are also general rules at a legal level in the Spanish Commercial Code, *Real Decreto de 22 de agosto de 1885 por el que se publica el Código de Comercio.*
47. Cfr. Article 2.1 ATAD.
48. *Real Decreto 1514/2007, de 16 de noviembre, por el que se aprueba el Plan General de Contabilidad.*

(1) 661 "interest on bonds and obligations";
(2) 662 "interest on payables";
(3) 664 "expenses arising on dividends payable on liability-classified instruments"; and
(4) 665 "interest on discounted bills and factoring transactions."

It must also be taken into account that tax restrictions over financial expenses have to be considered to determine the IDBR net financial expenses,[49] including those referred to in letters g), h) and i) of Article 15 CITA regarding expenses related to services rendered from tax havens,[50] financial expenses derived from intragroup debt incurred to acquire shares from a related entity[51] and expenses derived from hybrid transactions, as well as transfer pricing adjustments imposed by Article 18[52] and any other restriction posed in the CITA.[53]

Also, one must consider that certain nuances were established with regard to this definition in the interpretative ruling released on July 16, 2012, by which certain concepts that do not give rise to financial earnings or expenses from an accounting perspective must be taken into account in the calculation for IDBR purposes.[54] The best example regards hedging linked to specific borrowings, as it is stated that in these cases, even when accounting standards do not qualify the hedging as earnings or expenses, it must be reflected in the calculation of the IDBR limit displaying effects over debt incurred by the entity.[55] Other nuances were clarified through interpretative rulings, such as the fact that overdue interest (*intereses de demora*),[56], as well as financial payments derived from a debt restructuring[57] are considered financial expenses or that implicit financial earnings will be taken into account to calculate the net financial expenses.[58]

49. GDT rulings V1664 15 of May 28, 2015; V3004-17 of November 20, 2017.
50. The definition of what a tax haven for Spanish tax purposes is may be found in *Real Decreto 1080/1991, de 5 de julio, por el que se determinan los países o territorios a que se refieren los artículos 2.°, apartado 3, número 4, de la Ley 17/1991, de 27 de mayo, de Medidas Fiscales Urgentes, y 62 de la Ley 31/1990, de 27 de diciembre, de Presupuestos Generales del Estado para 1991.*
51. The seller must be a related entity, the shares may refer indistinctively to related or nonrelated entities. *See* section §8.03[A] of the present chapter for an examination of this rule.
52. *See* GDT ruling of July 16, 2012, first interpretative criterion. *See also* E. Cencerrado Millán & E. Gil García "Spain," fn.13, p. 640.
53. For instance, in GDT ruling V0165-17 of January 24, 2017, profit participating loans are considered as an equity instrument and thus give rise to nondeductible payments according to Article 15.a) CITA.
54. GDT ruling of July 16, 2012, first interpretative criterion.
55. GDT ruling of July 16, 2012, first interpretative criterion, letter c). *See also* GDT rulings V0152-17 of January 24, 2017; V0245-17 of January 31, 2017; V0595-16 of February 12, 2016; V3285-16 of July 13, 2016; V4789-16 of November 10, 2016; V3004-17 of November 20, 2017.
56. GDT rulings V0603-16 of February 15, 2016; V1403-16 of April 6, 2016; V1439-18 of May 29, 2018; V2068-16 of May 13, 2016.
57. GDT ruling V0165-17 of January 24, 2017.
58. GDT ruling V2155-15 of July 14, 2015.

The calculation of the operating profit results from operating activities (*resultado de explotación*) as configured in the profit and loss account (*cuenta de pérdidas y ganancias*), minus nonfinancial and other capital grants (*imputación de subvenciones de inmovilizado no financiero y otras*), minus impairments and gains (or losses) on disposal of fixed assets (*deterioros y resultado por enajenaciones de inmovilizado*), plus finance income derived from dividends or similar payments (*ingresos financieros de participaciones en instrumentos de patrimonio*) in which direct or indirect participation amounts to 5% or more, or the acquisition costs were more than EUR 20 million, except when shares were acquired from related parties according to what is established in Article 15.1.h) CITA.[59] It is relevant to note that the latter inclusion is in breach of the content of the IDBR contained in the ATAD, as it is stated in Article 4.2 *in fine* that "tax exempt income shall be excluded from the EBITDA of a taxpayer." This is the only aspect in which the Spanish IDBR is not in line with the rule contained in the ATAD and therefore changes in the calculation of the operating profits figure should be expected when the Directive is transposed into domestic law.[60]

Finally, one must not forget that, despite the calculation of the IDBR limit as described above, net financial expenses to the amount of EUR 1 million are allowed whatsoever. If the assessed tax period has a duration of less than one year, the EUR 1 million has to be limited and apportioned accordingly.[61]

[2] Outcome: Net Financial Expenses above or below the Limit

Net financial expenses below the limit. When net financial expenses are below the limit enshrined in the IDBR, no tax adjustments to commercial accounts will take place. In addition, the unused interest capacity may be added to the limit calculated for the next fiscal year;[62] that is a carryforward of the unused amount is allowed in the following five fiscal years so as to increase the limits existing in each period, as long as there is unused interest capacity to be compensated.[63] Therefore, the operating profit limit of the current fiscal year may be increased with the unused interest capacity.[64]

59. Some remarks on the interpretation of the "operating profits" concept may be found in GDT rulings V0012-17 of January 3, 2017; V0013-17 of January 3, 2017; V3727-15 of November 25, 2015.
60. Literature is unanimous in pointing out that this is the only aspect in which the Spanish IDBR goes against the ATAD. *See* B. Parejo García "La regla de delimitación de deducibilidad de intereses", fn. 33, p. 6. S. López Ribas "Financing Activities: Hybrid Mismatches and the Tax Deductibility of Interest in Spain," fn. 32, p. 454. E. Cencerrado Millán & E. Gil García "Spain," fn. 13, p. 648.
61. Article 16.4 CITA.
62. Cfr. Article 4.6.c) ATAD.
63. Article 16.2 CITA.
64. *See* STA interpretative note of February 3, 2015.

Example 2

Concept	*FY 0, Amount (EUR)*	*FY 1, Amount (EUR)*
Net financial expense	500,000	1,400,000
Operating profit	4,000,000	3,200,000
30% operating profit	1,200,000	960,000
Top-up limit	–	1,660,000
Amount to be deducted	500,000	1,400,000
Carryforward, net financial expense	0	0
Carryforward, unused interest capacity	700,000	260,000

In FY 0, net financial expenses are EUR 500,000 and thus below EUR 1,000,000 and also below 30% of the operating profit, that is EUR 1,200,000. Therefore, the whole amount is deductible, and no book-to-tax adjustments are needed. Additionally, there is unused interest capacity to the amount of EUR 700,000. In FY 1, the entity's net financial expenses rise to EUR 1,400,000, while the operating profit falls to EUR 3,200,000 and thus 30% of the operating profit equals EUR 960,000. As there was a balance of unused interest capacity, the top-up limit results from adding EUR 700,000 to that figure, which equals EUR 1,660,000. Therefore, the whole amount of net financial expenses, that is EUR 1,400,000, will be deductible and still there is an unused interest capacity of EUR 260,000 to be carried forward.

According to interpretative criteria issued by the tax authorities, the operating profits to be drained first are those of the current fiscal year and only when the amount has been completely exhausted, may the unused interest capacity that was carried forward be applied (last in first out).[65] This obviously makes the carryforward of prior unused capacity more difficult.

When net financial expenses are below EUR 1 million, a carryforward of the spread will not be possible if the 30% limit of the operating profit is below net financial expenses, as the calculation of the carryforward relies on the operating profit figure.[66] To put it in other words, the unused interest capacity calculation refers to the operating profit limit, not to the *de minimis* threshold. If this limit has been surpassed, there is no unused interest capacity, even despite the fact that the whole amount of net financial expenses may remain deductible due to the EUR 1 million *de minimis* threshold.

65. STA interpretative note of February 3, 2015 *in fine*.
66. GDT ruling of July 16, 2012, fourth interpretative criterion.

Example 3

Concept	*Amount (EUR)*
Net financial expense	700,000
Operating profit	600,000
30% operating profit	180,000
Amount to be deducted	700,000
Carryforward, net financial expense	0
Carryforward, unused interest capacity	0

Net financial expenses are EUR 700,000 and thus below EUR 1,000,000, but above the 30% operating profit, that is EUR 180,000. The whole amount is deductible, but no unused interest capacity may be carried forward because the entire amount of EUR 180,000 has been exceeded.

Net financial expense above the limit. When net financial expenses are above 30% of the operating profit and EUR 1 million, the amount over these limits will not be deductible, and a positive adjustment must be undertaken to raise the taxable base. Such an amount may be carried forward without temporal limits.[67] Pending net financial expenses have to be added to those of the fiscal year so as to compare the result with 30% of that fiscal year's operating profits.

Example 4

Concept	*FY 0, Amount (EUR)*	*FY 1, Amount (EUR)*
Net financial expense	1,300,000	1,500,000
Operating profit	2,000,000	2,200,000
30% operating profit	600,000	660,000
Top-up net financial expenses	-	1,800,000
Amount to be deducted	1,000,000	1,000,000
Carryforward, net financial expense	300,000	800,000
Carryforward, unused interest capacity	0	0

In FY 0, net financial expenses are EUR 1,300,000, while 30% of the operating profit is EUR 600,000. This exceeds the amount that can be deducted under the

67. Cfr. Article 4.6.a) ATAD.

IDBR. EUR 1,000,000 will be deductible according to the *de minimis* rule and a book-to-tax adjustment of EUR 300,000 will have to be performed. In FY 1, net financial expenses of EUR 1,500,000 have to be topped up with the carriedforward amount that in FY 0 was not deductible. Therefore, net financial expenses to be limited amount to EUR 1,800,000. Applying the *de minimis* rule, the result is that EUR 1,000,000 is deductible and therefore a book-to-tax adjustment of EUR 800,000 has to be performed. The same amount will be carried forward to the next fiscal year.

Due to the fact that, in taxable periods starting before January 1, 2015, the IDBR included a temporal limit of eighteen years on the carryforward of pending net financial expenses, rules on temporal allocation applied as follows: first, current net financial expenses were deductible and only when the limit still had not been reached, could pending net financial expenses be added (last in, first out). Nonetheless, for periods starting 2015 onward, such a rule is senseless, as the described temporal limitation no longer applies.

[D] Special Rules

[1] EIG and JVs

As regards the application of the IDBR, there are special rules applicable to EIG, European Economic Interest Grouping (hereinafter "EEIG") and JVs.

EIGs are entities with legal capacity that serve an instrumental purpose; that is they perform specific ancillary activities to their partners to enhance the profitability of the latter and not their own.[68] When partners are located in different EU Member States, an EEIG may be formed.[69] JVs, however, are entities allowing entrepreneurs to cooperate on the development of a specific project, service or supply.[70] JVs do not hold legal capacity but instead are considered as associative arrangements. Other relevant differences with respect to EIGs are that: (1) a JV has a limited lifetime aligned with the achievement of its purpose, while the EIG is not subject to time constraints; and (2) the EIG refers to auxiliary activities, while the JV may comprise the associates' core activities.

For tax purposes, a regime of semitransparency applies to EIGs, EEIGs and JVs, as the fraction of the taxable base corresponding to partners that are tax resident in Spain or nonresidents with a PE will be attributable to them and not to the EIG. Notwithstanding, the fraction of the taxable base corresponding to a nonresident entity with no PE in Spain will be taxed at the level of the EIG. It is important to emphasize that the attribution refers to the taxable base and thus, book-to-tax adjustments must be performed at the level of these entities.

68. Agrupaciones de Interés Económico, AIE. Their legal status is defined in *Ley 12/1991, de 29 de abril, de Agrupaciones de Interés Económico.*
69. Council Regulation (EEC) no. 2137/85 of July 25, 1985.
70. Unión Temporal de Empresas, UTE. Their legal status may be found in *Ley 18/1982, de 26 de mayo, sobre régimen fiscal de agrupaciones y uniones temporales de Empresas y de las Sociedades de desarrollo industrial regional.*

That said, as per the application of the IDBR, Article 43.1.b).1° CITA states that net financial expenses that were not deductible at the level of these entities have to be attributed to their partners. Hence, the limitation applies first to the calculation of the taxable base at the level of these entities, and then, if certain net financial expenses were not deductible, this amount will be attributable to partners that are tax resident in Spain or nonresidents with a PE in Spain.

Example 5

Company A, tax resident in Spain, holds a participation of 50% in a JV, being the other 50% held by Company B, tax resident abroad. Relevant numbers are the following.

Concept	*JV (EUR)*	*Company A (EUR)*
Net financial expense	4,000,000	500,000
Operating profit	5,000,000	700,000
30% operating profit	1,500,000	210,000

Assuming that there are no other book-to-tax adjustments relevant to the case, the amount to be deducted at the level of the JV is EUR 1,500,000. Therefore, the taxable base of the JV is EUR 3,500,000 (i.e., EUR 5,000,000–EUR 1,500,000) and the remaining nondeductible net financial expenses are EUR 2,500,000. Both amounts will be allocated at 50% to Company A, as it is a tax resident in Spain. The other 50% will be relevant for calculating the CIT at the level of the JV. Hence the result is as follows.

Concept	*Amount (EUR)*
Taxable base of the JV	1,750,000
Nondeductible net interest expense, to be carried forward	1,250,000

From the perspective of Company A, the adjusted numbers resulting from the allocation derived from the JV are as follows:

Concept	*Amount (EUR)*
Adjusted net financial expense	500,000 + 1,250,000 = 1,750,000
Operating profit	1,500,000
30% operating profit	210,000
Amount to be deducted	1,000,000
Carryforward of nondeducted net financial expenses	750,000

[2] *Fiscal Unity*

The Spanish fiscal unity regime is a specific, voluntary regime that entails that the components of a group of entities will not have to fulfill their CIT tax obligations individually, but the group will as a stand-alone CIT taxpayer.[71] Therefore, taxable bases generated by the group members will be aggregated and compensated so as to determine the taxable base of the group as a whole. Only entities that are tax resident in Spain and PEs of foreign entities located in Spain may form a fiscal unity; however, under certain conditions, it is permitted for the parent company to be located abroad—although it will not form part of the unity, as only resident entities or PEs located in Spain may do so.[72]

The taxable base in the fiscal unity regime is the sum of the individual tax bases of the entities forming part of it, modulated in accordance with items listed in Articles 62 and 63 CITA. Therefore, one must perform tax adjustments at an individual level and only when taxable bases are aggregated, the fiscal unity will display real effects, treating the group as a single taxpayer.[73] In this respect, one of the nuances to be taken into account is that Article 63.a) CITA states that the IDBR limit must be calculated at a group level and not at the level of each entity.[74] This means that, for calculation purposes, net financial expenses as well as the operating profit of the entities forming part of the fiscal unity must be aggregated and also modulated, which means *inter alia* that only indebtedness with parties not forming part of the group will be taken into account and not intragroup debt, as this is eliminated in the consolidation process.[75] Then, if nondeductible amounts of net financial expenses remain, these have to be allocated among the individual entities, to calculate their taxable base adequately before consolidation takes place.

Example 6[76]

Assume that entities A, B, C and D form part of a fiscal unity. No incorporations or eliminations take place on internal transactions. Assume that the operating profit of each entity is EUR 1,000,000. Net financial expenses are as follows:
- A: EUR 200,000
- B: EUR 100,000
- C: EUR 500,000
- D: EUR 600,000.

Article 63.a) CITA demands the calculation of the IDBR on an aggregated basis. Therefore the numbers are as follows.

71. Fiscal unity is envisaged in Articles 55-75 CITA.
72. Article 58.1 CITA.
73. GDT ruling of July 16, 2012, sixth interpretative criterion.
74. Cfr. Article 4.1.a) ATAD.
75. Article 64 CITA. GDT ruling of July 16, 2012, sixth interpretative criterion. *See* E. Cencerrado Millán & E. Gil García "Spain," fn. 13, p. 644.
76. Example contained in GDT ruling of July 16, 2012, eighth interpretative criterion.

Concept	*Amount (EUR)*
Aggregated net financial expenses	1,400,000
Aggregated operating profit	4,000,000
30% operating profit limit	1,200,000
Amount to be deducted	1,000,000
Nondeductible expenses to be allocated	200,000

The allocation of nondeductible expenses will take into consideration which of the entities exceed the 30% operating profit limit on their individual net financial expenses. In this example, all entities display a 30% limit of EUR 300,000. As only entities C and D exceed this limit, the EUR 200,000 nondeductible expenses will be apportioned among them. The total excess equals EUR 500,000 (i.e., entity C's EUR 200,000 plus entity D's EUR 300,000). Thus:

- in C, nondeductible expenses equal 200,000 x 200,000/500,000 = 80,000;
- in D, nondeductible expenses equal 300,000 x 200,000/500,000 = 120,000.

Therefore, for the purposes of calculating the individual tax bases of the members of the fiscal unity, entities A and B deduct all net financial expenses, while C deducts EUR 420,000 (500,000-80,000) and D deducts EUR 480,000 (600,000-120,000).

When an entity accesses the fiscal unity, pending net financial expenses will have to be adjusted according to the rules on eliminations and incorporations provided for in Articles 64 and 65 CITA[77] and will only be deductible up to 30% of the operating profits of the entity itself. Also, the carryforward of the unused interest capacity will take place on a stand-alone basis.[78] A similar rationale applies when a fiscal unit accesses another fiscal unit; in other words the mentioned pending amounts will be calculated in accordance with the composition of the former fiscal unit.[79] The nonapplicability of the fiscal unity regime or its termination entail that pending net financial expenses, as well as pending unused interest capacity, will be assumed by each individual entity proportionally according to its generation.[80] The same rationale applies when an entity abandons the fiscal unity.[81] It also has to be noted that the limit will not apply if an entity ceases to exist, unless such termination takes place within the fiscal unit. Additionally, credit institutions and insurance companies that form part of a fiscal unity are excluded from the calculation of the IDBR at a consolidated level.[82]

77. As per regulations on incorporations and eliminations, the referred provisions refer to regulations on the formulation of consolidated annual accounts provided for in *Real Decreto 1159/2010, de 17 de septiembre, por el que se aprueban las Normas para la Formulación de Cuentas Anuales Consolidadas y se modifica el Plan General de Contabilidad aprobado por Real Decreto 1514/2007, de 16 de noviembre y el Plan General de Contabilidad de Pequeñas y Medianas Empresas aprobado por Real Decreto 1515/2007, de 16 de noviembre*.
78. Article 67.a) CITA.
79. Article 74.3.b) CITA.
80. Article 74.1.b).1° CITA.
81. Article 74.2 CITA.
82. Article 63.a) second paragraph CITA.

In accordance with the described regime, it is easy to ascertain that the IDBR rule contained in the fiscal unity regime cannot be defined as group ratio rule as stated in BEPS as it neither complements the fixed ratio rule nor introduces a carve-out to escape the limitation posed in the IDBR.[83]

§8.03 SPECIAL INTEREST DEDUCTION LIMITATIONS

As indicated above, two additional rules on interest deduction limitations were introduced in Spain in 2012 and 2015. These rules are discussed in more detail in the following sections.

[A] Special Rule for Intragroup Acquisitions Using Debt Push Down Structures (Article 15.h of the CITA)

Together with the IDBR, a special rule was introduced in the CITA in 2012 establishing permanent nondeductibility of financial expenses incurred due to intragroup financing for either: (i) an intragroup purchase agreement referred to shares in any kind of entity; or (ii) capital contributions made to other companies of the group; unless, in both cases, the taxpayer proves the existence of valid commercial (economic) reasons for the transactions.

This special anti-avoidance rule (hereinafter "SAAR") was introduced as a reaction to *debt push down* financing structures used by MNEs in the late 2000s following transaction patterns identical (or very similar) to that described in the following example.

Example 7

A resident subsidiary of an MNE, enjoying exemption of foreign-sourced dividends—due to the Spanish special holding regime (Entidades de Tenencia de Valores Extranjeros)[84] *or due to the application of the Spanish participation exemption*[85]*—acquires significant participations of nonresident subsidiaries of the same group, financing the acquisitions by means of loans granted by another subsidiary of the same group (or a Bank). Inasmuch as its income is tax-exempt and interest paid for the loan is deductible, the (holding) company generates important tax losses. If one also takes into account that, since 2000, Spanish holdings (ETVEs) are also allowed to consolidate with other subsidiaries of the group for tax purposes, one can understand the important erosion of the Spanish tax base these transactions have generated.*

83. *See OECD 2015 BEPS Final Report on Action 4: Limiting Base Erosion Involving Interest Deductions and Other Financial Payments*, paras. 115-154.
84. Articles 107, 108 CITA.
85. Article 21 CITA.

As already mentioned in the introduction to this chapter, the Spanish Tax Authorities initially reacted to these structures resorting to different anti-avoidance devices in a long series of assessments, many of which are still pending before the Spanish Courts.[86] In any case, and despite the fact that the tax authorities have won the majority of these cases in Court,[87] the Spanish lawmakers finally decided to put a stop to (some) of these transactions by means of a targeted rule[88] along the following lines.

[1] Conditions for Application

The application of this special rule requires the accrual of financial expenses incurred due to intragroup financing (*source of funding condition*) for the acquisition of whatever shareholdings or for capital contributions from or to other companies of the group (*use of funding condition*). Both conditions must be analyzed separately.

Starting with the *use of funding condition*, the rule requires that the shareholdings be acquired from other companies of the group or the funds be contributed to other companies of the group. Even if the rule does not provide for it explicitly, the concept of "companies of the group" is defined in accordance with Article 42 of the Spanish Commercial Code (hereinafter "CC")[89] that establishes the duty to prepare consolidated accounts for "Groups of Companies."[90] This is not only a logical requirement but also the result of a systematic interpretation taking into account that when referring to the *source of funding condition* the rule refers to intragroup financing according to the same provision of the CC.[91] However, the acquired shareholdings do not need to be of companies already integrated into the group. The acquiring or contributing company whose deductions are excluded must obviously be resident in Spain or a PE located in Spain; however, the company whose shareholdings are acquired, the company from which the shareholdings are acquired or the company to which funds are contributed may or may not be resident in Spain.

As regards the *source of funding condition*, there are indeed some clear concepts in the law: as with the general interest deduction barrier there is no specific concept of financial expenses and therefore its meaning is that of accounting rules;[92] the qualification of *intragroup financing* is referred here explicitly to the concept of group

86. A brief description of these procedures in: J.J. Zornoza Pérez & A. Báez Moreno 2018 "Anti-avoidance Measures of General Nature and Scope. GAAR and Other Rules," fn. 2, pp. 13-14.
87. Until 2018 only two of the eleven cases analyzed by the Spanish Supreme Court have been decided in favor of the taxpayer.
88. In what prominent members of the Spanish Tax Authorities have called a *legal peacekeeping mission*: E. Sanz Gadea "Restricción y limitación a la deducción de intereses en el Impuesto sobre Sociedades", fn.32, p. 96.
89. *Real Decreto de 22 de agosto de 1885 por el que se publica el Código de Comercio.*
90. It must be pointed out that the requisite requires the existence of an intragroup acquisition or contribution and not that the involved companies are effectively obliged to render consolidated accounts. In this regard: M. Menéndez Álvarez & M. Linares Gil "Capítulo 10. Gastos no deducibles" in *Impuesto sobre Sociedades. Régimen General* (Eduardo San Frutos Gambín, dir., Thomson-Reuters-Aranzadi-EY Abogados 2013, 2ª ed.), p. 1110.
91. M. Menéndez Álvarez & M. Linares Gil "Capítulo 10. Gastos no deducibles", fn. 91, p. 1110.
92. *See* section §8.02[C][1] for an assessment of the definition.

contained in Article 42 CC. However, this condition might prove problematic regarding at least two circumstances:

(i) The rule requires the intragroup financing, that is the obtained funds, to be *used for* the described acquisitions or contributions (*direct link requirement*). Although the requirement may seem clear at first, it might prove problematic in practice since, at an accounting level, all liabilities finance all assets in the balance sheet.[93] Nevertheless, the rule requires a specific correspondence between a specific liability (intragroup financing transaction) and a specific asset (acquired shareholding or contribution). Reference has been made to cases in which this correspondence might be evident, such as express statements by the contracting parties in the financing contracts or the pledging of the acquired shares as collateral for the intragroup financing.[94] However, these cases are as clear as they are unusual[95] whereas, in addition, cases of contemporary intragroup and extra-group financing combined with intragroup and extra-group acquisitions or contributions are indeed common. Consider the following (rather simple) example:[96]

Example 8 In October 2012, a Company sells bonds depositing the amounts of the sale. In April 2013 this Company performs an intragroup acquisition. Later, in October 2013, the Company acquires shares in quoted Collective Investment Institutions concluding an intragroup loan on the same date.

It is apparent that in these rather common cases the proximity in time between the financing and the acquisition/contribution transactions—frequently suggested as decisive by several authors[97]—is of little help when trying to ascertain the existence of the direct link required by the law for the application of the special rule. If one of the advantages of SAARs is providing clarity with respect to the transactions which are effectively taxable (in our cases nondeductible), it seems obvious that the direct link requirement

93. E. Sanz Gadea "Restricción y limitación a la deducción de intereses en el Impuesto sobre Sociedades", fn. 32, p. 55.
94. M. Menéndez Álvarez & M. Linares Gil "Capítulo 10. Gastos no deducibles", fn. 91, p. 1112. E. Sanz Gadea "Restricción y limitación a la deducción de intereses en el Impuesto sobre Sociedades", fn. 32, p. 55. J.A. López-Santacruz Montes *Memento. Impuesto sobre Sociedades 2018* (Francis Lefebvre 2018), at 728.1.
95. M. Menéndez Álvarez & M. Linares Gil "Capítulo 10. Gastos no deducibles", fn. 91, p. 1112.
96. Taken from the same author who (ironically) attributed this rule a *legal peacekeeping mission*: E. Sanz Gadea "Restricción y limitación a la deducción de intereses en el Impuesto sobre Sociedades", fn. 32, p. 56.
97. M. Menéndez Álvarez & M. Linares Gil "Capítulo 10. Gastos no deducibles", fn. 91, p. 1112. E. Sanz Gadea "Restricción y limitación a la deducción de intereses en el Impuesto sobre Sociedades", fn. 32, p. 55.

totally undermines this goal, foreseeing significant litigation for its application.

(ii) The requirement of intragroup financing excludes the application of the rule if the lender is an independent third party and, particularly, a financial institution. Nobody has questioned such an obvious statement; however the clear limitation of the rule to intragroup financing raises some questions: (1) some decisions of the TS in which the special rule was not applicable *ratione temporis* denied deductibility of financial expenses in debt push down transactions even when the intragroup acquisition had been financed by loans granted.[98] These decisions pose a problem regarding the possible application of the Spanish GAAR to deny the deductibility of extra-group financial expenses in *debt push down transactions* where the special rule of Article 15.h of the CITA is not applicable (due to exclusive extra-group financing). Some authors close to the Spanish Tax Authorities have stated that the GAAR should be applied.[99] We believe, however, that the solution should be different. Applying the GAAR in this context would hardly be reconcilable with the principle of legal certainty and a bona fide application of tax law provisions. Indeed, this would lead to a limited approach to the two-faced reality of SAARs, inasmuch as these kinds of rules describe what is abusive according to the legislator and yet, at the same time, clarify *a contrario* what arrangements might not be considered abusive. To be more specific, despite the GAAR being in principle applicable, when the taxpayer is within the legal limits of the SAAR, at the end of the day the arrangement can never be considered artificial.[100] Applying these general reflections to our specific problem it would be unreasonable and rather haphazard for Article 15.h) CITA to refer to artificial *debt push down* transactions requiring intragroup financing while defending at the same time that the GAAR would allow for the nondeductibility of financial expenses generated in the context of extra-group loans. (2) The situation could be different if the intervention of an extra-group lender were considered abusive, for example if an extra-group financial institution borrows money from a company in the group to lend it to another (or the same) member of the group.[101] Several authors have suggested that the application of the Spanish GAAR to this situation would be

98. Decision of the Spanish Supreme Court of July 18, 2012 (case BICC). However, the Spanish Supreme Court, in its May 20, 2016 judgment (case Colgate Palmolive Holding), decided to allow interest deduction, pointing out that the acquisition had been financed by a Bank not integrated in the group, as we have denounced somewhere else.

99. A. López-Santacruz Montes *Memento. Impuesto sobre Sociedades 2018*, fn. 95, at 728.1. More ambiguous: E. Sanz Gadea "Restricción y limitación a la deducción de intereses en el Impuesto sobre Sociedades", fn. 32, pp. 95-96.

100. On this problem in general *see*: J.J. Zornoza Pérez & A. Báez Moreno 2018 "Anti-avoidance Measures of General Nature and Scope. GAAR and Other Rules," fn. 2, pp. 13-14. J.J. Zornoza Pérez & A. Báez Moreno "Chapter 33: Spain," fn. 2, at 33.4.

101. On this situation: E. Sanz Gadea "Restricción y limitación a la deducción de intereses en el Impuesto sobre Sociedades", fn. 32, p. 56. M. Menéndez Álvarez & M. Linares Gil "Capítulo 10. Gastos no deducibles", fn. 91, pp. 1110-1111.

feasible.[102] We agree with this position if the intervention of a "financing" third (nongroup) company were to be considered abusive according to the Spanish GAAR. As stated, if the SAAR is not applicable due to an artificial arrangement settled by the taxpayer, the normal relationship defined above between SAARs and GAARs would not be applicable. Indeed, in this case, one could never say that the legislator would consider the arrangement as not falling under the SAAR as nonabusive.[103] The only doubt arising in these cases is whether the whole debt push down transaction could be disregarded resorting to the GAAR or whether the GAAR could be used to disregard extra-group financing and restore the application of the SAAR rule on leveraged intragroup acquisitions. The reader might think this is a rather academic debate as, in any case, the deductibility of financial expenses would be denied for tax purposes. However, as will be shown immediately below, the consequences of applying the GAAR or the SAAR for leveraged intragroup acquisitions might be radically different. Once we have considered this problem in general, we will use an example to illustrate the differences.

[2] Legal Consequences

The obvious and primary consequence of the SAAR contained in Article 15.h) CITA is the permanent nondeductibility of financial expenses incurred due to the intragroup financing transactions. However, it should be noted that the rule does not deny the existence of intragroup financing and acquisition transactions which display their remaining legal and tax consequences. This means that the lender will be taxed on the corresponding financial income and the dividends or capital gains generated by the acquired shareholding attributed to the purchaser.[104] Therefore, the application of Article 15.h) of the CITA will inevitably generate economic double taxation inasmuch as the rule has foreseen no mechanism to correct or relieve it.[105]

A radical difference lies between the legal consequences of current Article 15.h) CITA and the correction of leveraged acquisition of intragroup companies under a GAAR. Indeed, the consequence of the application of the Spanish GAAR refers to the reconfiguration of the tax treatment of the arrangement according to its economic

102. M. Menéndez Álvarez & M. Linares Gil "Capítulo 10. Gastos no deducibles", fn. 91, p. 1110. A. López-Santacruz Montes *Memento. Impuesto sobre Sociedades 2018*, fn. 95, at 728.1. Other authors seem to simply confirm the direct application of the SAAR: E. Sanz Gadea "Restricción y limitación a la deducción de intereses en el Impuesto sobre Sociedades", fn. 32, p. 56.
103. J.J. Zornoza Pérez & A. Báez Moreno 2018 "Anti-avoidance Measures of General Nature and Scope. GAAR and Other Rules," fn. 2, p. 14.
104. *See* section §8.02[C][1] for an assessment of the definition of net financial expenses and operating profits.
105. No single existing International or European mechanism to correct double taxation would oblige the State of residence of the lender to correct this double taxation: Sanz E. Sanz Gadea "Restricción y limitación a la deducción de intereses en el Impuesto sobre Sociedades", fn. 32, p. 79; 82-84.

substance or—to put it more precisely—according to an appropriate (not abusive) fictive fact pattern. In this scenario, the application of the GAAR to a leveraged acquisition of intragroup companies should not only imply the nondeductibility of financial expenses incurred due to the intragroup financing transactions but additionally the disregard for tax purposes of both the intragroup acquisition and financing arrangements. This approach would eliminate economic double taxation in cases of domestic intragroup financing[106] (no interest would be taxed at the level of the lender) and potential unrelieved juridical double taxation in cross-border intragroup financing (no source taxation would be imposed on the payment of interest[107]). These differences justify the preference of certain Spanish authors for a GAAR (instead of a SAAR) approach for tackling leveraged intragroup acquisitions.[108] However, beyond this policy issue, these differences also show practical implications in the current legislative landscape. We recall here a problem that was left unresolved in a previous paragraph[109] by means of the following example.

Example 9

Company A, resident in Spain, is a member of an MNE. Company B, also resident in Spain and member of the Group, grants a loan to an "extra-group" financial institution which, in turn, grants a loan to Company A. Company A acquires all the shares of Company D from Company C which is also a member of the Group. Due to the existence of exclusive extra-group financing, the SAAR of Article 15.h would not be applicable at first sight. However, as stated before, the intervention of an extra-group lender might be considered abusive in this case, taking into account that all the funds originate from the group. In this situation, the doubt arises as to whether the whole debt push down transaction will be disregarded resorting to the GAAR or whether the GAAR will be used to disregard extra-group financing and restore the application of the SAAR rule on leveraged intragroup acquisitions. Even if the deduction of the interests corresponding to the intragroup loan were to be denied in either case, further consequences of both alternatives would be radically different: (i) in a domestic loan scenario, the application of the GAAR would imply the nontaxation of an interest for B (the financial institution intermediation would be disregarded) and the attribution of whatever dividends or capital gains generated by the shares in D to C. For its part, the application of the SAAR (after disregarding the financial institution due to the

106. *See* E. Sanz Gadea "Restricción y limitación a la deducción de intereses en el Impuesto sobre Sociedades", fn. 32, p. 97.
107. However, the Decision of the Spanish Audiencia Nacional of February 21, 2013 (case Accenture) seems to contradict this conclusion. The Spanish Court concludes that the nondeductibility of intragroup interests does not imply that interests were not paid to a nonresident corporation. This fact—and perhaps other procedural peculiarities of the case—justified the refusal by the Court to refund withholding taxes on accrued intragroup interests.
108. E. Sanz Gadea "Restricción y limitación a la deducción de intereses en el Impuesto sobre Sociedades", fn. 32, p. 97.
109. *See* section §8.03[A][1] *in fine*.

application of the GAAR) would imply the taxation of an interest for B and the attribution of whatever dividends or capital gains generated by the shares in D to A. (ii) In a cross-border loan scenario, similar differences arise. However, the application of the GAAR would not necessarily imply the nontaxation of an interest in the hands of B, inasmuch as the State of residence of the lender (different from Spain) does not need to recognize the adjustment made by the Spanish Tax Authorities. In any case, the application of the GAAR would imply the impossibility of levying a withholding tax on the payment of the interest. The application of the SAAR will affect neither the taxation of an interest obtained by B nor the levy of a withholding tax in Spain on the accrued interest.

[3] Escape Clause (Valid Economic Reasons)

The special rule does not apply if the taxpayer can demonstrate the existence of valid commercial reasons for undertaking such transactions.[110] The Preamble to Royal Decree-Law 12/2012—where the SAAR under scrutiny here was first introduced into the Spanish CITA, alongside the IDBR, as described in section §8.02[A]—mentioned, by way of example, two cases in which a valid commercial reason for the transaction may exist, thus precluding the application of the SAAR: (i) "Cases of restructuring within the corporate group as a consequence of shareholding acquisitions from third parties." As clear and straightforward as this valid commercial reason might look at first sight, its practical application raises new interpretative issues such as determining when an intragroup acquisition can be considered as a consequence of an acquisition from third parties.[111] Apart from the proximity of the extra-group and intragroup acquisitions, no other grounds have been provided on which to base this connection.[112] However, the similarity between the activity performed by both the acquiring and the acquired company might be a strong indication for the application of this valid commercial reason;[113] (ii) "Cases where the Spanish entity effectively manages the acquired shareholdings." Several authors have highlighted the ease with which the management of shareholdings may be reallocated in a group, thereby avoiding the application of the special rule.[114] This is why some authors linked to the Spanish Tax Authorities have claimed a mere geographical change in management to be insufficient

110. Critically on the proliferation in the Spanish legal order of SAARs based upon the existence or nonexistence of valid commercial reasons: J.J. Zornoza Pérez & A. Báez Moreno 2018 "Anti-avoidance Measures of General Nature and Scope. GAAR and Other rules," fn. 2, pp. 17-18.
111. E. Sanz Gadea "Restricción y limitación a la deducción de intereses en el Impuesto sobre Sociedades", fn. 32, p. 57.
112. *Ibid.*
113. *Ibid. See also* A. López-Santacruz Montes *Memento. Impuesto sobre Sociedades 2018*, fn. 95, at 729.
114. E. Sanz Gadea "Restricción y limitación a la deducción de intereses en el Impuesto sobre Sociedades", fn. 32, p. 97 indicating, however, that even in cases of effective management of the acquired shareholdings the existence of "exorbitant financial expenses"—whatever this should mean—should trigger the application of the special rule.

as a valid commercial reason, requiring evidence of a substantial change in management resulting in an increase in value of the business managed in Spain.[115] Unfortunately, the Rulings of the Spanish General Directorate of Taxes have provided little detailed guidance on this (required) substantial change in management.[116]

Of course, valid commercial reasons other than those exemplified in the Preamble must be admitted.[117] In this respect, it is worth mentioning those LAIC not reporting a tax advantage. While conceptually a transaction not reporting a tax benefit may not necessarily count on a valid commercial reason, this link might be assumed in the context of a rational business behavior. The lack of a tax advantage has served to justify the nonapplication of the special rule to: (1) loans between companies of the same tax group,[118] (2) loans between Spanish resident companies taxed at the same tax rate, (3) loans between Spanish and nonresident companies where the latter is taxed at a higher rate than the Spanish one or (4) intragroup acquisitions of shareholdings when the dividends distributed by the acquired company are not exempted.[119]

[B] Special Rule for *LBOs* (Article 16.5 of the CITA)

A special rule on the limitation of interest deductions was introduced in the 2014 comprehensive reform of the Spanish CITA[120] regarding financial expenses accrued in LBOs. The rule implies essentially that financial expenses associated with the acquisition of shareholdings of entities that subsequently merge with the acquiring company will be subject to an additional limit of 30% of the operating profit of the acquiring entity, without including the operating profit corresponding to any entity merging with that company. The new rule should be set in context. Its goal, at least theoretically, is to curb transactions that were very common in Spain in the years preceding the financial crisis, in which nonresident investors—normally Private Equity firms—took control of Spanish groups using a significant amount of debt that was subsequently warranted and paid by the acquired companies. These transactions have always been suspected of falling within the prohibition of financial assistance contained in Articles

115. A. López-Santacruz Montes *Memento. Impuesto sobre Sociedades 2018*, fn. 95, at 729.
116. By failing to provide a positive answer—due to an alleged lack of information—(Rulings no. V398/2013 of February 11, 2013 and V3644/2013 of December 19, 2013).
117. E. Sanz Gadea "Restricción y limitación a la deducción de intereses en el Impuesto sobre Sociedades", fn. 32, p. 57. A. López-Santacruz Montes *Memento. Impuesto sobre Sociedades 2018*, fn. 95, at 729.1. M. Menéndez Álvarez & M. Linares Gil "Capítulo 10. Gastos no deducibles," fn. 91, p. 1118. S. López Ribas "Financing Activities: Hybrid Mismatches and the Tax Deductibility of Interest in Spain," fn. 32, p. 451.
118. This has been confirmed by a Ruling of the Spanish General Directorate of Taxes no. V878/2013 of March 19, 2013.
119. However, all these cases (with the exception of intra(tax) group loans) generate additional interpretative issues such as what tax rate (nominal or effective, general or specific for interests) should be used as a reference, or whether a neutralization of financial income with (deductible) negative tax bases should be taken into account. *See*: E. Sanz Gadea "Restricción y limitación a la deducción de intereses en el Impuesto sobre Sociedades", fn. 32, p. 58.
120. *Ley 27/2014, de 27 de noviembre, del Impuesto sobre Sociedades.*

143.2 and 150 of the Corporate Enterprises Act.[121] Additionally, their elevated financial risk made LBOs—described jokingly in the jargon as *Large Bankruptcy Opportunity*—rather unpopular transactions. Perhaps for this reason and also due to the advantageous tax treatment of the transaction—before interest deduction barriers were introduced in 2012, interest accrued was fully deductible and so too was the depreciation of the merger goodwill—LBOs were frequently challenged by the Spanish Tax Authorities. However, in contrast to the cases of leveraged acquisitions of intragroup shares, tax authorities did not always succeed before the Courts. Even though in some notorious cases the tax administration incomprehensively managed to convince the TS that LBOs constituted simulated contracts,[122] there are also decisions upholding the (tax) legitimacy of LBOs[123] and, what is probably more important, there were senior officials of the Spanish Tax Administration who defended the economic substance of these transactions.[124] Indeed, there seems to be no traces of abuse, at least from a tax perspective, in acquiring companies—even with a high debt burden—or merging the acquiring and acquired companies after the acquisition particularly, in this last case, when the reorganization is imposed by the company (normally a financial institution) financing the transaction. These reasons might have led to the introduction of the special rule on LBOs—which cannot even be labeled as SAAR—on the basis of the following subsections.

[1] Conditions for Application

The rule limits the deductibility of financial expenses incurred by a resident company for the acquisition of shareholdings in whatever kind of entity if the acquiring company merges with any other company within four years following the acquisition and the merger benefits from the neutrality regime on restructurings contained in the CITA.[125] According to Article 67.b) CITA, the special rule also applies to limit financial expenses incurred by a resident company for the acquisition of shareholdings in an entity of any

121. *Real Decreto Legislativo 1/2010, de 2 de julio, por el que se aprueba el texto refundido de la Ley de Sociedades de Capital.*
122. *See* the comment of these decisions in: A. Martín Jiménez "Spain: Dividends, Leveraged Buyouts and the Concept of Abuse / Simulation in Domestic Law, EU Law and Tax Treaties" in *Tax Treaty Case Law Around the Globe 2017* (M. Lang et al. eds, IBFD 2018).
123. The Decision of the Spanish Supreme Court of February 26, 2015 (case Glaxosmithkline, S.A.) is often quoted on this matter. Even if the transactions under scrutiny are labeled as LBOs by a dissenting opinion incorporated in the decision it is rather unlikely that we are actually facing a transaction of the kind in that decision.
124. E. Sanz Gadea. *Gastos financieros: cada caso es un caso. Sentencia del Tribunal Supremo de 26 de febrero de 2015.* in http://www.loyolaandnews.es/masteresoficialesloyola/gastos-financieros-cada-caso-es-un-caso-sentencia-del-tribunal-supremo-de-26-de-febrero-de-2015/ (last visit July 10, 2019).
125. As stated before, this regime results from the implementation in Spain Council Directive 2009/133/EC of October 19, 2009, on the common system of taxation applicable to mergers, divisions, partial divisions, transfers of assets and exchanges of shares concerning companies of different Member States and to the transfer of the registered office of an SE or SCE between Member States.

kind that enters the fiscal unity to which the acquirer belongs (?), within the four years following the acquisition.

Article 16.5(3) CITA contains an escape clause according to which the special rule will not apply in the tax year in which the shares are acquired, if the acquisition is financed with debt that does not exceed 70% of the total purchase price of the shares; the special rule does not apply either in subsequent tax years if the amount of debt decreases following the acquisition, at least in the proportional part corresponding to the following eight years, until it reaches 30% of the total purchase price. Two observations must be made in relation to this escape clause: (i) this exception might result in a systematic nonapplication of the special rule, taking into account the high threshold fixed by the rule which, in the view of certain authors, follows the regular practice in LBOs.[126] According to these authors the most leveraged LBOs finance around 80% of the purchase price with debt;[127] (ii) the escape clause for subsequent tax years has been interpreted by the Spanish General Directorate of Taxes in its Ruling nº V1664/2015 of May 28, 2015. According to this interpretation, for the additional limit not to apply, the debt must be reduced according to the following formula:

[(Initial Debt percentage—30% of the initial debt percentage) x number of years passed after the acquisition] / 8.

The ruling poses two scenarios: (1) in a subsequent year, the debt is not reduced according to the formula. In this case, the additional limit would apply in that fiscal year, but in subsequent fiscal years, the additional limit would not apply when the debt was additionally reduced to reach the proportion set in the formula. In short, noncompliance with the debt reduction imposed in one year does not automatically involve the loss of the escape clause in subsequent years; (2) in a subsequent fiscal year, debt is reduced beyond the proportion set in the formula. In this case, of course, the additional limit will not be applied in the year in which an additional reduction was made; in subsequent years, the additional limit will not be applied even if debt is reduced below the proportion set in the formula if the total reduction complies with the proportion set in the formula.

[2] Legal Consequences

As previously stated, the rule implies that financial expenses incurred in LBO transactions will be subject to an additional limit of 30% of the operating profit of the acquiring entity, without including the operating profit corresponding to any entity merging with that company or entering the tax group of the acquiring company. Indeed, what the rule aims precisely to do is to avoid (or at least not promote) the high financial burden of the acquisition from falling on the acquired company. However, the additional limit,

126. E. Sanz Gadea "Anteproyecto y Proyecto de Ley del Impuesto sobre Sociedades. Nota sobre los Gastos Financieros" (Crónica Tributaria: Boletín de Actualidad 2014, no. 3), p. 59.
127. E. Sanz Gadea "El leveraged-buy-out en el Proyecto de Ley del Impuesto sobre Sociedades" in http://www.loyolaandnews.es/masteresoficialesloyola/el-leveraged-buy-out-en-el-proyecto-de-ley-del-impuesto-sobre-sociedades/ (last visit July 10, 2019).

like the IDBR contained in Articles 16.1-16.4 CITA is a mere timing rule, and, therefore, financial expenses exceeding the additional 30% limit of the operating profit of the acquiring company can be carried forward to the following fiscal years, without time limits. However, the additional limit applies before the IDBR.[128] Therefore: (1) if financial expenses are below the special limit for LBOs, they are added to the remaining financial costs of the company and deducted following the IDBR; (2) if financial expenses are above the special limit for LBOs, the excess can be carried forward to the following fiscal years and deducted according to the special rule of Article 16.5 and the IDBR.

It must be noted that, in the case of mergers, the application of the rule will be very difficult, if not impossible. Indeed, the mixture of assets, liabilities and equity generated by a merger will significantly hamper the identification of the separate operating profits of the acquiring and the acquired company.[129]

[3] LBOs and Prohibition of Financial Assistance

As stated before, LBOs have been suspected in Spain of falling within the prohibition of financial assistance contained in Articles 143.2 and 150 of the Corporate Enterprises Act according to which a company may not advance funds, nor make loans, nor provide securities, nor provide any kind of financial assistance with a view to the acquisition of its shares by a third party. The merger between the acquiring and the target company normally following LBOs might potentially be considered as (prohibited) financial assistance. This suspicion has been used by distinguished Spanish authors[130] to suggest the nondeductibility of interests paid in LOB transactions on the basis of a provision contained in the Spanish CITA prohibiting the deduction of illegal expenses for Corporate Income Tax Purposes (Article 15.f) CITA). In our view, this interpretation should be strongly rejected for the following reasons: (i) the reform operated in 2006 in the Second Company Law Directive significantly moderated the prohibition of financial assistance; (ii) Article 35 of the Corporate Restructuring Act[131] explicitly recognized merger LBO transactions. Even if it is true that the very article requires the issuance of an expert opinion stating whether the merger implies financial assistance, it is no less true that the provision has helped to acknowledge that LBOs are not per se prohibited; (iii) Article 16.5 CITA also implies an implicit recognition of LBOs within tax law. Should LBOs be prohibited, it would make little sense to regulate the deductibility of interest accrued in such transactions, particularly after a rule prohibiting the deduction of illegal expenses was introduced in the Spanish CITA in 2014. It

128. As indicated by the Spanish General Directorate of Taxes in its Ruling no. V1664/2015 of May 28, 2015.

129. E. Sanz Gadea "Anteproyecto y Proyecto de Ley del Impuesto sobre Sociedades. Nota sobre los Gastos Financieros", fn. 127, p. 59. A. López-Santacruz Montes *Memento. Impuesto sobre Sociedades 2018*, fn. 95, at 747.

130. E. Sanz Gadea "El leveraged-buy-out en el Proyecto de Ley del Impuesto sobre Sociedades", fn. 128. Less categorical in E. Sanz Gadea "Anteproyecto y Proyecto de Ley del Impuesto sobre Sociedades. Nota sobre los Gastos Financieros", fn. 127, pp. 59-60.

131. *Ley 3/2009, de 3 de abril, sobre modificaciones estructurales de las sociedades mercantiles.*

could be argued that the tax authorities should first analyze the LBO transaction from a commercial law perspective, prohibiting the deduction of interests accrued if they were incurred in as a result of financial assistance and applying Article 16.5 if that is not the case. Though this approach is sound in theory, it is problematic in practice, taking into account: (1) that the nondeduction of an illegal expense according to Article 15.f) CITA requires a previous statement of unlawfulness by the corresponding (nontax) Court or Administrative Body something that is still a contended issue in Spain; (2) the lawfulness of LBOs continues to be a matter of discussion among commercial lawyers,[132] and therefore the intervention of the tax authorities in this controversy might generate additional confusion.

132. *See*: Sánchez Calero, Juan; Fernández Torres, Isabel "Fusiones apalancadas, asistencia financiera y concurso (oportunidad y acierto del art.35 LME)" in *Documentos de Trabajo del Departamento de Derecho Mercantil* (2011, n. 38, 49 p.).

CHAPTER 9

The Netherlands

Harm van den Broek

---

§9.01 INTRODUCTION

As of 1 January 2019, all European Union (EU) Member States should have implemented most of the measures targeted at combating tax avoidance enshrined in the so-called Anti-Tax Avoidance Directive 1 (ATAD1). In this chapter, the author discusses the way in which Article 4 of ATAD1, the interest limitation rule based on companies' Earnings before interest, tax, depreciation and amortization (EBITDA), has been implemented in the Netherlands.

In section §9.02, the legislative process in the Netherlands is considered. Section §9.03 deals extensively with the various aspects of the calculation of the interest limitation. In section §9.04, the position of foreign permanent establishments is explained and in section §9.05, the Dutch provisions for the carry-forward of non-deductible interest charges. Sections §9.06 and §9.07 deal with the exceptions for group regimes and for public infrastructure projects. Section §9.08 discusses how the Netherlands restricts the possibilities for trade in companies carrying forward non-deductible interest. The compatibility of the Dutch interest limitation rule with primary EU law is discussed in section §9.09. The entry into force and the conclusions are dealt with in sections §9.10 and §9.11 respectively.

§9.02 THE DUTCH LEGISLATIVE PROCESS

In July 2017, the Dutch government published a consultation document[1] for the purpose of public debate concerning the implementation of the European Anti-Tax Avoidance Directive 2016/1164 (ATAD1). This consultation document contained a

---

1. https://www.internetconsultatie.nl/consultatiedocumentatad1.

draft legislative proposal with the various legislative options offered by ATAD1 to EU Member States. The then-existing government, which was at the end of its mandate, left it up to the present government to make the various policy choices involved.

In fact, in the autumn of 2017, the newly formed government presented its governmental legislative program[2] for the four years ahead which reflected the government's choices concerning the implementation of ATAD1. The government considered the interest limitation measure important in order to not only combat tax avoidance but also contribute to the approximation of the tax treatment of debt-financing and equity financing of business. The government opted for a robust implementation of the earnings stripping provision, with an interest limitation of up to 30% of the EBITDA and a threshold of only EUR 1,000,000 instead of EUR 3,000,000. The Dutch government decided not to exercise the possibility to make exceptions on the basis of the equity of the group, on the basis of the EBITDA of the group[3] or for stand-alone companies.[4] The government decided the new interest limitation rule should come into immediate force, without a grandfathering clause concerning existing loans.[5] Furthermore, it chose not to apply alternative equivalent interest limitation rules up to the year 2024. The legislator also considered it unnecessary to create an exception for financial institutions, assuming that the measure would be ineffective for banks[6] which generally receive more interest than they are charged. The government did, however, introduce a temporary measure concerning existing projects of public infrastructure.

Together with the introduction of the general earnings stripping provision of ATAD1, other existing general interest limitation rules have been cancelled in the Dutch Corporate Income Tax Act (CIT). This regards the interest limitation concerning the debt-financing of subsidiary companies (Article 13l CIT) and the interest limitation concerning the takeover by a fiscal unity of a subsidiary (Article 15ad CIT). Furthermore, the specific limitation of the carry-forward of losses of holding and financing companies (Article 20, paragraphs 4-6, CIT) has also been cancelled.

Altogether, taking into account the various choices that the Dutch government made as regards the options offered by ATAD1, the introduction of the new interest limitation rule in the CIT should result in an increase of revenues of EUR 1.1 billion in 2019 and EUR 2.0 billion on a structural basis.[7] Since the Dutch government did not generally intend to increase the tax burden for business, but rather to remain an attractive place for business, it has decided to use the additional revenues for a reduction of the general tax rate of the corporate income tax.

From 1 January 2019, by means of the *Wet implementatie eerste EU-richtlijn antibelastingontwijking*,[8] the Netherlands has implemented the provisions[9] of the

2. Regeerakkoord 2017, *Vertrouwen in de toekomst*, https://www.rijksoverheid.nl/regering/regeerakkoord-vertrouwen-in-de-toekomst.
3. Article 4, para. 5 ATAD1.
4. Article 4, para. 3 sub b ATAD1.
5. Article 4, para. 4 sub a ATAD1.
6. Article 4, para. 7 ATAD1.
7. Kamerstukken II 2018/19, 35030, nr. 3, p. 21.
8. Staatsblad 2018/508.

European ATAD1 of 2016. ATAD1 provides minimum rules and reflects the discussions concerning the Base Erosion and Profit Shifting (BEPS) project at the Organisation for Economic Co-operation and Development (OECD) level.[10] In the following sections, the various elements of the Dutch interest limitation rule are discussed, as laid down in a new Article 15b Corporate Income Tax (CIT).

§9.03 THE INTEREST LIMITATION

[A] Maximum Interest Limitation

Article 15b, paragraph 1, CIT provides:[11]

> 1. When computing the profits of a specific year, the surplus of interest charges shall not be deductible, to the extent that it exceeds the highest of the following two amounts:
>   a. 30% of the adjusted profits;
>   b. € 1,000,000.

Taxpayers shall apply the highest of the threshold either under a. or under b. An interest surplus up to EUR 1,000,000 does not effectively lead to an interest limitation. The threshold of EUR 1,000,000 cannot, however, be deducted from the amount of interest that is affected by subpar. a.[12] Parliamentary history provides the following example: in the case of a surplus of interest charges of EUR 1,700,000 and a maximum interest deduction (30% of EBITDA) of EUR 1,500,000, an amount of EUR 200,000 is excluded from tax deduction in the fiscal year concerned. Since the threshold of EUR 1,000,000 is lower than the 30% threshold of the EBITDA, the threshold of EUR 1,000,000 is irrelevant in this case.[13]

Where the ATAD1 allows a threshold of EUR 3,000,000, the Dutch legislator has chosen to apply a threshold of only EUR 1,000,000 and, consequently, a more severe approach. This choice was made in order to make the measure more effective in combating excessive interest deductions and in the approximation of the tax treatment of debt-financing and equity financing.[14] As such, this is in line with Article 3 ATAD1, which provides minimum rules of tax base protection. Member States are free to adopt more severe provisions, as long as they are in line with the fundamental freedoms. Various authors, however, have indicated that this severe approach could result in a competitive disadvantage for the Netherlands as an attractive place of business.[15] However, it should be specified that the government did not make use of the possibility

9. The Netherlands also implemented as of 1 January 2019 the provisions concerning seat transfers of companies as laid down in Article 5 ATAD1, despite the fact that the deadline for implementation of Article 5 ATAD1 is, by way of exception, 1 January 2020.
10. Compare OECD BEPS Report 2015, Action 4.
11. Translation, at this stage and further on, by the author.
12. Kamerstukken II 2018/19, 35030, nr. 3, p. 12.
13. *Ibid.*
14. Kamerstukken II 2018/19, 35030, nr. 3, p. 11.
15. S.A. Stevens, 'Implementatie van de earningstrippingmaatregel', *Tijdschrift Fiscaal Ondernemingsrecht* 2019/161.2, section 2.2.

to limit the deduction of interest to a lower percentage than 30% of the EBITDA. In that regard, the provisions are not particularly severe. Since the 'excessive' interest payments are not re-characterized as dividend, they often result in economic double taxation. In that respect, the aim to approximate debt-financing and equity financing has not been reached. According to parliamentary history, about 5,000 companies in the Netherlands have an EBITDA of more than EUR 3,300,000 and would be allowed to deduct an interest surplus of more than EUR 1,000,000.[16]

[B] The Surplus of Interest Charges

Article 15b, paragraph 2, CIT defines the 'surplus of interest charges':

> 2. The surplus of interest charges is the amount of interest charges relating to loans minus the amount of interest received in connection to loans, to the extent that the interest charged and interest received is, disregarding the application of this provision, taken into account for the computation of the profit of a specific year. The surplus of interest charges must be at least zero.

From paragraph 2 it follows that the interest limitation rule of the new Article 15b CIT only applies to interest payments that would otherwise have been tax-deductible. With this condition, the Dutch legislator intends to avoid the accumulation of various national interest limitation rules and the risk of a double adjustment of the company's taxable profits. This implies, for example, that the interest payments must be adjusted according to the arm's-length principle before the earnings stripping provision is applied.[17] Furthermore, for the purpose of Article 15b CIT, only interest received is taken into account if it is subject to tax in the hands of the creditor. For example, interest received that, by way of exception, is exempt under the participation exemption of Article 13 CIT is not taken into account.

If, in a specific year, the interest received were higher than the interest charged, theoretically the surplus of that year would be negative. Theoretically, a non-deductible positive surplus of the previous year that is carried forward could be set off against the negative surplus of later years. The legislator, however, did not accept such results and determined in section 2 that, 'The surplus of interest charges must be at least zero.'[18] Therefore, it is not possible to set off a positive surplus of interest charges against a negative surplus of interest charges in later years.

[C] The Adjusted Profit (EBITDA)

Since the interest limitation is calculated as 30% of the adjusted profits, it is necessary to provide a definition of the adjusted profit (EBITDA). This is done in paragraph 3:

16. Kamerstukken II 2018/19, 35030, nr. 7, p. 31.
17. Compare Stevens, section 4.5.
18. Kamerstukken II 2018/19, 35030, nr. 7, pp. 22-23; compare Stevens, section 4.1.

3. The adjusted profit, as referred to in par. 1, is the profit as computed without the application of par. 1:
   a. Increased by the amount of depreciations on assets of a specific year as determined without the application of par. 7;
   b. Increased by the amount of the amortizations to a lower book value of assets of a specific year and decreased by the amount of the recaptures of previous amortizations to lower values of assets during that specific year; and
   c. Increased by the surplus of interest charges of that specific year, except for the amount of interest charges referred to in par. 6, subpart d, as part of the surplus of interest charges;

   whereas the amount of adjusted profit is determined to be at least zero.

The starting point of the calculation of the adjusted profit is the amount of taxable profits of the company ('the profit as computed without the application of par. 1').[19] This results in exempted income not being included in the calculation and does not increase the amount of tax-deductible interest. With regard to the Netherlands, important exemptions are the participation exemption related to dividends and capital gains on shares in active and normally taxed companies in which the parent has an interest of at least 5%. Also, profits from foreign permanent establishments are not included in the taxable base. According to literature, foreign profits for which the company is entitled to a tax credit are included in the tax base. One may, however, wonder whether that is in line with the BEPS-4-report.[20] Moreover, the setting off of losses not yet compensated does not affect the EBITDA.[21]

In the initial draft of the consultation document, the profit would not be increased by the amortizations that had taken place. That would mean that the Netherlands would apply an EBITD (Earnings Before Interest, Taxation, Depreciation) instead of an EBITDA[22]. Van Strien, however, pointed out that this did not seem to be in line with Article 4, paragraph 2 ATAD1. Van Strien, however, also indicated that, since the Directive contains minimum rules, the legislator is generally allowed to apply more severe measures, such as the EBITD instead of the EBITDA.[23] In the end, the text of the draft tax act was changed in this respect, and the legislator embraced the EBITDA instead of the EBITD. In the text as adopted, for the calculation of the EBITDA, the taxable profits are also increased by the depreciation and amortization on assets. As literature noticed, this does not apply to the depreciation of stock.[24] The recapture of a previous amortization, however, decreases the EBITDA.

In some cases, interest charges cannot be deducted immediately but shall be capitalized as production costs of assets. Paragraph 3, subsection c provides that such interest charges must not be added to the taxable profits in order to calculate the

19. D.S. Smit, 'De Nederlandse implementatie van de earningstrippingbepaling uit ATAD 1', *Maandblad Belastingbeschouwingen* 2018/11, section 3.2.1.
20. BEPS-4-report, p. 44; Smit, section 3.2.1.
21. Kamerstukken II 2018/19, 35030, nr. 3, p. 35; Smit, section 3.2.1.
22. EBITDA also includes Amortization.
23. J. van Strien, 'Beperking renteaftrek via EBITDA-regels in ATAD1', *Weekblad Fiscaal Recht* 2018/19, section 4.2.
24. Smit, section 3.2.1.

adjusted profits (EBITDA). This makes sense because these interest charges have not (yet) been deducted tax effectively.

[D] Definitions of Loan, Interest Charges and Interest Received

[1] Introduction

Paragraph 6 provides definitions of the terms 'loan' and 'interest' for the purpose of Article 15b CIT:

> 6. For the purpose of this Article:
>   a. the following shall be considered as loan: a debt claim or a debt that results from an agreement of loan or from a comparable agreement;
>   b. the following shall also be considered as interest charges related to loans: costs related to loans and related to legal acts serving to cover the risks of interest or currency exchange fluctuations related to loans;
>   c. the following shall also be considered as interest charges related to loans and interest received related to loans: results from currency exchanges related to loans, as well as results related to legal acts serving to cover the risks of interest or currency exchange fluctuations related to loans;
>   d. the following shall also be considered as interest charges related to loans: interest charges related to loans which, before the application of par. 7 shall be registered as production costs of assets, not taking into account the fact that those interest charges as such are not taken into account for the computation of the profits of a specific year.

[2] Definition of Loan

Both for the calculation of the EBITDA and the surplus of interest charges, in paragraph 2 of the Dutch provision, interest is defined as 'interest (...) in connection to loans'. As pointed out by Stevens,[25] Article 2, paragraph 1 ATAD1 does not contain such a connection of 'interest' to 'loans'. Also, Van Strien[26] and Smit[27] noticed that the Dutch legislator did not adhere to the definitions of the Directive. In the Dutch text, it is therefore important to determine what loans are. The definition of 'loan' in paragraph 6 is decisive, not the Dutch civil law definition of a loan.[28] For tax purposes, as in civil law, there should at least be an obligation to pay the loan back.[29] Parliamentary history related to the earnings stripping rule indicated that 'loans' must be considered financial-lease agreements, but not provisions and reserves.[30] It also applies to hire-purchase systems.[31] Literature has highlighted that for the purpose of other

25. Stevens, section 4.2.
26. Van Strien, section 4.3.
27. Smit, section 3.2.2.
28. Kamerstukken II 2018/19, 35030, nr. 3, p. 39; Stevens, section 4.2.
29. Hoge Raad 8 September 2006, BNB 2007/104; Stevens, section 4.2.
30. Kamerstukken II 2018/19, 35030, nr. 3, p. 39; Stevens, section 4.2; Smit, section 3.2.2.
31. Kamerstukken II 2018/19, 35030, nr. 3, p. 39; Smit, section 3.2.2.

interest limitation rules (Article 10a CIT), the Dutch Supreme Court ruled that also obligations in the form of annuities constitute loans.[32] According to doctrine, factoring agreements, operational lease and rental agreements shall not be considered as loans.[33] With regard to certain payments related to securitization structures, there may be some doubt as to whether they shall be considered interest.[34] Literature, however, noticed that, unfortunately, parliamentary history provides only a limited explanation of the various terms and more extended guidelines would have been useful for practice.[35]

[3] Definition of Interest

The Dutch implementation act as well as ATAD1 apply a wide interpretation of the term ‘interest’ which includes payments that, from an economic point of view, are equivalent to interest payments.[36] This follows primarily from legislative history. Paragraph 6 does not provide an exhaustive definition of ‘interest’. It mentions which payments should *also* be considered as interest payments. These include costs related to loans and related to relevant legal acts, resulting from currency exchanges and from legal acts serving to cover the risks of interest or currency exchange fluctuations. If a swap-agreement turns a variable interest into a fixed interest, this fixed interest must be taken into account.[37] The accrual of the market value of a loan that, because of its low or absent interest rate, was acquired below its nominal value must also be considered as interest.[38] That does, however, not apply to the fluctuation of the value of a loan in general.[39] The definition also includes interest that as a result of an arm’s-length adjustment must be taken into account.[40] The definition does not include interest that has been carried forward pursuant to the earnings stripping provision.[41] In principle, interest charges are the mirror image of interest received,[42] *see also* paragraph 6, under c of Article 15b CIT. Obviously, such a mirror image does not exist in the case of costs related to interest charges as under paragraph 6, under b.

[4] Capitalized Interest

If companies produce new assets for their own use, the costs related to the production of such assets cannot immediately be deducted tax effectively, but must be added to the production cost of the asset and can be depreciated during the following years as part of the asset. This rule can be derived from case law of the Dutch Supreme Court

32. Hoge Raad 19 March 2019, BNB 2010/215; Stevens, section 4.2.
33. Stevens, section 4.2.
34. *Ibid.*
35. Smit, section 3.2.2.
36. Van Strien, section 4.3; Smit, section 3.2.2; Stevens, section 4.3.
37. Kamerstukken I 2018/19, 35030, nr. C, p. 12; Stevens, section 4.3.
38. Kamerstukken II 2018/19, 35030, nr. 3, p. 37; Stevens, section 4.3.
39. Kamerstukken I 2018/19, 35030, nr. C, p. 12; Stevens, section 4.3.
40. Kamerstukken II 2018/19, 35030, nr. 7, p. 41; Stevens, section 4.3.
41. Kamerstukken I 2018/19, 35030, nr. C, p. 13; Stevens, section 4.3.
42. Stevens, section 4.3.

concerning profit determination for tax purposes.[43] It may also apply to interest charges related to the production of assets. These interest payments must be capitalized. Despite the fact that this interest cannot (yet) be deducted, pursuant to paragraph 6, under d, such capitalized interest is included in the definition of 'interest' of Article 15b CIT and consequently increases the 'surplus of interest charges' and also the interest limitation.

Paragraph 7 of Article 15b CIT contains a specific provision concerning the tax deductibility of such interest charges that normally should be capitalized:

> 7. To the extent that a surplus of interest charges as referred to in par. 6, subpart d, exceeds the highest of the amounts mentioned in par. 1, those interest charges are, in contravention to Article 8 CIT in conjunction with Articles 3.25 and 3.29b of the Income Tax Act 2001, not registered as production costs of the business asset nor is such interest deductible in the computation of the profits of that year. For that purpose, if the surplus of interest charges in a specific year consists of interest charges as referred to in par. 6, subpart d and of other interest charges related to loans, then those other interest charges are the first to be excluded from tax deductibility.

In other words, if the interest limitation applies to interest that should normally be capitalized, this interest must, by way of exception, *not* be capitalized, but treated as regular interest payments that are affected by the earnings stripping provision. And if the surplus of interest charges consists both of regular interest and of interest that should be capitalized, the interest limitation applies in order of priority to the regular interest, while the other interest is capitalized as much as possible. Parliamentary history[44] provides an example that can be summarized as follows:

> Example
>
> A company has interest charges of 50 as part of the production costs of assets. Regular interest charges amount to 20. The adjusted profit is 100. The total amount of interest charges is therefore 70 (50 + 20). The maximum amount of deductible interest is 30 (30% of 100). Non-deductible interest is consequently 40 (70 - 30). This amount concerns in the first place the regular interest of 20, and for the rest (20) interest which would otherwise have been capitalized. These interest payments shall not be capitalized or deducted, but can be carried forward to future years and be deducted if there is unused EBITDA. The rest of the interest (30) must be capitalized as production cost of assets.

Pursuant to paragraph 7 (part of) the interest payments that otherwise would have been capitalized must now be carried forward to future years as part of the non-deductible interest. Stevens notes that this might even be advantageous for taxpayers, because it may result in an earlier effective tax deduction than in the case of the capitalization of the interest followed by the depreciation of the asset.[45] In the Netherlands, the depreciation of assets takes at least five years, depending on the type

43. HR 2 April 1969, nr. 16.101, BNB 1969/108.
44. Kamerstukken II 2018/19, 35030, nr. 3, pp. 40-41.
45. Stevens, section 4.4.

of asset. By contrast, if there is sufficient EBITDA in year two, all interest payments from year one that were forwarded can be deducted in year two.

In literature, there is some discussion as to whether the Dutch implementation measure concerning capitalized interest is identical to the provisions of ATAD1. Article 2, paragraph 1 of the Directive considers 'capitalized interest included in the balance sheet value of a related asset, or the amortization of capitalized interest' as interest. In practice, capitalized interest can be part of the balance sheet of an asset, but it can also simply be an anticipated interest payment to, for example, a bank. The definition of the Directive seems to apply to all forms of capitalized interest. Article 15b, paragraph 6, under d of the Dutch CIT, by contrast, considers as interest 'interest charges related to loans which, before application of par. 7 shall be registered as *production costs of assets (...)*' [emphasis added]. This definition seems to exclude capitalized interest that is not related to the production costs of assets, for example interest related to stock.[46] The author agrees with Smit[47] that it is appropriate for the Directive, in one way or another, to also apply to capitalized interest. Where a self-produced asset is depreciated, the interest element of an annual depreciation is as such not visible, and therefore it makes sense to apply the interest limitation at the moment of capitalization. However, if an anticipated interest payment to a creditor remains visible on the balance sheet, the earnings stripping rule can be applied in the year to which an interest payment is attributed. Capitalized interest should in any case, not escape from the earnings stripping provision.

§9.04 CARVE-OUT OF LOANS OF FOREIGN PERMANENT ESTABLISHMENTS

Since 2012, Article 15e of the CIT Act has contained a carve-out of the results of foreign permanent establishments. From that year onwards, the profits of foreign permanent establishments have no longer been considered part of the tax base of resident companies, except in the case of permanent establishments with so-called final losses in the sense of the Marks & Spencer ruling of the Court of Justice of the European Union.[48]

Until 2012, companies were in principle taxed on their worldwide income including the profits of foreign permanent establishments. Under this former regime, however, profits of foreign permanent establishments were generally exempt with progression as a result of bilateral tax treaties[49] or as a result of the unilateral Decree for the avoidance of double taxation.[50]

46. Stevens, section 4.4.
47. Smit, section 3.2.2.
48. CJEU 13 December 2005, Case C-446/03 (*Marks & Spencer*).
49. It is standing policy that in its tax treaties, the Netherlands adopts the exemption with progression system as a measure to avoid double taxation in the case of a permanent establishment.
50. The '*Besluit voorkoming dubbele belasting 2001*' applies in the absence of applicable tax treaties. It used to include an exemption with progression rule for the results of foreign permanent establishments of resident companies.

Since 2012, the profits of foreign permanent establishments have not been included in the CIT tax base and this also applies to interest charges related to loans that are attributed to foreign permanent establishments. Therefore, loans related to foreign permanent establishments can be excluded from the scope of the new earnings stripping rule because interest payments on such loans are already non-deductible on the basis of the aforementioned rule:

> 4. The surplus of interest charges does not include interest charges related to loans nor interest received related to loans to the extent that these constitute profit from another state as referred to in Article 15e on which the exemption for foreign business profits applies.

§9.05 CARRY-FORWARD OF NON-DEDUCTIBLE INTEREST CHARGES

Where the ATAD1 offers various options concerning the possibility of carrying forward non-deductible interest charges, the Netherlands has adopted the system of carry-forward without any time constraints:

> 5. To the extent that in a specific year pursuant to paragraph 1, the surplus of interest charges is not deducted, but is carried forward to the next year and is deductible for the computation of the profit of that year, to the extent that the surplus of interest charges of that later year is lower than the highest of the two amounts, mentioned in the first paragraph. The deduction of surpluses of interest charges which, pursuant to the first paragraph, were excluded from deduction, takes place in the order in which those surpluses have accrued. The tax inspector determines the amount of the surplus of interest charges that can be carried forward by means of a decision that is subject to appeal.

From paragraph 5 it follows that interest charges that could not be deducted pursuant to paragraph 1 can be carried forward and deducted in years in which the threshold for deduction has not been reached. This also leads to interest charges that are carried forward benefitting from the two thresholds.[51] The tax inspector determines the amount of interest charges that can be carried forward. Taxpayers can file an administrative appeal against such a decision in the event that it contains a miscalculation. This administrative decision in turn is subject to appeal at the administrative court. Once the deadline for the appeal has expired, the decision acquires a binding effect and cannot be reviewed in later years in which the interest payments should actually be deducted.

As an alternative, the Directive grants the option to carry back the surplus of interest charges that cannot be deducted to previous years, but the Dutch legislator rejected this option. Various authors have drawn attention to the fact that the current Dutch legislation has a procyclical effect[52] and may damage the economy. Companies that suffer losses have no EBITDA. That means that in addition to their losses, they are faced with an interest limitation. As the non-deductible interest charges cannot be

51. Compare Kamerstukken II 2018/19, 35030, nr. 7, p. 22; Stevens, section 5.1.
52. Van Strien, secs 3.8 and 4.5.

carried back, this immediately results in an additional tax burden (liquidity burden), besides the current operational losses. This immediate, additional tax burden increases the risk that such companies may not survive their difficult financial situations. If, by contrast, it were possible to carry back the non-deductible surplus of interest charges, then initially, the immediate, additional tax burden would be mitigated.

§9.06 GROUP REGIMES

As indicated above, the Netherlands has chosen not to make use of the various options for group regimes. Therefore, the interest limitation applies per taxpayer. Each separate taxpayer can therefore make use of the threshold of EUR 1,000,000. It should be noted, however, that the Netherlands applies the fiscal unity system, which is an optional system in group situations. Under that system, the profits of the companies that are part of the fiscal unity are taxed in the hands of the parent company of the fiscal unity as if they were branches of the parent company. Consequently, the fiscal unity can benefit from the threshold of EUR 1,000,000 only once. Instead, if the fiscal unity regime is not applied, each of the parent and subsidiary companies can benefit from a threshold of EUR 1,000,000. This is a disadvantage of the fiscal unity regime. However, the EBITDA will be determined at the level of the fiscal unity on the basis of the consolidated profits and losses of all the companies of the fiscal unity, which will generally result in a higher EBITDA. That is an advantage of the fiscal unity, in particular if one of the companies of a fiscal unity suffers losses and consequently has an EBITDA of nil. The recent Dutch tax act to bring the fiscal unity regime in line with the *Groupe Steria* ruling[53] of the Court of Justice of the European Union does not include any measures concerning the application of the fiscal unity regime in respect of the earnings stripping rule.[54]

§9.07 PUBLIC INFRASTRUCTURE PROJECTS

Article IIA of the *Wet implementatie eerste EU-richtlijn antibelastingontwijking* contains a specific rule concerning public infrastructure projects:

> For the purpose of the application of Article 15b of the Corporate Income Tax 1969:
>
> a. the surplus of interest charges does not include interest charges and interest received concerning loans that are connected to the financing of long-term public infrastructure projects existing on 25 October 2018 and approved by ministerial decrees for which a periodical fee is due by the public authorities for its availability on the basis of an integrated contract for the design, construction, financing, maintenance and exploitation; and
> b. profits resulting from projects as referred to under a. are not taken into account for the calculation of the adjusted profit.

53. Wet spoedreparatie fiscale eenheid, nr. 34 959, adopted by the Dutch Senate on 23 April 2019.
54. Stevens, section 2.3.

On the basis of this provision, only existing long-term public infrastructure projects are exempted from the interest limitation. The exemption only applies to those projects that have been approved by decree. The government held that this exemption does not apply to semi-public housing corporations that rent out low-cost dwellings to citizens with low incomes.

§9.08 TRADE IN COMPANIES WITH INTEREST CHARGES CARRIED FORWARD

The fact that a company is allowed to carry forward non-deductible interest charges means that the company will have to pay less tax in the future. That right has an economic value and might result in a practice of trading in shell companies carrying forward non-deductible interest charges. The Dutch legislator has introduced a legal provision to combat such trade, similar to the provisions to combat trade in companies with losses not yet compensated. This anti-abuse provision applies in case of a significant change in the economic interest in a company. Article 15ba, paragraph 1, first sentence CIT, that will apply from 1 January 2020 onwards provides:

> 1. If it appears that, compared to the beginning of the oldest fiscal year of which a surplus of interest charges in the sense of Article 15b CIT has not yet been fully deducted, the final economic interest in a taxpayer has changed significantly, then the surpluses of interest charges that have accrued before the moment that the change of economic interest took place, will not be taken into account anymore, by means of exception to Article 15b, par. 5, for the computation of the profits after the moment of such a change.

As a result of this provision, non-deductible interest charges can no longer be carried forward after a significant change in the economic interest in the company. A change of economic interest can be caused by the sale of shares, but also, for example, if the company issues shares to new shareholders or if an option on the company's shares is granted. Here, a substance over form approach is applied. This provision applies in the case of a significant change in the economic interest of at least 30%. Whereas the trade in companies with losses is only combated in the case of companies holding passive assets in particular or companies whose activities have ceased, the present anti-abuse provision applies without any exceptions. Also, other exceptions do not apply in a similar way to companies with interest charges carried forward, for example in the case of the inheritance of such shares. From that point of view, the present anti-abuse provision seems to contain overkill.

§9.09 COMPATIBILITY WITH PRIMARY EU LAW

[A] Fundamental Freedoms

The Dutch interest limitation rule of Article 15b CIT applies both to resident taxpayers and to non-resident taxpayers.[55] The rule applies to loans from group companies and to loans from external parties. Furthermore, the interest limitation rule applies to loans from domestic creditors and non-resident creditors. Therefore, as literature has pointed out,[56] at first sight, the rule does not seem to hamper the exercise of any of the fundamental freedoms.

After the *Groupe Steria*[57] ruling, it is, however, also useful to examine whether the application *at group level* of the interest limitation rule of ATAD1 is in line with the fundamental freedoms. In fact, in its *X BV* ruling,[58] the CJEU ruled that the application at group level of the Dutch interest limitation rule laid down in the Dutch Article 10a Corporate Income Tax infringed upon the freedom of establishment. In *X BV*, a Dutch company received a loan from its Swedish parent company in order to finance a capital contribution in its Italian subsidiary company. Under the Dutch Article 10a CIT, interest payments to associated companies are not deductible if the loan is historically connected to a capital contribution in another associated company. Consequently, the interest payments of X BV were not tax-deductible. By contrast, if the Italian subsidiary company had been resident in the Netherlands and if X BV and the Italian company had opted for the Dutch group regime (the so-called fiscal eenheid), then the interest limitation would not have applied. This possibility did not exist, however, since the Dutch 'fiscale eenheid' regime only applies to resident companies (or to Dutch branches of non-resident companies). The Dutch 'fiscale eenheid' regime is far-reaching and results in the various companies of the 'fiscale eenheid' being taxed as if they constitute together one single taxpayer, that is the parent company. Under the 'fiscale eenheid' regime, the activities and the assets and liabilities of the subsidiary companies are attributed to the parent company. Consequently, for tax purposes, the subsidiary companies are no longer treated as independent legal entities, but as branches of the parent company. As a result, for tax purposes, the loan of a parent company to a subsidiary company which is part of the same 'fiscale eenheid' is considered to be a capital contribution to a branch of the same legal entity, in which case Article 10a CIT does not apply. The option for the fiscale eenheidsregime may therefore, only in domestic situations, neutralize the interest limitation rule of Article 10a CIT, and this infringes upon the freedom of establishment. After the *X BV* ruling, the Dutch government presented a tax act[59] pursuant to which the fiscale eenheidsregime shall be disregarded for the purpose of the interest limitation rule of Article 10a

55. Smit, section 4.
56. Smit, section 4; Stevens, section 8.
57. CJEU 2 September 2015, C-386/14 (*Groupe Steria*).
58. CJEU 22 February 2019, C-398/16 (*X BV*).
59. Wet spoedreparatie fiscale eenheid, nr. 34 959, adopted by the Dutch Senate on 23 April 2019.

CIT, resulting effectively in an interest limitation also in the case of a domestic fiscal unity.

So, does the earnings stripping provision of ATAD1 in combination with the Dutch fiscal unity regime infringe upon the freedom of establishment? As pointed out by Smit,[60] during the European legislative process of ATAD1, with regard to the application of the earnings stripping provision at group level pursuant to Article 4, second sentence, under a, ATAD1, the Dutch presidency noted: '*The possible exclusion of national groups will need further refection: not only are there legal difficulties with such exclusions (...).*'[61] This further reflection did not, however, take place. An evident advantage of the application of the earnings stripping rule at fiscal unity level (group level) is that the interest limitation is calculated on the basis of the consolidated EBITDA of all the companies of the fiscal unity, which will generally be higher than the EBITDA of a company on a stand-alone basis. This advantage is limited to resident companies because only they can be part of the fiscal unity. The fact that the EBITDA of non-resident group companies cannot be taken into account hampers the freedom of establishment. The author agrees with Smit that the impossibility of consolidating foreign EBITDA is justified on the ground of the territoriality principle and the need to safeguard the cohesion of the tax system, in a similar way as the fact that losses of foreign subsidiary companies shall not be taken into account (unless these constitute final losses).[62] The fact that the foreign EBITDA is not taken into account is consistent with the fact that also interest payments by non-resident group companies are not taken into account. It should be further emphasized that the EBITDA of the non-resident group companies is already taken into account in their states of residence, and steps should be taken to prevent EBITDA from being taken into account twice, in two different states.

A third aspect that will be illustrated with an example is more worrying. A Dutch fiscal unity consists of three domestic companies, Parent BV, Subsidiary 1 BV and Subsidiary 2 BV. All the companies are loss making and have an EBITDA of zero. Subsidiary 1 grants a loan to subsidiary 2 at a fixed interest rate of 6%. If the companies were not part of a fiscal unity, subsidiary 2 would be faced with the earnings stripping rule, because its EBITDA is zero, while subsidiary 1 would anyhow be taxed on the interest received. As a result of the fiscal unity regime, the 'intra-fiscal unity' loan is disregarded for tax purposes and the group is not faced with the earnings stripping rule. By contrast, the earnings stripping rule would not be neutralized by the fiscal unity regime if subsidiary 1 were established in another EU Member State. In that case, it cannot be part of the fiscal unity regime and the loan is not 'intra-fiscal unity' and cannot be disregarded. Therefore, it appears that in order to bring the earnings

60. Smit, section 4. Also E.J.W. Heithuis expressed his doubts about the compatibility with EU law of the Dutch earnings stripping provision during the conference '50 jaar vennootschapsbelasting' which took place on 27 June 2019 at the Erasmus Universiteit Rotterdam.
61. Room document 1, Working Party on Tax Questions – Direct Taxation, 15 April 2016.
62. CJEU 25 February 2010, C-337/08 (*X Holding*).

stripping rule into line with the freedom of establishment, the recent amendment based on the *X BV* ruling should be extended to apply also to the earnings stripping rule.[63]

[B] Exemptions and State Aid Provisions

During the discussion in Parliament, various politicians requested the introduction of an exemption from the interest limitation rule for the so-called woningbouwcorporaties (*Dwelling-building-corporations*). These are semi-public organizations that build, manage and rent out dwellings of good quality to people with low income on a non-profit basis and are governed by the 2015 revised 'Woningwet' (*Act on dwellings*). It was considered undesirable to raise the tax burdens for these organizations with a public function and responsibility. The Minister of Finance, however, considered the introduction of such exemption as a potential breach of the prohibition to grant state aid which is in violation of Article 107 TFEU and rejected the proposals to that end. He also considered that this exemption would not fall under the exemption for public infrastructures as stated under Article 4 ATAD1.[64] In the end, the government financially compensated the 'woningbouwcorporaties' with a reduction of the general tax rate of the so-called verhuurderbelasting, a tax on the renting out of multiple dwellings.

§9.10 ENTRY INTO FORCE

Pursuant to its Article III, paragraph 1, subpart a, the *Wet implementatie eerste EU-richtlijn antibelastingontwijking* came into force as from 1 January 2019. The provisions concerning the interest limitation shall be applied to fiscal years starting on or after 1 January 2019. During the consultation process, various parties pleaded in favour of a grandfathering clause for existing loans. The Dutch legislator, however, chose to apply these new rules also to loans already in existence on 17 June 2016 and not to make use of the possibility to exempt such existing loans. The main reason for this is the fact that the earnings stripping provision replaces two existing interest limitation rules. Adopting a grandfathering clause would have meant that two parallel sets of interest limitation rules would exist, which was considered undesirable. Furthermore, the budgetary consequences also played a role in the decision.

§9.11 CONCLUSIONS

The interest limitation rule of Article 4 ATAD1 has been implemented in the Netherlands by the *Wet implementatie eerste EU-richtlijn antibelastingontwijking* and entered into force as from 1 January 2019 with a grandfathering clause for existing public

63. See also J.J. van den Broek, 'De earningstripping regeling in strijd met de vrijheid van vestiging', *Nederlands Tijdschrift voor Fiscaal Recht*, 2019/1991, pp. 1-4. By contrast, O.C.R. Marres, 'Waarom de earningsstrippingregeling niet in strijd met het primaire Unierecht is', *Nederlands Tijdschrift voor Fiscaal Recht*, 2019/3022, pp. 1-3, holds that the new provision is in line with primary EU law.
64. Idem Stevens, section 6.

infrastructure projects but not for other existing loans. The Dutch government considered the measure important in order to combat tax avoidance, but also in order to contribute to the approximation of the tax treatment of debt-financing and equity financing of business. Therefore, the government opted for a robust interest limitation rule. The interest cap is set at 30% of the EBITDA with a threshold for small- and medium-sized businesses of only EUR 1,000,000. The definitions of 'loan' and 'interest' in the Dutch implementation measure are not identical to those of the Directive, but have the same broad scope of application and do not seem to infringe upon the Directive. The regime does not contain any of the options offered by ATAD1 for safe havens based on a group test, nor an exception for stand-alone companies. However, if a group of resident companies is taxed as a fiscal unity, then the interest limitation rule applies at the fiscal unity level. There is no exception for financial institutions. An exception for public housing corporations, which various politicians had wished for, was not adopted. Non-deductible losses can be carried forward without any time restraint, but cannot be carried back, and may therefore have a procyclical effect. Furthermore, an anti-abuse rule was introduced to combat the trade in companies that carry forward such non-deductible interest. The implementation seems to be in line with the text of the Directive and with state aid provisions, but there is some debate over whether the application of the interest limitation rule at 'fiscal unity' level is in line with the freedom of establishment. The aim of the Netherlands to approximate the tax treatment of debt-financing and equity financing seems to have failed, however, because the interest limitation rule does not provide for the re-characterization of interest in dividend and results in 'inclusion without deduction'. Together with the introduction of the general earnings stripping provision of ATAD1, other general interest limitation rules have been cancelled. The additional revenues raised by the earnings stripping have been used to decrease the general tax rate of the CIT. One may wonder whether the stringent Dutch implementation of the earnings stripping rule makes the Netherlands a little less attractive as a place of business. Only time will tell.

ANNEX TRANSLATION BY THE AUTHOR OF ARTICLE 15B WET OP DE VENNOOTSCHAPSBELASTING 1969 (DUTCH CORPORATE INCOME TAX ACT)

(1) When computing the profits of a specific year, the surplus of interest charges shall not be deductible, to the extent that it exceeds the highest of the following two amounts:
  (a) 30% of the adjusted profits;
  (b) EUR 1,000,000.

(2) The surplus of interest charges is the amount of interest charges relating to loans minus the amount of interest received in connection to loans, to the extent that the interest charged and interest received is, disregarding the application of this provision, taken into account for the computation of the profit of a specific year. The surplus of interest charges must be at least zero.

(3) The adjusted profit, as referred to in paragraph 1, is the profit as computed without the application of paragraph 1:
  (a) increased by the amount of depreciations on assets of a specific year as determined without the application of paragraph 7;
  (b) increased by the amount of the amortizations to a lower book value of assets of a specific year and decreased by the amount of recaptures of previous amortizations to lower values of assets during that specific year; and
  (c) increased by the surplus of interest charges of that specific year, except for the amount of interest charges referred to in paragraph 6, subpart d, as part of the surplus of interest charges;

  whereas the amount of adjusted profit is determined to be at least zero.

(4) The surplus of interest charges does not include interest charges related to loans nor interest received related to loans to the extent that these constitute profit from another state as referred to in Article 15e on which the exemption for foreign business profits applies.

(5) To the extent that, in a specific year pursuant to paragraph 1, the surplus of interest charges is not deducted, but it is carried forward to the next year and is deductible for the computation of the profit of that year, to the extent that the surplus of interest charges of that later year is less than the highest of the two amounts, mentioned in the first paragraph. The deduction of surpluses of interest charges which, pursuant to the first paragraph, were excluded from deduction takes place in the order in which those surpluses have accrued. The tax inspector determines the amount of the surplus of interest charges that can be carried forward by means of a decision that is subject to appeal.

(6) For the purpose of this Article:
  (a) the following shall be considered as loan: a debt claim or a debt that results from an agreement of loan or from a comparable agreement;

(b) the following shall also be considered as interest charges related to loans: costs related to loans and related to legal acts serving to cover the risks of interest or currency exchange fluctuations related to loans;

(c) the following shall also be considered as interest charges related to loans and interest received related to loans: results from currency exchanges related to loans, as well as results/profits related to legal acts serving to cover the risks of interest or currency exchange fluctuations related to loans;

(d) the following shall also be considered as interest charges related to loans: interest charges related to loans which, before the application of paragraph 7, shall be registered as production costs of assets, not taking into account the fact that those interest charges as such are not taken into account for the computation of the profits of a specific year.

(7) To the extent that a surplus of interest charges as referred to in paragraph 6, subpart d, exceeds the highest of the amounts mentioned in paragraph 1, those interest charges are, in contravention to Article 8 CIT in conjunction with Articles 3.25 and 3.29b of the Income Tax Act 2001, not registered as production costs of the business asset nor is such interest deductible in the computation of the profits of that year. For that purpose, if the surplus of interest charges in a specific year consists of interest charges as referred to in paragraph 6, subpart d and of other interest charges related to loans, then those other interest charges are the first to be excluded from tax deductibility.

CHAPTER 10
Comparative Survey

Marco Barassi

§10.01 THE DEVELOPMENT OF COMPARATIVE TAX LAW

Comparative law developed in private law and then spread to different areas of law such as constitutional law, commercial law, procedural law and so on.[1]

Only in recent decades, have scholars studied comparative tax law[2] moving from the mere juxtaposition of different tax rules to their actual comparison, focusing on the methods of comparative tax law.[3] The use of proper methods of comparative law is crucial in order to reach correct results: for example, it is not sufficient to read a tax law rule in a code to understand how the rule is actually applied. One needs to know how courts, the Tax Authority and scholars all interpret the rule. In other words, the different legal formants and the *law in action* are relevant, rather than the *law in the books*.

This is also true in a particular field of application of comparative law that is commonly known as legal transplant.

1. According to Zweigert, K., Kötz, H., *Introduzione al diritto comparato*, Milan, 1998, p. 80, private law scholars especially engaged in the study of legal systems theory. Scholars agree that comparative law is not limited any longer to private law.
2. Moessner, J.M., *Why and How to Compare Tax Law*, in *Liber Amicorum Luc Hinnekens*, Bruylant, Brussels, 2003, pp. 306 et seq.; Barassi, M., *Comparazione (Dir. Trib.)*, in Cassese, S. (ed.), *Dizionario di Diritto Pubblico*, II, Milan, 2006, p. 1070; Barassi, M., *Comparazione giuridica e studio del diritto tributario straniero*, in Uckmar, V. (ed.), *Diritto Tributario internazionale*, 2005, pp. 1499 et seq.; Barassi, M., *La comparazione nel diritto tributario*, Bergamo, 2002; Turonyi, V., *Comparative Tax Law*, The Hague, 2003, and Ault, H.J., Arnold, B.J., *Comparative Income Taxation. A Structural Analysis*, 3rd ed., Alphen aan den Rijn, 2010.
3. Moessner, J.M., *Why and How to Compare Tax Law*, pp. 308 et seq.; Barassi, M., *Comparazione (Dir. Trib.)*, pp. 1073 et seq.

Although comparative law studies have focused mainly on pinpointing the differences and similarities between different legal systems, legal transplant and the circulation of models have also led to much comparison.

Moreover, due to globalization, comparative law focuses mainly on similarities and convergence processes.[4] Contamination and exchange among legal systems are frequent; the role of supranational and international organizations—such as the European Union (EU) and Organisation for Economic Co-operation and Development (OECD)—promotes the circulation of legal models and the harmonization of legal rules.

As a result, law is often inspired by foreign experience, so legal rules and legal instruments cross from one country to another. The result of a transplant is not always successful because the foreign rule must be consistent with the legal order in the country in which it is imported.

Transplants are frequent also in tax law where many rules circulate among different countries.

Tax law shares the reasons for legal transplants with other areas of law: a foreign rule is imitated when the legislator seeks solutions to new problems (already tackled abroad) or new solutions to old problems. Some examples are the concept of abuse of law, group taxation, participation exemption, interest deduction and so on.

A peculiar example of the circulation of models is the convergence of legal systems toward tax rules proposed by the OECD and G20 in the Base Erosion and Profit Shifting (BEPS) Project and the EU as concerns the phenomenon of the abuse of tax law. The taxpayer operates in a globalized world taking advantage of differences in national tax systems and in tax competition among States. As single States have inadequate tools for countering international tax evasion and tax avoidance achieved through aggressive tax planning and BEPS, States' action must be coordinated at international level. The international coordination follows two paths: tax cooperation through the automatic exchange of information[5] and BEPS Project Action Plan and EU Anti-Tax Avoidance Directive (ATAD).[6] Hence, tax rules converge in the aim of protecting tax revenue from tax evasion and tax avoidance.

This approach is a coordinated and cooperative one; it coexists with an opposing model by which single States' tax rules achieve a tax competition among States in order to attract foreign capital.[7] In fact, tax law is an important factor of a country's competitiveness and of its ability to attract foreign capital. Therefore, tax competition and internal limits (such as public expenditure) and external ones (such as EU prohibition of State aid or soft law as the code of conduct regarding harmful tax

4. Ferrarese, M.R. *Il diritto comparato e le sfide della globalizzazione. Oltre la forbice differenze/somiglianze*, in *Rivista critica del diritto privato*, 2013, p. 370.
5. With the OECD common reporting standard.
6. Directive (EU) 2016/1164 of July 12, 2016.
7. An example is the patent box regime that is widespread in Europe; another example is the *Corporate tax road map* project of the UK in order to render corporate income tax more competitive; the project is published on: https://www.gov.uk/government/uploads/system/uploads/attachment_data/file/193239/Corporation_tax_road_map.pdf.

competition) cause a convergence of tax laws toward rules and models that are not too restrictive, in order to attract foreign investment, compared with those of other States.

§10.02 THE PROBLEMS TO BE FACED

The issue of interest deduction relates to the different ways a company may finance its activity, the alternative being between debt and equity. While the return for debt—interest—is generally deductible for tax purposes, the return for equity—dividend—is not. In fact, in computing the tax base of the Corporate Income Tax (CIT), interests are cost related to income while dividends are the distribution of the net income to partners.

However, from a more general tax perspective, the debt-equity distinction has several aspects that, as far as is relevant to this chapter, may be summarized as follows.[8]

The first is the treatment of the income for the recipient. Where a participation exemption method applies, dividends are tax exempt for the recipient while interest income is subject to tax. In this case, the tax treatment is symmetrical for the payer (nondeductible dividend and deductible interest) and the recipient (dividend exempt and interest subject to tax). In a cross-border situation, symmetrical tax treatment is more difficult to achieve as different tax systems are involved, and the lack of symmetry between them may give rise to deduction in one country and nontaxation in another. The issue is dealt with by Action 2 of OECD-G20 BEPS Project.

At EU level, the symmetrical treatment became a legal rule with an anti-avoidance aim in the parent-subsidiary directive[9] and, as such, is to be implemented by the Member States.

The second aspect, despite the theoretically clear distinction between debt and equity,[10] is the existence of a large hybridization of debt and equity instruments. Although it is not possible to generalize, the existence of hybrid instruments that share the elements of a bond and of a stock is widespread:[11] this sometimes makes it difficult to distinguish what is debt from what is equity in order to apply the appropriate tax rules.[12]

8. For a more comprehensive approach to the debt-equity divide, *see* Schön, W., *The Distinct Equity of the Debt-Equity Distinction*, in *Bull. Int. Tax.*, 2012, pp. 490 et seq.; *see also* Vording, H., *The Debt/Equity Distinction in Corporate Taxation: Does It Work, Does It Matter?*, in Marres O., Weber D. (ed.), *Tax Treatment of Interest*, Amsterdam, 2012, pp. 5 et seq.
9. Article 4, 1., a) of the directive 2011/96/EU as modified by directive 2014/86/EU. The purpose of anti-avoidance is to counter base erosion by means of the well-known hybrid mismatch that allows MNEs, in a cross-border situation, to make deductions in one country with noncorresponding taxation in another country. From a wider perspective the issue is dealt with under directive 2016/1164 as modified by directive 2017/952.
10. The partner shares the risk of the business, has voting and participation rights, while the lender receives a return for the loan and has the right to the repayment of the loan itself.
11. Schön, W., *The Distinct Equity of the Debt-Equity distinction*, pp. 5 et seq.; Blessing, P.H., *The Debt-Equity Conundrum—A Prequel*, in Marres, O., Weber, D. (ed.), *Tax Treatment of Interest, supra.*, pp. 23 et seq.
12. Schön, W., *The Distinct Equity of the Debt-Equity distinction*, distinguishes debt treatment from equity treatment referring to the power of the company to decide on the distribution of funds. If

The abovementioned are not the only matters concerning interest deduction. Risks of base erosion exist if partners of a company finance the company itself, and the tax charge on interest perceived by partners is lower than the tax rate applied to the company that deduces interest. Profit shifting may arise in a cross-border situation and as far as Multinational enterprises (MNEs) are concerned, it may occur if a company of the group in a low tax jurisdiction makes a loan to another company of the group in a high tax country.

Depending on the situation mentioned above and on the aims pursued, the tax legislator may disadvantage the financing of partners by denying the deduction of interest, thus countering the arbitrage between different levels of taxation (interest deduction by the company and interest taxation at the partner's level). The tax legislator may also deny interest deduction if the company gains tax-exempt income (or income taxed at reduced rate) in order not to increase the benefit from tax exemption.[13]

§10.03 THE BEPS PROJECT

In order to combat BEPS in cross-border situations, the action of single countries is, of course, insufficient. Therefore, the BEPS Project is a way of countering international tax avoidance and evasion through the recommendation to States of best practices. The BEPS Project is soft law and is not a source of international law. Consequently, it is not binding on the States and, although States may choose the elements of the Project that they wish to introduce in their tax legislation, and will enact the best practices recommended by the BEPS Project, there the result will be a wide convergence of tax rules in the different States.

From a comparative perspective, it is worth noting that, like the ATAD, an EU Directive binds Member States and gives rise to harmonization because all Member States *have to* implement the rules contained in the directive.[14]

This chapter examines the interest deduction rule from a comparative perspective.

A brief survey of the rules concerning interest deduction in different countries is discussed below.

---

the company decides to retain income, the treatment should be that of equity, while if the lender claims the revenue—interest—and the company is, thus, obliged to pay, the treatment is that of debt. This approach refers to the right of the taxpayer to the income.

13. This situation may occur if a company borrows money in order to invest in tax-exempt activities.
14. The reasons why a directive has been chosen are explained in Recital 2 of the ATAD. Particularly: the need for "effective and swift coordinated implementation of the anti-BEPS measures at the EU level"; moreover "It is essential for the good functioning of the internal market that, as a minimum, Member States implement their commitments under BEPS and more broadly, take action to discourage tax avoidance practices and ensure fair and effective taxation in the Union in a sufficiently coherent and coordinated fashion. In a market of highly integrated economies, there is a need for common strategic approaches and coordinated action, to improve the functioning of the internal market and maximize the positive effects of the initiative against BEPS. Furthermore, only a common framework could prevent a fragmentation of the market and put an end to currently existing mismatches and market distortions. Finally, national implementing measures which follow a common line across the Union would provide taxpayers with legal certainty in that those measures would be compatible with Union law."

§10.04 COMPARATIVE SURVEY

[A] The Asian Countries[15]

[1] Singapore

Interest expense is deductible, without limitation, if it is wholly and exclusively incurred to produce the income; this is a general condition required for deducting expenses for income tax purposes.[16]

It is worth underlining that, from a comparative perspective, the Tax Authority may allow the deduction of interest expense that does not satisfy the condition set in the Income Tax Act, according to which the expense must be wholly and exclusively incurred in the production of the income, allowing the apportionment of the borrowing cost.[17] The Tax Authority allows what the Statute does not.

The interpretation of the rule by courts requires a close nexus between the interest expense and the production of income.[18]

Moreover, the arm's-length principle applies to loans between related parties and the Statute includes a General Anti Avoidance Rule (GAAR).[19]

[2] Hong Kong

The deduction of interest expense is allowed if the interest is "incurred in the production of profits that are chargeable to Hong Kong profit tax."[20] Specific anti-avoidance rules limit the deduction of interest paid to nonresidents requiring that the interest perceived be subject to Hong Kong tax.[21]

[3] Japan

Tax law limits the deduction of interest by means of three different rules: arm's length, thin capitalization and earnings stripping.

15. For information concerning the Asian countries, *see* Dong, Y., Kaur, B. *The Potential Effect of Action 4 of the OECD Base Erosion and Profit Shifting Initiative Regarding Excessive Interest Deduction in Companies in Asia*, in *Bull. Int. Tax.*, 2019, pp. 2 et seq., and IBFD online country guide.
16. Dong, Y., Kaur, B., *The Potential Effect of Action 4 of the OECD Base Erosion and Profit Shifting Initiative Regarding Excessive Interest Deduction in Companies in Asia*, in *Bull. Int. Tax.*7.
17. *Ibid.*
18. *Ibid.*
19. *Ibid.*
20. *Ibid.*
21. A more detailed explanation in Dong, Y., Kaur, B., *The Potential Effect of Action 4 of the OECD Base Erosion and Profit Shifting Initiative Regarding Excessive Interest Deduction in Companies in Asia*, pp. 7 et seq.

The amount of interest on a debt owed to an affiliated company exceeding the arm's-length value is treated as a donation with limited deductibility.[22]

The thin capitalization rule limits interest deduction paid to a foreign controlling shareholder if the debt to equity ratio exceeds 3:1;[23] it is possible to use a different debt to equity ratio if this can be demonstrated with comparable companies;[24] interest expense exceeding the deductible amount is permanently nondeductible.

The earnings stripping rule[25] restricts the deduction of net interest paid to related parties to 50% of the adjusted taxable income. Nondeductible interest may be carried forward for up to seven years.

[4] Republic of Korea

Interest expense is generally deductible unless the thin capitalization rule applies, or the debt is used to acquire assets that are not related to the business.[26]

Under the thin capitalization rule, a debt to equity ratio of 2:1 applies to debt toward foreign controlling shareholders and toward sister companies abroad.[27] The thin capitalization rule does not apply if the conditions and amount of the debt are comparable to those with an independent third party.[28]

From 2019, a fixed ratio rule of 30% of Earning Before Interest and Tax (EBIT) deduction applies to interest, in line with the rule suggested in Action 4 of BEPS Project. If both the thin capitalization rule and the fixed ratio rule are applicable, nondeductible interest is the greater amount computed under the thin capitalization rule or the fixed ratio rule.[29]

[5] India

From 2018, a limited interest deduction rule applies to interest on related foreign parties' debt; the deduction is limited to 30% of Earning Before Interest, Tax, Depreciation and Amortization (EBITDA) if the amount of interest expense exceeds a threshold of INR 10 million; the rule does not apply to banking and insurance businesses. Exceeding interest may be carried forward for the next eight years.[30]

22. IBFD online country guide.
23. The rule was introduced in 1992.
24. *Ibid*; IBFD online country guide.
25. In force from 2013.
26. IBFD online country guide; Dong, Y., Kaur, B., *The Potential Effect of Action 4 of the OECD Base Erosion and Profit Shifting Initiative Regarding Excessive Interest Deduction in Companies in Asia*, 8.
27. *Ibid*.
28. *Ibid*.
29. *Ibid*.
30. IBFD online country guide.

[6] Indonesia

A thin capitalization rule applies that limits the deduction of interest expense to a maximum debt to equity ratio of 4:1. The limit applies to domestic and cross-border loans if the lender is a related or third party.[31]

[7] China

A thin capitalization rule applies that limits the deductible interest expense to debts to related parties; the debt to equity ratio is 2:1.[32] Nondeductible interest paid to foreign related parties are recharacterized as dividend distribution and taxed as such.[33] However, the ratio does not apply if an enterprise can provide documentation to prove that the loan transaction is at arm's length and the effective tax rate of the borrower is no higher than that of the lender in China.[34]

[B] The South American Countries[35]

In Argentina, a fixed ratio rule of 30% of EBITDA as a limit of interest deduction applies but only to interest on debt to related parties.

In Peru, the Action 4 BEPS fixed ratio rule of 30% of EBITDA will apply as from 2021.

The tax law in Brazil, Chile, Colombia and Mexico includes a thin capitalization rule in order to limit the interest deduction on borrowing from related parties.

Brazil's thin capitalization rule restricts the deduction of interest connected to loans granted by related persons and to loans granted by persons located in low tax jurisdictions or subject to privileged tax regimes. In the first case (related persons), interest expense is deductible if it is necessary for the company's activities and, depending on the cases, if the debt to equity ratio of 2:1 is met.[36] In the second case, the Brazilian company's indebtedness to all lenders located in low tax jurisdictions or subject to privileged tax regimes must not exceed 30% of the equity of the Brazilian company.[37] In both cases, the exceeding part of interest expense is not deductible.

---

31. Dong, Y., Kaur, B., *The Potential Effect of Action 4 of the OECD Base Erosion and Profit Shifting Initiative Regarding Excessive Interest Deduction in Companies in Asia*, 10.
32. Dong, Y., Kaur, B., *The Potential Effect of Action 4 of the OECD Base Erosion and Profit Shifting Initiative Regarding Excessive Interest Deduction in Companies in Asia*, 10; the ratio is 5:1 for financial enterprises.
33. *Ibid.*
34. IBFD online country guide.
35. Manrique, D.C. et al., *BEPS in Latin America (Part II): A Review of the Implementation of Action 2, 3, 4 and 12*, in IBFD, November 1, 2018.
36. IBFD online country guide.
37. *Ibid.*

Costa Rica changed its tax law in order to limit interest deduction up to 30% of EBITDA, according to BEPS Action 4. The new rule will be effective as from 2021 and the deduction will gradually decrease to 20% of EBITDA.[38]

[C] The USA

Under the 2018 tax reform, the deduction of business interest cannot exceed the sum of: (a) business interest income, (b) 30% of the adjustable taxable income[39] and (c) the floor plan financing interest.[40] The nondeductible interest may be carried forward to the succeeding taxable year.

The adjustable taxable income corresponds to EBITDA and EBIT after January 1, 2022:[41] so the deduction of interest expense will be reduced after that date.

Small businesses are exempt from the limited deduction rule if the average gross receipts of the taxpayer are USD 25 million or less over a three-year testing period.[42]

Subject to some accounting requirements, interest paid to related parties is not deductible until interest is included in the taxable income of the receiver (matching principle); the same principle applies to foreign related parties' payments.[43]

[D] EU Member States

The Council directive 2016/1164 (ATAD) was adopted on July 12, 2016. The ATAD provides rules that implement the BEPS Actions in the EU including Article 4 concerning an interest limitation rule. The directive is considered to be the preferred vehicle for implementing BEPS conclusions at the EU level in order to guarantee the proper functioning of the internal market and to ensure that Member States implement BEPS commitment in a sufficiently coherent and coordinated way; moreover, instead of leaving it up to the Member States to implement the BEPS Actions, the implementation of the directive would lead to legal certainty and EU law compatibility.[44]

The ATAD provides for a model of interest deduction limitation based on a binding rule with different options granted to the Member States.[45] The rule is a minimum standard that Member States must apply as from January 1, 2019, although Member States that have national targeted rules as of August 8, 2016, against BEPS risk, which are equally effective to the interest limitation rule, may continue to apply their

38. https://www.pwc.com/us/en/tax-services/publications/insights/assets/pwc-costa-rica-tax-reform-includes-new-vat-capital-gains-tax.pdf.
39. Under section 163(8) of the US code, the "adjustable taxable income" does not include any business interest paid by the taxpayer, net operating loss deduction or, before January 1, 2022, deduction for depreciation and amortization.
40. Under section 163(9)(B) of the US code, the term "floor plan financing indebtedness" means indebtedness used to finance the acquisition of motor vehicles (including farm machinery or equipment) held for sale or lease and secured by the inventory so acquired.
41. IBFD country guide online.
42. *Ibid.*
43. *Ibid.*
44. ATAD, Recital 2.
45. For an in-depth analysis of Article 4 of the ATAD, *see* Chapter 4 of this book.

national rules for a certain period after the publication of the agreement between the OECD members on a minimum standard with regard to BEPS Action 4, but only until January 1, 2024, at the latest.[46]

[1] Austria[47]

Interest expense is generally deductible if connected with income or used to purchase business assets.[48]

Interest paid to related companies must comply with the arm's-length principle otherwise it is not deductible and qualified as hidden profit distributions.[49] Interest expense paid to generate exempt income is not deductible, but interest paid on loans to acquire shareholding in companies is deductible even where dividends are tax exempt due to participation exemption.[50]

As concerns interest paid to companies belonging to the same group or controlled by the same shareholder, it is nondeductible if the income of the recipient is not taxed or subject to a tax rate of less than 10%.[51]

Although there is no thin capitalization rule in Austrian tax law, the Supreme Administrative Court has established general guidelines that are used to determine if the equity is adequate for the purpose of taxation.[52] If it is not, a share of the debt toward shareholders may be considered as shareholders' equity and the referred interest is nondeductible and considered as hidden profit distribution.[53]

Although Austrian tax rules concerning interest payment deduction limitation within groups of companies provide a stem to profit shifting as suggested by the BEPS Project, if the recipient is not taxed or taxed at a low rate on interest received, the ambit does not comply with Article 4 of ATAD which addresses every interest payment without any differentiation being made on the type of recipient (be the lender a resident, nonresident, taxed at a high or low rate).[54]

---

46. Article 11(6), ATAD.
47. The information concerning Austrian tax law is mainly based on IBFD online country guide and Spindler-Simader, K., Wörer, V., *Implementation of the EU Anti-tax Avoidance Directive (2016/1164) in Austria*, in *Eur. Tax'n*, 2018, 286.
48. IBFD online country guide.
49. IBFD online country guide, Spindler-Simader K., Wörer V., *Implementation of the EU Anti-tax Avoidance Directive (2016/1164) in Austria*, 287.
50. *Ibid.*
51. *Ibid.*
52. IBFD online country guide.
53. *Ibid.*
54. Spindler-Simader K., Wörer V., *Implementation of the EU Anti-tax Avoidance Directive (2016/1164) in Austria*, 287-288. The Authors underline that Austrian scholars assume that national rules concerning interest deduction limitation are equally effective as Article 4 of the ATAD, while the European Commission rejected this assumption. Moreover, the Authors explain the economic reasons why Austria has traditionally rejected a general interest limitation rule.

[2] Belgium

New Belgian interest limitation rules were introduced as from 2019 in order to comply with the ATAD.[55] Interest paid in excess of interest received is deductible up to 30% of EBITDA or EUR 3 million. Special rules apply to taxpayers that are part of a group.[56] Nondeductible exceeding borrowing costs may be carried forward indefinitely. The Belgian interest limitation rule exercises options provided for by the ATAD: the rule does not apply to stand-alone companies and companies belonging to financial sector; moreover, the rule includes the grandfathering clause for loans concluded before June 17, 2016, and loans related to qualifying public-private cooperation projects are excluded if the project operator, borrowing costs, assets and income are all in the EU.[57]

The new rule replaces the previous thin capitalization rule that still applies in some cases excluded from the new interest limitation rule.

[3] France

There are many rules that limit interest deduction under French tax law.[58]

There are rules applicable to interest paid to shareholders or related companies. The deduction is limited to interest not exceeding the market[59] annual average rate; nondeductible interest is treated as a hidden distribution and taxed as a dividend. Interest paid to related companies is nondeductible if the interest is not subject, in the hands of the recipient, to taxation equal to at least 25% of the CIT. This rule was introduced in 2013 in order to prevent hybrid mismatches.[60]

As from 2019, France has implemented Article 4 of the ATAD. As a consequence, interest deduction is limited to EUR 3 million or 30% of the adjustable taxable profit. If the debt to equity ratio exceeds 1.5:1, the limit of deduction is reduced respectively to EUR 1.5 million or to 10% of the adjustable taxable profit.[61]

If a tax group consolidation applies, the limits are referred to the group.[62]

---

55. IBFD online country guide.
56. *Ibid*; interest paid and received by the taxpayer to a Belgian company of the same group is not included in the calculation of exceeding borrowing costs; the threshold of EUR 3 million must be allocated to Belgian companies belonging to the same group. Under certain conditions, companies of the same group may conclude an agreement in order to transfer the nonutilized threshold amount among them and amounts exceeding the threshold amount.
57. *Ibid.*
58. For an updated overview of the rules limiting interest deduction, *see* IBFD online country guide. *See also* Gutman, D., et al., *The Impact of the ATAD on Domestic Systems: A Comparative Survey*, in *Eur. Tax'*, 2017, p. 3.
59. Annual average rate of interest charged by financial institutions on variable interest rate loans; IBFD online country guide.
60. *Ibid.*
61. *Ibid.*
62. *Ibid.*

[4] *United Kingdom*

In 2017, interest deduction rules were changed in order to follow the BEPS Action 4 recommendation. A fixed ratio rule was introduced. The main features of the new rule are: the rule limits the amount of net interest a group may deduct up to 30% of EBITDA; a group ratio rule applies: the group ratio is based on the net interest expense to EBITDA ratio for the worldwide group based on its consolidated accounts; an exempt threshold, that is groups with interest of less than GBP 2 million do not apply the rule; restricted interest is carried forward indefinitely; unused interest allowance can be carried forward for up to five years; special rules apply to particular issues.[63]

[5] *The Netherlands*

Interest deduction under the Dutch tax law is limited by legal provisions and by case law.[64] Specific rules established by courts justify a separate paragraph, while the implementation of the ATAD in the Netherlands is dealt with in this book.[65]

According to the Supreme Court, interest is nondeductible if: (a) the loan is deemed to be an informal capital contribution, (b) the loan is subject to the *fraus legis* doctrine[66] unless the interest is sufficiently taxed in the hands of the recipient or (c) the interest is deemed to be a hidden profit distribution due to an excessive interest rate.[67]

As concerns case sub a) although the classification of a loan for tax purposes follows the civil law classification, according to case law this general rule does not apply if the loan is a sham loan, a bottomless pit loan or a participation loan.[68] The features of all these kinds of loans show that, despite the name of "loan," they resemble equity.[69]

From a comparative perspective, it is worth noting that the rules mentioned above are settled by courts and not by statute. The courts interpret facts keeping their legal form if it is coherent with the intention of the parties and the objective elements of the facts.

Other rules limit interest deduction in transactions with related parties.[70] Other rules were applied until December 31, 2018, to interest deduction related to acquisition by holding companies and excessive interest relating to a participation in a subsidiary;

63. Source: https://www.gov.uk/government/publications/corporation-tax-tax-deductibility-of-corporate-interest-expense/corporation-tax-tax-deductibility-of-corporate-interest-expense#background-to-the-measure. *See also* IBFD online country guide.
64. IBFD online country guide.
65. *See* van den Broek, H. *The Netherlands*, in this book.
66. Or falls under the just levy procedure that is a procedure settled by tax law and not commonly used; IBFD online country guide.
67. IBFD online country guide.
68. *Ibid*; Gutman, D., et al., *The Impact of the ATAD on Domestic Systems: A Comparative Survey*, 5.
69. A sham loan appears to be a loan, but in fact the parties' intention was to provide equity. When a bottomless pit loan is granted by a shareholder to its subsidiary, it is almost certain that the loan will not be repaid due to losses of the subsidiary. The features of a participation loan are that the remuneration of the loan is profit dependent, the loan is subordinate to claims from all creditors and the loan has no term or is perpetual: *Ibid*.
70. For more details IBFD online country guide.

from January 1, 2019, the ATAD has been implemented and the new limitation rule applies.[71]

The new rule limits the deduction of interest paid that exceeds interest received up to 30% of EBITDA as determined under the fiscal accounts. However, interest is deductible without limitation up to the amount of EUR 1 million.

The new interest deduction limitation applies only to interest payments that would otherwise have been tax deductible.[72] Nondeductible exceeding interest expense may be carried forward without a time limitation.[73] A specific anti-abuse provision has been introduced in order to avoid trade in companies with interest charges carried forward: nondeductible interest charges can no longer be carried forward after a significant (at least 30%) change of interest in the company.[74]

[6] Other EU Member States: An Overview

Other European States have changed the interest deduction rules in recent years. The first to be mentioned is Germany in 2007, followed by Italy in 2008 and by Portugal and Spain in 2012. The change was part of wider reforms that aimed, particularly in Germany and Italy, to reduce the corporate tax rate (the so-called race to the bottom) and enlarge the tax base. The reduction of the tax rate should increase the tax system's appeal to foreign investors in a competitive world; the enlargement of the tax base should balance the effects of tax rate deduction in order to safeguard tax revenue.[75] Germany, Italy, Portugal and Spain chose the fixed ratio rule that is the net interest deduction limitation of up to 30% of EBITDA; in Italy and Germany, the rule does not apply to bank and assurance companies. The rule applies to the interest expense exceeding interest income. In very general terms, there are differences between the German and Italian rules. The German rule applies to adjusted taxable income while the Italian one (and the Portuguese one) applied the rule to the financial value of EBITDA. Germany (and Portugal) has an exempt threshold that is to say the limitation does not apply if interest expense is less than EUR 3 million (EUR 1 million in Portugal; this was also the initial threshold in Germany; Italy has no exempt threshold). Germany has a stand-alone clause: the interest deduction limitation does not apply to nonaffiliated companies; Germany has an escape clause that allows a company belonging to a

71. IBFD online country guide.
72. VAN DEN BROEK, H. *The Netherlands Implementation of the ATAD1 Interest Limitation Rule*, Chapter 9, section §9.03[B].
73. VAN DEN BROEK, H. *The Netherlands Implementation of the ATAD1 Interest Limitation Rule*, Chapter 9, section §9.05; IBFD online country guide.
74. In *The Netherlands Implementation of the ATAD1 Interest Limitation Rule*, Chapter 9, section §9.08, VAN DEN BROEK, H. notes that, as the anti-abuse provision applies with no exception, it seems to contain overkill.
75. According to the German Government, the interest limitation rule was enacted in order to reduce German companies' debt ratio that was high compared to an international level while a high equity ratio protects against insolvency; however, scholars doubt that the increase of equity ratio, noticed in German companies after the enactment of the interest limitation rule, was due to the rule itself or to the reduction of debt financing forced by the financial crisis; EILERS, S. *Earnings Stripping*, in Marres, O., Weber, D. (ed.), *Tax Treatment of Interest for Corporations*, IBFD, 2012, 137.

group not to apply the deduction limitation, if the equity capital ratio of the company claiming the deduction of interest is no more than 2% lower than the equity capital ratio of the group. Both Germany and Italy allow the carry forward of interest and EBITDA.

These are the rules enacted before the ATAD.

As far as Germany is concerned, the interest limitation rule closely resembles the one of the ATAD and so it was already compliant with the directive.[76]

The German interest limitation deduction rule includes an anti-avoidance provision similar to the Dutch one that avoids the carryforward of nondeductible interest if the business is transferred.[77] Nondeducted interest expense may be carried forward without any time limit while unused EBITDA may be carried forward for the next five years. Similar rules apply under Italian legislation which also allows interest income exceeding interest expense to be carried forward. The Italian interest deduction rule has been amended in order to implement the ATAD, but without implementing the threshold of EUR 3 million (*de minimis* clause) up to which exceeding interest is deductible even if it is higher than the 30% of EBITDA and the stand-alone clause.[78] The EBITDA that was determined using data included in the profit and loss account is now computed by using tax-relevant values.

In Spain, the interest deduction limitation rule was enacted in 2012 inspired by the German rule;[79] the new rule replaced the thin capitalization with the aim of indirectly favoring equity financing and raising revenue.[80] The Spanish rule generally complies with the earnings stripping rule of Article 4 of the ATAD.[81] Spain opted for a *de minimis* threshold of EUR 1 million without a group ratio rule and without the exclusion of stand-alone entities.[82] Interest capacity may be carried forward in the next five years, and nondeductible interest expense may be carried forward without a time limit.

§10.05 SOME COMPARATIVE REMARKS

After the overview above of different rules concerning business interest deduction, it is possible to draw some concluding remarks from a comparative perspective.

76. For an analysis of the German rule *see* Reich, D., *The German Interest Barrier*, in this book.
77. Reich, D., *The German Interest Barrier*, Chapter 6, section §6.02[D], in this book.
78. Vanz, G., *EU Atad—Interest Limitation Rule—Issues Regarding Its Implementation—Italy*, Chapter 7, section §7.07, in this book, criticizes Article 4 of the ATAD, from a principle of proportionality perspective, because it does not oblige Member States to include a stand-alone clause.
79. Andrés Báez Moreno, Aitor Navarro Ibarrola, *Spain*, in this book, footnote 14.
80. *Ibid.*, Chapter 8, section§8.02[A], describes the aims of the new rule.
81. *Ibid.*
82. *Ibid.* The only aspect in which the Spanish rule is not in line with the ATAD is the inclusion of the exempt income in the calculation of EBITDA: *see* Moreno, A.B., Ibarrola, A.N., *Spain*, Chapter 8, section §8.02[C][1].

[A] Main Rules of Interest Deductibility

The main rules concerning interest deduction in different countries may be summarized as follows: interest must be incurred in producing taxable income (e.g., Singapore, Hong Kong and Austria) or to acquire business assets (Republic of Korea, Austria): these are general rules that usually apply to the deduction of business expenses. The first rule has a technical nature: if the company produces nontaxable income, the deduction of expenses incurred by this activity would increase the benefit consisting of nontaxable income.[83] Moreover, if the loan is between related parties, a matching condition may be required: the deduction is allowed if the interest received by the lender is included in the taxable income of the receiver. This rule aims to prevent mismatches, that is to say the deduction of the interest expense by a company without taxation in the hands of the related receiver.

Some countries apply a thin capitalization rule based on a given debt to equity ratio: the rule and its spread in different tax systems will be dealt with below. From a comparative viewpoint, it is worth remarking that the rule and the ratio in some cases may be disregarded if the company proves that its ratio or conditions of the loan are in accordance with those of comparable companies. The fixed ratio meets the need of a certain and simple rule, while the possibility to disregard it complies with the taxation of effective income constituting the taxpayer's ability to pay if the transaction is aligned with those concluded by comparable companies.

[B] The Spread of Earnings Stripping Rules and Related Problems

Part of the rules described above in section §10.4[D] was enacted before BEPS Action 4 and the ATAD. BEPS Action 4 recommended and the ATAD imposed on EU Member States the introduction of a fixed ratio rule.

The interest deduction limitation through a fixed ratio rule (earnings stripping rule) has spread among tax laws of different countries. BEPS Action 4 and the ATAD facilitated the spreading of this rule which, as noted before, was already part of German, Italian, Spanish and Portuguese tax law.[84] The introduction of a new legal rule in a legal system, particularly if a foreign rule is transplanted, raises the issue of its compatibility with the system itself.[85] In Germany, the fixed ratio rule (earnings stripping rule) may violate the ability to pay principle and particularly the objective net principle according to which the taxpayer's ability to pay is represented by his/her net income; the ability to pay principle is deduced by the principle of equality that is stated

83. Hong Kong has a territorial tax system so the reason behind the condition for deduction is different.
84. Rules which limit interest expense referring to a fixed ratio are applied by a number of countries as recognized by OECD/G20 BEPS Project, *Limiting Base Erosion Involving Interest Deductions and Other Financial Payments* — Action 4: 2016 Update, 25.
85. A directive, such as the ATAD, may also raise issues of conformity with EU principles like the one of proportionality but the issue is not dealt with in this chapter.

in Article 3 of the German Constitution.[86] The judgment is still pending before the German Constitutional Court. Scholars have raised a similar issue regarding the constitutional compliance of the Italian fixed ratio rule referred to the ability to pay principle: in fact, the Italian interest deduction limitation rule could result in the ban of the deduction of interest expense arising from the business activity that could entail income tax to be applied in violation of the taxpayer's ability to pay.

As the fixed ratio rule is included in an EU Directive, it prevails over national rules but, according to some Constitutional Courts, such as the Italian one, EU law may not conflict with and prevail over fundamental principles of a Member State; to the extent that principles regarding taxation are included in the fundamental principles of the Constitution—as may be the case for ability to pay that is considered to be closely related to the equality principle—the Constitutional Court may declare the law ratifying the Union treaties to be unconstitutional as it introduces rules into the Italian law that violate the fundamental principles of the Constitution.[87,88]

[C] Earnings Stripping Rule: Differences Compared with Thin Capitalization and Main Features

It has been outlined above that there is a convergence of the interest deduction rule toward a fixed ratio rule (earnings stripping rule) in different tax laws, more specifically 30% of EBITDA.

The convergence has been promoted by the recommendation contained in BEPS Action 4 and, as concerns EU Member States, by the ATAD.

However, the spread of such a rule precedes BEPS Action 4 and the ATAD.[89]

Many States used a thin capitalization rule before moving to the fixed ratio rule applied on EBITDA. This is true for Germany, Italy, Spain and many other States.

---

86. I R 20/15 (October 14, 2015); *see* Navarro, A., Parada, L., Schwarz, P., *The Proposal for an EU Anti-avoidance Directive: Some Preliminary Thoughts*, EC Tax Rev., 2016, p. 119; Dourado, A.P., *The Interest Limitation Rule in the Anti-tax Avoidance Directive (ATAD) and the Net Taxation Principle*, in EC Tax Rev. 2017, p. 112; for an analysis of the issue and the reasons why the interest barrier does not seem to violate the German Constitution, *see* Reich, D., *Germany*, in this book.
87. That is the so-called counter-limits theory expressed by the Italian Constitutional Court in judgment n. 183/1973; *see* Vanz, G., *The Italian Interest Limitation Rule: Constitutional Issues*, in Eur. Tax'n, 2018, p. 175; *Id.*, *Italy*, in this book. *See also* Italian Constitutional Court judgment n. 115/2018 after ECJ Case C-42/17.
88. As concerns the German Constitutional Court (Bundesvervassungsgericht), scholars point out that there are three exceptions that correspond to the counter-limits theory of the Italian constitutional court: the violation of fundamental rights, the lack of competence of an EU act and the violation of the guarantee of constitutional identity; *see* Luther, J., *Costituzionalizzare l'Integrationsgewalt: non solo querrelle de l'Allemagne*, in Bernardi, A., (ed.), *I controlimiti. Primato delle norme europeee difesa dei principi costituzionali*, Jovene ed., 2017,153. However, according to the judgment Solange II, BVerGE 73, 339 of 1986, the German Constitutional Court does not exercise its jurisdiction.
89. OECD/G20 BEPS Project, *Limiting Base Erosion Involving Interest Deductions and Other Financial Payments*—Action 4: 2015 Final Report, 58, states that a number of countries currently apply a fixed ratio rule.

The thin capitalization rule is a model toward which numerous tax systems converged[90] and, despite the spread of the fixed ratio rule, many countries have kept the thin capitalization rule, for example some Asian and South American countries, while in some cases both rules apply, for instance in Belgium and France.

The thin capitalization rule prevents the deduction of interest related to debt that exceeds a specified debt to equity ratio. Relevant debts are usually toward related parties and sometimes toward foreign related parties: the rules enacted by different States may vary significantly.[91]

The disallowing of excessive interest deduction is based on the idea that, over a given ratio, the partner should not have chosen to finance the company with loan but with capital contribution; therefore, as the remuneration for capital—i.e., dividend—is not deductible, the company may not benefit from the deduction of excessive interest expense.[92] So, the rule's aim is to protect the tax base.

Sometimes States combine the thin capitalization rule with arm's length and allow the deduction of interest at arm's length; moreover, in some cases, anti-avoidance rules are applied and interest payment may be recharacterized as dividend.[93] In the absence of thin capitalization provisions, similar effects may be achieved by the interpretation of courts which, as in Austria referred to above, established guidelines to determine if the level of equity is adequate for the purpose of taxation disallowing the deduction of excessive interest payments. As a consequence, although tax legislation does not include a thin capitalization rule, this is applied by courts.

The disadvantages of thin capitalization rules are highlighted in the BEPS Project Action 4: the limitation on the amount of debts leave significant flexibility to the rate of interest applied on such debts and groups may modify the level of equity in order to deduct more interest expense.[94] However, as noted above, some States still have a thin capitalization rule, sometimes combined with other rules and this approach is allowed by the BEPS Project Action 4.[95]

As noted above, many tax systems moved to a fixed ratio rule based on an EBITDA ratio. From a comparative standpoint, it would be interesting to determine if this model actually leads to the convergence of tax systems.

90. Kayis-Kumar, A. *Simulating Tax Minimization Strategies of Multinationals: Evaluating the Effectiveness of Changes in the United Kingdom's Corporate Interest Deductibility Rules*, in World Tax J., 2019, p. 127. Some Member States had to change their thin capitalization rule in order to comply with EU law; this was the case of Germany after Case C-324/00, *Lankhorst-Hohorst GmbH v. Finanzamt Steinfurt* and of the UK after Case C-524/04, *Test Claimants in the Thin Cap Group Litigation v. Commissioners of Inland Revenue*.

91. For a survey *see International Aspects of Thin Capitalization*, *Cahiers de Droit Fiscal International*, vol. LXXXIb, 1996.

92. The deduction of excessive interest may be coupled with low or no taxation of interest received by the lender as it may happen in a cross-border situation due to different levels of taxation in different countries, as already mentioned before.

93. Haslehner, W., *Interest*, in Reimer, E., Rust, A. (ed.), *Klaus Vogel On Double Taxation Conventions*, Alphen aan den Rijn, 2015, p. 929.

94. OECD/G20 BEPS Project, *Limiting Base Erosion Involving Interest Deductions and Other Financial Payments*—Action 4: 2015 Final Report, at 21.

95. *Ibid.*, at 82. Similarly, the ATAD: *see* Recital (6).

A fixed ratio rule using an EBITDA ratio connects the amount of net interest deductions with the taxable income generated by the company's economic activity[96] and so it implements one of the aims of the BEPS Project, that is to say to report profits where the economic activities generating them are carried out and where value is created.[97]

This seems to be the common element of the interest limitation rule since it may be supplemented by several other rules that imply a different extension of the rule itself. This approach is particularly evident in the ATAD which, together with a binding rule (excessive interest deductible up to 30% of EBITDA), provides many options to the Member States.[98] The options concern the personal scope of the rule related to groups,[99] the existence of a *de minimis* threshold of up to EUR 3 million where the fixed ratio rule does not apply,[100] stand-alone entities may be allowed a full deduction,[101] a grandfathering provision for preexisting loans[102] and the exclusion of long-term public infrastructure projects loans,[103] the application of a group equity ratio test[104] or a group's net third-party interest to EBITDA ratio,[105] the possibility to carry forward and back nondeductible exceeding borrowing costs and interest capacity[106] and the possibility to exclude financial undertakings.[107]

Moreover, the ATAD allows a derogation until January 1, 2024, to the interest limitation rule set out in the directive in favor of Member States that have national targeted rules preventing BEPS risks which are equally effective to the rule itself.[108]

The complete set of options allows the rule to be more consistent with the aim pursued which is mainly to counter the excessive deduction of interest expense especially by MNE in cross-border avoidance situations.[109] For example, the group ratio rule suggested in the BEPS Action 4 Final Report, which is similar to the one included in Article 4(5) of the ATAD, takes into account the fact that groups in different sectors may be leveraged differently or simply more highly, as explained in BEPS Action 4 Final Report,[110] with or without a low risk of BEPS.

---

96. *Ibid.*, at 12.
97. *Ibid.*, at 3.
98. Carmona Lobita, J., *The ATAD's Interest Limitation Rule—A Step Backwards?*, in Eur. Tax', 2/3, 2019; Schnitger, A., Zafirov, I., *Chapter 12: The Interest Limitation Rule in the Implementation of Anti-BEPS Rules in the EU: A Comprehensive Study*, in Pistone, P., Weber, D. (eds.), *IBFD 2018*, Online Books.
99. Article 4(1).
100. Article 4(3)(a).
101. Article 4(3)(b).
102. Article 4(a).
103. Article 4(b).
104. Article 5(a).
105. Article 5(b).
106. Article 4(6).
107. Article 4(7).
108. Article 11(6). The Commission Notice 2018/C 441/01 specifies the assumption utilized by the Commission to assess legal similarity and economic equivalence of the measures notified by the Member States.
109. ATAD, Recital (6).
110. OECD/G20 BEPS Project, Action 4 Final Report, paras. 115 et seq.

Another option concerning groups for tax purposes allows Member States to consider exceeding interest expense and EBITDA at the level of the group instead of the single companies composing the group.[111] Under Italian CIT,[112] it is possible to transfer to the tax group the nondeductible exceeding interest expense where it may be deducted if another member of the same group has interest capacity or has interest income exceeding interest expense. In the Netherlands, the fiscal unit regime applies, and EBITDA is determined at the level of the group where profits and losses of the company of the fiscal unit are consolidated.[113] In Spain, the fiscal unit regime may be applied with the determination of interest deduction at the level of the group and not of the single entities.[114] The risk of BEPS related to groups in cross-border situation does not emerge as, under Italian CIT, the tax group concerns only resident companies: in fact, the fiscal group to which CIT refers in order to transfer nondeductible exceeding interest expense or interest capacity is the one formed by resident companies;[115] the same is true under Dutch legislation[116] and also under Spanish legislation.[117] And it seems to be confirmed by the same directive whose Recital 7 states that: "Where a group includes more than one entity in a Member State, the Member State may consider the overall position of all group entities *in the same State*, including a separate entity taxation system to allow the transfer of profits or interest capacity between entities within a group, when applying rules that limit the deductibility of interest" (emphasis added).

So, the fixed ratio rule caps the exceeding deductible interest, and the limit may be exceeded if the group ratio rule or the other options (stand-alone, *de minimis* threshold) are implemented. One of the options is the carryforward of nondeductible exceeding interest or interest capacity: this seems to be one of the preferred choices.[118] The option shows that the ban of deduction is not definitive and if, in the following years, the exceeding interest decreases and/or EBITDA increases, nondeductible interest may become deductible. On the one hand, nondeductible interest due to a contingent situation—a temporary increase of interest or decrease of EBITDA—may be deducted if profitability improves; on the other hand, companies are driven to reduce their interest expense or improve their EBITDA although this aim is not always easy to reach.[119]

---

111. Article 4(1).
112. Article 96(14) of Corporate Income Tax.
113. VAN DEN BROEK, H., *The Netherlands*, Chapter 9, section §9.06.
114. MORENO, A.B., IBARROLA, A.N. *Spain*.
115. *See* Article 96 Italian CIT.
116. IBFD country guide online: all companies involved in the fiscal unit must be resident in the Netherlands.
117. MORENO, A.B., IBARROLA, A.N., *Spain*.
118. Only Slovakia and Latvia seem not to have chosen the interest carryforward: *see* Deloitte, *EU Anti-Tax Avoidance Directive. Implementation of Interest Expense Limitation Rule*, February 2019, p. 11, available at https://www2.deloitte.com/content/dam/Deloitte/global/Documents/Tax/dttl-tax-eu-anti-tax-avoidance-directive-implementation-of-interest-expense-limitation-rule.pdf.
119. It may be easy to achieve in a group but difficult to achieve, for example, by a stand-alone company in a negative economic situation.

From a comparative perspective, the spread of the earnings stripping rule which in many States replaced the thin capitalization rule may have been caused by the easier application of the former. In fact, both are basically anti-avoidance rules so, if no avoidance occurs, the rule should not be applied otherwise the application would be unreasonable.[120] As noted above, the thin capitalization in some countries may be disregarded if the company proves that its ratio or conditions of the loan are in accordance with those of comparable companies and so, arguably, no avoidance planning is at stake. The thin capitalization rule causes definitive nondeductibility of interest expense unless the taxpayer is able to demonstrate resemblance with comparable companies. This demonstration implies an activity on the part of the taxpayer and of the Tax Authority in order to control and respect the right to a fair hearing. The carryforward (and back) possibility of excessive nondeductible interest and interest capacity, included as an option in the ATAD, as well as in the BEPS Action 4 Final Report, allows the nondeductibility of excessive interest not to be made permanent, but this result is automatic and does not require any demonstration on the side of the taxpayer; moreover, the Tax Authority's control is easier.

Finally, as underlined in section §10.01, the different options provided by the ATAD allow Member States to counterbalance their aims of reaching a minimum standard of tax base protection through the interest deduction limitation, and of maintaining their tax attractiveness as is clearly expressed in the chapter regarding the Netherlands in this book.[121]

---

120. Unless the rule was not an anti-avoidance one but, for example, a rule to address a higher capitalization of companies.
121. VAN DEN BROEK, H., *The Netherlands*, Chapter 9, section §9.03.

PART III The Interest Limitation Rule in the ATAD: BEPS and CCTB

CHAPTER 11

The EU ATAD Interest Limitation Rule, BEPS and CCTB: The EU ATAD Rule and BEPS Action 4*

F. Alfredo Garcia Prats

§11.01 INTRODUCTION

The need to establish measures to counteract base erosion and profit shifting (BEPS) by multinational enterprises has led many States and international organizations to set aside well-founded traditional principles that previously settled the interjurisdiction allocation of income—profit—of multinationals, normally referred to as *at arm's-length* principle, or *at arm's-length* standards.

This is particularly relevant and evident in the area of limitation of deductibility of interest payments.[1] The recommendations suggested by the Organisation for Economic Co-operation and Development (OECD) in Action 4 of the BEPS action plan generate an outcome that is difficult to reconcile with the requirements of the *at arm's-length* standard, to the extent that it prevents the deductibility of certain (interest payment) expenses, regardless of whether the amount paid is clearly founded on the *arm's-length* principle or not. The application of a rather mechanical rule prevents the development of a market analysis in order to accept the deductibility of the expense, even if it becomes allocable to the entity bearing its cost from a pure market perspective and analysis.

---

* This work is part of the research carried on under the Project DER2017-88731-R "Globalización, multilateralismo y modulación de las garantías y derechos de los contribuyentes", granted by the Ministry of Economy, Industry and Competitiveness of Spain.

1. This is a situation that may also appear in other areas of action, such as the mechanisms foreseen to prevent double nontaxation outcomes.

At the same time, the outcome may be difficult to reconcile with some constitutional tax principles in different States, such as the ability to pay principle.[2] Moreover, the application of the suggested rules to counteract base erosion through the use of (cross-border) debt instruments may lead to unsolved and desired double taxation—at least temporarily—contrary to the traditional goals and objectives of international rules.

The action aims at a certain (natural) coordination among domestic tax rules dealing with the tax treatment (tax deductibility) of certain (excess) interest payments. Contrary to traditional international tax actions, the aim is not, and may not be, achieved by the introduction of certain treaty provisions, but, on the contrary, by the introduction of certain domestic tax rules. This is due to the fact that tax treaty rules do not normally deal, refer or influence the tax treatment of certain expenses, with the exception of the rules of business profits that can be allocated to permanent establishments and certain nondiscrimination clauses.

In any case, the objectives of such an action may be difficult to achieve since the rule lies on certain assumptions that are far from clear: a more-or-less common understanding of the concept of interest payment, and a certain assumption of the a priori deductibility of such payments at every domestic tax level. This is not to mention the lack of correspondence between the deductibility of the payment in the hands of the payer and the subject-to-taxation in the hands of the recipient which may lead to a different erosion mechanism that has been approached by means of another action plan of the BEPS project, based on the so-called single taxation principle.

Despite a coordinated approach between the European Union (EU) and the OECD in relation to the development of mechanisms and measures to tackle BEPS, the comparison of measures suggested by the OECD regarding the limitation of interest deductibility and the measures *imposed* by the EU—Article 4 of the Anti Tax Avoidance Directive (hereinafter "ATAD")—shows a clearly different path of enforceability and scope.

With regard to the introduction of domestic legislation to limit the deductibility of interest expenses, the OECD preferred a "best practice approach" instead of including minimum standard requirements. The OECD relied heavily on a natural convergence of legislations of different countries committed to achieving the outcome foreseen by the BEPS action plan. Faced with this approach, the EU reacted with the approval of a

2. In Germany, the corresponding domestic rule limiting deductibility of excess interest expenses is pending analysis of constitutionality by the German Constitutional Court. *See* Lampert, S., Meickmann, T., Reinert, M. "Article 4 of the EU Anti-tax Avoidance Directive in Light of the Questionable Constitutionality of the German 'Interest Barrier' Rule." European Taxation, August 2016, pp. 323-327. As regards other domestic legal orders *see*, Vanz, G. "The Italian Interest Limitation Rule: Constitutional Issues" European Taxation, April 2018, pp. 173-175. Sanz Gadea, E. "Restricción y limitación a la deducción de intereses en el Impuesto sobre Sociedades" Revista de Contabilidad y Tributación, 355/2012, pp. 47-104. López Pérez, M.J. "La limitación a la deducibilidad de los intereses en el impuesto sobre sociedades en España y Alemania: evolución y perspectivas de futuro" Gaceta Fiscal, 390/2018, pp. 50-71. Pontón Aricha, T. "Las medidas relativas a la limitación de intereses y a los instrumentos híbridos en la ATAD y su entorno", Documentos IEF, 14/2017. Calvo Vergez, J. "La nueva limitación a la deducción de gastos financieros en el Impuesto sobre Sociedades: Algunas consideraciones a la luz de la reforma fiscal", Actum Fiscal 95/2015, pp. 184-188.

mandatory rule included in the ATAD for all Member States. However, as we will analyze in the present article, the multiplicity of options, special regimes and exceptions included, in other words the special rules, still leave a certain relative level of discretion and manoeuvre for EU Member States in the midterm.

At the forefront, there is a need to consider, or reconsider, a certain coherence between the design of sound coordinated tax policies and the attribution of competences to the organizations and actors involved in the process. Lacking such attribution of competences, whether express or implicit, the development of partial measures of corporate tax policy aimed at preventing base erosion through the use of debt instruments may become more complex. In other words, the tax policy lying behind the proposal of limitation of deductibility would need, for the sake of coherence, to be made in a scenario where the basic standards of corporate taxation are coordinated if not shared among the participating States. This does not happen either in the G20 or in the EU itself, where the ATAD proposal has been approved before reaching a common understanding of the corporate tax base or establishing/introducing (?) a common corporate tax policy among its Member States. Without such a scenario, not only is the way to achieve efficient results far from clear but also the implementation of schemes devoted to deviate or shift profits through remuneration of debt is made more difficult. This is true also from a purely economic perspective, where the recommended measures may not necessarily reinforce the capitalization or the profitability of business that would be desirable to overcome economic crises and recession.

§11.02 BASE EROSION AND INTEREST LIMITATION RULES

The fight against the use of interest payment expenses and more specifically cross-border interest payment has centered the debate on corporate tax base erosion, harmful tax practices and profit shifting among jurisdictions. Cross-border interest payments were traditionally identified as one of the means used by multinational groups to shift profits between companies of the group and, therefore, among jurisdictions, eroding in some cases the (corporate income) tax base of such jurisdictions.[3] Therefore, international organizations, and especially the OECD, specified, after an extensive debate, what type of counteractive measures would effectively limit profit shifting using cross-border interest payments. Little debate emerged, however, after the Interest-Royalty Directive allowed cross-border interest payments (regardless of whether they were deductible or not) among associated enterprises free of withholding tax at source, without a clear counteractive measure ensuring a minimum level of taxation of this cross-border income.

This situation is not new and was identified long before the BEPS action plan was raised, promoted and developed by the OECD with the support of the G-20. In fact, the delocalization problems generated by cross-border interest payments generated the implementation of important counteractive tax measures in most domestic corporate tax systems to tackle the erosion generated by interest payments. These rules, adopting

3. OECD. Action 4 of the Action Plan on Base Erosion and Profit Shifting, p. 1

different approaches, scope or range could generally be categorized as thin capitalization rules and, in many countries, are still applied and in force.[4]

The selected measures suggest a limitation of the deductibility of interest payment expenses in relation to or with reference to the per asset value. Many alternative thin capitalization models coexisted in different countries and tax legislations. On the one hand, there were divergences in the definition of relevant equity and debt, whether limited to related parties relationships or considering relevant total debt ratios, applying either a formal or a substantial approach; some jurisdictions allowed a level of debt average (bed and breakfasting schemes); others allowed for a commercial justification from the borrower of the debt (would have approach); on the other hand, differences exist among the actual ratio approach selected (2:1; 3:1; or others), while some legislations opted for an earnings-stripping approach and some jurisdictions also introduced counteractive measures against back-to-back loans.

The OECD dealt with the thin capitalization rules and its compatibility with tax treaties several times. As early as 1987, the OECD presented its report on Thin Capitalisation,[5] which, sometime afterward, was substantially incorporated in the Commentaries of the OECD Model Convention (hereinafter "OECD MC"). The OECD also established under which circumstances these domestic measures could be considered compatible with the arm's-length standard and with the different nondiscrimination treaty clauses and, therefore, became applicable even despite the tax treaty primacy, although some tax treaty practices introduced specific treaty saving clauses to ensure such an outcome.[6] Thin capitalization rules varied from country to country as did its actual conception. Some countries considered that excessive deductions of interest paid by resident corporations to their nonresident creditors, as determined by reference to the amount of a corporation's debt relative to its equity, applied only to cross-border interest payments. Other countries considered thin capitalization rules as a shareholder equity disguised as debt issue, denying only the deduction of interest paid to nonresident shareholders who controlled or had a substantial interest in resident corporations.[7]

Thin capitalization measures received a stern warning, despite the OECD approval, when the European Court of Justice (ECJ) declared that "Article 43 EC is to be interpreted as precluding a measure such as that contained in Paragraph 8a(1), Head 2, of the Körpershaftsteuergesetz (Law on Corporation Tax)."[8] The ECJ considered that thin capitalization rules, while being applied only to cross-border interest payments, constituted an obstacle to the freedom of establishment that could be justified neither

4. OECD. Thin Capitalisation legislation. A background paper for country tax administrations. Draft. August 2012.
5. OECD. Issues in international taxation. num 2. Paris 1987.
6. OECD. Thin Capitalisation Report, adopted on November 26, 1986. *See* for details Piltz, D.J. International Aspects of Thin Capitalization. IFA Cahiers vol. 81b. IBFD, 1996. Hinny, P. New Tendencies in Cross-Border Treatment of Interest of Corporations. General Report. IFA Cahiers vol. 93b. IBFD, 2008.
7. Arnold, B. "Restrictions on Interest Deductions and Tax Treaties" 73 Bulletin for International Taxation. 4/2019.
8. Judgment of the Court (Fifth Chamber) December 12, 2002, Case C-324/00, *Lankhorst-Hohorst GmbH and Finanzamt Steinfurt*, ECLI:EU:2002:749.

by the reduction in tax revenue nor by the need to prevent tax evasion. If the seat of the recipient company lies outside the territory of a Member State, this does not entail per se a risk of tax evasion since the company "will in any event be subject to the tax legislation of the State in which it is established" and no abuse is proven. Despite that, the ECJ somehow softened the incompatibility criteria in cases of wholly artificial arrangements;[9] most States looked for alternatives to counteract the erosion of the tax base through cross-border interest payments or to preserve the tax base, thus leading to alternative standards and measures. At that point in time, the territoriality of the tax was not seen as a general, driving interest that could justify per se a reconsideration of the limitation of the exercise of the economic freedoms.

Germany, and other EU countries followed, adopted a "fixed ratio rule" with a structure similar to the earnings-stripping rules in force in other jurisdictions, such as the United States. The fixed ratio rule, which is applied regardless of the residence or domicile of the recipient, overcomes the requirements of the EU fundamental freedoms while maintaining some control against jurisdictional profit shifting. The main change related to a structural or substantially different approach; while thin capitalization rules are based on asset value standards, fixed ratio rules are based on profit value references, linking expenses with the profitability of the activities or the companies that need debt financing. Verification of the use of cross-border interest payment promoted the need to intensify a coordinated response at an international level, thus leading to Action 4 of the BEPS action plan seconded by the EU initiatives to counteract profit shifting and protect the EU Member States (hereinafter "MS") domestic corporate tax bases.

§11.03 OECD VERSUS EU APPROACH: A GENERAL COMPARISON

Although the approach toward the limitation of deductibility of interest payment expenses is similar in the measures suggested by the OECD and the ones that will eventually be implemented by the requirements of the ATAD Directive, there are some important differences between them that should be considered beforehand. We will examine the structural issues, referring to the relationship of the measure with the States enforcement obligations, and the technical issues, referring to the specific measures to be implemented and that affect the tax relationship between the taxpayer and the Tax Administrations separately.

The main difference is a structural one, deriving from the nature of the institution approving the approach and the legal effects. The OECD has adopted a simple recommendation for State policymakers to introduce some rules or mechanisms based on certain common patterns deriving from a fixed ratio rule. Action 4 of the BEPS did not lead to any minimum standard to be adopted mandatorily at an international or national level, whether on a tax treaty or on a domestic legislation basis.[10] Action Plan

9. Judgment of the Court (Grand Chamber) March 13, 2007, Case C-524/04, *Thin Cap Group v. Commissioners of Inland Revenue*, ECLI:EU:2007-161.
10. Action 4 of the BEPS action plan did not lead to any measure that is to be considered a minimum standard, or that is affected by the so-called inclusive framework of the OECD. However, the

4 only recommends the adoption of certain rules with some alternatives and exceptions regarding its final implementation. It is difficult to conceptualize such an approach as a soft law mechanism since the recommendation to the States will be followed by an *implementing* measures verification process involving an indirect mechanism of evaluation.

On the contrary, Article 4 of the ATAD Directive has to be mandatorily implemented by EU Member States and failure to do so entails legal consequences for violating EU Law, although the different alternatives, exceptions, exemptions and deferred implementation dates may leave Member States some room for manoeuvre.

Therefore, as the OECD opted not to introduce a minimum standard requirement in that regard, and instead, opted for a recommendation with coordinated implementations of the recommended approach, the EU tries to guarantee a minimum standard with a mandatory minimum requirement

Despite some criticism, it is not correct to maintain, in this respect, that the EU should have followed the OECD proposal, allowing Member States to decide how to comply with the Recommendations of the BEPS action plan. On the contrary, it must be seen as a measure or policy choice that reinforces the international approach expressed under the consensus of the OECD and the G20 and forces the EU Member States to follow a more coordinated approach, since, as will be seen immediately below, Article 4 of the ATAD still leaves some leeway for Member States.

As regards the technical rules (either suggested or imposed), both the OECD and the EU have important similarities and, although the general approach is similar, they also have some discrepancies concerning the formulation of the so-called fixed ratio rule to limit the possibility of deducting interest expense payments. The "fixed-ratio rule" consists of three main elements: a benchmark net interest/EBITDA (earnings before interest, tax, depreciation and amortization) ratio; a group ratio rule as a complementary rule; and targeted rules, formulated as exclusions, exceptions or safe harbor rules at the EU level, to address specific situations. The fixed ratio rule depends, for its part, on the formulation of the "net interest amount", the identification of the relevant EBITDA reference and the establishment of the specific ratio.

The main similarity is the consensus reached at international and EU level regarding the legal technique for counteracting profit shifting through interest payments[11] which is the establishment of a fixed ratio rule as the main countermeasure

initial report (OECD. Limiting Base Erosion Involving Interest Deductions and Other Financial Payments. Action 4: 2015 Final Report. Paris. 2015) has been followed up by an important discussion and debate: OECD. Discussion Draft on BEPS Action 4 related to Banking and Insurance sectors. July 28, 2016. OECD. Additional Guidance on Action 4 of the BEPS Action Plan to curb international tax avoidance. December 22, 2016, which develop further elements concerning the design and operation of the rule and the technicalities for its implementation, not for changing or increasing the international consensus achieved. *See* OECD. Limiting Base Erosion Involving Interest Deductions. 2015 Report. October 2015. OECD. Limiting Base Erosion Involving Interest Deductions. 2016 Update. December 2016. OECD. Inclusive Framework on BEPS: Progress Report. June 2019.

11. The OECD report identifies three main scenarios where this outcome may arise: (i) groups placing higher levels of third-party debt in high tax countries; (ii) groups using intragroup loans to generate interest deductions in excess of the group's actual third-party interest expense; and (iii) groups using third-party or intragroup financing to fund the generation of tax-exempt

accompanied by a group ratio that tends to loosen the strict requirements of the automatic ratio rule. For the OECD Recommendation, the group ratio rule is only a policy option, either to apply a different group ratio rule or simply not to apply any group ratio rule. The OECD, furthermore, considers that other measures producing an equivalent result may also be implemented. Instead of the fixed ratio rule, the ATAD Directive also agrees to maintain alternative measures in force at a certain date if they "are equally effective" (Article 11.6 ATAD).

The difference, however, consists in the establishment of the specific ratio, which is considered, only as a recommendation in the Report of Action 4 of the BEPS plan, to be between 10% and 30%. Therefore, the recommendation of the OECD opts for the establishment of a bracket of suitable deductibility. The actual ratio (10%/30%) is not fixed at random but as a result of the analysis of the indebtedness ratio of most publicly traded multinational groups, which showed a net third-party interest ratio as compared to EBITDA of less than 10% according to its consolidated financial reports. The ATAD, on the contrary, establishes a 30% fixed rule (as a maximum) allowed deductible expense, despite the fact that, although the ATAD is a *de minimis* rule, Member States are *allowed* to implement a lower deductible threshold, as occurs in some domestic tax systems.[12]

The ATAD Directive does not include a minimum threshold deductibility like the 10% suggested by the OECD reports, but, despite its consideration of a minimum standard, a denial of deductibility of net interest expenses under that threshold could raise issues of proportionality and lack of respect for the ability principle. Following its wording, the ATAD also allows MS to establish different cap/ratio rules for related and nonrelated interest expenses or for some specific sectors.

The OECD completes its recommendation with the recognition of some suitable supplementary rules that serve to complement the fixed ratio rule. Among these complementary rules, the OECD advocates the inclusion of a *de minimis* threshold (on either a separate or group basis); the exclusion of public-benefit projects under certain conditions, considering that, in those cases, the BEPS risks are reduced; specific treatment for the banking and insurance sectors; the possibility to carry forward disallowed interest expenses or unused interest capacity; the transfer pricing rules implications (ongoing process), or the need to establish a monitoring process of the implementation of the recommended measures.

---

income. Being the second scenario a BEPS situation, the alternative/complementary rule of the EBIDTA Group should be placed not as an optional broadening clause to benefit the deductibility of intragroup interest payments if the group ratio is higher, but as a requirement to reduce the single entity ratio and consider only the group ratio as lower. Some countries' practice includes, in that regard, a different ratio rule that is lower for intragroup interest payments. As for the third scenario, it is foreseeable that exempted income will be excluded from the EBITDA, even if it may lead to several interpretative issues.

12. This is the outcome of Article 3 of the ATAD Directive, devoted to the "minimum level of protection" of the respective financial interests of Member States—protection for domestic corporate tax bases—although the ECJ case law on the requirements of the principle of proportionality should counterbalance this enabling provision of secondary EU Law.

The ATAD, on its side, complements the main rule with a list of options,[13] derogations,[14] taxpayer's rights (grandfather clause),[15] the equity escape rule for members of a consolidated group,[16] exclusions,[17] deferrals[18] and carryforward or carryback mechanisms[19] that may certainly serve to better accommodate the limitations of the rule to the requirements of the ability to pay principle. The alternatives of implementation for MS that arise from the combination of these complementary rules and the differences in interpretation of the different specialities, specificities and alternatives of the rule, which may arise from country to country until the ECJ reaches a common valid interpretation, assimilates, to a certain extent, the requirements of the ATAD and the coordinated follow-up of the Recommendations of the BEPS action plan of the OECD in that regard. This is especially true taking into consideration the escape clause included in Article 11.6 with reference to the equally effective rules in force as at August 6, 2016.[20]

---

13. Optional fixed group ratio rule, Article 4.1.a) applicable both to the group total borrowing costs or to a single entity belonging to a group, Article 4.1.b) ATAD.
14. Article 4.3 ATAD, derogations referred to the *de minimis* rule and the stand-alone entities.
15. Article 4.4 ATAD, referring to the grandfather clause for loans concluded before June 17, 2016, if not subsequently modified.
16. Article 4.5 ATAD allows certain exceptions to the fixed ratio rule that softens the requirements of the general clause contained in Article 4.1 ATAD for entities belonging to a consolidated group when the equity over total assets ratio is broadly equal to or higher than the equivalent group ratio.
17. Article 4.7 ATAD allows MS to exclude financial undertakings from the application of the fixed ratio rule—the whole Article 4—even if such an undertaking is part of a consolidated group for financial accounting purposes. The rule is intended to exclude only highly regulated institutions, not including, for instance, securitization vehicles of Regulation 2017/2402. Article 4.4. ATAD also allows the application of the rule to be excluded from long-term public infrastructure project loans, which is probably due to the business model of these projects and not necessarily related to the exclusion of BEPS risks which may also exist.
18. Article 11.6 ATAD allows, by way of derogation, the application of rules equally effective to the fixed ratio rule that had national targeted rules as at August 8, 2016, until the first full fiscal year following the date of publication of the agreement between the OECD members on the official website on a minimum standard with regard to BEPS, and at the latest until January 1, 2024.
19. Article 4.6 ATAD contains three different alternatives to include a carryforward or a carryback rule:
    a) Carryforward of excess borrowing costs that cannot be deducted in the corresponding tax period without time limitation;
    b) Carryforward—no limit—**and** carryback—3 years—of exceeding borrowing costs that cannot be deducted in the corresponding tax period;
    c) Carryforward without time limitation of exceeding borrowing costs and carryforward up to five years of unused interest capacity to deduct excess borrowing costs that cannot be deducted under the applicable rules.
20. For the analysis of the differences of implementation among the different Member States and the asymmetries that can be generated, *see* IBFD. The implementation of Anti-Beps rules in the EU: A comprehensive Study. Chapter 12. 2018. Hillmann, L., Hoehl, R. "Interest Limitation Rules: At a Crossroads Between National Sovereignty and Harmonization" European Taxation, April 2018, pp. 140 ff. A good example of what is being related is the case of the Irish tax system. While it does not contain any ratio-rule limitation, the Irish government considers that it can be argued to be, at least, equally as effective. Under Irish legislation, a deduction is available for borrowing costs where the use to which the related funds were put satisfies certain conditions, or where the interest is incurred for the purposes of the trade and is not otherwise disallowed under Ireland's existing anti-avoidance provisions.

In order to determine the maximum amount of deductible interest expenses, both the OECD and the EU refer to the ratio between two magnitudes: exceeding borrowing costs and taxpayer's EBITDA. As for the determination of the denominator of the ratio, the OECD refers initially to the EBITDA, with the possibility to complement it with an alternative measure (reference to the EBIT).[21]

In its 2016 Update Report, the OECD devotes a chapter to establish the calculation of net third-party interest expenses (Chapter 7 and Chapter 12 for the group) and another to calculating the EBITDA (Chapter 7 and Chapter 13 for the group). Following its nonbinding recommended approach, the OECD recognizes different approaches to calculating net third-party interest expenses: (a) to take the figures from the consolidated/individual income statements, (b) to make adjustments to the first figure to reflect items included in the definition of interest and payments economically equivalent to interest in Chapter 2 or (c) measure those items based on how they are treated in the group's consolidated financial statements. As for the concept of EBITDA, the OECD also recognizes that some differences of calculation may exist from one to another, considering the EBITDA either for tax or for accounting purposes. Therefore, the idea of treating these Guidelines as a soft law needs to be carefully considered, taking into account the coherence and specific relationship between the concrete domestic tax provision to be interpreted and the OECD reports' reference to the specific alternative to which it can be assimilated.

The ATAD, on the contrary, defines on a *unanimous basis*, the "borrowing costs", the "exceeding borrowing costs" and the "EBITDA" and, for that reason, may represent some important structural changes for countries that did not have a similar rule implemented beforehand and other moderate adaptations for countries that had implemented a similar system before the approval of the ATAD. Member States need to consider and carefully analyze the different alternatives and possibilities of regulations that remain open as a proper implementation of Article 4.

Despite the fact that the ATAD contains a definition of the objective of the rule (interest expenses on all forms of debt), many interpretative and applicative issues may arise with regard to each of the definitions of such interest as comprised in the Directive. In that regard, the OECD Report (paragraph 34) might be used in its supportive role, but it does not solve all applicative issues that will arise concerning certain complex settlements, structures, schemes or financial products and instruments (for instance upstream loans, loans to fund dividends, loans to fund-related party acquisitions, acquisition vehicles subsequently merged into a target company and so on). The need for clarity in the proper interpretation of such rules will certainly require an appropriate EU legal framework of protection for taxpayers considering the important economic and legal consequences that a retrospective declaration of the ECJ may have in that regard.

Similar problems may arise regarding the understanding of the meaning of the EBITDA definition contained in the ATAD. According to Article 4.2 of the ATAD, "the EBITDA shall be calculated by adding back to the income subject to corporate tax in the

21. EBITDA: earnings before interest, tax, depreciation and amortization. EBIT: earnings before interest and tax.

Member State of the taxpayer the tax-adjusted amounts for exceeding borrowing costs as well as the tax-adjusted amounts for depreciation and amortization. Tax exempt income shall be excluded from the EBITDA of a taxpayer."

Many different issues arise as regards the concrete meaning of such an EU Law concept. Despite the fact that it is an EU Law concept, some of the references such as "income subject to tax," "depreciation" or "amortization" force us to conclude that these references must be completed according to the respective domestic tax law—lacking a harmonized tax rule—that is to be applied. In that regard, it must be considered that the ATAD cannot be truly considered a harmonization tax Directive, but, on the contrary, a Directive devoted to protect the respective financial interests of the Member State regarding the corporate tax base.

In the same way, the mandatory exclusion of tax-exempt income leads to some interesting issues, for instance, with regard to the consideration of foreign-source income, when it is included in the tax base, but exempted, or alternatively fully credited via a tax credit. In other terms, in order to determine exemption or lack of taxation, it should be clarified whether exemption is referred to exemption in the State applying the measure or whether foreign taxes being paid that correspond to the "exempt" income would enable consideration of exempted—*de iure* or de facto—foreign income to be included in the calculation of the EBITDA. Not taking into account such technical situations may lead to international economic double taxation which runs contrary to the single taxation principle. Moreover, considering the reasons that justify the exclusion of exempted income—especially as regards scenario 3 that leads to interest BEPS results—it should be decided whether the rule should or could also be applied to income subject to limited or reduced taxation. The lack of definition, at international or at EU level, of minimum taxation for corporate tax purposes may make the development of such reasoning difficult. As another example, reference to tax-exempt income leads us to question whether CFC income has to be considered subject-to-tax income for that purpose or a specific charge such as the capital gains tax. Similar problems arise as to whether losses of previous taxable years carried forward have to be considered as determining the corresponding income generating the EBITDA or not.

What seems clear, however, is that reference to the exclusion of tax-exempt income for the determination of the EBITDA, a rule that runs counter to the practice in some EU countries up until now, leads us to conclude that the EBITDA reference is a tax concept and cannot be simply derived from accounting law or practices.

Lacking a proper EU Law body that defines the minimum corporate taxation that should be preserved (such as the CCTB or the CCCTB Draft proposals), the correct and logical integration mechanism should be to refer to those concepts in the domestic law with which the ATAD will need to be integrated, a mechanism that also worked for the integration of the technical elements of the Parent-Subsidiary and the Interest-Royalties Directive until they were defined, unanimously, by the ECJ.

§11.04 SOME CONSIDERATIONS AND ISSUES NOT (NECESSARILY OR PREVIOUSLY) DEALT WITH

The format of the present work and its limited scope does not allow us to make an in-depth analysis of the many implications, alternatives and difficulties of interpretation that will certainly arise from: (a) the verification of the proper or improper implementation of the requirements of the Directive; (b) from the interpretation or the requirements and implications of such a Directive when the specific rules will have to be applied. However, we consider it worthwhile to elaborate some arguments on the coherence, appropriateness, efficiency, automatism and reasonability of the ATAD regulation regarding the limitation of deductible interest payments.

The measure needs to be understood in the light of the new, international and political context in order to counteract profit shifting and base erosion. In times of crisis, the formulation of tax policy guidelines from an international perspective seems to be governed by the need to increase tax revenues or prevent their loss instead of formulating proposals to incentivize the capitalization of business sectors or disincentivizing external/debt funding. Nonetheless, there seems to be some distance between international political consensus and the technicalities needed in order to proceed to a proper and efficient implementation of the corresponding regulations in the different corporate tax systems of the EU (or the world).

The first important failure is the obvious, and necessary, lack of consensus among the different tax systems of the treatment that should refer to investors and creditors as far as their capital remuneration is concerned. Despite the fact that the general assumption is to distinguish the basic tax treatment at the level of the paying entity (the correspondence of deductible debt/nondeductible equity), there are important deviations from this assumption that make the follow-up and implementation of the recommended/mandatory rules difficult and unequal.

Following this line of reasoning, the analyzed measures are recommended or imposed despite the total lack of consensus, and natural disparity, of the basic elements that are needed to properly integrate these measures in each of the domestic tax systems. The measures were developed, and approved, even though there was a lack of consensus on: (a) the concept of interest payment/income at an international/comparative level; (b) the consideration and requirements for an interest payment to be deductible for corporate tax purposes; (c) the lack of correspondence between the treatment of the payment on the side of the payer and the treatment of the income paid on the side of the recipient;[22] and (d) finally, the divergences, asymmetries and double taxation situations that may still appear as a result of the interaction between the implemented rules with Action 4 of the BEPS action plan, and Article 4 ATAD neither raise nor solve the basic issues, deriving from the lack of coordination and correspondence between corporate tax systems of different countries, and opt to

22. For a detailed consideration and analysis *see* Gadwood, J., Morton, P. General Report. Interest Deductibility: The Implementation of BEPS Action 4. Cahiers de Droit Fiscal International. IFA. London Congress 2019. pp. 15-ff.

start building the house from the roof, suggesting a capped maximum interest deductibility ratio.

Connected to this reasoning, it is convenient to consider whether the suggested measures are coherent with the underlying BEPS action plan rationale: taxes should be paid where value is created and activities take place. The limitation of the deductibility of interest expenses by a fixed ratio rule does not seem to be *ab initio* in line with such an underlying principle. The denial of deductibility is based on a purely "prudential" protection of the corporate (territorial) tax base but does not appear to be directly or indirectly linked to the taxable income generated by the economic activities taking place in the territory of the protected State. Neither Action 4 of the BEPS action plan nor Article 4 ATAD establishes a link between the interest expense and the taxed income or the generating activities as a requirement for deductibility. The limitation rule is not made dependent at any point on a commercial analysis, but, on the contrary, is applied automatically, when all the interpretative and applicative problems have been solved. Unless there is express recognition that debt funding deductibility and, therefore, its remuneration under corporate tax policy leads to inefficient and undesirable results, it does not seem to reflect the aforementioned underlying principle. Moreover, the possibilities to implement the mandatory measure with a relatively high level of disparities and asymmetries do not necessarily ensure that they will contribute toward a neutral allocation of debt capital and expenses.

In fact, the establishment of a cap to limit the deductibility of interest payment expenses may lead to (economic) double taxation, either domestic or international. Neither the OECD Recommendations nor the ATAD ensures that this negative result will be eliminated. Therefore, no proposals on how to deal with resulting (temporal) double taxation are included either in the Directive or in the debate. Apparently, this double taxation can hardly be eliminated by tax treaty provisions and will necessarily have to be dealt with at a domestic level. The potential generation of (economic) double taxation by an EU Law secondary provision opens very interesting questions of adequacy, and even constitutionality of the rule, that can only be mentioned here, but not properly developed.[23]

It is doubtful whether this outcome may be justified as a necessary deterrent to prevent corporate base erosion. It is also doubtful whether the double taxation outcome may be justified and/or in line with the need to ensure single taxation or minimum taxation. Moreover (temporal) double taxation arising from the measures neither ensures a proper jurisdictional allocation of income and can be (solely) justified by the need to prevent tax base erosion, although it is not necessarily in line with the requirements of the territoriality principle. Finally, the basic question regarding the allocation of interest expenses that is who should bear the cost of external financing, the investor or the investment, remains to be solved, despite the fact that the measures suggested by the OECD and finally approved by the ATAD seem to underline and favor the investment bearing a (temporarily) limited charge of that cost.

23. Among others, whether the arbitration mechanisms enshrined in Directive 2017/1852/EU of October 10, 2017, on tax dispute resolution mechanisms in the EU could be used to avoid this outcome.

From the perspective of efficiency, the suggested measures are also subject to debate. Despite the fact that the OECD considered that the limited ratio rule should establish a "minimum protection" of the tax bases and the executive summary regarded the fixed ratio as "a minimum" (p. 11), the final Report did not include a minimum standard in that regard and, therefore, the effectiveness of the measures will depend on the follow-up analysis and the review process of the implemented measures. Even if the ATAD transformed the recommendation into mandatory rules to be implemented by EU MS, the options, exceptions and the acceptance of alternative measures might endanger the effectiveness of the measure. The competition for capital markets is still high and a consensus, even if minimum, is difficult to reach.

The effectiveness of the measure is also subject to its legal and (pending) constitutional verification. The pending constitutional analysis before the German Constitutional Court has already been mentioned. Moreover, it is difficult to predict whether the finally approved measures would pass the compatibility test developed by the ECJ regarding domestic anti-avoidance measures.

We need to bear in mind that EU ATAD Directive can be considered a coordination measure and should not be seen as a direct tax harmonization mechanism. Its goal consists of establishing different measures designed to protect Member States' corporate tax base. In fact, the provisions of the Directive may lead to several alternative implementation situations and, therefore, still leave some leeway for asymmetries, safe harbor, exclusions, options and exceptions, increasing the possibilities of tax planning on certain cross-border structures. What is more, group taxation rules seem to soften the rules instead of reducing the possibilities of profit shifting.

To opt for a cap-limited deductibility, which is of a preventive nature and not a reactive mechanism that applies automatically, and, therefore, does not allow the taxpayer to prove that valid economic reasons exist, apart from the ones foreseen by the legislator, for having such a debt finance position, and that the payment does not belong to a wholly artificial arrangement, may put judges in a difficult position (at a domestic and EU level) if they have to decide whether the measures finally implemented and Article 4 of the ATAD itself are compatible with the existing interpretation of the compatibility criteria of anti-avoidance tax rules in connection with the requirements of fundamental freedoms. From the principle of proportionality perspective, a comparative legal analysis shows that less restrictive measures for establishing—and denying—the deductibility of interest payments protecting the tax base exist and the following alternatives could have been suggested: (a) conditional deductibility related to the need to incur interest expenses in order to generate taxable income; (b) conditional deduction, related to the treatment of the interest received by the recipient, which can be transformed into a minimum tax on the income generated by the interest; (c) targeting a correspondence and symmetry of treatment measures that establish a relationship between the deductibility and the taxation/exemption of the income; (d) recharacterization of income/expense if it can be assimilated to capital/equity.

Nevertheless, it is necessary to remind ourselves that the measures required by the ATAD are considered by the ATAD itself to be a minimum standard, thus leading to some interesting questions, regarding how the "minimum Directive standard" is to be (?) dealt with, that is to say, whether the minimum standard can be accomplished by one provision and each provision, by any provision, or by the whole package of measures.

Bearing in mind the ECJ case law, it would be wise to consider that Member States would accomplish the minimum standard rule, Article 3 ATAD, by including in their domestic legislation provisions that respect one—and the main—anti-abuse rule, Article 6 ATAD. This line of reasoning would prevent an analysis giving an outcome of incompatibility as the one developed in the previous paragraphs. However, this does not seem to be the correct answer.

Another alternative that could ensure the compatibility outcome would be to establish the proper relationship between the different provisions of the ATAD. The ATAD itself does not establish any criteria of preference or subsidiarity between the different provisions, so it is difficult in principle to figure out whether the fixed ratio rule has preferential application over the mismatch arrangement provisions or vice versa, or whether the limited ratio rule can be applied simultaneously, or, on the contrary, is excluded, when the general anti-abuse rule demands its application (preference of the general rule), or if it is the GAAR that is not applicable when the interest limitation rule becomes applicable (*lex specialis* criteria). However, our understanding is that the ATAD implicitly allows the simultaneous application of all and each rule to a single scenario, provided that the situation falls under its respective scope of application. Therefore, the application of the GAAR and/or the interest limitation rule will depend greatly on the circumstances of the case. Therefore, it can be concluded that, in such a case, both would conform to the minimum level of protection of financial interest of the Member State concerned derived from ATAD and the compatibility and proportionality analysis should be developed accordingly. The same would be true if MS decided to apply a higher or alternative degree of protection of the tax base,[24] in which case the compatibility and proportionality analysis will become crucial for the appropriate balance between primary EU Law, secondary EU Law and implemented domestic law.

24. For instance, when countries apply alternative measures such as recharacterization (partial or total) disallowance of deductibility, *fraus legis* or recharacterization in cases assimilated to capital/equity, application of the arm's-length test, the application of withholding taxes on certain (excess) interest payments, limitation of level of interest of expense or debt (thin cap rules), group limited expenses or disallowance of interest expenses in certain transactions.

CHAPTER 12

The ATAD and the CCTB

Werner Haslehner

§12.01 INTRODUCTION

This short chapter analyses the relationship between the interest limitation rules laid down in the Anti-Tax Avoidance Directive (ATAD)[1] and the Proposed Directive[2] on a Common Corporate Tax Base (CCTB). Both are substantially congruent with very few differences in their content. Nevertheless, there are several aspects of the relationship between the two directives that raise fundamental questions as to their respective impacts on national law. Accordingly, this contribution aims to highlight, first, the general relationship between European Union (EU) directives, second, the specific relationship between the ATAD and the CCTB – if and when it is adopted – and, third, comments on the few variations in their respective provisions on interest limitation.

§12.02 RELATIONAL POSITIONING OF EU DIRECTIVES

EU directives are a key component of secondary EU law and, arguably, are the most important source of 'EU tax law'.[3] As explained in Article 288 TFEU, a directive 'shall be binding, as to the result to be achieved, upon each Member State to which it is

1. Council Directive (EU) 2016/1164 of 12 July 2016 laying down rules against tax avoidance practices that directly affect the functioning of the internal market, OJ L 193/1, 19.7.2016.
2. Proposal for a Council Directive on a Common Corporate Tax Base, 25 October 2016, COM(2016)685 final (hereinafter referred to as the '2016 CCTB Proposal' or simply – synonymously with the abbreviation for the resulting common corporate tax base – as the 'CCTB').
3. EU tax law is used here to refer to the totality of EU law governing taxation matters, including: (i) primary law rules and principles governing the division of competences in that field (particularly Article 113 and Article 115 TFEU), (ii) primary law directly affecting national legislation and administration (particularly the fundamental freedoms and the prohibition of State aid), and (iii) secondary law laid down with a view to (partial) harmonisation of national taxation.

addressed, but shall leave to the national authorities the choice of form and methods', meaning that they require implementation in national law. This principle not only governs the relationship between directives and national law, but also necessarily affects the relationship between national law and primary law, directives and primary law, and directives vis-à-vis each other. This section aims to address these three relational aspects of EU directives.

[A] Directives and National Law

The relationship between directives and national law has been the subject of many fundamental developments. Most notable among these developments is the creation and evolution of the doctrine of 'direct effect'. According to this doctrine, directives can be directly applicable to override national law despite a lack of any implementation action taken by Member States, if three conditions are fulfilled: (i) the rules laid down in the directive are clear, precise, and unconditional; (ii) the deadline for implementation has lapsed; and (iii) the directive provides rights to individuals.[4] A corollary of those conditions, when combined with the fact that – per the wording of Article 288 TFEU – a directive is only binding upon *each Member State to which it is addressed*, is that a directive cannot be invoked against a legal subject by a Member State that has failed to implement it.[5] This consequence, which is firmly grounded in both the estoppel principle[6] and the principle of legal certainty,[7] according to which any State interference with general freedoms of individuals needs to find a basis in properly implemented law, has become a bedrock protection for taxpayers. The Court of Justice of the European Union (CJEU or Court) explicitly confirmed that result in its landmark case on the Tax Merger Directive:[8] in *Kofoed*,[9] the Court held that Denmark could not rely on the anti-tax avoidance proviso laid down in Article 11(1)(a) of Directive 90/434/EEC in the absence of a domestic implementation measure. According to the CJEU, 'the principle of legal certainty precludes directives from being able by themselves to create obligations for individuals. Directives cannot therefore be relied upon per se by the Member State as against individuals'.[10] Nevertheless, such an implementation measure does not necessarily require legislative action in response to the directive as long as the full extent of the taxpayers' rights and obligations from the

4. *See* Judgment of 19 January 1982, *Becker*, Case 8/81, ECLI:EU:C:1982:7; for further details *see*, for example, Robert Schütze, European Constitutional Law (2012) pp. 323-327.
5. *See*, for example, Judgment of 5 April 1979, *Ratti*, Case 148/78, ECLI:EU:C:1979:110, para. 22; Judgment of 26 February 1986, *M.H. Marshall v. Southampton*, Case 152/84, ECLI:EU:C:1986:84, para. 48.
6. Herwig C.H. Hofmann, Gerard C. Rowe and Alexander H. Türk, Administrative Law and Policy of the European Union (2011) p. 93; Robert Schütze, European Constitutional Law (2012) p. 327.
7. *See*, for example, Judgment of 7 January 2004, *Wells*, Case C-201/02, ECLI:EU:C:2004:12, para. 56.
8. Council Directive 90/434/EEC of 23 July 1990 on the common system of taxation applicable to mergers, divisions, transfers of assets and exchanges of shares concerning companies of different Member States, OJ L 225, 20.8.1990, p. 1 (repealed).
9. Judgment of 5 July 2007, *Kofoed*, Case C-321/05, ECLI:EU:C:2007:408.
10. *Ibid.*, para. 42.

directive are clear from national law. In the CJEU's words, 'the transposition of a directive may, depending on its content, be achieved through a *general legal context*'.[11] While this meant that a general principle prohibiting abuse of rights or other (general) anti-avoidance provisions could be sufficient to allow Denmark to deny a taxpayer the benefits of the directive,[12] it still seemed clear that in the absence of such national doctrine or provision, the taxpayer would be able to claim a directive's benefits even in what may be considered an abusive situation.

In 2019, the CJEU moved beyond its traditional understanding of the doctrine of direct effect in the context of tax directives. In a series of combined judgments (the 'Danish Cases') concerning the Parent Subsidiary Directive[13] and the Interest and Royalties Directive, respectively,[14] it held that the general principle of EU law that establishes that EU law cannot be relied on for abuse or fraudulent ends not just permits, but in fact obliges, Member States to deny a directive's benefits where they are invoked for abusive or fraudulent ends.[15] The CJEU specified - in what seems a clear departure from its earlier case law - that this obligation was not affected by 'the absence of domestic or agreement-based anti-abuse provisions'[16] that would implement such a principle. That result came as a surprise to many commentators,[17] particularly in the context of direct taxation.[18]

One explanation for the CJEU's stance might be found in its case law on indirect horizontal effect - which it had largely used to the benefit of individuals, to give full effect to the principle of non-discrimination in private disputes;[19] it appears that the Court has expanded that concept to the EU anti-abuse principle. Advocate General (AG) Kokott had reached a similar conclusion prior to the Danish Cases:[20] according to her analysis of the CJEU jurisprudence, the general anti-abuse principle could be

11. *Ibid.*, para. 44 (emphasis added).
12. *Ibid.*, para. 48.
13. Council Directive 2011/96/EU of 30 November 2011 on the common system of taxation applicable in the case of parent companies and subsidiaries of different Member States (recast), OJ L 345, 29.12.2011, p. 8 (as amended).
14. Council Directive 2003/49/EC of 3 June 2003 on a common system of taxation applicable to interest and royalty payments made between associated companies of different Member States, OJ L 157, 26.6.2003, p. 49 (as amended).
15. Judgment of 26 February 2019, *N Luxembourg 1 et al.*, Joined Cases C-115/16, C-118/16, C-119/16 and C-299/16, ECLI:EU:C:2019:134, para. 111 and Judgment of 26 February 2019, *T Danmark et al.*, Joined Cases C-116/16 and C-117/16, ECLI:EU:C:2019:135, para. 83.
16. *Ibid.*
17. *See*, for example, Alfredo García Prats et al., Opinion Statement of the ECJ Task Force on the Danish Cases, European Taxation 2019, 487-502; Daniel Gutmann, Contre la théorie du bénéficiaire effectif en droit fiscal européen et international, 2 Fiscalité Internationale 2019, 1; Arne Schnitger, Entscheidungen des EuGH zum Begriff des Nutzungsberechtigten und Missbrauch, Internationales Steuerrecht (IStR) 2019, 304 at 306.
18. The CJEU previously ruled in favour of the direct applicability of the anti-abuse principle only in the much more harmonised field of value added taxation, for example, in Judgment of 18 December 2014, *Italmoda*, Joined Cases C-131/13, C-163/13, C-164/13, ECLI:EU:C:2014:2455, and Judgment of 22 November 2017, *Cussens and Others*, Case C-251/16, ECLI:EU:C:2017:881.
19. *See*, for example, Judgment of 22 November 2005, *Mangold*, Case C-144/04, ECLI:EU:C:2005:709; Judgment of 19 January 2010, *Kücükdeveci*, Case C-555/07, ECLI:EU:C:2010:21.
20. *See* Juliane Kokott, Das Steuerrecht der Europäischen Union (2018) p. 59.

directly applied in cases in which no directive provides a more specific anti-abuse standard. She pointed out, however, that such an approach would lead to the surprising result that a merely declaratory anti-abuse provision found in a directive could shield a taxpayer from the denial of benefits in abusive situations when that provision had not been implemented. The latest Court decisions do not appear to make the same distinction identified by AG Kokott,[21] but rather seem to suggest that all that is required of a Member State to deny certain tax benefits is its reliance on the general principle rather than on the directive's anti-abuse provision.[22]

Such an expansion of the anti-abuse doctrine is subject to criticism on at least two points: first, the earlier case law on indirect horizontal effects has already been criticised as undermining the EU's constitutional structure set up by the treaties as it erodes the limits set for the applicability of secondary law.[23] Second, while the CJEU could argue that, in that particular case, direct applicability was necessary even to the detriment of individuals because those individuals' interests had to be balanced against the rights of discriminated individuals, here the CJEU gives superior weight not to individual rights, but to the general interests of the EU and the Member States, albeit couched in terms of 'general principle of law'.

In addition to such criticism, this new development in the CJEU's jurisprudence raises a number of questions regarding the extent of its reach beyond the directives considered in those cases. For the purposes of this chapter, the question of interest is whether the direct application of the anti-abuse principle has: (1) any influence on the interpretation of the interest limitation rule laid down in EU legislation and (2) whether its importance varies between the ATAD, on the one hand, and the 2016 CCTB Proposal, on the other. As a starting point, it is worth pointing out that the CJEU's case law on the application of the anti-abuse principle concerns the granting of benefits that directives confer upon taxpayers rather than the interpretation of provisions which themselves aim to limit tax planning opportunities such as the interest limitation rule. It is, thus, questionable whether that case law has any impact on the relevant provisions for this chapter. However, a benefit under EU law may already be identified in certain existing exceptions to tax-aggravating provisions, making reliance on such exceptions contingent upon there not being an abuse. The Court's strong emphasis on the direct applicability of the general anti-abuse principle may also mean that seemingly clearly circumscribed anti-avoidance provisions (without special exceptions or carve-outs) will need to be interpreted in light of that principle, which may significantly affect their scope.

Furthermore, the Court's case law may have an impact on the relationship of different anti-abuse rules, both those found within one and the same directive and

21. Notably, the CJEU did not embrace the conclusion reached by AG Kokott on that point in her Opinion in the Danish Cases. *See* Opinion of 1 March 2018, *N Luxembourg et al.*, Case C-115/16, ECLI:EU:C:2018:143, paras 98-107; and Opinion of 1 March 2018, *T Danmark*, Case C-116/16, ECLI:EU:C:2018:144, paras 94-103.
22. Thus, the CJEU distinguished its result in the Danish Cases from the conclusion in *Kofoed*. *See* Judgment of 26 February 2019, *N Luxembourg 1 et al.*, Joined Cases C-115/16, C-118/16, C-119/16 and C-299/16, ECLI:EU:C:2019:134, para. 117.
23. *See* Robert Schütze, European Constitutional Law (2012) p. 336.

those included in different directives. The question has been posed as to whether the new general anti-avoidance rule (the 'GAAR') contained in Article 6 ATAD requires the denial of a tax advantage in circumstances that fall within the scope of other, more specific anti-abuse rules found in EU legislation – be it in the ATAD itself, or in other corporate tax directives.[24] According to one view, the more specific provisions categorically define the meaning of abuse within their field and leave no room for the application of the GAAR. That position, which conforms with the legal reasoning adopted by German tax courts,[25] may not be applicable in the context of EU law, given the importance the CJEU seems to assign to the general anti-abuse principle. As a result, existing special and targeting anti-avoidance rules may not give legal certainty to taxpayers as to their explicit scope of application, as the direct applicability of the anti-abuse principle would be readily available to fill any gap left open by the drafters of the directive.

[B] Directives and Primary EU Law

The diagnosis that a general anti-abuse principle may be applied in the context of directives and indeed override the conditions and rights laid down in such directives signifies that the relationship between directives and primary EU law becomes a potential concern to be addressed. At the beginning of such an enquiry must stand the obvious fact that directives are part of secondary EU law and must, therefore, comply with primary EU law, including both the written fundamental freedoms[26] and unwritten fundamental principles.[27] At the same time, the CJEU is often reluctant to find secondary law to be in breach of the EU Treaties. Instead, it will often aim to interpret the former in light of the latter in order to conclude that they are compatible.[28] This is particularly relevant in the context of potentially restrictive tax measures because the CJEU tests national implementation measures only against the rules of secondary law and not directly against primary law – at least in cases of 'exhaustive harmonisation'.[29] As a consequence, if the CJEU scrutinises secondary law less closely in comparison to

24. *See* Alfredo García Prats et al., EU Report on Anti-avoidance Measures of General Nature and Scope, IFA (ed), Cahiers de droit fiscal vol. 103a (2018) p. 66.
25. *See*, for example, Dietmar Gosch, Missbrauchsabwehr im Internationalen Steuerrecht, in Markus Achatz (ed), Internationales Steuerrecht – DStJG vol. 36 (2013) p. 213; Werner Haslehner, Tax Treaty Disputes in Germany, in Eduardo Baistrocchi (ed.), A Global Analysis of Tax Treaty Disputes (2017) p. 316.
26. *See*, for example, Judgment of 26 October 2010, *Schmelz*, Case C-97/09, ECLI:EU:C:2010:632, para. 50; Judgment of 25 June 1997, *Kieffer and Thill*, Case C-114/96, ECLI:EU:C:1997:316, para. 27; Judgment of 9 August 1994, *Meyhui*, Case C-51/93, ECLI:EU:C:1994:312, para. 11; Judgment of 17 May 1984, *Denkavit Nederland*, Case 15/83, ECLI:EU:C:1984:183, para. 15.
27. *See*, for example, Judgment of 7 March 2017, *RPO*, Case C-390/15, ECLI:EU:C:2017:174; Judgment of 23 April 2009, *Puffer*, Case C-460/07, ECLI:EU:C:2009:254.
28. Rita Szudoczky and Dennis Weber, in Peter Wattel, Otto Marres and Hein Vermeulen (eds). Terra/Wattel: European Tax Law – Volume 1 (7th edn 2018) p. 30, refer to the 'principle of reconciliatory (or consistent) interpretation'.
29. *See*, for example, Judgment of 8 March 2017, *Euro Park Service*, Case C-14/16, ECLI:EU:C:2017:177, para. 19; Judgment of 7 September 2017, *Eqiom and Enka*, Case C-6/16, ECLI:EU:C:2017:641, para. 15. The corollary of this is that the Court will accept potentially incompatible secondary law where it leaves Member States a sufficiently wide margin of appreciation to

national law with regard to the potentially restrictive effects of anti-avoidance provisions, the attendant lower standard of protection for taxpayers' freedoms could be 'imported' from a directive into national law. Hence, the question as to whether the CJEU does, indeed, apply a different standard of review to secondary legislation is placed centre stage.

While the CJEU does review secondary law in light of primary law, most of its case law in this respect concerns compatibility with the rules of competence and legislative procedure. In other words, the cases concern not only the content of secondary law (its substantive legality), but also its formal legality. In that context, it has long been established that the EU legislature is afforded broad discretion with respect to the substantive conditions for creating secondary EU law, namely: competence, subsidiarity, and proportionality. In those fields, the CJEU will invalidate laws only when they lead to an undermining of legislative procedure[30] or if it finds the legislative measure to be tainted by a manifest error in that regard.[31] By contrast, the procedural conditions of co-legislation, such as the effective consulting of parliament prior to the adoption of an act, are applied rather stringently, as they represent an 'essential factor in the institutional balance intended by the [EU] Treaty'[32] that reflects the democratic principle.

The question of interest for the purposes of this chapter, however, is the standard of review applied by the CJEU to secondary law when it reviews its content, for instance, if it were to test whether an anti-abuse provision restricts a fundamental freedom more than is strictly necessary. In this respect, it has been argued that the EU legislature would be afforded broader discretion than Member States since the EU is naturally more inclined to protect the internal market than individual Member States, in particular insofar as economic laws are concerned.[33] Indeed, the CJEU has explicitly endorsed the use of a different standard of review by transplanting its earlier case law on the principle of proportionality as an element of the formal legality of a legislative act to the substantive review of the content of such an act: in *Alliance for Natural Health*,[34] it referred to its conclusion in *British American Tobacco* concerning the proper exercise of the EU's competence as a matter of the principle of proportionality[35] in order to conclude that:

enable implementation in a way that complies with primary EU law. *See* Rita Szudoczky and Dennis Weber, *supra*, footnote 29, p. 30.

30. *See* the distinction the CJEU makes in its Judgment of 10 December 2002, *British American Tobacco (Investments) and Imperial Tobacco*, Case C-491/01, ECLI:EU:C:2002:741, para. 109.
31. *Ibid.*, para. 123.
32. Judgment of 7 March 2017, *RPO*, Case C-390/15, ECLI:EU:C:2017:174, para. 25; Judgment of 5 July 1995, *Parliament v. Council*, Case C-21/94, EU:C:1995:220, para. 17; Judgment of 10 June 1997, *Parliament v. Council*, Case C-392/95, EU:C:1997:289, para. 14.
33. *See*, for example, Juliane Kokott, Das Steuerrecht der Europäischen Union (2018), p. 45; for another view, *see*, for example, Axel Cordewener, Anti-abuse Measures in the Area of Direct Taxation: Towards Converging Standards under Treaty Freedoms and EU Directives?, 26 EC Tax Review (2017) pp. 60-66.
34. Judgment of 12 July 2005, *Alliance for Natural Health and Others*, Joined Cases C-154/04 and C-155/04, ECLI:EU:C:2005:449.
35. As laid down – since the Lisbon Treaty – in Article 5(1) and (4) TEU.

> 'the Community legislature must be allowed a broad discretion in an area such as that involved in the present case, which entails political, economic and social choices on its part, and in which it is called upon to undertake complex assessments. Consequently, the legality of a measure adopted in that area can be affected only if the measure is manifestly inappropriate having regard to the objective which the competent institution is seeking to pursue'.[36]

It subsequently extended this understanding more broadly to tax measures in *RPO*,[37] again referring exclusively to earlier cases where the exercise of the EU competence was at stake, rather than the compliance of secondary law with substantive rules of the internal market.[38]

While this convergence of interpretation of the different guises of the principle of proportionality may seem entirely logical, it is not an inevitable conclusion, since the two uses of the principle of proportionality concern two, rather different balancing exercises: in the first instance (Article 5(1) TEU), the proportionality principle is used to balance the EU's interests in adopting harmonising measures against the Member States' autonomy; in the second instance (proportionality as a condition for justifying the interference with internal market rules), the proportionality principle is used to balance the political, social, and economic interests of the EU legislature against the general interests of the EU internal market as expressed in the fundamental freedoms. It should be apparent that the margin of discretion afforded to the EU legislature is not necessarily the same for both of these balancing exercises, since the weight of the internal market rules may differ from that of Member State's legislative autonomy. Nevertheless, this observation does not amount to an objection to the convergence of standards for review in the CJEU's jurisprudence; it is merely intended to clarify the different contexts in which the Court has made those judgments.

The concrete balancing issue with respect to tax abuse is further complicated by the fact that it is not merely a balance between (national or EU) 'general interest', on the one hand, and an EU primary law rule, on the other hand. Rather, in this context, two principles of primary EU law must be balanced against each other: here, the EU's primary law anti-abuse principle is pitted against the EU's primary law principle of free movement. As the anti-abuse principle, arguably, has evolved and become ever-stronger in the Court's recent case law, it is no longer clear that the balance between the two found in the Court's earlier case law, which has become known as the 'wholly artificial' standard, still holds in this scenario, let alone whether it remains binding on the EU legislature.[39]

36. Judgment of 12 July 2005, *Alliance for Natural Health and Others*, Joined Cases C-154/04 and C-155/04, ECLI:EU:C:2005:449, para. 52.
37. Judgment of 7 March 2017, *RPO*, Case C-390/15, ECLI:EU:C:2017:174, para. 54.
38. References are made, there, to Judgment of 10 December 2002, *British American Tobacco (Investments) and Imperial Tobacco*, Case C-491/01, ECLI:EU:C:2002:741, para. 123 and Judgment of 17 October 2013, *Billerud Karlsborg and Billerud Skärblacka*, Case C-203/12, EU:C:2013:664, para. 35.
39. For a similar conclusion *see*, Adam Zalasinski, The ECJ's Decisions in the Danish 'Beneficial Ownership' Cases: Impact on the Reaction to Tax Avoidance in the European Union, 2 International Tax Studies 4 (2019), section 4.2.2.1, referring to the surprising possibility that the

Another question with regard to the relationship between primary and secondary law in this context is whether the purpose of the directive or provision, which is to combat avoidance and abuse, has any bearing on the result. Two brief observations can be made in this respect: on the one hand, in that situation, the principle of effectiveness of EU law would weigh in on the side of the anti-abuse principle and, thus, might tip the balance against free movement and the taxpayer's freedom to benefit from tax planning. On the other hand, one might assume that such a directive or provision was drafted for the purpose of defining the content of the anti-abuse principle more precisely, such that there would be no justification for extending the reach of the principle beyond the clear wording of secondary law.

What does all this mean for the relationship between the primary law aspects of the ATAD, on the one hand, and the 2016 CCTB Proposal, on the other? The ATAD, as a whole, was adopted to 'strengthen the average level of protection against aggressive tax planning in the internal market'[40] and to combat 'the erosion of tax bases in the internal market and the shifting of profits out of the internal market',[41] while the CCTB's primary objective is to 'facilitate business within the EU by subjecting taxpayers to a single rulebook of corporate tax legislation to apply across the internal market',[42] but also aims to 'make the system more robust and resilient to aggressive tax planning'.[43] That difference in outlook is complemented by their rather different ambitions with regard to the extent of harmonisation. The ATAD was explicitly intended to achieve a mere minimum standard of anti-avoidance rules, while the 2016 CCTB Proposal is intended to achieve a rather more comprehensive harmonisation, which is reflected in the existence of multiple options for Member States implementing the former, but not the latter. The CCTB sets definitive standards, including those regarding the level of strictness of anti-avoidance rules.[44] As a consequence, it could be argued that the CCTB, if adopted as proposed, will more likely establish exhaustive harmonisation in the relevant field and, thus, effectively shield national law from direct scrutiny in light of primary EU law. The ATAD, in contrast, sets out a minimum standard and, thus, cannot generally be seen to achieve exhaustive harmonisation. Nevertheless, insofar as a national norm does not go beyond the standard set by the ATAD, it would be surprising if the CJEU were to test it against anything other than that directive as the Member States have no discretion to be more lenient.[45]

As a result, it seems most probable, first, that the relevant provisions of secondary law will shield national law from direct scrutiny under primary EU law at least to the extent that they do not go beyond it and, second, that the rules laid down in secondary law will benefit from a more revenue-friendly interpretation of the

heretofore 'rock solid' approach allowing taxpayers to be motivated by tax reasons as long as their arrangements are 'genuine' may be abandoned.

40. Recital 3 ATAD.
41. Recital 5 ATAD.
42. 2016 CCTB Proposal, p. 4.
43. *Ibid.*
44. For examples of such options in the interest limitation rule, *see* infra section §12.04.
45. *See*, for example, Daniel Smit in Peter Wattel, Otto Marres and Hein Vermeulen (eds), Terra/Wattel: European Tax Law – Volume 1 (7th edition 2018) p. 495.

anti-abuse principle than has been the general assumption in earlier case law on the fundamental freedoms.

[C] The Interrelationship of Directives

What then, lastly, is the relationship between different directives? In principle, they stand next to each other on the same step in the hierarchy of norms – above national law but below primary EU law. As a result, the relationship between different acts of secondary law (such as two directives) is determined by the intention of the EU legislature that adopted them in the same way as ordinary national law. Consequently, potential conflicts with respect to the legal effects ordered by different directives will have to be resolved following general principles of interpretation: that is, in the absence of a specific rule resolving any apparent differences, reference will typically be made to the *lex specialis derogat de lege generali* and the *lex posterior derogat de lege anteriori* rules; yet, the overarching ordering principle continues to be the determination of the legislative intention.

Due to the peculiarly fragmented nature of the EU legislature, however, the legislative intent may be both difficult to determine with any certainty and especially unsatisfactory from a constitutional standpoint. While different parliamentary chambers – roughly equivalent to the EU Parliament and the Council – as co-legislative institutions are not uncommon, several aspects are unique to the EU legislature.

First, the completely different personal composition of the Council of Ministers, which depends on the subject matter of a particular piece of legislation, may lead to overlapping and potentially contradictory rules passed by different groups of government representatives. This, however, may be considered the least significant difference, as national legislators also congregate in specialised committees in parliament and the members of parliament can change dramatically following elections.

Second, the EU legislature passes significantly different forms of what one might call 'ordinary' legislation under Article 288 TFEU: regulations, directives, and decisions. While one might expect these to have some order of priority among them, no such priority can be derived from the EU Treaties or CJEU case law. The unspoken assumption of the EU Treaties may be that they will not overlap, let alone contradict each other, but this may not always be true.

Third, the EU legislative process differs markedly from one subject matter to another: while parliament has only a consultative voice in tax matters and the Council must pass legislation unanimously under the special legislative procedures set up by Articles 113 and 115 TFEU, most other legislation is passed by majority vote in the Council and parliament under the ordinary legislative procedure. However, the EU Treaties do not provide for any explicit order of priority among legislative instruments on the basis of the different rules of creation required to pass legislation in various areas. While politicians initially called for a proper legislative hierarchy in the course of earlier treaty negotiations,[46] and EU law scholars have suggested a possible hierarchy between such 'ordinary' and 'special' legislative acts, they ultimately concluded that the assumption of an unwritten rule of priority 'proves unmanageable in terms of methodology and implausible in terms of substance'.[47]

The relationship between directives – in general and in the various potentially conflicting provisions found in them – remains one of uncertain and, a priori, indeterminable character.

§12.03 THE RELATIONSHIP BETWEEN THE ATAD AND CCTB

Although closely connected, the ATAD and the CCTB have quite different historical backgrounds, scopes, and objectives. While the idea of a common corporate tax base dates back to the early days of EU tax approximation[48] – with the idea of reaching a holistic solution for corporate taxation in the internal market – the Member States and EU institutions developed the ATAD as a response to the OECD/G20 BEPS project, which was intended to address base erosion and profit shifting within groups of related companies.[49] As most EU Member States had already committed to implementing the results from that project in 2015, the EU Commission saw a clear need to harmonise approaches in order to prevent further fragmentation within the internal market.[50] By the time this need became apparent, the original 2011 CCCTB Proposal[51] had been up for discussion by the Council for a number of years without an apparent route for its adoption. The best path towards implementing the BEPS recommendations was identified in late 2015 by splitting off various anti-avoidance provisions found in the 2011 CCCTB Proposal and including them in a separate 'anti-BEPS directive',[52] which led to the Commission's ATAD Proposal published on 28 January 2016. Following an uncharacteristically short period of Council-level negotiations that resulted in relatively few amendments to the Commission's original proposal, the ATAD was adopted on 12 July 2016. Subsequently, the Commission withdrew the 2011 CCCTB Proposal and replaced it with a relaunched project that followed a 'staged approach' – separating the

---

46. *See* Jürgen Bast, Legal Instruments and Judicial Protection, in A. Van Bogdandy and Jürgen Bast (eds), Principles of European Constitutional Law (2009) p. 362.
47. *Ibid.*, p. 390.
48. The idea of a CCTB had already been floated in the 1992 'Ruding Report', although it was meant to coincide only with 'Phase III' of corporate tax harmonisation 'concurrently with full economic and monetary union'; *see* European Commission, Report of the Committee of independent experts on company taxation (1992), pp. 201-209.
49. For a comprehensive account of the development at the institutional level, *see* Katarina Köszeghy, Corporate Tax Harmonization: C(C)CTB 2.0? in Werner Haslehner, Georg Kofler and Alexander Rust (eds), EU Tax Law and Policy in the 21st Century (2017) pp. 305-333.
50. Proposal for a Council Directive laying down rules against tax avoidance practices that directly affect the functioning of the internal market, 28 January 2016, COM(2016) 26 final (hereinafter 'Commission ATAD Proposal'), p. 6.
51. Proposal for a Council Directive on a Common Consolidated Corporate Tax Base (CCCTB), COM(2011) 121/4 (hereinafter '2011 CCCTB Proposal').
52. Katarina Köszeghy, in Werner Haslehner, Georg Kofler and Alexander Rust (eds), EU Tax Law and Policy in the 21st Century (2017) p. 315; *see* the ECOFIN Proposal for a Council Directive on a Common Consolidated Tax Base (CCCTB), 14544/15 FISC 171.

goal of harmonising the tax base from the further objective of consolidation – to make it more palatable to the Member States.[53] The only other significant change from the 2011 CCCTB Proposal lies in the mandatory nature of the common rules for groups over a certain size while leaving the option open for smaller companies to calculate their tax base under the same rules.[54] Both chronologically and genealogically, the ATAD and 2016 CCTB Proposal are thus intertwined in complex ways. As already pointed out, however, they differ in both their objective and their scope.

With regard to the EU's competence to adopt either directive, both are based on the internal market competence of Article 115 TFEU. In the case of both directives, concerns have been raised regarding their compatibility with the treaty conditions of Article 115 TFEU (in the case of the ATAD)[55] or the principles of subsidiarity and proportionality (in the case of the 2011 CCCTB Proposal[56] and the 2016 CCTB Proposal[57]). In light of the broad discretion which the CJEU generally affords the EU legislature, any substantive objections raised against the legality of such further harmonisation – ranging from the argument that the ATAD goes beyond the minimum standard agreed to by OECD Members to the view that mere minimum harmonisation does not properly address the risk of fragmentation as a consequence of unilateral implementing measures – are likely to be ineffectual. It is, of course, notable that the 2016 CCTB Proposal relies significantly on the same rationale as the ATAD to justify a common approach, namely its anti-avoidance function.[58] That follows from the fact that it proposes a mandatory application of its rules and, thus, itself creates a certain amount of fragmentation between its own – common – rules and the Member States' national regimes that would continue to apply to companies that do not fall under such mandatory application of ATAD rules and that do not otherwise choose to opt into the EU system. This stands in stark contrast to the 2011 CCCTB Proposal, which was 'primarily designed to serve the needs of companies that operate across borders'[59] and, while it also included anti-avoidance rules, these were far less developed.[60]

What does this mean, finally, for the relationship of the ATAD and the 2016 CCTB Proposal if the latter eventually becomes law? Since their scope is different, the CCTB would not entirely replace the ATAD. Even if it incorporated all of the ATAD's

53. 2016 CCTB Proposal, p. 3.
54. *Ibid.*
55. *See*, for example, Arnaud de Graaf and Klass-Jan Visser, ATA Directive: Some Observations Regarding Formal Aspects, 25 EC Tax Review (2016), p. 199 (at pp. 204 et seq.); Werner Haslehner, EU-US Relations in the Field of Direct Taxes from the EU Perspective: A BEPS-Induced Transformation?, in Pasquale Pistone and Dennis Weber (eds), Implementation of Anti-BEPS Rules in the EU: A Comprehensive Study (2018) pp. 44-48.
56. The 2011 CCCTB Proposal was opposed under the so-called yellow card procedure laid down in Article 6 of Protocol (no. 2) on the application of the principles of subsidiarity and proportionality by the national parliaments of Bulgaria, Ireland, Malta, the Netherlands, Poland, Romania, Slovakia, Sweden and the United Kingdom. *See* Rita Szudoczky, Is the CCCTB Proposal in Line with the Principle of Subsidiarity?: Negative Opinions Submitted by National Parliaments in the 'Yellow Card Procedure', in Dennis Weber (ed). CCCTB: Selected Issues (2012), at p. 111.
57. The 2016 CCTB Proposal was opposed by the parliaments of Denmark, Ireland, Luxembourg, Malta, the Netherlands, Sweden and the United Kingdom.
58. *See* 2016 CCTB Proposal, p. 2.
59. Recital 8 of the 2011 CCCTB Proposal.
60. For a comparison, *see* infra section §12.04.

provisions, the CCTB would only apply to groups above a certain size and, thus, would not cover all corporate taxpayers subject to the ATAD. While large multinational groups would be subject to both directives – unless the 2016 CCTB Proposal is amended to partially repeal the ATAD – smaller groups and stand-alone companies would continue to be subject to the ATAD rules, unless they opted into the new CCTB regime. As their coexistence seems unavoidable, the question of priority comes to the fore to the extent that their scopes would overlap but impose different obligations on Member States with respect to the introduction of anti-abuse rules. Member States would, in any event, have to implement both regimes, although they may try to fully harmonise the rules: the main difference lies in the fact that the ATAD grants more options to Member States than the 2016 CCTB Proposal; consequently, any potential differences would be eliminated by exercising options in the ATAD in line with the chosen solution in the 2016 CCTB Proposal (if adopted without modification). The question, thus, is whether the Member States would be obliged to do so.

Certainly, no such obligation exists outside the scope of application of the CCTB, at least, that is, with respect to companies that are not part of a large group. What is the obligation of Member States with regard to applying anti-abuse rules to such groups following the adoption of the CCTB? In this respect, the anti-abuse rules of the CCTB must be seen both as *lex posterior* and *lex specialis*. Although the ATAD has the narrower objective and scope by merely partially harmonising Member States' approaches towards tax avoidance, the CCTB's anti-abuse rules would apply to a narrower set of facts than the ATAD. Also, considering that the CCTB's objective 'to provide for a holistic solution to creating a fairer and more efficient corporate taxation'[61] arguably encompasses the goals of the ATAD entirely within its scope of application, one can derive a legislative intent to supersede the earlier 'quick response to follow up on the OECD/G20 BEPS project'.[62] Finally, it would be entirely illogical (and otherwise undermine the effectiveness of the CCTB) if Member States were able to continue to apply optional rules from the ATAD to groups that otherwise fall within the mandatory scope of application of the CCTB.

If the CCTB is adopted as proposed, it will incorporate the objectives of the ATAD completely, but it also intends – at least in its latest iteration[63] – to go beyond mere minimum harmonisation. Rather, it would seek to harmonise the corporate tax base completely. As a consequence, the concrete approach taken by the ATAD provisions, particularly the various options given to Member States on how to implement them, would be an odd fit for the CCTB. It is no surprise, then, that the 2016 CCTB Proposal

61. Bart Van Raaij, Where Do We Go from Here? The Steady Move Towards a Common Corporate Tax Base, in Werner Haslehner et al. (eds), A Guide to the Anti-Tax Avoidance Directive (Edward Elgar 2020, in print).

62. *Ibid.*

63. While the 2011 CCCTB Proposal had been intended to apply only optionally – that is to say, taxpayers could opt into the regime – the 2016 CCTB Proposal foresees a mandatory application of its rules for large corporate taxpayers. *See* 2016 CCTB Proposal, p. 9.

does not generally include such options (although one may wonder to what extent greater optionality may result from further Council negotiations).[64]

Nevertheless, a full-blown common consolidate corporate tax base (CCCTB), as a final destination for EU corporate taxation, would hardly be compatible with many optional derogations from the rules, as it could make consolidation exceedingly burdensome in practice.

§12.04 A COMPARISON OF THE RULES ON INTEREST LIMITATION

The 2011 CCCTB Proposal contained an interest limitation rule, which was, however, entirely different from the one included in the ATAD.[65] Indeed, Article 81 of the 2011 CCCTB Proposal, included as one of three explicitly named 'anti-abuse rules',[66] only concerned interest payments made to associated enterprises in third countries if the recipient was subject to a low tax rate and no effective exchange of information was available. While there may seem to be little reason for a substantive comparison between that proposed rule and the one found in the ATAD, it should be emphasised that a general interest limitation was not considered a necessary element of corporate tax rules until as late as 2011. It is also worth noting that the OECD's final report on BEPS Action 4 only considered the adoption of such a rule to be a 'best practice' and not a 'minimum standard', thus making it all the more interesting that the EU Commission changed its 2011 approach in both the ATAD and the relaunched 2016 CCTB Proposal, which included a fixed ratio non-deductibility clause.[67]

The interest limitation rules in the ATAD[68] and the CCTB[69] are broadly identical, with the main difference being the expectedly greater optionality available to Member States under the ATAD. The main difference between the ATAD and the 2016 CCTB Proposal, on the one hand, and the 2016 CCCTB Proposal, on the other, follows from the fact that under the 2016 CCCTB Proposal's approach, the 'group' would be the taxpayer so that all calculations relating to deductibility of interest would have to be made at the group level.[70] As a corollary of that change, the Commission proposed to increase the safe-haven threshold of deductible interest from EUR 3 million to EUR 5 million.[71]

64. Cf. Van Raaij in Haslehner et al. (ed): 'The ATAD includes various derogations for which Member States may opt. The derogations in the CCTB that derive from the ATAD are not optional but mandatory. However, not all of these derogations have been included in the CCTB proposal, since it would not match with the objective and purpose of the CCTB to have the same degree of flexibility as in the ATAD.'
65. The 2016 CCTB Proposal goes as far as to note (on p. 10) that 'this is a new rule (absent from the proposal of 2011)'.
66. Chapter XIV of the 2011 CCCTB Proposal.
67. For a more detailed review of the interaction of BEPS Action 4 and the ATAD rule, *see supra* Chapter 11.
68. Article 4 ATAD.
69. Article 13 2016 CCTB Proposal.
70. *See* Article 69(1) 2016 CCTB Proposal.
71. Article 69(3) 2016 CCTB Proposal.

In general, while the ATAD interest limitation rule is characterised by a multitude of options for Member States, the equivalent in the 2016 CCTB Proposal makes a definitive choice for the Member State (and thus taxpayers across the EU). Indeed, while the initial Commission Proposal for the ATAD already offered broad discretion to Member States on how to design the limitation rule, an even greater level of flexibility was added in subsequent negotiations at the Council level.[72] A number of differences between the ATAD and the 2016 CCTB Proposal concern the calculation of the interest limitation. For instance:

- in the definition of 'borrowing costs', the CCTB includes deductions made under its Allowance for Growth and Investment;[73]
- while the ATAD contains the option to calculate the 30% threshold and safe harbour at group level,[74] this is mandatory under the CCTB;[75]
- while the CCTB provides for the unlimited carry-forward of non-deductible exceeding borrowing costs,[76] the ATAD also gives Member States the option to allow a carry-back of exceeding borrowing costs for up to three years[77] and to carry forward unused interest capacity for up to five years;[78]
- only the ATAD gives Member States the option to allow consolidated groups to use consolidated financial statements prepared under rules different from International Financial Reporting Standards (IFRS) or national accounting standards.[79]

The other differences between the ATAD and the CCTB concern the various exceptions granted from the interest limitation rule. At times, the differences mean that the ATAD is potentially harsher on taxpayers than the CCTB, while at other times, the opposite is true. The first is the case where:

- the ATAD makes the safe-haven deduction of exceeding borrowing costs up to EUR 3 million optional,[80] while the same is mandatory under the CCTB;[81]
- the ATAD allows Member States to exclude stand-alone entities from the scope of the interest limitation,[82] while under the CCTB, the interest limitation rule can never apply to such entities;[83]

72. Katarina Köszeghy, in Werner Haslehner, Georg Kofler and Alexander Rust (eds), EU Tax Law and Policy in the 21st Century (2017) p. 328.
73. Article 4(12) 2016 CCTB Proposal includes the 'defined yield on net equity increases as referred to in Article 11 of this Directive'.
74. Article 4(1) ATAD.
75. Article 13(2) 2016 CCTB Proposal.
76. Article 13(6) 2016 CCTB Proposal.
77. Article 4(6)(b) ATAD.
78. Article 4(6)(c) ATAD.
79. Article 4(8) ATAD. Cf. Article 4(10) 2016 CCTB Proposal for the definition of 'consolidated group' in that directive.
80. Article 4(3)(a) ATAD.
81. Article 13(2) 2016 CCTB Proposal.
82. Article 4(3)(b) ATAD.
83. Article 13(4) 2016 CCTB Proposal.

- the ATAD grants Member States the option to apply a standstill clause to exclude interest payments under loans concluded prior to 17 June 2016 as well as payments made under loans funding long-term infrastructure projects,[84] while the CCTB includes both rules (with an as yet undetermined date) as mandatory exceptions;[85]
- the ATAD allows Member States to exclude financial undertakings from the scope of the rule,[86] while the CCTB excludes such undertakings outright.[87]

The ATAD is potentially more taxpayer-friendly in respect of the optional group carve-outs: the 2016 CCTB Proposal does not include an equivalent to the ATAD's group ratio rule and the equity escape rule.[88]

§12.05 CONCLUSION AND OUTLOOK

This chapter aimed to analyse the interaction between the ATAD and the 2016 CCTB Proposal, particularly with respect to the interest limitation rules contained in both. Beyond a mere comparison of the differences between the provisions, which shows primarily that the already adopted ATAD allows much more flexibility in this respect than the CCTB Proposal, some general observations were made on the relationship between directives, as well as their interaction with national law and primary law. What this brief analysis demonstrates is that the object of secondary law has an important impact on its position in the multilevel EU legal order, especially now that the CJEU's recent case law aims to strengthen the anti-abuse principle in EU law and thus, indirectly, strengthen laws that aim to implement that principle (or can at least be read in that sense). As a consequence, anti-abuse rules are more likely to both affect national law directly (even in the absence of their proper transposition) and withstand scrutiny under the EU fundamental freedoms.

The ATAD interest limitation rule has mostly been implemented already, although the directive grants Member States that had 'equally effective' rules in place on 8 August 2016 a transitional period for implementation until 2024. The Member States that rely on that exception may, then, wait for further negotiations and the eventual adoption of a CCTB before committing to any particular version of the option-ridden Article 4 ATAD. The main reason for the many options found there – the time pressure to act within a short period – is not present in negotiations for the CCTB, suggesting that even though the final outcome of further discussions at the Council level will look different from the 2016 CCTB Proposal, it will likely contain fewer options than the ATAD.

84. Article 4(4) ATAD.
85. Article 13(5) 2016 CCTB Proposal.
86. Article 4(7) ATAD.
87. Article 13(7) 2016 CCTB Proposal.
88. Article 4(5) ATAD.

The 2018 French-German Common Position Paper annexed to the so-called Meseberg Declaration gives an outlook on the status of these negotiations.[89] According to that jointly issued position, both countries take the following view on the concrete version of the interest limitation rule to be included in the CCTB directive: 'France and Germany are in favour of the inclusion of, notably, the group escape clause, the carry-forward of unused interest deduction volumes ("EBITDA[90] carry forward"), and the deletion of exceptions for long-term public infrastructure projects and financial undertakings.'[91] If these elements were found in a unanimously adopted CCTB directive, especially the deletion of the latter two exceptions, the differences between the ATAD and any such CCTB directive would continue to have a potentially significant impact on certain companies' decisions to opt into the CCTB regime. Ultimately, if the French-German position could command unanimous support, it would, in any case, seem appropriate to change the ATAD rule accordingly.

89. A Joint Declaration adopted by the French and German governments on 19 June 2018. *See* https://www.bundesfinanzministerium.de/Content/EN/Standardartikel/Topics/Europe/Articles/2018-06-20-Meseberg-att2.pdf?__blob = publicationFile&v = 3 (last accessed 6 July 2019).
90. EBITDA stands for earnings before interest, taxes, depreciation, and amortization.
91. German-French Common Position Paper on CCTB Proposal, 19 June 2018, p. 3.

CHAPTER 13

The Interplay Between Interest Limitation Rules and Anti-hybrid Rules: Inverting the Paradigm

Leopoldo Parada

§13.01 INTRODUCTION

Interest limitation rules and anti-hybrid rules have been at the core of both the Organisation for Economic Co-operation and Development (OECD) Base Erosion and Profit Shifting Project (hereinafter the 'BEPS Project')[1] and the European Union (EU) Anti-Tax Avoidance Directive (hereinafter 'ATAD').[2] However, they aim at two different goals. While interest limitation rules aim in general at controlling an enterprise's excess indebtedness, anti-hybrid rules aim at avoiding specific mismatches

1. OECD, *Limiting Base Erosion Involving Interest Deductions and Other Financial Payments – Action 4: 2015 Final Report*, OECD/G20 Base Erosion and Profit Shifting Project (OECD Publishing, 2015). *See also* OECD, *Limiting Base Erosion Involving Interest Deductions and Other Financial Payments, Action 4 – 2016 Update: Inclusive Framework on BEPS*, OECD/G20 Base Erosion and Profit Shifting Project (OECD Publishing, 2016). For the complete OECD BEPS Project, *see* OECD, *Addressing Base Erosion and Profit Shifting* (OECD Publishing, 2013). *See also* OECD, *Action Plan on Base Erosion and Profit Shifting* (OECD Publishing, 2013). For an early analysis of the OECD BEPS Project, *see* Y. Brauner, *BEPS: An Interim Evaluation*, 6 World Tax J. 1 (2014).
2. This reference to the ATAD, which includes both the ATAD 1 and the ATAD 2, is singularized in this work. Council Directive (EU) 2016/1164 of 12 July 2016 laying down rules against tax avoidance practices that directly affect the functioning of the internal market [19 July 2016] OJ L193/1 (hereinafter 'ATAD 1'). *See also* Council Directive (EU) 2017/952 of 29 May 2017 amending Directive (EU) 2016/1164 as regards hybrid mismatches with third countries [7 June 2017] OJ L 144/1 (hereinafter 'ATAD 2').

originated by the use (or misuse) of hybrid financial instruments (HFIs)[3] or hybrid and reverse hybrid entities.[4]

At first sight, therefore, one may argue that the interplay between the two rules is nothing else than a classic relationship between *lex generalis* and *lex specialis*, thus preventing a priori any potential conflicts. Moreover, to reinforce this idea one may also argue that since both rules have the same economic effect on taxpayers, that is increasing the taxable base of the taxpayer in the same amount of non-allowable deductions in the payer state, the logical result is that the application of anti-hybrid rules (*lex specialis*) is prioritized – as argued by the OECD and followed by the EU secondary legislation.[5] This conclusion is nonetheless premature, and perhaps also, short-sighted.

Even though it is evident that the economic effect of interest limitation rules and anti-hybrid rules is rather similar, giving priority to the application of one rule over the other should be a more carefully evaluated decision, especially in light of potential economic double taxation conflicts. In this regard, the author argues for inverting the 'official paradigm'[6] as regards the conflicting application of these rules, thereby giving priority to the application of interest limitation rules over anti-hybrid rules in all those cases in which hybrid mismatches come into play.[7] This proposal, in the author's view, may bring more consistent outcomes both from a practical and from a tax policy perspective, ultimately avoiding economic double taxation.

Section §13.02 briefly analyses the interest limitation rules in the context of the EU ATAD 1, with a short outline of its legal precedent: the German interest barrier. Section §13.03 summarizes the functioning of the anti-hybrid rules that originated within the OECD BEPS Action 2 and were subsequently introduced also in the EU ATAD 1 and 2. Section §13.04 illustrates how the simultaneous application of interest limitation rules and anti-hybrid rules in cases involving either HFIs or hybrid entity structures raises the question of priority of these rules, and how choosing one position or the other may have completely different outcomes. In addition, this section argues that giving priority to the application of anti-hybrid rules in cases involving hybrid

3. For a recent analysis on the anti-hybrid rules in the ATAD 1 and 2 applied specifically as regards hybrid financial instruments, *see* L. Parada, *Hybrid Financial Instruments and the New Anti-Hybrid Rules in the EU ATAD 1 and 2: Implementation Challenges*, in: W. Haslehner (ed), *The Anti-Tax Avoidance Directive* (Edward Elgar Publishing 2019), forthcoming. For a complete analysis on issues related to hybrid financial instruments and BEPS, *see* F. Martínez Laguna, *Hybrid Financial Instruments, Double Non-Taxation and Linking Rules* (Kluwer Law International 2019). *See also*, J. Bungaard, *Hybrid Financial Instruments in International Tax Law* (Kluwer Law International 2017).
4. For a further analysis on issues related to hybrid entities and BEPS, *see* L. Parada, *Double Non-taxation and the Use of Hybrid Entities. An Alternative Approach in the New Era of BEPS* (Kluwer Law International 2018).
5. *Infra* section §13.04[B].
6. This author refers to the 'official paradigm' as the position argued by the OECD in the OECD BEPS Action Plan 2 – reinforced in the EU ATAD 1 and 2 – that is when anti-hybrids and interest limitation rules apply concurrently, the former rules (anti-hybrids) have priority. *See* analysis at *infra* section §13.04[B].
7. This author has already raised this argument before. Parada, *supra* note 4, 343-347. *See also*, L. Parada, *Hybrid Entity Mismatches and the International Trend of Matching Tax Outcomes: A Critical Approach*, 46 Intertax 12, 988-990 (2018).

mismatches may ultimately result in permanent economic double taxation. Section §13.05 makes a claim for inverting the official paradigm that anti-hybrid rules should apply before interest limitation rules. This section argues that this approach is not only more consistent with the aim of avoiding economic double taxation but also aligns the interplay of these rules better under the tax policy aims of coherence and ease of administration. Section §13.06 provides the conclusions.

§13.02 INTEREST LIMITATION RULES IN A NUTSHELL

Countries around the world provide for rules limiting the deductibility of interest expenses in cross-border financial structures in order to maintain the equity/debt balance in a company. The foregoing is strictly connected with the unequal tax treatment between debt and equity, which encourages companies to prefer debt to equity when it comes to determining how to invest in a company.[8]

In a nutshell, provisions limiting the deductibility of interest expenses consist in either a fixed debt-equity ratio, also known as *thin capitalization rules*, or a limitation in the excess of interest expenses calculated as a percentage of the taxable EBITDA (Earnings Before Interest, Taxes, Depreciation and Amortization), also known as *earnings stripping rules*. The majority of the countries opt for this latter option, providing for a limitation in the deductibility of net interest expenses up to 30% of the amount of taxable EBITDA to the extent that the net interest expenses do not exceed certain thresholds, in some cases, and, in other cases, only if the entity in excess of indebtedness is part of a group.

The application of the interest limitation rule therefore implies that a certain amount of interest expenses, which are normally deductible within a taxable year, will now not be deductible, regardless of the fact that under certain circumstances the amount of non-deductible expenses may be carried forward to future taxable years.

[A] The German Interest Barrier as Legal Precedent

The German interest limitation rule (or 'interest barrier') is perhaps one of the best examples of interest limitation rules around the world.[9] After all, these rules have served as inspiration for the design and implementation of other similar domestic rules

8. *See*, for example, W. Schön et al., *Debt and Equity in Domestic and International Tax Law– A Comparative Policy Analysis*, BTR 2 (2014). Another important difference between debt and equity is the timing of taxation of payments since most countries accrue interest income or deductions throughout the term of an instrument that leads to an additional income or a reduction of taxable income, and therefore an increase or decrease in taxes. That is, taxes can be reduced or have to be paid even though no cash flow of interest payments takes place. *See* L. Parada, *Is It Debt or Is It Equity? The Problem with Using Hybrid Financial Instruments*, 74 Tax Notes Int'l 4, 348 (2014).
9. For a detailed analysis of these rules, *see*, e.g., C. Knöller, *The Efficacy of Thin Capitalization Rules and their Barriers: An Analysis from UK and German Perspective*, 39 Intertax 6/7 (2011). For a specific analysis on the German rules in this book, *see* D. Reich, *Germany*.

in many countries (especially in Europe), including the interest limitation rules introduced in the ATAD 1.[10]

Under German law, a business [*Betrieb*][11] is limited to deducting net interest expenses, that is the amount after offsetting the interest expenses against the interest earnings of the business, as business expenses up to 30% of the amount of the taxable EBITDA.[12] If there is thus an excess of net interest expenses, this is not deductible in the fiscal year, although it can be carried forward indefinitely and deducted in subsequent fiscal years subject to the same threshold limitation.[13] The non-deductible amount of interest is not re-characterized as dividends.[14]

For the purposes of this rule, the term 'interest expenses' includes all remuneration for borrowed capital that has reduced the relevant profits,[15] including not only interest expenses in a restrictive manner but also other considerations paid to the lender, for example, prepayment fees, provisions and other fees.[16] In contrast, considerations not payable to a lender or considerations for other services such as arrangement fees, commitment fees, letter of credit or others are not included.[17] Likewise, interest income is considered as income from all types of cash receivables.[18]

---

10. The German interest barrier is codified in §4h of the EStG [*Einkommensteuergesetz*], which provides the general rule and the exceptions applicable to this rule. Accordingly, §8a(2) and §8a(3) of the KStG [*Körperschaftsteuergesetz*] provide some special rules regarding the exceptions when applied specifically to corporate entities. This rule replaced the former thin capitalization rule. *See* K. von Brocke and E. Garcia Perez, *Group Financing: From Thin Capitalization to Interest Deduction Limitation Rules*, 16 Intl. Transfer Pricing J. 1, 31 (2009).
11. German or foreign corporations, partnerships and commercial partnerships limited by shares [*Kommanditgesellschaft auf Aktien* or KGaA] constitute one business. Accordingly, companies that form a tax group [*Organschaft*] are also considered as one business. Permanent establishments, on the contrary, do not qualify as one business. *Id.*
12. DE: §4h(1) of the EStG. The taxable EBITDA is different from the financial EBITDA stated in the balance sheet. The taxable EBITDA comes indeed from the taxable profits of the business and is adjusted by adding and/or deducting interest expense and/or interest income as well as ordinary tax depreciation and/or amortization. However, §4h(1) of the EStG takes only regular depreciation and amortization into account. Thus, extraordinary write-offs do not increase the volume of taxable EBITDA. M. Scheunemann and T. Müller-Duttiné, *New German Tax Rules on Financing Expenses*, 35 Intertax 8/9, 519 (2007).
13. DE: §4h(1) of the EStG. The carry-forward of disallowed interest expenses should be carefully considered because there are situations in which the denial of interest expenses deductions does indeed become final. For example, when the volume of the debt financing and the volume of taxable EBITDA remain unchanged in future fiscal years, or in the case of restructuring measures, particularly the change of control under §8c of the EStG, or if more than 50% of the shares in a corporation are directly or indirectly transferred within a five-year period, or if less than 50%, but more than 25% of the shares in a corporation are directly or indirectly transferred within a five-year period. In this latter case, the use of the interest carry-forward is disallowed on a pro rata basis. *Id.*, 520.
14. A. Fross, *Earnings Stripping and Thin Cap Rules: Maintaining an Arm's Length Distance*, 53 Eur. Taxn. 10, 514 (2013). Under the old German thin cap rules, there was a re-characterization. That is, the excess interest income was treated as dividend at the level of the shareholder. The above implied that it was exempted from taxation (95% exempt). Today, however, the interest income is fully taxed at the shareholder's level. Scheunemann and Müller-Duttiné, *supra* note 12.
15. DE: §4h (3) of the EStG.
16. Scheunemann and Müller-Duttiné, *supra* note 12.
17. *Ibid.*
18. Von Brocke and Garcia Perez, *supra* note 10, at 32.

This rule applies to both related and unrelated parties and provides for some exceptions as well. First, the limitation of 30% of taxable EBITDA applies only to the extent that the amount of net interest expenses exceeds EUR 3 million, which is known as the '*de minimis rule*'.[19] Second, the general rule does not apply when a business does not belong, or only partially belongs, to a group, which is known as 'stand-alone provision'.[20] Third, and finally, even if a business belongs to a group, the interest limitation rule does not apply if the business' equity ratio does not fall short of the group's equity ratio by more than 1%. This latter rule is known as 'escape clause'.[21]

[B] The Interest Limitation Rules in the ATAD 1

Article 4 of the ATAD 1 provides for a rule similar to the German interest barrier. Indeed, the ATAD rule states a limit to the amount of *borrowing costs* (interest expenses)[22] that can be used as business expenses up to 30% of the amount of taxable EBITDA.[23] Accordingly, the non-deductible amount of expenses can be carried forward for up to five years or carried back for up to three years.[24] The excess of EBITDA can only be carried forward for up to five years.[25]

The ATAD interest limitation rule applies only when the exceeding costs are over EUR 3 million.[26] In other words, like the German rule, it includes a de *minimis rule* mainly to prevent small- and medium-size companies from falling into the scope of the rule.[27] Accordingly, Member States would be able to exclude stand-alone companies from the application of the interest limitation rules.[28] The ATAD also introduces an 'escape clause'; that is, the taxpayer belonging to a group may not be subject to the interest limitation rule if the taxpayer demonstrates that the ratio of its equity over its assets does not fall short of the group's ratio by more than 2%.[29]

The foregoing will be illustrated below with a very simple example.

19. DE: §4h(2)a of the EStG. The original amount was nonetheless EUR 1 million. DE: Citizen Relief Act [*Bürgerentlastungsgesetz*] of 16 July 2009, BGBl 1, 1959 (2009) and Growth Acceleration Act [*Wachstumsbeschleunigungsgesetz*] of 22 Dec. 2009, BGBl 1, 3950 (2009). This exception has, in principle, the purpose of protecting small- and medium-size enterprises falling within the scope of the rule.
20. DE: §4h (2)(b) of the EStG.
21. DE: §4h(2)(c) of the EStG.
22. According to Article 2(1) of the ATAD 1, the term 'borrowing costs' means interest expenses and other equivalent costs that a taxpayer incurs in connection with the borrowing of funds. The distinction between 'borrowing costs' and 'interest expenses' appears nonetheless to lack a substantive significance. *See* S. Lampert, T. Meickmann and M. Reinert, *Article 4 of the EU Anti Tax Avoidance Directive in Light of the Questionable Constitutionality of the German 'Interest Barrier' Rule*, 56 Eur. Taxn. 8, 324 (2016).
23. Article 4(1) of the ATAD 1.
24. Article 4(6)(a) and (b) of the ATAD 1.
25. Article 4(6)(c) of the ATAD 1.
26. Article 4(6)(c) of the ATAD 1.
27. Article 4(3) of the ATAD 1.
28. A stand-alone entity 'means a taxpayer that is not part of a consolidated group for financial accounting purposes and has no associated enterprise or permanent establishment'. Article 4(3)(b) of the ATAD 1.
29. Article 4(5)(a) of the ATAD 1.

Let us assume a company (Co1), incorporated in state MS1, with a subsidiary (Co2), incorporated in MS2, which subsequently owns Sub 1 and Sub2, two resident companies in MS2. Co1 and Co2 are considered associated companies.[30] Accordingly, Co2, Sub 1 and Sub2 are part of the same group under the laws of MS2, although their results are not consolidated for tax purposes. We will assume that Co1 grants a loan to C2o which pays interest back in year X for the amount of EUR 5 million. Co2 also has interest income in year X, which amounts to EUR 1 million. Sub 1 and Sub2 have no income or interest expenses that year. The taxable EBITDA of the group (Co2 + Sub1 + Sub2) amounts to EUR 10 million. We will finally assume that the Co2 ratio of its equity over assets does not fall below 2% of that of the group (Figure 13.1).

Figure 13.1 Interest Limitation Rule

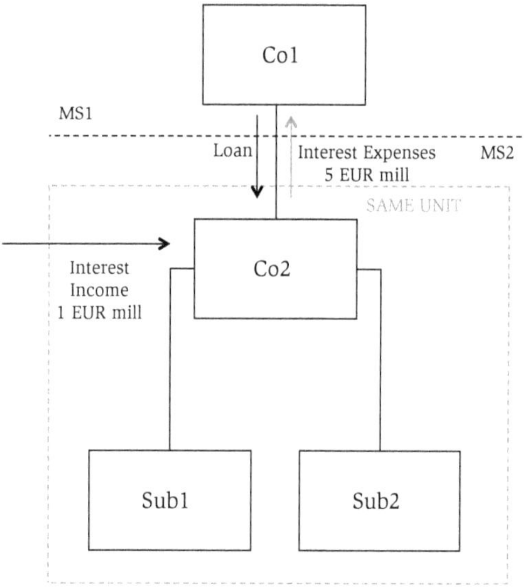

In this case, the amount of net deductible expenses - 'borrowing costs' - (EUR 4 million) will be limited to up to 30% of the taxable EBITDA from the group composed by Co2 + Sub1 + Sub2.[31] The *de minimis* exception does not apply because the net borrowing costs are not over EUR 3 million. Accordingly, neither the *stand-alone* nor *escape clause* may apply. Therefore, the amount of allowable interest expenses in year X will amount to EUR 3 million. The amount of EUR 1 million of non-deductible expenses in year X can be carried forward to the subsequent year.[32]

30. Article 2(4) of the ATAD 1 (including the definition of 'associated enterprises').
31. Article 4(1) of the ATAD 1 (EBITDA in this case is calculated at the level of the group).
32. Article 4(6) of the ATAD 1.

§13.03 ANTI-HYBRID RULES IN A NUTSHELL

Anti-hybrid rules aim at counteracting what is known in doctrine as *hybrid mismatch arrangements*, that is arrangements that make use (or misuse) of the different tax characterization of the same financial instrument or the same legal entity, which ultimately result in a double deduction (DD) or a deduction/non-inclusion (D/NI) outcome.

This Section briefly explains the rules created to counteract these specific mismatches, known as 'linking rules', which were originally suggested in the OECD BEPS Action 2 and subsequently replicated in the EU ATAD 1 and 2.

[A] Hybrid Mismatch Arrangements

The OECD BEPS Action Plan 2 refers to *hybrid mismatch arrangements* as arrangements that 'exploit differences in the tax treatment of an entity or instrument under the laws of two or more jurisdictions to achieve double non-taxation, including long term deferral'.[33] Similarly, the ATAD 1 states that a hybrid mismatch is '... a situation between a taxpayer in one Member State and an associated enterprise in another Member State or a structured arrangement between parties in Member States where the following outcome is attributable to differences in the legal characterization of a financial instrument ... a) a deduction of the same payment, expenses or losses occurs both in the Member State in which the payment has its source, the expenses are incurred or the losses are suffered and in another Member State ("double deduction"); or b) there is a deduction of a payment in the Member State in which the payment has its source without a corresponding inclusion for tax purposes of the same payment in the other Member State ("deduction without inclusion")'.[34]Hybrid mismatch arrangements therefore constitute the objective scope of the anti-hybrid rules.

It is important to highlight as well that in general the scope of application of the rules is limited to mismatches between a taxpayer and its associated enterprises. That is, mismatches regarding the use of HFIs or hybrid (or reverse hybrid) entities fall into the scope of the anti-hybrid rules to the extent that there is a sufficient ownership connection between payer and payee.

33. OECD, *Neutralizing the Effects of Hybrid Mismatch Arrangements – Action 2: 2015 Final Report, OECD/G20 Base Erosion and Profit Shifting Project*, 11 (OECD Publishing 2015).
34. Article 2(9) ATAD 1. This scope is widely extended in the ATAD 2, which includes not only hybrid mismatches related to the use of hybrid financial instruments (and hybrid entities) but also cases of reverse hybrid mismatches, PE mismatches and tax residence mismatches. K. Spindler-Simader and V. Wöhrer, *Implementation of the EU Anti-tax Avoidance Directive (2016/1164) in Austria*, 58 Eur. Taxn. 7, 296 (2018).

[B] Anti-hybrid Rules and the OECD BEPS Action Plan 2

The OECD BEPS Action Plan 2 recommends a two-level reaction to deal with hybrid mismatch arrangements, that is a *primary response* and a *defensive rule*, which are known together in literature as 'linking rules'.

A *primary response* consists in denying a deduction of a hybrid payment to the extent that this is made twice (DD outcome) or, when the deduction is granted in the payer state, there is no corresponding inclusion of income in the recipient state (D/NI outcome). These mismatches in the tax outcomes may of course be the result of the use of either HFIs or hybrid entity structures. Accordingly, a *defensive rule* requires either a deduction to be denied (DD outcome) or taxation to be applied as regards a hybrid payment (D/NI outcome) in those cases in which the primary response was not effective for solving the hybrid mismatch. Again, these mismatches in the tax outcomes may be the result of the use of either HFIs or hybrid entity structures.[35]

Therefore, these rules have the special characteristic of being contingent both as regards the tax outcomes in the jurisdictions involved in the hybrid transactions and as regards their own application. In other words, a denial in a deduction (*primary response*) is contingent on the fact that such a deduction was not made in the other jurisdiction involved, or, that being made in the payer state, this was not recognized as income in the payee state. Accordingly, a denial of a deduction or taxation of the hybrid payment as a secondary rule (*defensive rule*) is contingent on the denial of the deduction in the other state.

Moreover, a *primary response* applies at first to counteract a hybrid mismatch arrangement. Therefore, and only to the extent that this rule was ineffective for solving the hybrid mismatch arrangement, the *defensive rule* comes into play.

[C] Anti-hybrid Rules and the EU ATAD 1 and 2

In light of the recommendations in the OECD BEPS Action Plan 2, the ATAD 1 and 2 also introduced linking rules in order to ensure that hybrid payments resulting from the use of both HFIs and/or hybrid entity structures do not remain untaxed.[36] Generally speaking, and unlike some minimal differences in the scope, the ATAD anti-hybrid rules in effect resemble the recommendations in the OECD BEPS Action Plan 2.

The ATAD 1 introduces a *primary response*, which denies a deduction if the same financial instrument is treated as debt in the payer Member State and as equity in the payee Member State, or that the same entity is regarded as opaque in its place of incorporation and as tax transparent in the jurisdiction of the investors, and due to these disparities a DD or a D/NI outcome comes into play. In particular, the primary

35. For an analysis of these rules from the perspective of hybrid entity structures, *see* Parada, *supra* note 7. For a recent analysis from the perspective of hybrid financial instruments, *see* Martínez Laguna, *supra* note 3. *See also*, Bungaard, *supra* note 3.
36. The focus on double non-taxation rather than on the core of the disparities (i.e., different tax characterization of entities or instruments) is still arguable. *See*, for example, Parada, *supra* note 4, 279-352.

response denies the deduction of the hybrid payment in the Member State where that payment has its source (DD outcome) or the Member State where the payer is located (D/NI outcome).[37]

Considering that the geographical scope of the ATAD 1 is limited to hybrid mismatches within the EU, there was of course no need to introduce a defensive rule. That is, the mandatory enforcement of directives by Member States makes a defensive rule unnecessary.[38]

The ATAD 2, which extended the scope of linking rules to mismatches with third states outside the EU, also provides for a *primary response* that denies a deduction in the Member State that is the 'investor jurisdiction'. This reference to the 'investor jurisdiction' is not exempt from criticism, especially because it appears to be inconsistent with the ATAD 1 (which refers to the 'source state')[39] and with the specific outcome of D/NI, which calls for a denial of the deduction in the 'payer jurisdiction'.[40]

The ATAD 2, however, also introduced a *defensive rule*, which applies in those cases where the primary response did not. In particular, the defensive rule requires a deduction to be denied in the payer jurisdiction in situations in which a primary response did not apply before denying the deduction in the investor jurisdiction in cases of a DD outcome.[41]

[D] Basic Illustrations of the Anti-hybrid Rules in the ATAD

The application of the ATAD rules can be illustrated using examples of either HFIs or hybrid and reverse hybrid entities. For the purposes of these basic illustrations, the author will distinguish between DD and D/NI cases.

[1] DD Cases

Let us assume that XCo is a company resident in state X, which controls YCo, a company resident in state Y, which subsequently holds a subsidiary (YSub), which is also a resident in state Y.

Accordingly, YCo and YSub are part of the same group, although they do not consolidate their results for tax purposes. YCo borrows money from a third-party lender, which is unrelated to the group (bank). We will also assume that YCo is a taxable entity in state Y, while it is treated as a tax transparent entity in state X. Therefore, the interest paid by YCo will be deducted against the income of the group in state Y. However, the same deduction can be used in state X due to the tax transparent

37. Article 9 of the ATAD 1 reads as follows: '1. To the extent that a hybrid mismatch results in a double deduction, the deduction shall be given only in the Member State where such payment has its source. 2. To the extent that a hybrid mismatch results in a deduction without inclusion, the Member State of the payer shall deny the deduction of such payment.'
38. Article 1 of the ATAD 1 (scope). *See also*, recital 13.
39. Article 9(1)(a) of the ATAD 2.
40. For example, G. Fibbe and T. Stevens, *Hybrid Mismatches under the ATAD I and II*, 3 EC Tax Rev., 156 (2017).
41. Article 9(1)(b) of the ATAD 2.

treatment of YCo in that state. In simple words, the same deduction is used twice, once in state Y and once in state X (Figure 13.2).

Figure 13.2 Example of DD

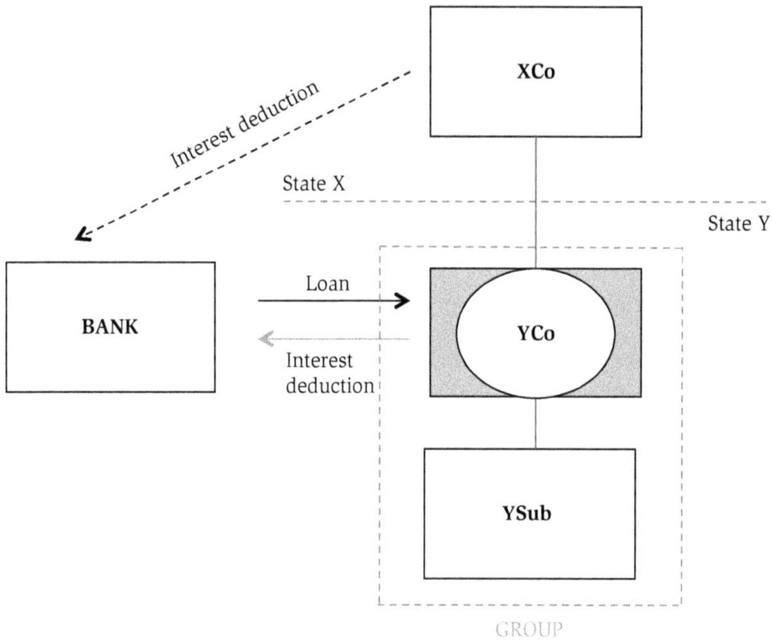

The ATAD 1, which limits its geographical scope to hybrid mismatch arrangements within the EU,[42] contemplates the denial of a deduction in the source state as a *primary response* in cases involving hybrids and DD outcomes. That is, state Y will deny the deduction to YCo in order to counteract the mismatch.[43]

However, the application of the rules may become a bit trickier if either state X or state Y is not considered as EU Member State, thus giving rise to the application of the ATAD 2. Here, the effects of the rules will depend on which state is actually the non-EU Member State.

42. *Supra* section §13.03[C].
43. Although the determination of the source state might appear straightforward to reach in the example above, it is not always an easy task, especially because 'source' is not a uniform concept. The issues regarding the determination of source have been largely discussed in the international tax literature. *See*, for example, L. Lokken, *What Is This Thing Called Source?* 37 Int'l Tax J. 3, 21-26 (2011). *See also* F. Vanistendael, *Reinventing Source Taxation*, 6 EC Tax Rev. 3, 152-161 (1997). For a tax treaty approach as regards issues on source, *see* J. Avery Jones et al., *Tax Treaty Problems Relating to Source*, BTR 3 (1998).

If state X is a non-EU Member State, the ATAD 2 provides, as a primary response, that the deduction shall be denied first in the 'investor jurisdiction',[44] that is state X in our example. Yet, the enforcement of this primary response becomes a difficult task, unless state X has also introduced a primary response domestically and decides to apply it.[45] That is the reason why the ATAD 2 also introduces a defensive rule, which in this case means that state Y shall deny the deduction of interest payments.[46] Accordingly, as state Y is an EU Member State, the application of the defensive rule is not left to the discretion of state Y and should therefore be applied.[47]

On the contrary, if state Y is a non-EU Member State, state X ('investor jurisdiction') is obliged to apply the primary response. Therefore, the mismatch in the outcome will be solved without the need to apply a defensive rule in the non-EU Member State.[48]

[2] D/NI Cases

A classic example of a D/NI outcome could be shown using an HFI case. Let us assume that XCo is a company resident in state X, which has a subsidiary in state Y (YSub). Accordingly, we will assume that the same instrument (e.g., a contingent debt) is treated as debt in the payer state Y while it is considered as equity in the payee state X. The different tax qualification of the same financial instrument will result in a deduction in state Y while a non-corresponding inclusion of income in state X, where the interest payments are treated as equity, and therefore, generally subject to a participation exemption.

44. ATAD 2 does not use the concept of 'source state' anymore. Fibbe and Stevens, *supra* note 40, 156.
45. State X is a non-EU Member State. Thus, there is no mandatory EU secondary law to be respected for this state.
46. Article 9(1)(b) of the ATAD 2.
47. Parada, *supra* note 3 (forthcoming) (where the author explains that unlike the ATAD 2, the ATAD 1 applies only to mismatches among Member States, which means that a primary response introduced in a directive must be implemented and is enforceable for all Member States).
48. *Id.*

Figure 13.3 Example of D/NI Using HFIs

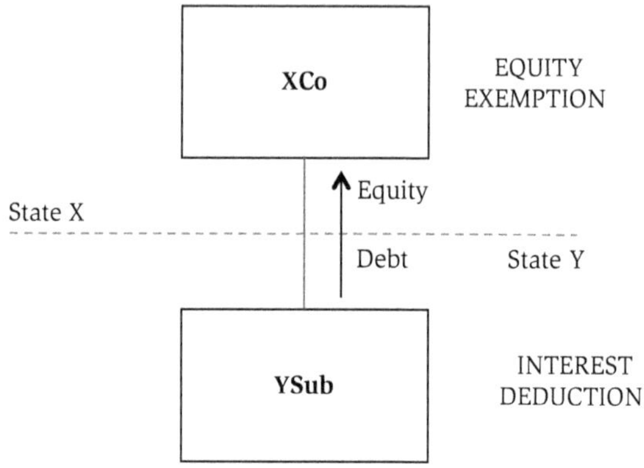

The same outcome could be achieved in the example above if, instead of a divergent opinion as regards the tax characterization of the same financial instrument, the states X and Y do not agree on the existence of YCo as a taxable entity.[49] In other words, if YCo were considered as a taxable entity in state Y while as a tax transparent entity in state X, a deduction would be granted in state Y, but a non-inclusion of interest payments would occur in state X because the transaction is indeed disregarded for tax purposes in that country.[50]

Figure 13.4 Example of D/NI Using Hybrid Entities

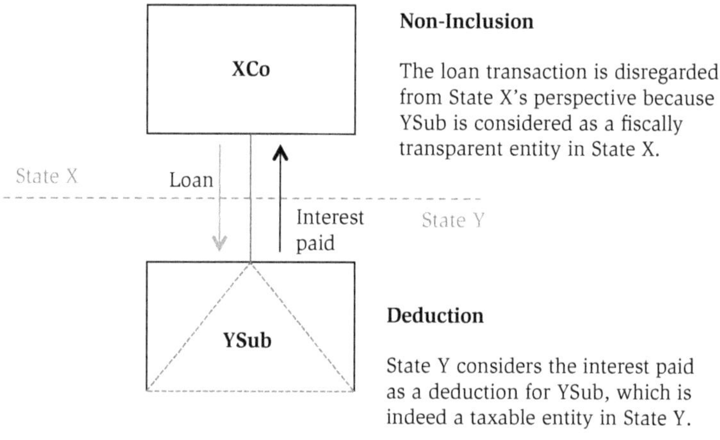

49. For an in-depth analysis on the topic of hybrid entities, *see* Parada, *supra* note 4. For an analysis of hybrid entities in the EU context, *see* G. Fibbe, *EC Law Aspects of Hybrid Entities* 15, Doctoral Series, IBFD, 2009.
50. *See* more on this in Parada, *supra* note 4, 291-299.

If we assume that states X and Y are EU Member States, the ATAD 1 provides only for a primary response to solve the mismatch in the outcomes; that is, it denies the interest deduction in the payer state Y in our example.[51] In contrast, if either state X or Y were non-EU Member States, the ATAD 2 provides for both a primary response and a defensive rule.

If state Y were a non-EU Member State - and granted a deduction for those interest payments - state X (EU Member State) would have to apply a defensive rule; that is, it would be obliged to tax those interest payments, or, in the same way, not apply the participation exemption in the case of a mismatch originated by the use of an HFI. In the case in which the mismatch is the result of the different tax qualification of YCo (hybrid entity), the outcome is the same, that is, taxation in state X because of the application of the defensive rule. In other words, the loan transaction is recognized for tax purposes as if YCo were not a tax transparent entity in state X.

In contrast, if state X were a non-EU member, state Y (EU Member State) must deny the deduction of those interest payments (primary response) either because the disparity is due to the different tax characterization of the same financial instrument (Figure 13.3) or the same entity (Figure 13.4). In other words, since state Y is obliged to comply with EU law, and therefore to apply the directive, the mismatch is expected to be solved without the need for a defensive rule in the non-EU state.

§13.04 THE CONFLICTING INTERPLAY BETWEEN INTEREST LIMITATION RULES AND ANTI-HYBRID RULES

As already stressed in this work, the interplay between interest limitation rules and anti-hybrid rules is due to the fact that both rules may concur together in situations involving either HFIs or a hybrid entity structure. Therefore, the concurrent application of both rules raises the question as to which one of these rules should apply first, affecting both the scope of a primary response and a defensive rule.

This Section analyses the question and argues - in contrast to the OECD approach - for the application of interest limitation rules taking precedence over anti-hybrid rules. This approach is not only more consistent with the aim of avoiding economic double taxation but also aligns better the interplay of these rules under the tax policy aims of coherence and ease of administration.

[A] Using a D/NI Outcome and Hybrid Entities as an Example

The best way to illustrate the interplay between interest limitation rules and anti-hybrid rules is to use a simple example involving a hybrid entity structure and a D/NI outcome.

Let us therefore take a company (XCo) incorporated in state X, which holds a subsidiary (YCo) that then holds a sub-subsidiary (YSub), being the latter two

51. It is evident that no defensive rule is necessary, because the mismatch would be solved by the mandatory application of the primary response (EU secondary law) in the payer state Y.

incorporated in state Y. We will also assume that XCo grants a loan to YCo which pays interest back in year 1. Accordingly, YCo and YSub are part of the same group, although they do not consolidate results for tax purposes. In addition, let us also assume that while state Y considers YCo as a taxable entity, state X regards the same entity as tax transparent.[52] Consequently, we will have a hybrid entity structure with the result of a payment being deducted in state Y but not recognized as income in state X.

Figure 13.5 Interplay Between Int. Lim. Rules and Anti-hybrid Rules

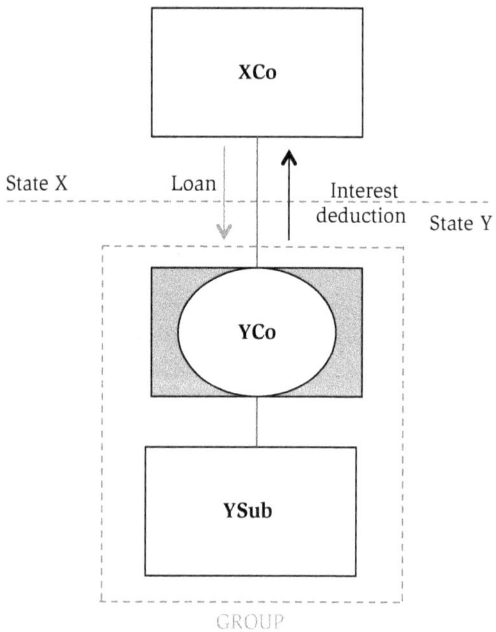

For purposes of this example, the following amounts shall also be considered as regards the payer entity (YCo).[53]

Interest Expenses	200
Interest Income	0
Net Interest Expenses	200
EBITDA[54]	400

52. We will assume that YSub is considered in both state X and Y to be a taxable entity.
53. We will assume that YSub does not have interest income or interest expenses in year 1.
54. The amount of EBITDA includes both YCo and YSub, which are part of the same tax unit or group.

Therefore, if state Y includes both an interest limitation rule and a *primary response* in its domestic laws, the question will be which rule should apply first. The outcome may nonetheless vary depending on the answer. After all, an interest limitation rule would limit the deductibility of interest up to 30% of the amount of taxable EBITDA, while a primary response will disallow the full amount of deductible interest to the extent that those interest payments are not recognized as income in state X, which indeed occurs here because the deductible interest is paid by an entity considered as taxable in state Y but as tax transparent in state X (the recipient of the income), giving rise to a D/NI outcome.

The implications regarding the interplay between interest limitation rules and anti-hybrid rules are, however, not exclusively limited to the application of a primary response. Indeed, they will also affect the application of a *defensive rule* in the other state (payee state X), because a defensive rule applies only to the extent that a primary response was not effective to counteract a hybrid mismatch first, that is when a deduction was not denied in the payer state.[55] In this case, therefore, the defensive rule will apply according to the amount of deductible expenses actually allowed in the payee state.

[B] The OECD Approach

Assuming the conflicting interplay between interest limitation rules and anti-hybrid rules, the OECD BEPS Action Plan 2 opts for prioritizing the application of anti-hybrid rules.

This approach is based on the fact that anti-hybrid rules are considered to make adjustments regarding particular items that are taken into account for the purposes of calculating a taxpayer's overall income or expenses. Therefore, they should be applied before any overall limitation as a matter of logic.[56] As stated by the OECD: '[r]ules to address hybrid mismatch arrangements should be applied by an entity before the fixed ratio rule and group ratio rule to determine an entity's total net interest expense. Once this total net interest expense figure has been determined, the fixed ratio rule and group ratio rule should be applied to establish whether the full amount may be deducted, or to what extent net interest expenses should be disallowed'.[57]

Let us return to our example in Figure 13.5, but now using the OECD approach.

In this case, a primary response would apply first, denying the full amount of deductible interest expenses (200) in state Y. This amount of non-deductible interest will not allowed to be carried forward to subsequent years, which may be possible under interest limitation rules in general. In other words, the taxpayer will suffer a permanent economic burden of economic double taxation if for any reason (such as a timing difference) those interest payments are finally recognized as income in state X.

55. This proves once again that both a primary response and a defensive rule are strictly linked to each other.
56. OECD (2015), *supra* note 33, 97.
57. *Id.*, 103.

In contrast, if the amount of deductible expenses is granted anyway in state Y, it is state X that must now apply a defensive rule taxing the interest income (200).[58]

[C] Criticism

Although the OECD approach regarding the interplay between interest limitation rules and anti-hybrid rules appears, in principle, to be logical, this conclusion is still arguable for different reasons.

First, the argument that anti-hybrid rules are deemed to make adjustments for particular items taken into account for the purpose of calculating the taxpayer's overall income or expenses appears to be overrated. Indeed, economically speaking, both interest limitation rules and anti-hybrid rules are used to calculate the taxpayer's overall income and expenses, because both rules have the same effect; that is, they increase the taxable base of the payer entity with regard to the amount of non-deductible interest in the payer state. For example, if an amount of 1,000 of deductible expenses is limited to 400 because of the EBITDA rule or it is fully disallowed, the effect is exactly the same; that is the amount of disallowed interest expenses must be added back to the taxable profits of the payer entity, and therefore, it increases the tax base of the taxpayer for that taxable year. In both cases, therefore, the limitation in the deduction of expenses is used to calculate the taxpayer's overall income and expenses. In other words, it is not self-evident that an interest limitation rule may accomplish a role other than helping the taxpayer to determine his overall income and expenses too.[59]

Second, if the principle underlying the application of a *primary response* is that this rule should be applied only to the extent that the taxpayer is effectively entitled to deduct interest in the payer state, there is no reason to exclude, but rather to encourage, the prior application of interest limitation rules as part of this analysis. Indeed, interest limitation rules, as part of the general domestic corporate tax system of a state, determine whether or not – and to which amount – a taxpayer is entitled to deduct interest payments. Therefore, a *primary response* should not apply insofar as the taxpayer is subject to other limitations in the deductibility of payments, such as general interest limitation rules. The foregoing also appears to be recognized in the OECD BEPS Action Plan 2, when it says: 'The hybrid entity rule (Recommendations 3 to 7), however, only operate to the extent a taxpayer is actually entitled to a deduction for a payment under local law. Accordingly, these rules will not apply to the extent the taxpayer is subject to transaction or entity specific rules under the parent or payer jurisdiction that prevent the payment from being deducted.'[60]

It is true that the foregoing does not clarify entirely that interest limitation rules should apply before anti-hybrid rules. However, if one agrees that interest limitation rules are part of the general rules of a corporate tax system, one should also agree that they ought to be considered before the application of a specific rule with a different aim

58. The author originally argued this in Parada, *supra* note 4, 316-319 and 343-347.
59. Parada, *supra* note 4, 344.
60. OECD (2015), *supra* note 33, 97.

but a similar economic outcome, that is denying a certain amount of deductible expenses but in connection with a specific hybrid structure.[61]

Third, the application of a *primary response* before interest limitation rules may generate a permanent situation of economic double taxation for the taxpayer in the payer state, which is indeed reinforced by the fact that no carry-forward of non-deductible expenses is offered in the cases of D/NI outcomes when the anti-hybrid rule applies. Therefore, if a deduction is denied in the payer state because of the application of a *primary response*, this denial becomes permanent if interest payments are included as income later on in the payee state, for example, due to a timing issue.[62]

Let us take our example in Figure 13.5 to illustrate the foregoing. If YCo is denied the full amount of 200 interest payments in year 1, that deduction is neither reinstalled for tax purposes in year 1 nor is it carried forward to the subsequent year 2. In other words, assuming that state X did not include the payment of 200 in year 1, but rather in year 2, there is no possibility of using the non-deductible payment in year 2. In sum, the double taxation on YCo becomes permanent.[63]

In addition, and although both *interest limitation rules* and a *primary response* may equally raise questions as regards the ability-to-pay principle,[64] interest limitation rules have the advantage of providing the possibility of carry-forward, which, to a certain extent, appears to be more in compliance with ability-to-pay, at least from the perspective that a denial of expenses does not become permanent.[65] Nonetheless, this argument should be given careful consideration because there may be situations in

61. 'In the author's view interest limitation rules accomplish this role of preventing that a payment (i.e. interest) is deducted in the country of the payer and should therefore be considered before applying a different rule, whose aim is also different, but whose result is similar, i.e. limitation in the deductibility of certain payments.' Parada, *supra* note 4, 345.
62. Parada, *supra* note 4, 318 (where the author also stresses the inclination to solve double non-taxation issues even at under the cost of creating economic double taxation).
63. It is evident that a carry-forward does not completely alleviate economic double taxation, especially if the inclusion of income occurred in state A in year X. However, it is undeniable that if that inclusion occurred in year Y, the carry-forward mitigates the double tax effect.
64. J. Lüdicke, *'Tax Arbitrage' with Hybrid Entities: Challenges and Responses*, 68 Bull. Intl. Taxn. 6/7, 317 (2014) (where he argues that the OECD *linking rules* contravene the ability-to-pay principle and may hit minority shareholders).
65. Although a full analysis regarding *linking rules* and the ability-to-pay principle certainly exceeds the purpose of this contribution, it is perhaps interesting to note that issues concerning the limitation in the deductibility of payments and ability-to-pay principle have even achieved the level of judiciary in some countries, for example, in Germany where the ability-to-pay principle is specifically recognized in Article 3 of the German Constitution, which grants equal treatment to taxpayers in similar circumstances, including corporations through the objective net principle or *objektives Netto Prinzip*, which is a sort of recognition of the ability-to-pay principle as regards corporations. Under this principle, corporations should consider for their calculation of annual taxes all the income and expenses related to the business, without exceptions. Therefore, a limitation in the deductibility of ordinary expenses, regardless of the policy reasons given for their establishment, would in principle be violating the ability-to-pay principle. This debate has been reinforced in a recent landmark decision of the German Federal Fiscal Court [*Bundesfinanzhof*], which confirmed most of the constitutional concerns already expressed in the past with respect to the German interest limitation rule [*Zinsschranke*]. DE: BFH, 14 October 2015, I R 20/15. The final decision depends on the German Federal Constitutional Court [*Bundesverfassungsgericht*, BVerfG), which is still pending. For an analysis of the arguments of the BFH, *see* Lampert, Meickmann and Reinert, *supra* note 22, 324-327.

which the denial of interest expenses under interest limitation rules may also become final.[66] The definitive answer will depend on the specific features of the rule in the state where it is applied.

§13.05 INVERTING THE PARADIGM: A CLAIM FOR CONSISTENCY

This section supports the claim for inverting the paradigm that anti-hybrid rules should apply before interest limitation rules. This approach appears to be more consistent not only with the aim of avoiding economic double taxation but also with that of providing coherence and ease of administration as regards hybrid mismatches. Ultimately, this approach has positive implications both from a practical and from a tax policy perspective.

[A] Illustration

Let us take the example of Figure 13.5 to illustrate this claim. In this case, the deductibility of interest will be limited first to an amount of 30% of the taxable EBITDA (interest limitation rule), that is 120. Likewise, the amount of non-deductible interest will be reduced to 80, which may nonetheless be carried forward to subsequent years according to the domestic rules of state Y.

Therefore, as a consequence of the foregoing the scope of both the *primary response* and the *defensive rule* is reduced. The *primary response* will be applied only on the amount of 'effectively deductible interest', namely the amount of 120. This also means that the *defensive rule* in the payee state (state X), in the event that the primary response did not apply in state Y, will be limited to the same amount (120). In other words, the payee may be obliged to include only 120 of interest as income in state X. Likewise, the amount of non-deductible expenses (80) can be carried forward and used in future years, subject to the same limitation of 30% of taxable EBITDA.

[B] Practical and Tax Policy Implications

[1] Practical Implications

From a practical perspective, rooting for the application of interest limitation rules may first partially avoid a permanent economic double taxation outcome and it may even indirectly solve the issues of hybrid mismatches without the need for applying complex *linking rules*.[67]

66. Scheunemann and Müller-Duttiné, *supra* note 12, 520 (referring to the German interest barrier).
67. On this opinion, *see* R. de Boer and O. Marres, *BEPS Action 2: Neutralizing the Effects on Hybrid Mismatch Arrangements*, 43 Intertax 1, 40-41 (2015) (where these authors state that 'the introduction of a more generic interest deduction limitation, such as the limitation of excessive interest deduction through thin cap or earning striping rules, or via global allocation of interest expenses by formulary apportionment' could work).

As noted already, the amount of non-deductible expenses when interest limitation rules apply is generally carried forward to subsequent years. The foregoing prevents the denial of a deduction in the payer state, which is meant to increase the taxable base of the payer in an equivalent amount of disallowed deductions, from subsequently being included as income in the payee state leaving the taxpayer in a situation of permanent and unrelieved double taxation. Taking again the example of Figure 13.5, this implies that if the interest limitation rules apply first in state Y, only 80 out of 200 of the deductible interest will be disallowed in state Y. However, the foregoing does not prevent YCo (taxpayer) from using the disallowed expenses in subsequent taxable years, thus avoiding double taxation.

Accordingly, using interest limitation rules first may help to control the application of the defensive rule. Indeed, taking the example of Figure 13.5 again, only the amount of allowable deductions (120) will be potentially subject to a defensive rule in state X to the extent that a primary response did not apply in state Y. As a result, the scope of application of the defensive rule (which means taxing the deductible payments in state X) is reduced, first, and second, even if a primary response affects the amount of 120 in state Y, denying this deduction with no carry-forward, appears to be more proportionate for the taxpayer than denying the full amount of 200 at once.

Yet, prioritizing the application of interest limitation rules also has a downside, which is the possibility for the taxpayer to manipulate the amount of taxable EBITDA in order to obtain a higher amount of deductible expenses. The foregoing is indeed possible if the taxable EBITDA is calculated on a group of companies.[68] However, this likelihood decreases if the payee state has actually included a *defensive rule* and taxes the amount of deductible interest there.

[2] Tax Policy Implications

From a policy perspective, giving priority to the application of interest limitation rules over anti-hybrid rules may provide coherence and ease of administration as regards issues of hybrid mismatches in general.

As hybrids are complex matters, anti-hybrid rules should aim to be - at least - simple and coherent.[69] However, this is certainly not the case of *linking rules*. These rules, as stressed somewhere else too,[70] pose some obvious troubles (and extra burden) for taxpayers and tax administrations without truly focusing on the core reason for mismatches in the case of either financial instruments or entities. In contrast, they are designed in an ad hoc manner to target specific tax outcomes, generally connected with the - arguable - avoidance of double non-taxation.[71] The

68. *See* the example in Figure 13.5.
69. Emphasizing the importance of these tax policy aims too, *see* Parada's proposal on hybrid entity mismatches ('reactive coordination rule'), in Parada, *supra* note 4, 358-360.
70. Parada, *supra* note 4, 353 et seq. (proposing a rule that disregards double non-taxation as the core of the problem regarding hybrid entities).
71. For the conceptual analysis on double non-taxation, *see* Parada, *supra* note 4, 13-51.

foregoing drives us to inconsistent results, such as the fact that it is not always the country producing the mismatch that is the one called to counteract it.

Still, even if single taxation were an accepted objective, this aim could be perfectly accomplished by giving priority to the interest limitation rule over the primary response. The foregoing does not mean to acknowledge that the aim pursued by the OECD in Action 2 is correct. However, it means that having coherence in mind, it would not really matter whether the application of the interest limitation rule were to be given priority over anti-hybrid rules.

Accordingly, giving priority to interest limitation rules may also lead to greater ease of administration. Indeed, although it is evident that interest limitation rules are not less technical than anti-hybrid rules, they have some advantages. First, they are not contingent on the results occurring in the other contracting state. In other words, they simply depend on the decision of a single state (payer state).[72] Second, the denial of a deduction contemplates the possibility of a carry-forward of non-deductible expenses, which could indirectly mitigate a potential economic double taxation outcome resulting from the inclusion of income in the payee state. This option is certainly not contemplated by anti-hybrid rules, in particular with regard to the primary response.[73] Third, and as a consequence of the foregoing, both tax administrations and taxpayers may benefit. While the former group would require less knowledge of the tax implications in another state in order to apply interest limitation rules, the latter would certainly face a reduction in the transaction costs associated with hybrid transactions, generating a double-win scenario.

§13.06 CONCLUSIONS

This contribution has demonstrated that the interplay between interest limitation rules and anti-hybrid rules is more conflictual than it might appear at first sight. However, this conflicting interplay should not be prematurely solved by simply differentiating these two rules using the classic distinction between *lex generalis* and *lex specialis* in order to justify the application of anti-hybrid rules first. Such a paradigm is far from being just a matter of logic as argued by the OECD.

As the author has demonstrated here, strong practical and tax policy reasons justify changing this paradigm, that is by giving priority to the application of interest limitation rules over anti-hybrid rules. This approach not only avoids economic double taxation – an aim generally forgotten in the discussion on hybrids – but also provides coherence and ease of administration, two tax policy aims that together with simplicity should be the basis for the design of tax rules anywhere in the world.

72. The contingent application of *linking rules* also involves surrendering sovereignty that countries are not always likely to enjoy. G. Cooper, *Some Thoughts on the OECD's Recommendations on Hybrid Mismatches*, 69 Bull. Intl. Taxn. 6/7, 346 (2015).
73. *Supra* section §13.05[B][1].

CHAPTER 14

Some Reflections on Interest Limitation Rules and Financial Institutions

Federica Pitrone

§14.01 INTRODUCTION

Interest limitation rules within the financial sectors may be considered an evergreen issue to which a straightforward answer has not yet been found at European or international level.

This is clearly stated by both the Anti-Tax Avoidance Directive[1] ('ATAD') and the Action 4 Report of the BEPS Project.[2] The former, when referring to the interest limitation rule introduced by Article 4, states the following: 'Although it is generally accepted that financial undertakings, i.e., financial institutions and insurance undertakings, should also be subject to limitations to the deductibility of interest, it is equally acknowledged that these two sectors present special features which call for a more customised approach. As the discussions in this field are not yet sufficiently conclusive in the international and Union context, it is not yet possible to provide specific rules in the financial and insurance sectors and Member States could therefore exclude them from the scope of interest limitation rules.'[3] According to the wording used, financial undertakings should be excluded from the scope of the interest limitation rule as it stands. This is due both to the special features that financial undertakings present and to the scarce clarity of this issue.

1. Council Directive (EU) 2016/1164 of 12 July 2016 laying down rules against tax avoidance practices that directly affect the functioning of the internal market ('ATAD').
2. The Base Erosion and Profit Shifting ('BEPS') Package presents fifteen Actions that provide governments with the domestic and international instruments needed to tackle tax avoidance.
3. Preamble, para. 9, ATAD.

Also, according to the Organisation for Economic Co-operation and Development (OECD) and, more specifically, its report on Action 4,[4] the established common approach to tackling 'BEPS' involving interest, that is the fixed ratio rule and group ratio rule, was not meant to be extended to the banking and insurance sector. In fact, the OECD highlights that a different approach is needed to address risks posed by entities in the banking and insurance sector, considering their unique features. Therefore, also according to the OECD, countries should exclude entities in the banking and insurance sectors from the scope of the proposed common approach.

Bearing the above in mind, this contribution aims to clarify that BEPS risks involving interest posed by entities in the financial sectors are minor and that, in any case, if those risks are identified, they must be addressed without introducing limitations to the deductibility of interest. This is internationally accepted and is a consequence of the nature of the activities performed by a banking group and the specific regulatory requirements under which financial institutions operate. Such an issue is of the utmost importance because badly designed interest limitation rules may reduce the effectiveness of regulatory requirements which were introduced to tackle the financial crisis and to avoid future crises.

§14.02 FINANCIAL INSTITUTIONS: THEIR SPECIFIC FEATURES

The Action 4 Report of the OECD is aimed at defining 'recommendations regarding best practices in the design of rules to prevent base erosion through the use of interest expense, for example through the use of related-party and third-party debt to achieve excessive interest deductions or to finance the production of exempt or deferred income, and other financial payments that are economically equivalent to interest payments'. In fact, according to the OECD, the use of third-party and related-party interest is one of the simplest of the profit-shifting techniques available in international tax planning. Against this background, the OECD has established a common approach[5] to tackling BEPS involving interest. At the heart of the common approach is a fixed ratio rule which restricts an entity's net interest deductions to a fixed percentage of its earnings before interest, taxes, depreciation and amortisation (EBITDA) calculated using tax principles.

This common approach, however, is not adequate when it comes to the financial sector. In fact, in the case of interest limitation rules within the financial sectors, it must be considered that financial institutions present key features that differentiate them from other industries.

First, banks hold financial assets and liabilities as an integral part of their main business activities, and, therefore, interest plays a different role in the banking sector comparable with the cost of sales for entities in non-financial sectors. Second, financial sector businesses are subject to strict regulations which impose restrictions on their

4. OECD, Limiting Base Erosion Involving Interest Deductions and Other Financial Payments Action 4 – 2016 Update, 2017.
5. It is worth mentioning that the EU has passed the ATAD which includes requirements for an interest limitation rule based on Action 4 of the OECD's BEPS Project.

capital structure, and, therefore, BEPS risks involving interest posed by entities in the financial sectors are minor if any. Third, in the majority of cases, entities engaged in the banking business will have net interest income rather than net interest expense and, therefore, the common approach is unlikely to be effective anyway.

[A] Role and Nature of Interest

Banks rely on interest income to ensure their profitability and liquidity. Indeed, for financial institutions, interest income and expenses are the most significant item of operating income and operating expense and play a role comparable with revenue and cost of sales for entities in non-financial sectors. Therefore, there is a fundamental difference compared with other businesses. Moreover, entities engaged in the banking business aim at making profits and do so by lending money at a higher rate than the rate at which it borrows. Accordingly, in most cases, they will have net interest income rather than net interest expense and, therefore, rules such as a fixed ratio rule or a group ratio rule which limit the level of an entity's net interest expense are unlikely to be effective and would make the system unnecessarily complex.

[B] Regulatory Requirements

Banks are subject – usually on a consolidated basis – to capital requirements that require them to hold minimum amounts of equity and limit their ability to place an excessive level of debt in some entities or to use debt to fund equity investments in subsidiaries. In other words, these regulatory requirements provide protection against excessive leverage for tax purposes limiting de facto any BEPS risk involving interest. This means that the regulations effectively constrain interest-related BEPS risks at least as well as the general fixed ratio rule.

Just to give an example, the use of 'hybrid' instruments is quite inconvenient and expensive for banks within the European Union (EU) because, from a regulatory perspective, and the Directive on access to the activity of credit institutions and the prudential supervision of credit institutions and investment firms (so-called CRD IV Directive) in particular, there are very strict conditions to be satisfied in order to meet a proportion of the minimum capital requirements through non-equity instruments, for example Alternative Tier I capital. Accordingly, scarce use is made of these instruments.

In any case, other issues which do not involve specific, interest-related BEPS risk, such as 'hybrid' regulatory capital issued in the legal form of equity but treated as debt for tax purposes and borrowing to invest in equity-funded vehicles in low tax jurisdictions, are the target of the work under BEPS Action 2 for hybrid mismatches and Action 3 for controlled foreign company regimes and should not be solved via interest limitation rules.

Tax rules cannot avoid considering these elements that place financial institutions in a different situation compared with other industries. Overall, significant regulatory and commercial factors reduce the risks of BEPS involving interest posed by banking and insurance groups, and tax rules should not weaken the effectiveness of capital regulation in providing protection against default, insolvency and a future financial crisis.

[C] Preliminary Conclusions

Based on the foregoing, due to the nature of the activities performed by financial institutions and the specific regulatory requirements imposed on banks, financial institutions should be excluded from the scope of interest limitation rules which would only create complexity and may put financial groups at a disadvantage compared to other sectors. For the reasons explained above, BEPS risks involving interest posed by entities in the financial sectors are minor. Being minor, if (and when) BEPS risks somehow involving interest are identified, they must be addressed without introducing limitations to the deductibility of interest. This is particularly important in order to avoid a disproportionate impact on banking groups as a result of rules applied in other sectors.

Having clarified that there is no need to introduce limitations to the deductibility of interest within the financial sector, the other unanswered question is whether we need any additional tax rules to tackle the problem of BEPS somehow involving interest posed by banking groups if these risks are identified. This will be discussed in the next section.

§14.03 DO WE NEED ADDITIONAL TAX RULES?

From a general perspective, it is fundamental to stress that if BEPS risks involving interest are identified, a country has only one possibility right now and that is to introduce domestic targeted rules. Both the OECD and the EU have clarified that as the discussions in this field are not yet sufficiently conclusive, it is still not possible to provide specific international and/or European rules in the financial sector. However, the implementation of new, domestic, targeted rules gives rise to quite a few relevant issues. First, it requires further analysis on how the regulatory regime is implemented in each country and on whether there is a specific need for them in the first place: generality is dangerous and may lead to undesirable results. This means that domestic tax rules should always consider and take into account the regulatory regime imposed on banking groups and, broadly speaking, tax and regulatory experts should work together to find solutions that do not undermine the effectiveness of regulatory requirements.

Therefore, if an interest-related BEPS risk is identified, tax authorities should first engage with regulators to understand why that risk is not constrained and whether any tax rules proposed would conflict with the aims of regulators. Second, unilateral action may result in uncertainty and unrelieved double taxation and, therefore, should not be encouraged.

Having clarified that, one could ask which BEPS risks involving interest could be posed by banks. It is worth mentioning that the use of third-party or intragroup interest to fund non-taxable income was identified by some countries as a risk posed by banks. The latter arises where interest is used to fund equity investments giving rise to income which benefits from a tax exemption or is taxed in a preferential manner.

In this context, the question to be answered is whether there is any need to introduce new tax rules or whether governments already have instruments at their disposal for tackling potential tax avoidance schemes. In this context, in the author's opinion, most of these risks are already addressed and there is no need for additional tax rules because BEPS risks, like the one described above, can be solved using ordinary tax avoidance rules. We should not forget that many countries have already introduced various rules in their tax systems aimed at tackling different kinds of tax avoidance such as General Anti Avoidance Rules (GAARs), Specific Anti Avoidance Rules (SAARs), transfer pricing rules and controlled foreign companies' rules referring to companies artificially located in low-taxed jurisdictions. Moreover, in the context of the 'BEPS project 2.0' on digital taxation[6] and the 129 members of the OECD/G20 Inclusive Framework, a global agreement is under discussion for taxing multinational enterprises. The second pillar of this project explores the design of a system to ensure that multinational enterprises pay a minimum level of tax and, therefore, to protect their tax base from profit shifting to low or no-tax jurisdictions. The proposal is aimed at developing two rules: (1) an income inclusion rule and (2) a tax on base eroding payments. Accordingly, the BEPS risks that could be linked to income which benefits from a tax exemption or is taxed in a preferential manner will be tackled at international level. There is, therefore, no need for countries to introduce unilateral measures at this stage.

§14.04 CONCLUSIONS

The role that interest plays in the banking sector is different from that in other commercial and industrial companies. Funding and sourcing within a banking group are driven by various commercial and regulatory considerations, that is non-tax considerations, including the need to borrow in order to generate income. Moreover, the regulatory environment significantly constrains banking groups from engaging in activity that may pose a potential BEPS risk arising from the tax-deductibility of interest. Accordingly, the application of interest limitation rules to banking groups is unnecessary from a BEPS perspective. As the interest-related BEPS risk associated with the banking group is low, countries should be permitted to apply a full exemption for banking groups from the application of interest limitation rules.

If further protection is considered necessary, targeted tax rules should be coordinated with regulators. This will prevent unfair and arbitrary outcomes for the banking sector which could give rise to wider, unintended consequences for the global economy. However, combined with the fact that many countries already have tax rules to counter tax avoidance, we believe the correct approach is to avoid domestic and

6. OECD/G20 Inclusive Framework on BEPS, Programme of work to develop a consensus solution to the tax challenges arising from the digitalisation of the Economy, 2019.

unilateral tax measures which may result in uncertainty and unrelieved double taxation.

To avoid this, at the current stage, countries may want to wait for the evolution of the BEPS project 2.0 aimed at finding a global solution to tax avoidance and act only once this global solution becomes reality.

Chapter 15
Conclusions

Giuseppe Melis

Interest deductibility limitation rules raise a number of complex theoretical and practical issues.[1]

Starting from the *rationale* underlying these rules, the history of thin capitalization rules providing for maximum debt/equity ratio constitutes a perfect example of this complexity.

Originally, thin capitalization rules were introduced in many countries with a clear anti-tax avoidance purpose. They were, in fact, limited to payments of interest between related parties resident in different States, thereby demonstrating their aim to avoid an asymmetrical and favorable treatment of interest payments among companies belonging to the same group where the debt/equity ratio of the debtor exceeded a physiological level. Moreover, in some States such rules were not applied if the debtor could prove that he would have been able to obtain a similar loan from unrelated parties, thus confirming their anti-tax avoidance purpose on the one hand and ruling out the possibility that the legislator's aim was to prevent companies from overindebtedness on the other.

The nature of these rules changed substantially after the *Lankhorst-Hohorst* judgment of the European Court of Justice (ECJ) (December 12, 2002, C-324/00): as an immediate consequence of that judgment, thin capitalization rules were also extended to purely domestic payments of interest. The rationale underlying the rules changed and became more "economic," in order to stimulate the financing of companies through equity rather than through debt.

It is highly questionable whether "negative" rules such as thin capitalization rules denying, in certain cases, the deduction of interest are the most appropriate way to pursue that economic aim or if such an aim can be better achieved using solely

1. On this issue *see*, in the Italian literature, the monograph of A.E. La Scala, *Gli interessi passivi nella determinazione del reddito di impresa*, Aracne, Roma, 2016.

"positive" rules such as *Dual Income Taxes*, *Allowance for corporate equity* or other similar measures providing directly for a favorable tax treatment of equity financing.

More in general, one may also wonder if this aim to reduce debt through tax measures is desirable both from a general perspective—as it may hamper companies' competitiveness—and from an individual perspective, as there may be physiological cases that fall anyway within the interest limitation rule.

At the same time, we have to consider that the individual access to bank financing has been deeply influenced in these last years by the rating systems adopted by banks following the new regulations on bank capital adequacy, stress testing, market liquidity risk, non-performing loans and so on, therefore contributing to the prevention of the risks deriving from a potentially excessive debt/equity ratio in a far more efficient way than tax measures could do. This of course implies that the financial institutions themselves, being subject to capital requirements that oblige them to hold minimum amounts of equity, cannot place an excessive level of debt in some entities or use debt to fund equity investments in subsidiaries.[2]

In any case, in addition to the anti-tax avoidance purpose with reference to the asymmetrical tax treatment of interest, two other tax justifications for this kind of limitation rules exist.

On the one side, interest payments are deductible as a business expense when calculating the company's taxable income, while dividends are nondeductible. Of course, there is normally a symmetrical treatment in the sense that interest income is taxed with the lender while dividends are almost exempt. But, of course, the State of the debtor is mainly interested in the deduction aspect.

On the other side, three additional factors contribute to the legislator's suspicion toward passive interest. First, by virtue of their intrinsic nature, interest expenses cannot easily be referred exclusively to the economic activity carried on by the company; second, interest is the most mobile of all the production factors and can easily be located anywhere without generating capital gains; third, identification of the beneficial owner can be made very difficult.[3]

This difficult balance between tax and nontax purposes has not been solved with the shifting that has taken place in recent years in many countries from thin capitalization rules to earnings stripping rules, which were also adopted as a countermeasure at Organisation for Economic Co-operation and Development (OECD) and European Union (EU) levels.[4]

These latter rules are in fact ambiguous too, as they are often linked to anti-avoidance or anti-erosion purposes, but their structure is not always compliant with the underlying rationale.

For rules of this kind, the deduction of passive interest exceeding active interest is allowed on a lump sum basis which is connected with the company's income before interest, amortization and depreciation. Under this perspective, it could be observed

2. *See* Chapter 14, F. Pitrone.
3. *See* S. Giannini, D. Stevanato, R. Lupi, *Quali giustificazioni per l'indeducibilità degli interessi passivi?*, in *Dialoghi di diritto tributario*, 2008, p. 13 ss.
4. On the differences between the OECD and the EU approach, *see* Chapter 11, F.A. Garcia Prats.

that such rules try to establish a link with the economic performance of the company—rather than with the equity and with the debt of the company itself as occurs with thin capitalization rules—and in this sense they can be classified as an attempt to reach an optimal level of debt in the sense that it can be paid back through the company's profits. This would also be testified to by the fact that the limitations to interest deduction apply notwithstanding the origin of the debt.

However, the fact that the interest deduction cannot exceed a certain level of Earnings Before Interest, Taxes, Depreciation and Amortization (EBITDA) also means that interest cannot erode the *whole* income, thus making it impossible to shift the excess profit from the debtor to the lender or to transform equity into debt over a certain amount. In view of this, the anti-avoidance and anti-erosion purpose is more evident, although this does not imply that such rules cannot affect physiological cases too, where such negative conditions do not occur at all. There could be cases where the debt is acceptable from a business perspective and also cases regarding particular stages in the life of a company, for example start-up and renovation, where this limitation has no sense. These rules are, moreover, procyclical and companies in trouble with a lower EBITDA also have to face the extra tax burden determined by the interest limitation rules.

In actual fact, the risk of applying this kind of rule to cases of real business costs can be mitigated or wholly eliminated through exemption rules for stand-alone entities—which are normally small entities—or through a *de minimis* rule that, in any case, allows the deduction of passive interest whose amount is under a certain threshold. These are, however, mere options whose introduction is left at the discretion of the States by the Anti-Tax Avoidance Directive (ATAD),[5] with the consequence that some Member States including Italy have not exercised them.[6] The fact that these safe-harbor clauses linked to the entity's small size and to the lack of related parties—where the risk of tax avoidance is likely to be relatively low—are optional and not binding demonstrates that this ambiguity also affects the aforementioned Directive. The same happens with the mere option given to Member States to exclude the limitation of interest in the case of long-term public infrastructure projects, whose *rationale* lies in the very limited risk of tax avoidance deriving from the connection with the public sector or with the option to exclude the financial sector.[7] Probably all this has been the price that had to be paid in order to reach a political agreement on the Directive.

The possibility to carry forward or carry back nondeductible exceeding borrowing costs and the unused interest capacity is another ambiguous element as it appears to be more a provision aimed at countering the deduction of interest expenses in the absence of congruous positive revenues rather than a strict juridical anti-abuse instrument.

5. *See* Chapter 3, M. Grandinetti and Chapter 4, A. Vicini Ronchetti.
6. *See* Chapter 7, G. Vanz.
7. For instance, Dutch legislation does not provide for any exception with regard to financial institutions: *see* Chapter 9, H. van den Broek.

This ambiguous nature of the provisions aimed at limiting interest deduction makes it difficult for the interpreter to give a precise evaluation of them, as it could be observed that the economic aim, which is to avoid an overindebtedness of national companies, maintains its validity even in the absence of any aim to avoid tax.

Furthermore, the constitutional point of view is affected by this ambiguity. From the German Report [8] it is clear that the position of the First Senate of the German Federal Fiscal Court referring the German rule for constitutional review on the grounds that it violates the principle of equality enshrined in Article 3(1) of the Constitution from the objective net principle point of view could find both tax (securing the German tax base; anti-avoidance purpose) and nontax (strengthening the equity ratio of German enterprises; creating incentives for domestic investment) justifications.

Even the compatibility with the EU proportionality principle is influenced by this ambiguity as one could state that the ATAD rule introducing a predetermined and statutory binding evaluation of what is an appropriate level of deductible interest may go far beyond the sole anti-avoidance purpose, but this conclusion would have to take into account all the nontax justifications mentioned before.[9]

It is also evident that the measures adopted at world level have not yet reached an appreciable level of coordination and this even applies in the EU after the ATAD.[10]

First, it is very difficult to draw a line between debt and equity and/or between interest and dividend. Different proposals have been developed in this regard yet no single approach is globally predominant. It has even been argued that a line simply does not exist so that this distinction should be eliminated for purposes of characterizing taxable income (or deductible expenses).[11] The choices of the different States may, therefore, differ one from another in this respect.

Second, there are States that still adopt thin capitalization rules while there are States that adopt earnings stripping rules. However, it can also happen that such rules coexist with the application of a general anti-avoidance rule and/or specific anti-avoidance rules including anti-hybrid rules [12] and/or transfer pricing rules. This may of course generate conflicts among the different rules: the one existing between interest limitation rules and anti-hybrid rules is a perfect example of the complexity of this issue.[13]

Third, even the way the measures are designed differs greatly from State to State. On this last point, suffice it to think of their different subjective scopes of application (i.e., individuals, partnerships, corporations and other commercial or noncommercial entities, and groups of companies). This means that different tax regimes for interest limitation may coexist in the same country while the deduction of passive interest

8. *See* Chapter 6, D. Reich.
9. *See* Chapter 5, G. Bizioli.
10. *See* Chapter 10, M. Barassi.
11. *See* Chapter 2, J. Bundgaard & M. Tell.
12. *See* Chapter 8, A. Baez Moreno & A. Navarro Ibarolla, regarding the special rule for intragroup acquisitions using debt push-down structures and the special rule for leveraged buyout transactions.
13. *See* Chapter 13, L. Parada.

should never depend upon the legal form adopted by the taxpayers but rather on their economic fundamentals; otherwise the neutrality of the market would be hampered.

In conclusion, if we also consider the extreme technical complexity of these limitation rules and the fact that in a world where the financing of companies and financial institutions themselves depends more and more on nontax regulations the traditional interest limitation rules start to seem anachronistic, it would be more appropriate and efficient to introduce two separate rules: on the one side, a real anti-avoidance rule targeted at passive interest paid in circumstances where the company would not have been able to obtain a similar loan from an unrelated party and, on the other side, a "positive" measure aimed at strengthening the financing by equity rather than by debt as we mentioned before.[14]

14. On other possible solutions, among which the introduction of a "Comprehensive Business Income Tax" (CBIT) combined with a system based on the dependent entity model that considers a foreign subsidiary primarily to be an extension of its parent/head office as if it were a permanent establishment, *see* Chapter 1, P. Essers.

Index

H

I

EUCOTAX Series on European Taxation

(1) Peter HJ Essers, Guido JME de Bont & Eric CCM Kemmeren (eds), *The Compatibility of Anti-Abuse Provisions in Tax Treaties with EC Law,* 1998 (ISBN 90-411-9678-1).

(2) Gerard TK Meussen (ed.), *The Principle of Equality in European Taxation,* 1999 (ISBN 90-411-9693-5).

(3) Michael Lang (ed.), *Tax Treaty Interpretation,* 2001 (ISBN 90-411-9857-1).

(4) Pasquale Pistone, *The Impact of Community Law on Tax Treaties: Issues and Solutions,* 2002 (ISBN 90-411-9860-1).

(5) René Offermanns, *The Entrepreneurship Concept in a European Comparative Tax Law Perspective,* 2002 (ISBN 90-411-9887-3).

(6) Michael Lang & Mario Züger, *Settlement of Disputes in Tax Treaty Law,* 2002 (ISBN 90-411-9904-7).

(7) Carlo Pinto, *Tax Competition and EU Law,* 2003 (ISBN 90-411-9913-6).

(8) Michael Lang, Hans-Jörgen Aigner, Ulrich Scheuerle & Markus *Stefaner, CFC Legislation, Tax Treaties and EC Law,* 2004 (ISBN 90-411-2284-2).

(9) Mattias Dahlberg, *Direct Taxation in Relation to the Freedom of Establishment and the Free Movement of Capital,* 2005 (ISBN 90-411-2363-6).

(10) Michael Lang, Judith Herdin & Ines Hofbauer, *WTO and Direct Taxation,* 2005 (ISBN 90-411-2371-7).

(11) Dennis Weber, *Tax Avoidance and the EC Tray Freedoms: A Study of the Limitations under European Law for the Prevention of Tax Avoidance,* 2005 (ISBN 90-411-2402-0).

(12) Félix Alberto Vega Borrego, *Limitations on Benefits Clauses on Double Taxation Conventions,* 2005 (ISBN 90-411-2370-9).

(13) Michael Lang, Josef Schuch & Claus Staringer, *ECJ-Recent Developments in Direct Taxation,* 2006 (ISBN 90-411-2509-4).

(14) Reuven S. Avi-Yonah, James R. Hines Jr. & Michael Lang, *Comparative Fiscal Federalism. Comparing the European Court of Justice and the US Supreme Court's Tax Jurisprudence,* 2007 (ISBN 978-90-411-2552-1).

(15) Christiana HJI Panayi, *Double Taxation, Tax Treaties, Treaty-Shopping and the European Community,* 2007 (ISBN 978-90-411-2658-0).

(16) Dennis Weber, *The Influence of European Law on Direct Taxation: Recent and Future Developments,* 2007 (ISBN 978-90-411-2667-2).

(17) Michael Lang & Pasquale Pistone, *The EU and Third Countries: Direct Taxation,* 2007 (ISBN 978-90-411-2665-8).

(18) Oskar Henkow, *Financial Activities in European VAT: A Theoretical and Legal Research of the European VAT System and Preferred Treatment of Financial Activities,* 2007 (ISBN 978-90-411-2703-7).

(19) Michael Lang (ed.), *Tax Compliance Costs for Companies in an Enlarged European Community,* 2008 (ISBN 978-90-411-2666-5).

(20) Michael Lang (ed.), *Source versus Residence. Problems Arising from the Allocation of Taxing Rights in Tax Treaty Law and Possible Alternatives*, 2008 (ISBN 978-90-411-2763-1).
(21) Ioanna Mitroyanni, *Integration Approaches to Group Taxation in the European Internal Market*, 2008 (ISBN 978-90-411-2779-2).
(22) Rolf Eicke, *Tax Planning with Holding Companies. Repatriation of US Profits from Europe:Concepts, Strategies, Structures*, 2008 (ISBN978-90-411-2794-5).
(23) Peter Essers et al. (ed.), *The Influence of IAS/IFRS on the CCCTB, Tax Accounting, Disclosure and Corporate Law Accounting Concepts: 'A Clash of Cultures'*, 2008 (ISBN 978-90-411-2819-5).
(24) Tonny Schenk-Geers, *International Exchange of Information and the Protection of Taxpayers*, 2009 (ISBN 978-90-411-3142-3).
(25) Raymond Adema, *UCITS and Taxation: Towards Harmonization of the Taxation of UCITS*, 2009 (ISBN 978-90-411-2839-3).
(26) Michael Lang, Jianwen Liu & Gongliang Tang (eds), *Europe–China Tax Treaties*, 2010 (ISBN 978-90-411-3216-1).
(27) Michael Lang, Pasquale Pistone, Josef Schuch & Claus Staringer (eds), *Procedural Rules in Tax Law in the Context of European Union and Domestic Law*, 2010 (ISBN 978-90-411-3376-2).
(28) Sjaak J.J.M. Jansen, *Fiscal Sovereignty of the Member States in an Internal Market: Past and Future*, 2011 (ISBN 978-90-411-3403-5).
(29) Dennis Weber & Bruno da Silva, *From Marks & Spencer to X Holding: The Future of Cross-Border Group Taxation*, 2011 (ISBN 978-90-411-3399-1).
(30) Claus Bohn Jespersen, *Intermediation of Insurance and Financial Services in European VAT*, 2011 (ISBN 978-90-411-3732-6).
(31) Sabine Heidenbauer, *Charity Crossing Borders: The Fundamental Freedoms' Influence on Charity and Donor Taxation in Europe*, 2011 (ISBN 978-90-411-3813-2).
(32) Michael Lang, et al., *The Future of Indirect Taxation: Recent Trends in VAT and GST Systems around the World*, 2012 (ISBN 978-90-411-3797-5).
(33) Harm van den Broek, *Cross-Border Mergers within the EU: Proposals to Remove the Remaining Tax Obstacles*, 2012 (ISBN 978-90-411-3824-8).
(34) Michael Lang, et al. (eds), *Tax Treaty Case Law around the Globe – 2011*, 2012 (ISBN 978-90-411-3876-7).
(35) Dennis Weber (ed.), *CCCTB: Selected Issues*, 2012 (ISBN 978-90-411-3872-9).
(36) Daniël Smit, *EU Freedoms, Non-EU Countries and Company Taxation*, 2012 (ISBN 978-90-411-4041-8).
(37) Rita de la Feria, *VAT Exemptions: Consequences and Design Alternatives*, 2013 (ISBN 978-90-411-3276-5).
(38) Karin Simader, *Withholding Taxes and the Fundamental Freedoms*, 2013 (ISBN 978-90-411-4842-1).
(39) Madeleine Merkx, *Establishments in European VAT*, 2013 (ISBN 978-90-411-4554-3).
(40) Carla De Pietro, *Tax Treaty Override*, 2014 (ISBN 978-90-411-5406-4).

(41) G.K. Fibbe & A.J.A. Stevens (eds), *Hybrid Entities and the EU Direct Tax Directives*, 2015 (ISBN 978-90-411-5942-7).
(42) Gerard Staats, *Personal Pensions in the EU*, 2015 (ISBN 978-90-411-5953-3).
(43) Michael Lang & Ine Lejeune (eds), *VAT/GST in a Global Digital Economy*, 2015 (ISBN 978-90-411-5952-6).
(44) Massimo Basilavecchia, Lorenzo del Federico & Pietro Mastellone (eds), *Tax Implications of Environmental Disasters and Pollution*, 2015 (ISBN 978-90-411-5611-2).
(45) Cristina Trenta, *Rethinking EU VAT for P2P Distribution*, 2015 (ISBN 978-90-411-6137-6).
(46) Marie Lamensch, Edoardo Traversa & Servaas van Thiel (eds), *Value Added Tax and the Digital Economy: The 2015 EU Rules and Broader Issues*, 2016 (ISBN 978-90-411-6612-8).
(47) Raffaele Petruzzi, *Transfer Pricing Aspects of Intra-Group Financing*, 2016 (ISBN 978-90-411-6732-3).
(48) Mario Grandinetti (ed.), *Corporate Tax Base in the Light of the IAS/IFRS and EU Directive 2013/34: A Comparative Approach*, 2016 (ISBN 978-90-411-6745-3).
(49) Bruno da Silva, *The Impact of Tax Treaties and EU Law on Group Taxation Regimes*, 2016 (ISBN 978-90-411-6905-1).
(50) Michael Lang, Alfred Storck & Raffaele Petruzzi (eds), *Transfer Pricing in a Post-BEPS World*, 2016 (ISBN 978-90-411-6710-1).
(51) Marta Papis-Almansa, *Insurance in European VAT: Current and Preferred Treatment in the Light of the New Zealand and Australian GST Systems*, 2017 (ISBN 978-90-411-8360-6).
(52) Wolfgang Speckhahn, *Real Estate Investment Trusts In Europe: Europeanising Tax Regimes*, 2017 (ISBN 978-90-411-8360-6).
(53) Frank J.G. Nellen, *Information Asymmetries in EU VAT*, 2017 (ISBN 978-90-411-8837-3).
(54) Erik Ros, *EU Citizenship and Direct Taxation*, 2017 (ISBN 978-90-411-8584-6).
(55) Werner Haslehner, Georg Kofler & Alexander Rust (eds), *EU Tax Law and Policy in the 21st Century*, 2017 (ISBN 978-90-411-8815-1).
(56) Claudia Sanò, *National Legal Presumptions and European Tax Law*, 2018 (ISBN 978-90-411-6613-5).
(57) Christoph Marchgraber, *Double (Non-)Taxation and EU Law*, 2018 (ISBN 978-90-411-9410-7).
(58) Dennis Weber & Jan van de Streek (eds), *The EU Common Consolidated Corporate Tax Base: Critical Analysis*, 2018 (ISBN 978-90-411-9233-2).
(59) Werner Haslehner (ed.), *Investment Fund Taxation: Domestic Law, EU Law, and Double Taxation Treaties*, 2018 (ISBN 978-90-411-9669-9).
(60) Jérôme Monsenego, *Selectivity in State Aid Law and the Methods for the Allocation of the Corporate Tax Base*, 2018 (ISBN 978-90-411-9413-8).
(61) José Manuel Almudí Cid, Jorge A. Ferreras Gutiérrez & Pablo A. Hernández González-Barreda (eds), *Combating Tax Avoidance in the EU: Harmonization and Cooperation in Direct Taxation*, 2019 (ISBN 978-94-035-0154-3).

(62) Werner Haslehner, Georg Kofler & Alexander Rust (eds), *Time and Tax: Issues in International, EU, and Constitutional Law*, 2019 (ISBN 978-94-035-0354-7).
(63) Nathalie Wittock, *Sales Promotion Techniques and VAT in the EU*, 2019 (ISBN 978-94-035-0861-0).
(64) Carla De Pietro (ed.), *New Perspectives on Fiscal State Aid: Legitimacy and Effectiveness of Fiscal State Aid Control*, 2019 (ISBN 978-94-035-1415-4).
(65) Giorgio Beretta, *European VAT and the Sharing Economy*, 2019 (ISBN 978-94-035-1435-2).
(66) Claudio Cipollini, *Special Tax Zones and EU Law: Theory, Implementations, and Future Challenges*, 2020 (ISBN 978-94-035-1885-5).
(67) Gianluigi Bizioli, Mario Grandinetti, Leopoldo Parada, Giuseppe Vanz & Alessandro Vicini Ronchetti (eds), *Corporate Taxation, Group Debt Funding and Base Erosion: New Perspectives on the EU Anti-Tax Avoidance Directive*, 2020 (ISBN 978-94-035-1170-2).

www.ingramcontent.com/pod-product-compliance
Ingram Content Group UK Ltd.
Pitfield, Milton Keynes, MK11 3LW, UK
UKHW020249290926
15470UKWH00002B/827

9 789403 511702